DATE DUE

The Freedmen's Bureau and Reconstruction

RECONSTRUCTING AMERICA
Paul Cimbala, series editor

1. Hans L. Trefousse, *Impeachment of a President: Andrew Johnson, the Blacks, and Reconstruction.*
2. Richard Paul Fuke, *Imperfect Equality: African Americans and the Confines of White Ideology in Post-Emancipation Maryland.*
3. Ruth Currie-McDaniel, *Carpetbagger of Conscience: A Biography of John Emory Bryant.*

The Freedmen's Bureau and Reconstruction

RECONSIDERATIONS

edited by

PAUL A. CIMBALA
and
RANDALL M. MILLER

Fordham University Press
New York
1999

ISBN 0–8232–1934–8 (hardcover)
ISBN 0–8232–1935–6 (paperback)
ISSN 1523–4606

Reconstructing America, no. 4

Library of Congress Cataloging-in-Publication Data

The Freedmen's Bureau and Reconstruction / [edited by] Paul A. Cimbala
and Randall M. Miller. — 1st ed.
    p.   cm. — (Reconstructing America ; no. 4)
    Includes index.
    ISBN 0-8232-1934-8 (hardcover). — ISBN 0-8232-1935-6 (pbk.)
    1. United States.   Bureau of Refugees, Freedmen, and Abandoned
Lands.   2. United States—Politics and government—1865–1877.
3. Reconstruction—Southern States.   4. Freedmen—Southern States.
5. Southern States—History—1865–1877.   6. Afro-Americans–
–History—1863–1877.   7. Southern States—Race relations.
I. Cimbala, Paul A. (Paul Allan), 1951–   .   II. Miller, Randall M.
III. Series: Reconstructing America (Series) ; no. 4.
E185.2.F858   1999
975'.041—dc21   99-34974
                                                                      CIP

03   02   01   00   99   5   4   3   2   1
Printed in the United States of America
First Edition

To the Memory of Samuel E. Day (1834–1925),
who saw the war as a beginning
and went north to a new life.—R.M.M.

and

To the Memory of George Cimbala (1874–1924),
who found opportunity in a reunited nation.—P.A.C.

CONTENTS

PREFACE

In 1955, George R. Bentley published *A History of the Freedmen's Bureau*, the last full account of the federal Reconstruction agency that Congress had charged with supervising the South's transition from slavery to freedom. Since that time, a sea change in Reconstruction historiography has occurred. At the center of much discussion about how Republicans tried to translate Union victory and emancipation in war into a new order in peace has been the role of the Freedmen's Bureau. The Bureau, after all, stood as the principal expression and extension of federal authority in the defeated South. Through the Bureau, the federal government would assume new responsibilities in providing relief to refugees and ex-slaves, trying to settle the ex-slaves on land (and then removing them from land), overseeing labor contracts and adjudicating labor disputes, building schools, and more. Through the Bureau, the Republican party would carry its ideas about a free-labor political economy southward. But, as histories of Reconstruction reiterate, the Bureau did not get its way. In the end, black freedom and free-labor ideas were only partly, and often precariously, planted.

Historians have disagreed on the effectiveness of the Bureau in securing freedom and remaking the South. Some have argued that the Freedmen's Bureau, along with the army, undercut black freedom by seeking to restore agricultural production and minimize social and political change. Others have viewed the Bureau as fundamental in tearing down the old order and helping blacks claim equality before the law and opportunity on the land. Still others have suggested that however much the Bureau might have preferred continuity over revolution in a postwar South, at least in the short run, the Bureau's long-term commitment to basic civil rights for blacks worked against the unyielding white commitment to keep blacks down forever. Whatever the true assessment of the Bureau's role—and the debate continues—it is now time to revisit the Bureau as a whole, to bring scholarship on the Bureau together, to take stock of the literature, and to point new directions for inquiry. Thus this book.

Much of the best recent work on the Bureau and Reconstruction has observed ideas and people in action. In doing so, scholars have come to appreciate that the story of the Bureau was more than the political wrangling between Andrew Johnson and Radical Republicans in Washington. Scholars now remind us that no single story or typology represented the whole of the Bureau. There were in fact many Bureaus, as agents, freedpeople, and white southerners negotiated, sometimes violently, the meaning of freedom in their local areas. Getting down to cases revealed the permutations of Bureau agents' beliefs, strategies, and personalities. It also showed that black and white southerners approached the Bureau as suited their own particular needs. As such, the Bureau was in a constant state of evolution and adaptation. Considering the obstacles of racism, southerners' distrust of outsiders, the temporary status of the Bureau as an agency, the Bureau's limited resources, the lack of a significant military presence to support the Bureau, among a host of constraints, it is a wonder the Bureau succeeded at all. At the same time, the many state and local studies of the Bureau all seem to suggest that, however weak institutionally or racist personally, the Bureau altered the assumptions and calculus of local power and race relations. Simply by being there to oversee a labor contract or hear the complaint of an ex-slave or a planter was to interrupt, even disrupt, the complete economic and social power claimed by whites over blacks before emancipation. If nothing else, the Bureau showed that slavery was dead. On that point, the scholars agree.

Despite the recognition of the Bureau's significance, the agency has yet to be presented in a comprehensive book-length study that addresses the new historiographical trends and integrates questions, such as the role of gender in the formation of Bureau policy, that would have surprised Bentley and his generation of scholars. That the Bureau still wants a new history is the consequence, in part, of the agency's own voluminous archive. The National Archives houses thousands of linear feet of loose papers and bound volumes and hundreds of rolls of microfilm of Bureau material. It is almost too much for anyone but the most devoted Bureau scholar to peruse in a lifetime. Scholars have not ignored the Bureau, but few have actually devoted full-dress studies to the agency at the state and local levels.

This need is significant, if for no other reason than it is necessary to obtain the building blocks before one can construct the edifice. Although scholars have identified broad region-wide themes in the Bureau's history, they also have begun to show that, because of the diversity of conditions and personalities in the Reconstruction South, there were distinct variations on those themes in different settings.

Until recently, only three book-length state studies of the Bureau existed. During the past several years, four new studies of the Bureau in Texas, Arkansas, and Georgia have joined them. Fortunately, the article literature on the Bureau is ever on the increase. This growing corpus of monographs and articles will be most useful for the brave soul who takes up the challenge of producing a new study of the Freedmen's Bureau as a whole. In the meantime, the editors of the present volume believe that a multifaceted look at the agency will serve as an essential intermediate measure for bringing interested students of Reconstruction up to date on the current status of Bureau research.

This book brings together many of the scholars who have been working through the Freedmen's Bureau papers and other sources to rethink the Bureau's place in securing freedom and remaking the South. Without any claim to being comprehensive or providing the definitive account of the Bureau and Reconstruction, this book represents a sampling of the range and variety of new work being done on the Bureau. The editors asked only that the authors provide original essays that raised questions hardly asked before, explored issues still needful of examination, drew on sources not previously sampled or much analyzed, or ventured onto new settings. No consensus among the authors emerged regarding the Bureau's character and effect, though many authors found Bureau agents trying to transplant Yankee ideas about a free-labor society and economy to southern soil and found black southerners pushing the Bureau to stand up for them, even as they turned to their own community resources to build churches, schools, and lives independent of whites. But collectively the essays do show that understanding Reconstruction anywhere in the South is impossible without factoring in the presence of the Bureau. The Bureau stands at the vital center of Reconstruction history and historiography.

In the gestation period from idea to publication, this book has benefited much from the interest and assistance of historians and librarians. The contributors were enthusiastic about the project from the outset, which made the editors' job an exciting one. Staff at Fordham University, Saint Joseph's University, Haverford College, and the University of Pennsylvania libraries further eased the editorial burden by assisting the editors in checking sources and facts. Saverio Procario, the director of Fordham University Press, and Mary Beatrice Schulte, executive editor of the Press, gave their whole-hearted support to this project from the time the editors first proposed it to them. Their interest is but one example of their commitment to publishing new studies of America's Civil War and the nation's Reconstruction, the present volume being one of the inaugural works appearing in the Press's new series titled "Reconstructing America."

INTRODUCTION

The Freedmen's Bureau and Reconstruction: An Overview

Randall M. Miller

In December 1865, Private Calvin Holly, a black Union soldier detailed to the Mississippi branch of the Freedmen's Bureau, wrote to General Oliver O. Howard, head of the Bureau in Washington, describing conditions in postwar Mississippi. Blacks there, he reported, were "in a great many ways being outraged upon beyound humanity." Women and children were having their houses "tourn down from over the[ir] heads," two black women were found dead along the Jackson road with their throats slit, a church was burned, and "The Rebbles are going a bout in many places through the State and robbing the colered pe[o]ple of arms money and all they have and in many places killing." Private Holly then advised the general that "the safety of this country depenes upon giving the Colered man all the rights of a white man, and especialy the Rebs, and let him know that their is power enough in the arm of the Government to give Justice, to all her loyal citizens." The Union must put down the rebel spirit still alive in Mississippi, he argued, or risk losing the war during the peace. Holly concluded by urging Howard and friends of the Union in Congress to pass "some laws that will give protection to the colered man and meet out Justice to traters in arms." More to the point, he instructed Howard: "now if you have any true harted men send them down here to carry out your wishes through the bureau in regaurde to the freedmen." Failing that, "get Congress to stick in a few competent colered men as they did in the army and the thing will go right."[1]

Holly's letter echoed concerns from across the South in 1865, and after, about the need for the federal government to secure the victory by punishing treason and protecting freedom. Reports from the field also reminded those in the nation's capital that the government must establish its authority by means of a direct presence in the South, that respect for the Union demanded a new assertion of federal power. For Holly, as for so many other Union veterans and freedpeople over the next several years, the Freedmen's Bureau promised to do the job. But confidence in the Bureau, and in blacks' own abilities, to make good the peace was not so readily realized. Republicans wrangled among themselves as to what powers the Bureau should have and how far the government should reach into local affairs and private lives in defining and defending freedom, while President Andrew Johnson and the Democrats thought the Bureau should not exist at all. And white southerners resisted almost every effort of the Bureau or any northern interest to give southern blacks a chance. Therein lay much of the hope and tragedy of Reconstruction.

With the war over, no question burned more intensely than what did freedom mean. The emancipation of almost 4 million slaves set in motion an unprecedented effort to define a new social, economic, and political order. Indeed, as Frederick Douglass observed, "Verily, the work does not end with the abolition of slavery, but only begins."[2] The question of freedom involved not only the newly emancipated slaves but also the defeated southerners and victorious northerners. No guidelines were at hand to point the way, and no consensus existed to ensure an easy transit from slavery to freedom, from a slave society to a free one, from a world premised on white rule and black subjugation to one founded on equality before the law.

Even before the Confederacy's last days, the Union struggled to lay the groundwork for a "reconstructed" South and give life to the "new birth of freedom" heralded in Lincoln's Gettysburg Address. The Thirteenth Amendment, adopted in February 1865 amid cheers and tears by a Republican-controlled Congress, in one sentence ended slavery and in another granted Congress enabling power to ensure that freedom. But the Amendment, ratified in December

1865, did not spell out the dimensions of that new authority, which remained more promise than accepted constitutional writ among most Americans. All the while, conditions in the South cried out for immediate action. Abandoned lands, a growing and desperate refugee population, starvation, devastation, and the collapse of organized civil authority in the South demanded federal efforts to provide relief, begin the rebuilding process, and restore order. Private organizations and provisional southern state governments, as yet in constitutional limbo and often in disarray, lacked the means. So, too, blacks meeting in conventions and churches across the South looked to Congress to protect their "rights" as "citizens," even to extend the franchise to them.

In March 1865, Congress took steps to smooth the path from war to peace and slavery to freedom when it established the Bureau of Refugees, Freedmen, and Abandoned Lands (known as the Freedmen's Bureau) under the authority of the War Department. The Bureau bill provided for a coordinated national program of relief and supervision and management of "all abandoned lands, and the control of all subjects relating to refugees and freedmen from rebel states . . . under such rules and regulations as may be prescribed by the head of the bureau and approved by the President." The act limited the tenure of the Bureau to "the present war of rebellion and for one year thereafter." Thus began the most ambitious (if also temporary) experiment to date in extending federal authority into the states. Moreover, in a clause authorizing the Bureau to "set apart, for the use of loyal refugees and freedmen," abandoned and confiscated lands, the act carried an implied promise of government aid to blacks and Unionists in staking new lives as independent farmers in a reconstructed South.[3] In many ways, the Freedmen's Bureau, more than any other agency, embodied what the Union would have freedom mean—in constitutional, ideological, and practical terms.

As such, the Bureau became a focal point for Reconstruction. For newly freed blacks, it was "the government." Indeed, Bureau agents often constituted the only federal presence in much of the South and, insomuch as white-controlled local and state governments refused to recognize blacks' claims as citizens to testify in their own behalf and have their contracts respected in law, the Bureau became the only place for them to get a fair hearing. To many white southerners, and even their northern Democratic Party allies, the Bureau symbolized the "tyranny" of Reconstruction and the corruption of government. Bureau agents, they cried, intruded into local affairs by setting up schools for freedpeople, negotiating or overseeing labor contracts, arguing for blacks' rights in law, and more. By their presence alone, Bureau agents upset the old ways wherein white southerners had ruled blacks as they saw fit. Blacks wanted the Bureau protected and its authority enlarged, while southern whites wanted it disbanded and local government restored. Different expectations regarding the Bureau persisted throughout Reconstruction—and dogged the Bureau's legacy and reputation long after its demise, as historians' judgments about the Bureau's success or failure attest.

During its brief life, the Bureau lacked a clear mandate as to its proper authority and the extent of its responsibilities in the face of ever-changing social, economic, and political conditions and interests. The Bureau never was master of its own fate. Its principal source of funding was cut off almost as soon as the Bureau went into operation, and it depended on private charity and annual congressional appropriations to survive. The Bureau did not function as a freestanding institution, and its "life" was by design short-lived. When the Bureau was established in March 1865, Republicans rejected Senator Charles Sumner's proposal to make the Bureau a permanent agency with cabinet rank. The Bureau, virtually all Republicans believed, was intended to meet an extraordinary crisis with extraordinary means, but only until freedom was established and southern "reconstruction" safely under way. It was organized under the War Department and made subject to presidential authority by a Republican Congress that increasingly sought to invest the agency with new responsibility for making congressional Reconstruction work (though unwilling to fund the Bureau adequately). The structural aspects of the Bureau's authority and responsibility derived significantly from wartime experience when the military organized land and labor in the occupied South, yet after the war the Bureau had to operate almost alone in much of the South because no viable Union military presence existed anywhere outside the towns. In addition, the politics of Reconstruction clouded the Bureau's mission and hobbled its authority.

The Bureau's fortunes became entangled in the politics of Reconstruction at every level. Throughout Reconstruction, the Bureau suffered from uneven support in Washington and sustained opposition in the South. Fundamental to the Bureau's difficulties in realizing the ambitions of its most ardent supporters was its uneasy relationship with the president, who doubted the agency's legality, distrusted its mission, and, in the end, disrupted its operations. The problems with the president began in early 1866 and lasted throughout Johnson's tenure.

Following reports from the South of atrocities committed against freedpeople and Union supporters and fearing that the discriminatory "black codes" passed by the provisional southern governments would leave freedpeople in a condition of vassalage, Republicans of all stripes put forward a Freedmen's Bureau bill in February 1866 to extend the Bureau's life and give it new legal powers. Especially significant were the provisions authorizing the Bureau to build and support schools and to assume jurisdiction of cases in which state officials denied blacks the "civil rights belonging to white persons."[4] In conjunction with the Civil Rights bill of 1866—which guaranteed basic civil rights (e.g., the right to make and enforce contracts, the right to have equal access to the courts as witnesses or parties to suits), defined citizenship in such a way as to include the freedmen, and ordered the transfer of legal proceedings from state to federal courts whenever state courts denied citizens' rights on the basis of race—the Freedmen's Bureau bill signaled a broad new federal role in civil rights and the protection of freedpeople. But the Republicans again forswore any interest in making the Bureau a permanent institution. The bill was a response to immediate exigencies and the black codes. Republicans fully expected President Johnson to sign both bills.

In March 1866, Johnson vetoed the bills. A constitutional literalist ever distrustful of encroaching federal power, Johnson rejected the Freedmen's Bureau bill on the grounds that it favored one class of citizens over another, threatened to create an "immense patronage" and overburden the nation's finances, invaded the jurisdiction of state courts, and would make freedpeople wards of the state. Johnson's veto dismayed Republicans and delighted Democrats. Whatever Johnson's political motivations in his veto, the effect on the Bureau was to cast its legitimacy in doubt. To be sure, the Republicans passed a revised Freedmen's Bureau bill, over Johnson's veto in July 1866, that granted the Bureau new authority to establish special courts in former Confederate states, but the Bureau would thereafter be held captive to Johnson's presidential ambitions and constitutional strictures, Democrats' obstructionism, and politics in general. The Supreme Court added to Johnson's and other Bureau opponents' conviction that the Bureau operated without constitutional authority when it ruled, 9–0, in *ex parte Milligan* (April 1866, with opinions released in December 1866) that military courts could not try civilians in areas where civil courts remained open. Republicans' insistence that the Bureau's courts were necessary and legal because the war was not over until Congress restored the rebellious states hardly settled the matter in the public mind and gained no credence with Johnson.

Johnson refused to accept the Republicans' plans for Reconstruction in any case. He became increasingly strident in his denunciation of Republicans, whom he termed *traitors*, and increasingly aligned with Democrats. In the ensuing bitter battles over Reconstruction policy, the Bureau became one of the lightning rods of controversy. Republicans increased the Bureau's responsibility and the federal government's direct interest in protecting the freedpeople and giving Unionism a foothold in the South, which included placing ten "unreconstructed" states under military jurisdiction in 1867. In 1866, Republicans passed a new Civil Rights bill over Johnson's veto and drafted the Fourteenth Amendment to ensure citizenship and civil rights for freedpeople. Johnson responded to these challenges with stubbornness, new charges of Republican conspiracies, and mistimed appeals to northern public opinion. Johnson sealed his political isolation from Republicans with his disastrous "swing around the circle" during the 1866 congressional elections, which served only to discredit him among moderates, embarrass his office, and ensure the election of a veto-proof Republican majority to the next Congress.

An unbowed Johnson turned to his executive powers to undo Republicans' handiwork and have his way. The Bureau lost in the process. By pardoning former Confederates wholesale and restoring their property, Johnson undercut the Bureau's ability to raise money and to settle blacks on their own land. By removing military officers and Bureau commissioners he thought too sympathetic to the freedpeople and replacing them with men closer to his own views on the need to get freedpeople working and land restored, he undermined Bureau morale and authority. Such actions confused the Bureau's practices as personnel changed and different interpretations about free labor and the meaning of freedom clashed. By refusing to enforce Republican Reconstruction, he encouraged white southerners to oppose it as well. For these and other acts of obstruction, the Republicans impeached the president in 1868. A chastened Johnson relaxed his interference, but, by then, the Bureau's days were numbered.

The president did not defeat the Bureau, and, indeed, his policies led some Republicans to live with the Bureau longer than they otherwise might have done. But Johnson's actions weakened the Bureau sufficiently to frustrate its objectives, discourage its supporters, and limit its authority. In a constitutional world where most Americans, irrespective of region or political party, harbored deep suspicions of federal governmental power, he kept the Bureau on the political and ideological defensive.

Further complicating and compromising the Bureau's ability to oversee Reconstruction in the former Confederate states were the conflicting aspirations about Reconstruction held by many of the Bureau's supporters. Republicans generally subscribed to a free-labor ideology rooted in the belief that economic mobility ensured social and republican order. By their reckoning, personal habits of industry, frugality, integrity, and self-discipline would lead to independence and prosperity for both individuals and society. The key was unfettered access to opportunity, which in an agricultural and artisanal world meant land and tools. Slavery had denied the slaves individual responsibility and bred bad habits among slaves and slaveholders alike; in a larger sense, argued free-labor advocates, slavery had suffocated initiative across the South by degrading labor and concentrating wealth in few hands. Now freed of slavery's clutches, supposedly the ex-slaves and the South generally could be transformed into a free-labor economy and society akin to that in the North. But in working out the details of how to plant free-labor values in newly freed soil, Republicans and Bureau agents alike disagreed on how much governmental aid was necessary and for how long.

Most Republicans believed that the freedmen could best make themselves free men by working for land, rather than looking to the government for handouts and relying on federal governmental protection and direct interference beyond the immediate problems of restoring civil order and putting people to work after the war. Others thought that making over the South required more strenuous, sustained federal intervention. A few even called for the confiscation and redistribution of former Confederates' lands as the best way to give ex-slaves a start and bury forever the "lords of the lash" who had bullied the South into secession and remained unrepentant even in defeat.

No issue proved more vexing for the Bureau and Reconstruction than land and labor. The freedpeople expected land that they could work on their own account to be the one sure way to liberty, but white southerners refused to part with their property. And the Bureau was expected to satisfy the freedpeople's legitimate interest in acquiring land while also getting them to work on land still owned by others.

The legacies of slavery and wartime Reconstruction in different areas confused Bureau policies and practices regarding land and labor. Army practice established the boundaries of action open to the Bureau after the war, but no uniform policy toward land and labor had been developed during the war. In fact, in many instances, the army's use of black "free" labor borrowed from a variety of planting practices used during slavery. The demands of rice cultivation differed significantly from those of cotton or sugar, for example, and led to distinctive ways of organizing and managing labor. In the task-oriented system that had governed the South Carolina and Georgia low country, slaves had "claim" to the rest of the day once they had completed their assigned tasks to the satisfaction of the overseer or driver. Slaves then had used "their own time" to tend gardens, raise chickens and livestock, fish, and hunt and thereby had entered a petit-market economy in which they learned to work for themselves. In the Mississippi Delta region and the Louisiana sugar parishes, by contrast, gang labor prevailed and slaves had fewer opportunities to work for themselves. Expectations about control over time and working the land, born of local custom and circumstance, carried over into the army's and then the Bureau's policies during and after the war.

The freedpeople's expectations for land—for "forty acres and a mule"—owed much to the particular circumstances of emancipation and governmental policy in the South Carolina and Georgia sea islands and low country during the war. From the "day of the big-gun shoot" in November 1861, when Union forces entered Port Royal

Sound and sent planters fleeing, the "Port Royal experiment," operated by the Treasury Department and freedmen's aid societies, became the showcase of abolitionists' and Radical Republicans' efforts
to transform the war for the Union into one against slavery by demonstrating that the blacks who stayed on the abandoned sea island
plantations could be organized to work productively and act respon-
sibly. There, the widely reported successes in planting crops and
even raising the first regiment of black troops did much to persuade
northern public opinion that blacks would work without compulsion
and would defend their own freedom, and they also fed the idea
that, in time, blacks would have their own land. Here, many Republicans intoned, was the model for a new South.

Likewise, in January 1865, General William Tecumseh Sherman,
desperate to relieve his army of the large entourage of fleeing slaves
that it had attracted during its "march to the sea," arranged to get
rid of blacks by giving them land. Sherman issued his famous Special
Field Orders, No. 15, which set aside the sea islands and low-country
area thirty miles inland from Charleston, South Carolina, to Jacksonville, Florida, for resettling blacks. Each family would receive a "pos-
sessory title" to forty acres of land, and, as Sherman later authorized,
the loan of mules and horses from the army to work that land. Although Sherman had acted in part on the advice of black leaders in
Savannah, who insisted that the surest route to freedom was for the
ex-slaves to till and own their own land, Sherman's interest in "reconstruction" was less visionary than military, and his authority for
doing so was more circumstantial than constitutional. Still, Sherman's order established a precedent with profound implications for
what blacks and their friends wanted out of Reconstruction land and
labor policy.

The promise of "forty acres and a mule" was seemingly incorporated into the March 1865 bill creating the Freedmen's Bureau and
became the mantra thereafter for blacks eager to gain autonomy and
self-reliance and for Radical Republicans eager to break up the
landed wealth and power of the "old South." By June 1865, roughly
10,000 families of freedpeople, with the assistance of the Freedmen's Bureau, had taken up more than 400,000 acres under the
Sherman order. They had put in crops with the expectations of reap-
ing what they sowed and having Congress convert their temporary
claims into ownership. At the same time, in several other places

across the South, the Bureau was leasing land and providing tools and draft animals to ex-slaves.

Away from South Carolina and Georgia, a very different story unfolded. The largest "experiment" organizing black labor during the war took place in the lower Mississippi Valley. As elsewhere, slaves pouring into Union army camps forced the army to find ways to alleviate the strains on limited army supplies, to bring order to the camps, and to exploit the slaves' labor. Although some army officers appealed to northern missionary and voluntary aid associations to provide relief and even open schools for the "contrabands," as the slaves coming into Union lines were known, the army assumed principal responsibility for them and sought to put them to good use. Military interest, rather than humanitarianism, drove this army policy, though the appallingly high mortality rates in the contraband camps, as much as 25 percent during the war before the army instituted its labor policies, figured in military thinking. The army employed the contrabands in a host of tasks, almost wholly in fatigue duty, at little pay, and often to the disgust of the contrabands who felt abused and of Republicans who thought an opportunity for social reform was being lost.

Important in defining army policy toward the contrabands were the labor regulations issued by General Nathaniel Banks in 1863 for occupied Louisiana, and later extended northward in the Mississippi Valley to encompass more freedpeople than anywhere else in the occupied South. Those regulations made "idleness" and "vagrancy" crimes. Banks's motives in forcing contrabands to work were complicated by wartime political considerations of trying to nurture Unionism among planters by assuring them of labor and order on the plantations, along with his desire to get the contrabands out of the camps, but the effect was to make the army the enforcer of plantation discipline. Able-bodied freedmen were expected to work, and the army's provost marshals would see that they did.

Most such freedmen found work on plantations owned by loyal southerners whose land had not been confiscated and for whom the Emancipation Proclamation did not apply, or on army-controlled "abandoned" or confiscated plantations leased to northern investors or southerners who had taken the oath of allegiance. After choosing their employer, the freedmen were obliged to sign year-long contracts. Such contracts provided for either a share of the crop at year's end or a monthly wage, in addition to food and shelter, but also imposed deductions for days lost due to illness or irregular work and almost complete submission to the authority of the plantation owner or lessee.

This compulsory system of labor was a wartime expedient and, said its defenders, promised an orderly transition to "freedom." In large measure, though, it consigned the freedpeople to lives as plantation workers, with little prospect of becoming landholders.

As responsibility for "reconstruction" passed from the army to the Freedmen's Bureau in 1865 and 1866, the earlier experiences and expectations came with it. Many Bureau agents had been army officers, and the Bureau was under the authority of the War Department. To be sure, army thinking about freedpeople's policy had not been of one mind during the war. Generals with abolitionist sympathies, such as Rufus Saxton, military governor of the South Carolina and Georgia sea island and low-country district, and Bureau head O. O. Howard, known as the "Christian general," viewed the end of slavery as an opportunity to plant a free-labor society and a new moral order in the South. They wanted ex-slaves to have land, equality before the law, and schools, and they sought to use army resources to facilitate the ex-slaves' march into freedom. Outnumbering the Saxtons and Howards, though, were army officers who regarded "reconstruction" primarily as a problem of management. For them, returning workers to the fields as soon as possible remained the priority. The written contract, they believed, would protect the freedpeople while also ensuring a peaceable transition from slavery to a wage-based labor system. Virtually all of them agreed, however, that respect for law must prevail and that the freedpeople must have basic civil rights and protection from abuses.

The various land and labor policies developed during the war strongly influenced thinking about the determination of land and labor management during Reconstruction. The more publicized efforts in South Carolina and Georgia had obscured the army's less-known but more widely applied practices in the Mississippi Valley region and contributed to the sense of "betrayal" some Republicans, many Bureau agents, and most freedpeople felt when the "promise" of land from the South Carolina and Georgia experiments was not extended across the South and, indeed, was retracted in South Carolina and Georgia. Adding to the freedpeople's expectations of receiving land were the many rumors circulating during and immediately after the war that the federal government would confiscate rebels' land and give it to former slaves. Ex-slaves thought such redistribution their just due for years of unremitting toil and suffering, and many Bureau agents and Union soldiers thought so too. But so radical a scheme as confiscating land after the war died aborning in Congress. Few Republicans and no Democrats countenanced any policy that would violate the sanctity of property. In any case, President Johnson ended the prospect in 1865 by adopting a generous amnesty and pardon policy toward former Confederates and ordering all abandoned and confiscated lands still in the hands of Union forces at war's end to be returned to their "rightful" owners. General Howard and the Bureau grudgingly complied with the order. Although more than 2,000 freed families would acquire title to lands on the South Carolina and Georgia sea islands under special provisions in the 1866 Freedmen's Bureau Act, most blacks were dispossessed of land they had occupied during the war. Thus did the Mississippi Valley wartime arrangements (which emphasis on getting ex-slaves back to work and restoring social order also reflected army practices in occupied Virginia and the Tennessee Valley), more than the "promise" of the "Port Royal experiment" and the "Sherman lands" in South Carolina and Georgia, stake the boundaries of federal government policy in regard to land and labor.

Enforcement of Johnson's policy left the Bureau compromised in blacks' minds for not fulfilling the promise of land and bereft of the independent resources that came from selling abandoned land to run its programs. However much Radical Republicans and freedpeople decried Johnson's policy and considered the ex-slaves as the rightful owners of the land they occupied, the fact of land restoration altered forever the role of the Bureau and the freedpeople's relationship with it, their former masters, and government itself.

The passage of the Southern Homestead Act in June 1866 opened up 46 million acres of public land in five southern states for settlement, with first claim given to freedmen and Union veterans, but the act succeeded mostly on paper, for only about 1,000 freedmen ever gained title to this land. Much of the land was poor in quality and inaccessible. The Bureau tried to facilitate movement to Homestead land but with halting efforts and very limited success. Lacking information, capital, and even transportation to reach the land, and tied to yearlong labor contracts, most freedpeople after 1865 had to turn to negotiating the best terms possible for working land that others would own. They could hope to earn and save enough to buy a parcel on their own account some day, but they were increasingly trapped by low returns and onerous conditions.

The Bureau moved out of the land business to assume its principal roles as labor mediator and school builder. Achieving a free-labor South would take time—more time than the temporary, under-manned, and poorly supplied Bureau could achieve alone. Soon enough, blacks, Bureau agents, and white southerners realized this and acted accordingly.

The Bureau became the principal intermediary between planters and freedpeople as they worked out new labor arrangements. Bureau agents adapted to local circumstances and crop conditions in trying to negotiate agricultural contracts that promised fair wages in return for steady work. The contracts varied across the South, but generally they specified the terms of payment (wages or a share of the crop, or some combination thereof) and any other allotments (such as food, housing, clothing, medical care) due the freedmen. The contracts were made with men, usually heads of households, which reflected the basic nineteenth-century belief that men were legally and morally responsible for finding work, and detailed the workers' duties and employers' authority. Freedpeople often chafed at the conditions, and planters complained of their lack of control over workers. The Bureau stepped in to remind freedpeople of their contractual obligations to work until the crop was in and to remind planters to respect the terms of the contract regarding pay, allotments, and workers' rights to do as they pleased on their own time.

The most difficult days were in late 1865 and early 1866 when many freedpeople balked at signing contracts for yearlong labor because they anticipated getting land from the government. Also, many freedpeople moved to reunite families, find better conditions, and acquire land—a process of migration and expectation that continued throughout Reconstruction and left some areas short of labor and others crowded with laborers. By most accounts, the contract system failed to satisfy the ambitions of the freedpeople. Also, many planters cheated the freedpeople out of their wages and allotments, abused them, and otherwise violated the terms and spirit of the contracts because most whites refused to acknowledge that blacks had any rights that whites were bound to respect. Not surprisingly under such conditions, Bureau agents spent most of their time settling disputes.

The Bureau's ability to adjudicate disputes was limited, even as its responsibility for doing so grew. Bureau agents were thinly scattered across the South, which meant that most conflicts between freedpeople and planters did not reach the Bureau. Undermanned and often unschooled in local custom and crop patterns, the Bureau agents initially let local civil courts handle the load of complaints, once southern states allowed blacks to testify in civil cases. Until the summer of 1866, the Bureau lacked the legal authority to do otherwise.

The revised Freedmen's Bureau Act of 1866 granted the Bureau authority to establish special courts and boards of arbitration with civil and criminal jurisdiction over minor cases involving freedpeople. The so-called freedmen's courts meted out an ad hoc justice. With no legal precedents to guide their decisions and little or no military support to compel obedience to the courts' findings, Bureau agents had to rely on persuasion, cajoling, and threats of further legal action to win compliance from planters, many of whom refused to concede that the Bureau, or anyone, had any right to interfere in their relations with black workers at all. Also, the doubtful constitutionality of the freedmen's courts in the wake of *ex parte Milligan* led many Bureau agents to look to the civil courts for relief, as did the revisions in state law during 1866 and 1867 that accorded black litigants basic civil rights in courts of law.

Still, the willingness of a Bureau agent to listen to the complaint of a freedperson and that agent's ability to bring suit against a planter in a civil court (the local court's likely favoritism to a white over a black litigant notwithstanding) or to send a case involving civil rights to a federal court gave Bureau agents leverage in negotiating settlements. That informal process of advocacy and intervention, more than legal proceedings, became the main line of Bureau "adjudication" and the heart of individual agents' strategy across the South. Thus did Bureau agents' practices in the various states, more than did federally prescribed regulations and law, make policy. Bureau "policy" in negotiating, monitoring, and enforcing labor contracts, as in every other activity, remained in a state of evolution and adaptation—a fact that led to confusion in understanding the Bureau's role in Reconstruction.

Among the Bureau's several responsibilities, none was more enduring than its role in building schools for the freedpeople. But here, too, the purposes of the Bureau and its authority were not wholly clear, and Bureau practices varied from locale to locale. Bureau officials from O. O. Howard down to agents in the field agreed that education was the "talisman of power" for the freedpeople, the necessary adjunct to the "education" of working for themselves and the foundation of a free society of self-reliant people. To be sure, much of the impetus for education came from blacks, who filled makeshift schools in the contraband camps, struggled to set up their own schools in churches and abandoned buildings after emancipation, and constantly pressed the Bureau for financial and material aid for education, but the Bureau eagerly joined in the process. The Bureau invested heavily in education. It established or supported day, evening, Sunday, mechanical arts (or industrial), and special schools and founded such colleges as Hampton Institute, Howard University, and Fisk University, among several, to train teachers. Between 1865 and 1870, the Bureau spent $5 million on freedmen's schools, more than half of the total recorded expenditures from all sources for such education during that critical period. In addition, Bureau agents spent much of their time in sponsoring and managing schools from 1866 onward.

The Bureau did not run freedmen's education according to any set plan. Their education remained more a philosophy than a clearly demarcated program, for the Bureau lacked the resources and authority to establish and maintain a public school system anywhere. Rather, the Bureau offered a framework for education that would be carried on by others. It provided materials to build schools, transported northern teachers (and sometimes paid them) to freedmen's schools, and coordinated efforts with freedmen's aid and missionary societies to manage schools. The American Missionary Association (AMA), more than any of the other Protestant-based aid societies, became a virtual partner with the Bureau in education. This was due in part to the congruent free-labor philosophy and personal friendship of AMA and Bureau officers, but also to convenience. Such arrangements caused confusion about who actually ran the schools, indeed sometimes who was supposed to pay the teachers. Overall, though, working closely with northern aid societies and local black churches allowed the Bureau to enlarge its geographic reach, so that schools were located in most counties of the former Confederate states by the late 1860s, and it maximized Bureau resources by leaving many problems of staffing to the aid societies and, increasingly by 1870, to blacks.

In conjunction with the aid societies, the Bureau brought thousands of northern teachers, many of them women, to the South to redeem its benighted white natives from their political and social "heresies" and to lift up the freedpeople through the three "Rs" and northern Protestant enlightenment. Whatever the paternalism of such attitudes, the effect was profound. The second "northern invasion" made possible freedmen's education and boosted the Bureau's efforts to lead the freedpeople toward middle-class values. It also spurred both blacks to gain control over their own schools and whites in "reconstructed" governments to assume responsibility for establishing a permanent public education system, if only to get the "Yankee schoolmarms" out and southern culture back into schools.

By 1870, when the Bureau's educational and other responsibilities ended, there were over 4,300 freedmen's schools with almost a quarter million students in the South. The statistics in some ways disguise the unevenness and poverty of freedpeople's education. Most of the schools were located in or near towns, and, by 1870, most black school-age children still did not attend school at all (and those who did went to school for but a few months out of the year and often only for a few years overall). And virtually every school was segregated by race, for whites refused to attend freedmen schools and the Bureau and Republicans did not push for racial integration in education. Yet, to discount the Bureau's educational achievements misses the dynamic of the Bureau's role in Reconstruction. The Bureau could not take credit for all of those schools, many of which were then staffed by blacks and even some southern whites, but without the Bureau's resources and resolve, freedmen's education would have been even more sporadic and poorer than it was. The Bureau laid a foundation, but, as in land and labor policy and relief efforts, the overtaxed Bureau agents and the overextended Bureau alone could not remake the southern educational system. Nor did the Bureau seek to do so. Its goal in education was to set a course for others to follow rather than carry the load by itself, and its efforts should be judged on that basis.

The effectiveness of the Bureau in Reconstruction—whether in land and labor policy, education, or relief—hinged on the ability of individual agents to make their case before blacks and whites and to gain respect for law. The Bureau lacked the institutional resources to effect fully relief, recovery, and reform, and local permutations of custom and circumstance meant constantly having to adapt broad Bureau philosophy and interest to very particular conditions. The result was that the Bureau suffered from overworked agents in the field. There were never enough agents (according to the best count available, a total of 2,441 men served as agents over the life of the Bureau and only 900 were spread across the South at the height of Bureau staffing). Agents often lived and operated alone, with diminishing military support and unrelenting local white opposition. Outsiders by birth and culture, they had to find their own way through a thicket of expectations and local norms amid a social revolution in the making.

The caseload of individual agents was staggering. Blacks presented the agents with a constant stream of complaints and concerns, including family and personal matters, and, even as they decried the Bureau's interference, whites regularly pressed the agents to make the freedpeople work and abide by their contracts. The end of the planting year was especially taxing for agents, as they were called on to settle disputes over payments for the crop just harvested and, at the same time, to arrange contracts under favorable terms for the next year. Also, throughout the year, agents had to file reports on schools, civil order, labor, and so much more—a constant round of reportage and correspondence whereby agents explained their doings, sought authority to act, and prodded officials to help. Agents knew no rest. Broken health, exhaustion, and even mental depression afflicted the Bureau agent who was "on call" every day. As Georgia agent James Davison described the problem: "I am *tired out* and *broke down*. . . . Every day for 6 months, day after day, I have had from 5 to 20 complaints, *generally trivial* and of no moment, yet requiring consideration & attention coming from both Black & White. . . . The result is my time is consumed, and I virtually become a 'pack horse' for the whole county."[5]

Also faced with social ostracism and violence, exhausted agents left the Bureau. Georgia agent J. W. Barney spoke for many agents who resigned because of overwork and threats of violence when he wrote in 1868, "I have endured this as long as mortal man can" and observed that the "great mystery to the many is that a man of my stamp could live in that section of the country for one year." To be sure, many agents stayed longer than Barney, who longed to return to "a country where life is protected by law," but few stayed more than two years or so.[6] Thus did the daily demands on Bureau agents make even more temporary the Bureau's presence than did the congressional legislation limiting its life to five years.

All this said, the Bureau accomplished much during Reconstruction. Its relief efforts alone saved many southerners from starvation and started up the resettlement and rebuilding process for countless refugees. Its educational work laid the groundwork for public education across the South, and its provisions for school buildings, supplies, and even teachers made it the midwife of much of the freedpeople's own educational effort. However restricted by philosophy and circumstance, its land and labor policies at least established the rights of freedpeople to own their labor and the duty of all parties to respect the law. That most southern blacks remained a landless and despised class and most southern whites remained "unreconstructed rebels" in their racial attitudes and refusal to accept freedpeople as citizens and Republican governments as legitimate owed less to Bureau failings than to the larger social, economic, and political context in which the Bureau operated and Reconstruction policy and practice evolved. If the experience of the Bureau showed the limitations of Republican policy and federal authority, it also suggested their possibilities. Despite all the structural and political constraints on the Bureau, it demonstrated that government could (and would) act. In so doing, it provided psychological as much as material relief. The Bureau helped awaken Americans to the promise of freedom, and, for a time, the Bureau's physical presence in the South made palpable to many citizens the abstract principles of equal access to the law and free labor.

The essays in this book show the Bureau in action. They also suggest how racial attitudes, political ambition and interest, and economic and social advantage, among several factors, affected the ways that the army, the president, the Congress, and the various state and local governments understood and engaged the Bureau. Most of all, they point to the importance of getting down to cases. Read together, these essays reveal that the Bureau was never a single unified force or even a coherent philosophy on how to inculcate "free-labor" values and "reconstruct" the South. The Bureau often worked at cross-purposes of recovery and reform. And the Bureau did not work alone, as its negotiations and alliances with various congeries of freedpeople and white landholders, among others, in the South and with freedmen's aid societies, especially the AMA, demonstrate. Out of such activity a new synthesis of expectation and effort developed so that the Bureau of 1866 and after evolved into a much larger, and also more contentious, idea and institution than what reformers had envisioned in 1865. It also had become weaker institutionally on the "national" level, while it grew in importance in many localities. The commitment, courage, and ingenuity of individual Bureau agents made the difference. In that regard, the essays point to the vital roles that these agents played in shaping "reconstruction" into several forms, all contingent on local culture, custom, and condition but also derived from common assumptions about class and gender regarding work. Personality counted, just as local culture did (the Catholic Creole milieu of the sugar parishes of lower Louisiana was worlds apart from the cotton Piedmont or the low-country rice cultures). Finally, the essays remind us that by viewing the Bureau and Reconstruction as interlocking processes, it is possible to move from sterile debates about the "good" or "bad" of the Bureau to appreciate anew Frederick Douglass's wise counsel that we should understand that the abolition of slavery was a beginning more than an end. So it was with the Bureau as well.

NOTES

1. Calvin Holly to O. O. Howard, December 16, 1865, in Ira Berlin, Barbara J. Fields, Steven F. Miller, Joseph P. Reidy, and Leslie S. Rowland, eds., *Free at Last: A Documentary History of Slavery, Freedom, and the Civil War* (New York: The New Press, 1992), 523–25.

2. Frederick Douglass quoted in Eric Foner, *Reconstruction: America's Unfinished Revolution, 1863–1877* (New York: Harper & Row, 1988), 76. My overall narrative of the Bureau and Reconstruction draws on Foner's essential history and on the recent work on the Bureau cited in the various essays in this volume. For a very useful survey of the literature on the Freedmen's

Bureau, see John David Smith, " 'The Work It Did Not Do Because It Could Not': Georgia and the 'New' Freedmen's Bureau Historiography," *Georgia Historical Quarterly* 82 (summer 1998): 331–49.

3. Quotations from "An Act to Establish a Bureau for the Relief of Freedmen and Refugees" (March 3, 1865), reprinted in Deirdre Mullane, ed., *Crossing the Danger Water: Three Hundred Years of African-American Writing* (New York: Doubleday Anchor, 1993), 301–2.

4. For the texts of the two 1866 Freedmen's Bureau bills, the one vetoed by Johnson and the revised bill passed over his veto, see Edward McPherson, *The Political History of the United States during the Period of Reconstruction* (Washington, D.C.: Philip and Solomons, 1871), 72–74, 78–80. My discussion of the meaning of the Freedmen's Bureau legislation relies on Donald G. Nieman, *To Set the Law in Motion: The Freedmen's Bureau and the Legal Rights of Blacks, 1865–1868* (Millwood, N.Y.: KTO Press, 1979), 106–9.

5. James Davison quoted in Paul A. Cimbala, *Under the Guardianship of the Nation: The Freedmen's Bureau and the Reconstruction of Georgia, 1865–1870* (Athens: University of Georgia Press, 1997), 64–65.

6. J. W. Barney quoted in ibid., 79.

The Freedmen's Bureau and Reconstruction

1

Ulysses S. Grant and the Freedmen's Bureau

Brooks D. Simpson

LATE IN LIFE, when Ulysses S. Grant reflected on his achievements during the American Civil War, he did not restrict himself to what he had accomplished on the battlefield. In his *Memoirs*, he departed from his narrative of military events during the fall of 1862 to describe his efforts to take care of the black refugees in West Tennessee and northern Mississippi. In November, he had placed Chaplain John Eaton of the 27th Ohio Infantry in charge of organizing camps and putting blacks to work to bring in the fall cotton and corn corps from the then deserted plantations. Those planters who remained could hire black workers, with Eaton supervising the relationship. Grant recorded the result: "At once the freedmen became self-sustaining. The money was not paid to them directly, but was expended judiciously and for their benefit. They gave me no trouble afterwards." Eventually, blacks were paid to cut wood to fuel Union steamers; the resulting income served "to feed and clothe all, old and young, male and female," as well as "to build them comfortable cabins, hospitals for the sick, and to supply them with many comforts they had never known before." Proud of these accomplishments, Grant ruminated, "It was at this point, probably, where the first idea of a 'Freedman's Bureau' took its origin."[1]

In advancing this claim, Grant wrote in ignorance of other efforts along the Atlantic coast, from the banks of the mouth of the James River to South Carolina's Sea Islands, to establish the foundations for freedom for the freedpeople. At the same time, he inadvertently revealed some of his own assumptions about what form freedom for blacks would take. The federal government would supervise the transition from slavery to freedom by managing labor relationships to maximize order and productivity while also providing for the freedpeople's welfare. Ever pragmatic, Grant realized that his program curtailed the impact that a refugee population might have on military operations, including disorder, disease, and the draining of supplies from the soldiers.

It would be left to Eaton, writing some twenty years after Grant's account first appeared, to shed additional light on the general's thinking. When the chaplain, surprised to receive Grant's order, reluctantly reported for duty at headquarters, he believed that he had been given "an impossible undertaking doomed to bring only suffering and failure." Grant explained how military necessity "and the dictates of mere humanity" demanded a solution to the problems posed by the refugees flooding into Union lines; "in view of the condition out of which they sprang, the General believed it to be necessary that for a while, at least, some form of guardianship should be exercised over them." But the general did not stop there. The blacks, he argued, could be put to good use in support of military operations. "He went on to say that when it had been made clear that the Negro, as an independent laborer—for he was not yet a freedman—could do these things well, it would be very easy to put a musket in his hands and make a soldier of him, and if he fought well, eventually to put the ballot in his hand and make him a citizen." It was a remarkable vision, Eaton recalled. "Obviously I was dealing with no incompetent, but with a man capable of handling large issues. Never before in those early and bewildering days had I heard the problem of the future of the Negro attacked so vigorously and with such humanity combined with practical good sense."[2]

Some scholars read too much into these wartime plans as precursors of postwar policy toward the freedpeople in the South: for most military commanders, what to do with the former slaves took a backseat to the primary obligations of defeating enemy armies and subduing occupied populations.[3] Nevertheless, Grant's conversation with Eaton was noteworthy for what it forecast as well as for what it omitted. That the general was a former slaveholder (he had freed his slave in 1859) and had married into a slave-owning family made his vision of the future even more unexpected. To foresee a future where black men would wield bayonets and ultimately ballots placed Grant with Frederick Douglass in predicting how far the revolution set in place by the war and emancipation might go. At the same time, Grant said nothing about blacks as independent landowners, tilling the soil of their own farms: implicit in his forecast was a world where blacks worked for other people, who most likely would be white. As someone who labored hard (and unsuccessfully) to establish his own economic independence as a farmer in the 1850s, Grant understood the pride involved in working the land. He still held fast to this belief in 1863, when he welcomed the chance to use the plantations of Jefferson and Joseph Davis as an example of black independence, and expressed the hope that these experiments would become "a Negro paradise." For the moment, however, wartime priorities demanded that Grant concentrate on subduing an insurrection rather than fostering a revolution—although, in many eyes, the very acts of emancipating blacks, securing compensation for their labor, and enlisting them in the Union army were revolutionary enough.[4]

A soldier instinctively wants to restore order, even in a war that promises revolutionary change; even as he wields the tools of violence, he seeks a peace born of victory. That Union war aims during the Civil War came to embrace both the restoration of order and the revolution wrought by emancipation complicated matters still more, especially when it became apparent that it would be extraordinarily difficult (if not impossible) to achieve both reconciliation with whites and justice for blacks in the postwar South. For those scholars who measure the extent of change wrought by the Civil War and Reconstruction in terms of a revolution based on the redistribution of land from whites to blacks, the Freedmen's Bureau proved a disappointment, an exercise in northern paternalism. And yet, in the end, the army was only following orders. Republican policymakers were unwilling to institute a far-reaching program of land confiscation and redistribution during the war, and whatever initiatives existed at war's end were stifled by President Andrew Johnson. Moreover, the army's commitment to preserve order had revolutionary consequences, for the use of the Freedmen's Bureau, military courts, and military commissions protected blacks when southern state legislators, local authorities, and civil courts proved unable or unwilling to meet that challenge.

Army personnel became the primary administrators of Reconstruction policy in the South during and after the war. Despite efforts by Senator Charles Sumner to place the proposed Freedmen's

Bureau under the auspices of the Treasury Department (which at the time was headed by fellow Radical Republican Salmon P. Chase), the Bureau that came into being in March 1865 was controlled by the War Department, a decision supported by none other than Eaton. Thus it was inevitable that Grant came to play a role in the shaping of the postwar order in the South. Eventually, he sought to exercise more direct control over the process by integrating the Freedmen's Bureau with occupation forces and having department and district commanders double as assistant commissioners for the Bureau. The general-in-chief never became engaged in debates over the Bureau's power to distribute confiscated lands to the freedpeople: indeed, he expressed concern that Bureau agents were promoting disorder by allowing blacks to entertain thoughts that eventually they would each receive forty acres to call their own. At the same time, he saw in the Bureau a useful instrument for restoring order throughout the South and for supervising the transition from slavery to freedom. If that meant a commitment not to homesteads but to wage labor contracts, it also meant a commitment to the protection of black civil rights. Thus the desire to restore order in just fashion placed Grant in the role of a reluctant revolutionary.

In arraigning the Freedmen's Bureau for its failure to achieve a revolution in social and economic (and thus ultimately political) relationships between whites and blacks, many historians have given short shrift to the efforts of Bureau agents and army personnel to secure protection for the freedpeople from intimidation, violence, and the operation of southern civil courts. Yet supporters of the rights of the emancipated noted that without such protection, it would be hard to achieve any significant or lasting progress. If blacks were not allowed to exercise basic civil rights, they would have little chance to maintain their title to property, including land, or to market their crops. The restoration of civil government, including the reestablishment of state and local courts, offered no relief, in large part because white southerners passed legislation to ensure that justice would not be color-blind. For all of the attention given to the passage of so-called black codes by several southern states, just as remarkable was the decision to restrict or to deny altogether black participation in the civil courts as witnesses or jurors. It was unlikely that all-white juries would find in favor of black plaintiffs or defendants; lacking black testimony, many white defendants would go unpunished for crimes committed against blacks. Thus the restoration of civil rule guaranteed injustice for blacks, especially when local authorities demonstrated little interest in protecting black rights.[5]

Major General Oliver O. Howard, who headed the Freedmen's Bureau, understood the problem. At the end of May 1865—just a day after President Johnson issued the first of his proclamations outlining how those southern states that lacked an existing government recognized by Washington could go about restoring civil rule— Howard authorized assistant commissioners to adjudicate cases in which blacks were parties. Even Johnson understood that prohibiting black testimony and service as jurors made a mockery of civil processes: repeatedly, he warned those white southerners who were engaged in erecting postwar political institutions to rectify these shortcomings. Otherwise, the president predicted, reports of wrongdoing would fuel calls for a more radical intervention in southern affairs by the federal government in accordance with the preference of those Republicans who advocated fundamental change.

During the summer, both blacks and whites looked to the United States Army and the Bureau to preserve order. Of course, they did not always agree on what constituted "order." White landowners believed that both agencies would compel blacks to work, whereas blacks looked to them to offer a shield against violence and to serve as an arbiter to ensure that landowners did not violate labor contracts. "The military officers of the United States are in fact the only tribunal to which under present circumstances differences between whites and blacks can be submitted with equal satisfaction to both parties," Carl Schurz, a former Union general and a Republican spokesman who toured the South during the summer of 1865, observed, "and I am certain, the decisions of no other tribunal would be so readily acquiesced in." For many whites, this held true only so long as the institutions of local justice were not restored. They pursued efforts to revive state militias and local police forces to displace federal authorities and reassert white hegemony. What intensified this demand for the restoration of civil authority was the antipathy that many southern whites had toward the black regiments that formed a good portion of the occupation forces—and the proportion of the occupation forces composed of black soldiers increased as white units were mustered out.[6]

Grant had nothing to do with the framing of the legislation that established the Freedmen's Bureau or with the naming of Howard as its head; for that post, he had preferred Eaton. In fact, despite his expressions of concern about the importance of reconstructing the nation upon the foundation of a lasting peace, Grant paid little attention to matters in the South throughout the summer of 1865. He presided over demobilization of the volunteer army and urged a reduction in the number of soldiers left on occupation duty in the South; only the rapid departure of white volunteers deterred him from limiting the responsibilities of black soldiers. Restoring order and reconciling white southerners remained his foremost priorities. Grant showed no interest in discussions about the confiscation and redistribution of planter lands; rather, he rested content with the notion that free labor meant wage labor, with black workers negotiating contracts with white landowners. He encountered Howard at commencement at Bowdoin College on August 4; perhaps it was then that Grant assured Howard that he would make enough army officers available to provide a Bureau agent for every county in the South.[7]

Only once during the summer of 1865 did a matter concerning the operations of the Bureau compel Grant to take action. In Georgia, General Edward A. Wild, the officer in charge of the Bureau on most of the state's mainland, won quite a reputation for himself and his rather rough handling of southern whites, especially in his endeavor to discover the whereabouts of the Confederacy's gold reserves. His efforts included torturing and searching the persons of Wilkes County residents, confiscating Robert Toombs's residence at Washington, Georgia, and seizing the county courthouse for a black school. Schurz, who traveled through Georgia in early August on a journey to report on conditions in the South, noted that Wild had neglected to organize the Bureau's operations, which left military commanders to devise makeshift arrangements between planters and workers; the general preferred to address blacks at mass meetings, where he and the Reverend Mansfield French held forth on the rights and responsibilities that came with freedom. General James B. Steedman, commanding the Department of Georgia, deemed Wild "entirely unfit for the discharge of the duties incumbent upon him." Learning of Wild's adventures, Grant, without pausing to investigate the lurid reports, recommended his removal. "Men should be appointed who can act from facts and not always be guided by prejudice in favor of color," he added; perhaps one of his staff officers should travel south to Mississippi, Alabama, and Georgia to report "upon the situation and management of the freedmen in those States."[8]

Grant did not follow up on that recommendation, nor did he participate in the exchange of letters between Howard and President Johnson that effectually terminated the Bureau's activities in redistributing confiscated land to blacks. Instead, his involvement with Bureau affairs during 1865 was intermittent and sporadic. Grant thought that the Bureau had erred in operating desegregated schools in Charleston, South Carolina; he authorized the retention of officers in the volunteer service who were serving as agents until Howard secured full-time replacements. However, he was not engaged with the framing of Bureau policy or the carrying out of its responsibilities: the relationship between the Bureau and the army remained undefined, leading to bureaucratic confusion.[9]

By the time Grant returned to Washington in the fall of 1865, Reconstruction was only one of several priorities confronting him. He continued to supervise the demobilization of the wartime army and helped to frame the organization of its postwar successor; he remained interested in supporting efforts to overthrow the French-backed regime of Maximilian in Mexico. What concerned him most was the dilemma posed by demobilization at a time when some military presence, however slight, remained advisable, for as white volunteers returned home, black volunteers remained in uniform and on duty despite angry protests by white southerners that their presence was abrasive. Grant concluded that as of the summer of 1865 "every where submission was perfect," a sign that he was not well informed about conditions in the South (and had yet to take the trouble to become informed). He acknowledged that the mission of the occupation force was "to secure order and protect the freedmen in the liberty conferred upon them" and recommended a force of 80,000 men in part because of "the possibility of future local disturbances arising from ill feeling left by the war or the unsettled questions between the white and black races at the south." He remained reluctant to see things for himself by undertaking a personal inspection tour, however, despite the advice of one staff officer, Cyrus B. Comstock: "I thought he had better go so that he might be able to speak decidedly on questions of reconstruction." President Johnson agreed, and at the end of November Grant took a short swing though the southern Atlantic states. In a span of two weeks, he visited Virginia, the Carolinas, Georgia, and East Tennessee and stopped at several cities along the way.[10]

Inevitably Grant's conclusions were impressionistic, even sketchy; in traveling from city to city, he neglected conditions in rural areas and small towns. Moreover, he allowed his discussions with South Carolina landowners too much weight in forming his conclusions about the operations of the Freedmen's Bureau. For several months, General Rufus Saxton, assistant commissioner of the Bureau in South Carolina, had struggled to provide blacks with their own land. White southerners resisted. A delegation of white landowners informed General George G. Meade, who toured the state in September, that confiscation of their lands would render their efforts to rebuild their lives "absolutely impossible." Meade attempted to check Saxton; Howard, after failing to negotiate a compromise with President Johnson that would have offered partial restoration in exchange for a limited redistribution of plantation lands to blacks, had to urge Saxton to press forward with complete restoration. At Johnson's behest, Howard had traveled to the Sea Islands in October to explain the new policy. He found white southerners understandably receptive to the president's conciliatory efforts, whereas Bureau agents and blacks realized that they had been betrayed in their efforts to create a brave new world. Saxton resisted the administration's edict for Edisto Island. South Carolina whites pressed upon Grant their argument that Bureau agents were fomenting disorder and raising false hopes. Although Grant visited the Sea Islands on December 3, he seems to have been more impressed by what he observed of Charleston's whites during the previous two days. One newspaper reported the general's "great pleasure and satisfaction at the general good feeling, spirit and disposition which he had observed along his route, evinced by the Southern people toward the government, and their cheerful adaptation to the new orders of affairs."[11]

Grant returned to Washington on December 11, a week after Congress convened. Johnson, pleased by what the general had found, asked him to file a report: the president planned to pair Grant's letter with Schurz's far more detailed and documented report that the Senate, acting on Charles Sumner's suggestion, had asked him to provide. If Grant's letter did not constitute a ringing endorsement of presidential policy, it did not offer the sustained indictment contained in Schurz's lengthy missive. Grant featured the Bureau in his letter. He admitted that he had not given Bureau affairs careful examination, but he nevertheless offered some observations and recommendations. The impression he received from conversations with fellow officers, including Bureau administrators, "lead me to think that in some of the States its affairs have not been conducted with good judgment or economy." He blamed some Bureau agents for encouraging the freedmen in the belief that confiscation and redistribution remained possible, thus complicating the negotiation of labor contracts for the coming year. Noting that Howard had done what he could to dissuade blacks of this notion, Grant observed that "the complaint in South Carolina was, that when he left things went on as before." Nor were the agents entirely responsible for the resulting chaos. Although "many, perhaps the majority" of agents "advise the freedmen that by their own industry they must now expect to live" and supervised labor contracts under that assumption, blacks did not always cooperate. "In some instances, I am sorry to say, the freedman's mind does not seem to be disabused of the idea that a freedman has the right to live without care or provision for the future." Expecting to receive their own parcels of land, some blacks remained idle or congregated "in camps, towns, and cities"; the resulting "vice and disease will tend to the extermination, or great reduction of the colored race." Such conclusions went beyond Grant's limited exposure to southern conditions, although they reflected assumptions held by others, including the president. However, they followed from the general's belief that the best way to restore southern economic health for both blacks and whites was if blacks worked for whites: that arrangement would produce a prosperous and orderly social order.

If Grant was critical of some Bureau practices, he nevertheless believed that "in some form the Freedmen's Bureau is an absolute necessity until civil law is established and enforced, securing to the freedmen their rights and full protection." After all, no one could expect that the racial prejudices (or "opinions," as Grant called them) long held by white southerners "can be changed in a day." The freedmen "require for a few years not only laws to protect them, but the fostering care of those who will give them good counsel, and in whom they rely." What Grant wanted to do was not to abolish the Bureau but to place it under direct military control. Bureau officers and army commanders often issued conflicting orders; the army and the Bureau worked at cross-purposes that created confusion exacerbated by the presence of so many officers on detached duty with the Bureau. Better, Grant thought, to empower every army officer to act as a Bureau agent, with orders for them transmitted through normal department channels. This proposed reorganization "would secure uniformity of action" while cutting expenses. Efficiency, economy, and order, not revolution, were to be the guiding principles in securing emancipation. Howard took the hint. On December 22, he instructed his assistant commissioners to investigate Grant's charges and correct what needed to be corrected. He reminded them that the Bureau was part of the army and urged them to cooperate with department commanders.[12]

Grant's report revealed his ambivalence about the progress of reconciliation and the fruits of emancipation. In arguing for the maintenance of military occupation and the Freedmen's Bureau, he made the case for continued federal intervention; in his reflections on black behavior, he expressed his preference for having black laborers work for white planters and suggested that both races were to blame for current racial friction. That most historians have argued that the report constituted an endorsement of Johnson's policy reflects the degree to which Johnson himself was able to frame perceptions of the document. After all, the president had sought it precisely because he wanted to counter the conclusions reached by Schurz. Although the president had ostensibly approved of Schurz's trip, the German-American had undertaken it with the determination to uncover proof that presidential reconstruction fell short of providing blacks protection for their newfound freedom. That Schurz's resulting report, bulging with testimony documenting violence against blacks, served as an indictment of Johnson's policy came as no surprise. By pairing it with that of the Union's foremost war hero, the president sought to muffle its impact and correctly concluded that the public would find more credible the findings of the hero of Appomattox.

Schurz's extensively documented report impressed Grant. Within a week of reading it, he directed his commanders in the South to file reports on interracial violence. At the same time, Illinois Senator

Lyman Trumbull announced that he planned to introduce legislation to protect the freedpeople's civil rights. During the second half of 1865, neither the state constitutional conventions that met in accordance with the dictates of presidential reconstruction nor the state legislatures that followed them labored to secure equality before the law for blacks. Instead, white southerners aimed to eliminate blacks from serving on juries or testifying as witnesses in most cases and forged new legal discriminations in framing civil codes. Nor did southern law enforcement and civil courts do better. First, local authorities often allowed acts of violence against blacks to go unpunished by failing either to offer protection or to apprehend the perpetrators of such acts. Second, even when authorities brought whites to trial for committing acts against blacks, convictions were rare, for all-white juries and the obstacles placed in the way of black testimony thwarted prosecutors. Third, the combination of discriminatory clauses in state legislation—usually called "the black codes"—and the tendency of southern courts and juries to hand down harsher punishments on blacks worked together to create a multitiered classification for citizenship, in which blacks had few rights that whites were bound to respect. The treatment of freedmen in southern civil courts necessitated the construction of an alternative forum to provide real justice for southern blacks.[13]

Even Johnson pressed (without success) for allowing blacks to serve on juries, for the president realized that unless white southerners provided minimal legal safeguards for black rights, Congress might well demand more far-reaching protection. The president approved Howard's May 1865 circular authorizing assistant commissioners to exercise jurisdiction in cases where blacks were not allowed to testify. Some southern legislatures took the hint, although not without reluctance. In December 1865, Governor Charles J. Jenkins urged the Georgia state legislature to provide blacks with an opportunity to testify in court; the legislature responded by limiting that opportunity to civil cases in which a black was a party and to criminal cases in which the defendant was black or those that concerned an infringement of a black's rights to person or property. That did not satisfy Bureau officials, who pressed for complete civil equality.[14]

They found an ally in Grant. He was impressed by evidence forwarded by his commanders that demonstrated the persistence of violence and injustice toward blacks in the South, as well as the continuing hostility toward and harassment of army personnel (including Bureau agents) and those whites who sought to assist the freedmen. To Schurz, he confessed to feeling "very bad about his thoughtless move" in submitting his report and thus arming Johnson with the means to assail Schurz's findings. His change in attitude was evident in his response to Alabama Governor Robert M. Patton's request to form a state militia: "For the present, and until there is full security for equitably maintaining the right[s] and safety of all classes of citizens in the states lately in rebellion, I would not recommend the withdrawal of United States Troops." On January 12, 1866, the War Department issued General Orders, No. 3, which authorized military commanders to intervene to protect from civil prosecution military personnel arrested for actions done under orders, loyalists charged with offenses against the Confederacy or in connection with the use of abandoned land and property in compliance with military directives, and blacks "charged with offenses for which white persons are not prosecuted or punished in the same manner and degree"—a direct blow at the black codes.[15]

Issuing an order was one thing; enforcing it was another, and the implementation and interpretation of the directive varied from command to command. In Florida, Bureau agents, with Howard's support, struck at some provisions of the black codes, but they left others untouched; in Mississippi Department Commander Thomas J. Wood and Assistant Commissioner Samuel Thomas battled over the application of the order. Elsewhere, however, the order empowered military commanders in Georgia and Virginia to strike telling blows at discriminatory legislation.[16]

General Orders, No. 3, appeared the day after Trumbull reported his two bills out of committee. The first bill extended the life of the Freedmen's Bureau and expanded its powers. Much has been made of the provisions in the bill expanding the powers of the Freedmen's Bureau that addressed the confiscation and redistribution of land and the efforts to offer occupants of lands seized during the war extended use, if not ultimate possession, of such property, but of equal importance were the sections that authorized Bureau agents to intervene to provide justice for blacks where local courts, laws, or practices denied equality under the law to them and that incorporated the protection offered blacks under General Orders, No. 3—as

dence. On April 2, 1866, Johnson issued a proclamation declaring that a state of insurrection no longer existed in ten of the eleven states of the former Confederacy—Texas being the lone exception. What that meant for the continued exercise of federal power in the South remained something of a puzzle. Although the president declared that "standing armies, military occupation, martial law, military tribunals, and the suspension of the writ of habeas corpus" were inconsistent with a state of peace, he did not at first explicitly end such measures; moreover, it was not clear how the proclamation bore on the life span of the Freedmen's Bureau in light of the Texas exception. Its appearance took the cabinet by surprise; it was not issued until late afternoon.[21]

A possible reason for the president's haste appeared the next day, when the Supreme Court issued its ruling in ex parte Milligan, a case that involved the trial of several Indiana antiwar protestors by a military commission after their arrest in October 1864. Although the Court would not issue the justices' opinions until December, it did announce that it had decided that, as civil courts were in operation in Indiana at the time of the case, the military commission had no jurisdiction in the matter. Johnson, who had approved the military commission's finding of guilty against the accused as well as its initial sentence of death (only to commute the sentences to life imprisonment at hard labor), welcomed the court's decision because of its implications for Reconstruction. If, after all, he found that peace had been restored and the civil courts had resumed operation, there would be no need for the army or the Bureau to intervene in civil or criminal proceedings.[22]

Congressional Republicans, Grant, and Howard all reacted to what appeared to be a coordinated effort to repudiate efforts to provide federal protection for black civil rights in the South. On April 6, the Senate overrode Johnson's veto of the Civil Rights Bill, and the House followed suit three days later. At the same time, Grant, Howard, and Secretary of War Edwin M. Stanton sought clarification of the impact of the president's proclamation on military commissions and Bureau courts. Initially, the president directed that such mechanisms were to be employed only when civil authorities failed to enforce the law. On May 1, however, the president instructed Stanton to issue General Orders, No. 26, which declared: "Hereafter, whenever offenses committed by civilians are to be tried where civil tribunals are in existence which can try them, their cases are not authorized to be, and will not be, brought before military courts-martial or commissions, but will be committed to the proper civil authorities." Nothing was said about what would happen if the civil authorities failed to act or acted in ways that denied real justice to blacks. Grant believed that the new directive prohibited military authorities from protecting blacks who were being treated unfairly by removing their cases to military courts or commissions. That interpretation seemed confirmed when Supreme Court Associate Justice Samuel Nelson directed military authorities to release a man accused of murdering a young black in Lexington, South Carolina, on the grounds that civil courts were now in operation.[23]

The challenges raised by Johnson's vetoes, proclamations, and directives to color-blind justice were made palpable in Nelson's decision. A far more vivid illustration of the consequences of remanding blacks to the tender mercies of white authorities occurred in Memphis on the day that Stanton issued orders putting into effect Johnson's decision to use civil courts. That day, blacks, many of them recently discharged soldiers, clashed with whites; over the next several days, white mobs descended on black sections in south Memphis. By the time military forces restored order, forty-six blacks had been killed. Among the instigators of the riot were local policemen and the mayor of Memphis. How one could deem civil authorities ready to dispense justice to blacks when many of them participated in such activities transcended rational thought. In response, Grant and Howard began working together to use both the army and the Bureau to protect the freedpeople from the workings of justice, southern style. One means toward that end was to unify the Bureau and the army in order to minimize conflict. In reorganizing military departments in the South, Grant made sure that the generals placed in charge of North Carolina, South Carolina, Georgia, and Alabama were also appointed commissioners for the Freedmen's Bureau; he reiterated the need for a military presence "to give a feeling of security to the people," although he expressed the hope that "this force will not be necessary to enforce the laws either State or National."[24]

Another way to offer protection for blacks—and those who protected them—was to issue new orders authorizing military intervention when necessary. Within days of the appearance of General Orders, No. 26, Grant decided that military commanders could still protect blacks from the enforcement of discriminatory state laws. It looked, however, as if the president had terminated the activities of military commissions to punish serious crimes against blacks, thus robbing Bureau agents of an essential weapon. By July 1866, it was obvious that such intervention was essential to protect the freedpeople and army personnel (including Bureau agents). Howard informed Grant of the failure of local authorities in several southern communities to apprehend or prosecute people accused of assaulting or murdering Bureau agents and blacks. At the same time, Howard forwarded to Grant a letter from Mrs. L. E. Potts of Paris, Texas, that informed the president: "It is not considered [a] crime here to kill a negro." If civil authorities would not act, the army would. Endorsing Potts's plea, Grant instructed General Philip H. Sheridan "to furnish, upon application of agents of the Freedmen's Bureau, such assistance as the means of his command will permit, either for the protection of refugees, freedmen, and Union men, or to enforce punishment for crimes." The same day, July 6, 1866, he issued General Orders, No. 44, directing military commanders "to arrest all persons who have been or may hereafter be charged with the commission of crimes and offenses against officers, agents, citizens and inhabitants of the United States, irrespective of color, in cases where the civil authorities have failed, neglected, or are unable to arrest and bring such parties to trial; and to detain them in military confinement until such time as a proper judicial tribunal may be ready and willing to try them."[25]

These orders were soon implemented by Grant's subordinates. Also, they soon came under the scrutiny of the administration; on the very day that Grant issued General Orders, No. 44, he instructed General George H. Thomas to identify and locate the principal actors in the Memphis riots of May 1866. The next day, Grant learned from Stanton that the president thought that the Civil Rights Act offered blacks "ample means for judicial protection"; thus, "it is not deemed necessary for military authority to intervene in such cases, or in any way interfere with the action of judicial tribunals having cognizance of them." The case in question concerned an effort to cite General Orders, No. 3, in support of a case regarding a suit against a treasury agent; nevertheless, the inference was that General Orders, No. 44, would not receive Johnson's approval.[26]

That this interpretation was a reasonable one soon became evident. When Grant learned of Johnson's opposition to military intervention under General Orders, No. 3, he forwarded to Stanton a report just received from Thomas on the Memphis riot with the recommendation "that the leaders in this riot be arrested by the Military, and held by them, until the civil authorities give evidence of their ability, and willingness, to take cognizance of their cases and to give them a fare [sic] trial"—in short, to apply General Orders, No. 44. The letter went from Stanton to Johnson, who passed it on to Attorney General James Speed. The attorney general's response understandably troubled Grant. Speed admitted that what had happened was "disgraceful to human nature, subversive of good order and peace, and derogatory to the dignity of the laws of the State of Tennessee"; nevertheless, "it constitutes no offence against the laws and dignity of the United States of America." The courts were open: victims should seek redress there. Although Speed did not specifically mention the Civil Rights Act, he observed that the appropriate courts included federal as well as state courts. Speed remained silent about what should happen in the absence of action by state authorities; he said nothing about how anyone would seek recourse from local authorities when some of them aided the rioters; he offered no advice on how an "injured party" would go about seeking "redress" if the party in question was dead.[27]

These exchanges occurred in the wake of the passage of the Fourteenth Amendment by Congress in June 1866 and its almost immediate ratification by Tennessee, which happened the day before Speed offered his opinion. The attorney general had a point: if Republicans welcomed the actions of Tennessee Governor Parson Brownlow and the Tennessee state legislature in ratifying the amendment, it stood to reason that the same government should punish the perpetrators of the Memphis riot. But congressional Republicans agreed with Grant and Howard that state and local authorities and institutions throughout the South offered blacks, their white allies, and army personnel little if any protection from crime and violence. At the same time that Grant framed General Orders, No. 44, Congress sent to the president a new Freedmen's Bureau bill. Absent this time were the previous provisions looking toward the distribution of confiscated lands (several sections addressed outstanding issues related to land policy). The new legislation continued to muddle the relationship between the Bureau and the army, for the president could appoint civilians as agents or assistant commissioners (although such appointees would be "so far deemed in the military service of the United States as to be under the military jurisdiction and entitled to the military protection of the Government while in the discharge of the duties of their office.") It authorized the retention in military service of those volunteer officers whose regiments had been or were being mustered out (at that time, virtually all of the volunteer regiments still in service were composed of black soldiers).[28]

Critical in the context of the present debate over civil authorities and institutions was Section 14. It authorized the president to use the Bureau and occupation forces to "extend military protection and have military jurisdiction over all cases and questions concerning the free enjoyment of such civil immunities and rights" as enumerated by the Civil Rights Act of 1866 until representatives from the state in question were readmitted to Congress; it also prohibited discriminatory punishments by race, color, or previous condition of enslavement. As expected, Johnson vetoed the bill on July 16, three days after Speed offered his opinion concerning the Memphis rioters. The president declared that civil courts were "in full practical operation" throughout the South, "open to all, without regard to color or race." Congressional Republicans immediately overrode the veto.[29]

The new legislation appeared to support Grant and Howard in their efforts to counter southern civil authorities and courts, although in *authorizing* Johnson to act as opposed to *mandating* action, the legislation left open a loophole for inaction. Nevertheless, Grant expressed optimism for the future and argued that "any unnecessary interference by the military with the civil authorities would not only tend to embitter the whites against the government, but delay the consummation of that harmony between the races so much to be desired." But that, in many cases, military interference remained a necessity became evident on July 30, 1866, when a clash between rival political factions in New Orleans turned into yet another race riot, again with local authorities looking on and failing to act or assisting the white rioters in subduing the blacks and their white allies.[30]

What happened at New Orleans reminded Grant that much remained to be done before anyone could pretend that civil authorities were able and willing to protect black civil rights. In light of Johnson's unwillingness to call for punishment of the rioters—indeed, the president claimed that the whole clash had been staged by Republicans in an effort to secure political advantages—Grant expected his directives to be countermanded. He revealed his uncertainty when, in mid-August, he received word from Thomas that the perpetrators of the Memphis riots had been identified. As the civil authorities had failed to act, Thomas asked if he should arrest them in compliance with General Orders, No. 44. Grant, mindful of Speed's opinion (although Speed had since resigned his office in an expression of disgust with Johnson's reconstruction policy), forwarded Thomas's missive to Stanton with the following endorsement: "I do not feel authorized to order the arrest of the Memphis rioters but I think it ought to be done with a strong hand to show that where the civil authorities fail to notice crime of this sort there is a power that will do so." Convinced of the need for General Orders, No. 44, Grant decided that Speed's opinion applied only to the case of the Memphis rioters and left the orders in force; after all, Speed's opinion had been delivered before the passage of the Freedmen's Bureau Act.[31]

Less than a week later, Johnson delivered another blow to the efforts of Grant and Howard to protect blacks from injustice. On August 20, the president declared the insurrection at an end in Texas and proclaimed that "peace, order, tranquility, and civil authority" existed throughout the republic. A draft of the proclamation stated that directives concerning the Freedmen's Bureau and military authority throughout the South remained in force, but no such statement appeared in the final proclamation. From Louisiana, with the New Orleans riot still fresh in his mind, Sheridan expressed concern: "If civil authorities are to be looked to for justice, I fear that the condition of affairs will become alarming." Grant, however, believed that Johnson's proclamation left no alternative; in October, he informed Sheridan that the proclamation nullified General Orders, No. 3 and No. 44.[32]

A month later, Grant was not so sure. Perhaps he was emboldened by the election results of 1866, which indicated that a majority of northern voters rejected the president's policy by voting Republican. Perhaps he was responding to his own increasing disgust with the president's behavior during the campaign. In any case, in November, he reminded Stanton that he had never actually revoked General

Orders, No. 3 and No. 44, nor had he received instructions to do so. He now wanted to revisit the question of whether Johnson's August proclamation rendered them void and added that he believed that General Orders, No. 44, was critical to the enforcement of the Civil Rights Act. Even General Edward O. C. Ord, no friend of the freedpeople, wanted to know what he could do to protect Arkansas blacks.[33]

When Congress reconvened in December 1866, Grant and Howard worked together to push Republicans to pass additional legislation that would empower the army to work with the Bureau to protect southern blacks. The opinion of the Supreme Court in *ex parte Milligan*—and Johnson's interpretation of that opinion—suggested the need for such intervention. Both the majority opinion, penned by Justice David Davis, and a concurring opinion, composed by Chief Justice Chase, were released to the public on December 17. Both opinions agreed on the propriety of negating the operations of the military commission in the specific case before the Court; where they diverged was over the broader implications of whether Congress possessed the authority to establish such courts in proper circumstances—a matter not necessarily before the Court. The implications of the case for military commissions and Bureau courts were momentous. Had peace been restored in the South? Were civil courts in operation? Did the decision deal a death blow to military commissions and Bureau courts? Would the decision leave the freedmen to the tender mercies of southern civil courts?

Much has been made of Justice Davis's later comment in private correspondence concerning the decision's applicability to southern policy. "Not a word said in the opinion about reconstruction & the power is conceded in insurrectionary States," he asserted, claiming that to attach a broader implication to his words was wrong. Both supporters and opponents of congressional Reconstruction, however, viewed Davis's opinion as implying that efforts to shield southern blacks from the consequences of facing unfair trials in southern civil courts were unconstitutional. Stanton barked that *Milligan* struck "at the roots of the Freedmen's Bureau law, and as leading directly to its entire abrogation, as well as other legislation looking to the protection of loyal men, white and black, by the Federal Government, from the persecution of the disloyal and rebellious, whose bogus State power is thus confirmed to them." Not everyone shared the war secretary's disgust. Andrew Johnson specifically cited Davis's opinion in support of his decision to release from military custody Dr. James L. Watson of Rockbridge County, Virginia, who had been arrested by military authorities when civil magistrates had refused to prosecute him for the murder of William Medley, a black man. In ordering his men to apprehend Watson, General John M. Schofield had specifically cited the Freedmen's Bureau Act of 1866 and General Orders, No. 44, as authority; he chose to try Watson before a military commission in order to provide a test case of the meaning of Johnson's peace proclamation in light of army directives and congressional legislation. Howard approved of the proceeding. The inaction of the Virginia civil authorities to punish a white man for the cold-blooded and premeditated murder of a black man was precisely what had moved Grant, Howard, and Congress to erect what protections they could for black civil rights.[34]

As congressional Republicans began to frame new Reconstruction legislation, they requested the president to provide them with information concerning violations of the Civil Rights Act. Grant asked Howard to compile a list of murders and other acts of violence to enable the general-in-chief "to make a report showing the courts in the states excluded from Congress afford no security to life or property." Grant provided Stanton with additional information toward the same end. In his annual report, Howard called on Congress to pass new legislation to strengthen the military's ability to protect blacks. Congressional Republicans responded to these reports as they crafted new legislation. The Reconstruction Act, which passed Congress in February 1867, rendered the existing civil governments in the ten former Confederate states that had failed to ratify the Fourteenth Amendment subject to military authority; it authorized the five district commanders who would supervise the reestablishment of civil governments in compliance with Republican guidelines to employ military tribunals, if necessary, to protect the freedpeople. Subsequent legislation empowered the district commanders to remove uncooperative civil officials. In his veto message, Johnson singled out for criticism the section authorizing district commanders to organize military commissions as introducing arbitrary justice; he argued that the courts were open and in operation; he made reference to *ex parte Milligan*. As expected, Congress overrode the veto on the day it was issued, March 2.[35]

If the Reconstruction Act appeared to sanction military action in support of the Bureau's efforts to secure justice for blacks, it was not the perfect solution. Although Bureau officials welcomed the revival of military assistance, the legislation entrusted the district commanders, not the Bureau agents, with deciding whether military commissions were necessary. Because the legislation left the appointment of district commanders in the hands of the president, one could not be sure what the district commanders would do, especially after the president commenced removing those generals who were most in sympathy with the cause of the freedpeople. The legislation also clouded the exact nature of Grant's authority over district commanders; subsequent legislation sought to remedy that shortcoming by offering him concurrent authority concerning the suspension or removal of civil officials. The result was that relations between the district commanders and Bureau officials varied from district to district and from commander to commander. Adding to the problems facing the Bureau was a shortage of personnel, and Grant found himself unable to spare any more officers for Bureau duty. Moreover, the administrative apparatus for which the legislation provided was, in any case, temporary because the main purpose of the Reconstruction Act (and subsequent additional legislation) was to provide for the reestablishment of civil governments; once Congress expressed itself satisfied with the result by seating a state's congressional delegation, the act ceased to operate in that state.[36]

Grant and Howard continued to work together to protect the freedpeople—and each other. When Bureau agents seemed less than enthusiastic to treat blacks fairly, Grant was willing to investigate. And he was willing to protect Howard as well. In the summer of 1867, when Grant battled unsuccessfully to prevent the suspension of Stanton as secretary of war and the removal of Sheridan as a district commander, he succeeded in saving Howard when Johnson sought to replace him; the following year Howard supported Grant for president. The new president urged Howard to stay on as head of the Bureau even as its activities wound down; however, with the restoration of civil governments in the South, the Bureau's role in offering blacks protection from violence and injustice ended— although violence and injustice continued.[37]

Nor did Grant always favor the Bureau's agenda. In the same letter where Grant recommended that Clinton B. Fisk, a hard-working advocate for the freedmen, be placed in command of the District of Tennessee (which also made him the assistant commissioner for the state), he proposed that General Jefferson C. Davis serve in the same capacity in Kentucky—although Davis's racial prejudices were evident to all and never more than when he abandoned black refugees several times during Sherman's March to the Sea. Although Grant wanted the Bureau to operate under military supervision, he resisted the idea of using army appropriations to subsidize its operations.[38] Nor did he envision a substantial long-term mission for the Bureau after the restoration of civil governments throughout the states of the former Confederacy, even though it was evident that much remained to be done to protect blacks' lives, liberty, property, and happiness—as events in Georgia made manifest in 1868. If he stood by Howard when the general found himself charged with mismanagement of Bureau affairs, he also was willing to let the agency expire. In such ways did he raise questions about his commitment to protecting blacks; it is one thing to envision equality before the law and a bright future for the ex-slaves and another to act effectively to achieve that vision.

All too often scholars critical of the Freedmen's Bureau or of Grant's commitment to emancipation confuse intentions with results, or they fault nineteenth-century individuals and institutions for failing to live up to certain twentieth-century notions of what "should" have been done during Reconstruction. Such simplifications distort historical reality. In their rush to pass judgment, scholars risk trampling over the obligation to render the complexities of the past in ways that those living at the time would have understood. Grant's relationship with the Bureau tells much about his understanding of emancipation and the Bureau's role in securing that result; his concern with restoring postwar order in the South cut in both conservative and revolutionary ways. Establishing a labor system based on contracts between black workers and white landowners promoted conciliation and prosperity (especially for the landowners); however, Grant's willingness to use the military to protect black rights supported a revolution in race relations, one that some people today overlook.

Where Grant and Howard failed was in effectively using the combined resources of the Bureau and the army to achieve this goal. At best, they reduced the incidence of violence and discriminatory justice meted out to blacks. The decision to restore civil governments throughout the South meant that federal intervention by the army and the Bureau to secure equality before the law would be short term: in the future, it would be up to regimes friendly to the purposes of congressional Reconstruction and acting in accordance with different legislation to call for assistance from the federal government. Moreover, the evidence that Howard gathered concerning violence in the South in 1866 testified to the failure of both the Bureau and the army to prevent such incidents, to protect blacks, or to punish the perpetrators. Both agencies failed the freedpeople in spectacular fashion at Memphis, New Orleans, and several other interracial clashes, to say nothing of thousands of other encounters throughout the South. Whether, under the circumstances, it would have been possible to devise policies and institutions that would have secured a different result remains open to debate. Then, as today, there were no easy answers.

NOTES

1. Ulysses S. Grant, *Personal Memoirs*, 2 vols. (New York: Charles L. Webster and Co., 1885–86), 1:424–6.

2. John Eaton, *Grant, Lincoln, and the Freedmen* (New York: Longmans, Green & Co., 1907), 5–15.

3. See Louis S. Gerteis, *From Contraband to Freedman: Federal Policy Toward Southern Blacks, 1861–1865* (Westport, Conn.: Greenwood Press, 1973).

4. Eaton, *Grant, Lincoln, and the Freedmen*, 85–6.

5. See Dan T. Carter, *When the War Was Over: The Failure of Self-Reconstruction in the South, 1865–1867* (Baton Rouge: Louisiana State University Press, 1985).

6. Carl Schurz to Andrew Johnson, July 28, 1865, in Brooks D. Simpson, LeRoy P. Graf, and John Muldowny, eds., *Advice after Appomattox: Letters to Andrew Johnson, 1865–1866* (Knoxville: University of Tennessee Press, 1987), 83; see also Brooks D. Simpson, "Quandaries of Command: Ulysses S. Grant and Black Soldiers," in David W. Blight and Brooks D. Simpson, eds., *Union and Emancipation: Essays on Politics and Race in the Civil War Era* (Kent, Ohio: Kent State University Press, 1997), 133–49.

7. William S. McFeely, *Yankee Stepfather: General O. O. Howard and the Freedmen* (New Haven: Yale University Press, 1968), 109. Grant was not

alone in taking a much needed but ill-timed vacation: Oliver O. Howard fled the humidity of the nation's capital for his home state of Maine that August (ibid., 106).

8. Carl Schurz to Andrew Johnson, Aug. 13, 21, 1865, in Simpson et al., *Advice after Appomattox*, 94, 97n–98n, 99; Ulysses S. Grant to Edwin M. Stanton, Aug. 28, 1865, in John Y. Simon et al., eds., *The Papers of Ulysses S. Grant*, 20 vols. to date (Carbondale: Southern Illinois University Press, 1967–   ), 15:310; see also Paul A. Cimbala, *Under the Guardianship of the Nation: The Freedmen's Bureau and the Reconstruction of Georgia, 1865–1870* (Athens: University of Georgia Press, 1997), 23–7, 225. Other Bureau officers apparently did not see Wild's removal as a warning against radical action. Wild ended his days by prospecting for silver; he died in Medellín, Colombia.

9. Grant endorsement of Nov. 10, 1865, on Q. A. Gillmore to George D. Ruggles, Oct. 28, 1865, in Simon et al., *Papers of Ulysses S. Grant*, 15:386; Donald G. Nieman, *To Set the Law in Motion: The Freedmen's Bureau and the Legal Rights of Blacks, 1865–1868* (Millwood, N.Y.: KTO Press, 1979), 13.

10. Grant to Stanton, Oct. 20, 1865, in Simon et al., *Papers of Ulysses S. Grant*, 15:357–8; Grant to Meade, Nov. 6, 1865, ibid., 15:398–9; Cyrus B. Comstock Diary, Nov. 22, 1865, Comstock Papers, Library of Congress, Washington, D.C.

11. McFeely, *Yankee Stepfather*, 130–48; quotation in Simpson et al., *Advice after Appomattox*, 208–9.

12. Ulysses S. Grant to Andrew Johnson, Dec. 18, 1865, in Simon et al., *Papers of Ulysses S. Grant*, 15:434–7; Meade to Grant, Nov. 8, 1865, in ibid., 5:400; Bureau of Refugees, Freedmen, and Abandoned Lands, Circular No. 22, Dec. 22, 1865, in ibid., 15:438; Meade to Stanton, Sept. 20, 1865, in Simpson et al., *Advice after Appomattox*, 233.

13. Brooks D. Simpson, *Let Us Have Peace: Ulysses S. Grant and the Politics of War and Reconstruction, 1861–1868* (Chapel Hill: University of North Carolina Press, 1991), 127–8.

14. Charles Fairman, *Reconstruction and Reunion, 1864–88: Part One* (New York: Macmillan, 1986), 1243–4.

15. Grant, endorsement, Jan. 9, 1866, in Simon et al., *Papers of Ulysses S. Grant*, 16:54; Department of War, General Orders No. 3, Jan. 12, 1866, ibid., 16:7–8.

16. Simpson, *Let Us Have Peace*, 128–9.

17. Edward McPherson, *The Political History of the United States during the Period of Reconstruction* (Washington, D.C.: Philip & Solomons, 1871), 72–4; Simpson, *Let Us Have Peace*, 128.

18. Ely S. Parker to Theodore S. Bowers, Jan. 27, 1866, and Cyrus B. Comstock to John A. Rawlins, Feb. 1, 1866, enclosed in Grant to Andrew

Johnson, Feb. 14, 1866, in Simon et al., *Papers of Ulysses S. Grant*, 16:458–61; Simpson, *Let Us Have Peace*, 129–30.

19. Simpson, *Let Us Have Peace*, 132; McPherson, *Political History*, 68–74.

20. McPherson, *Political History*, 74–8.

21. Johnson, "Proclamation re End of Insurrection," Apr. 2, 1866, in LeRoy P. Graf et al., eds., *The Papers of Andrew Johnson*, 15 vols. to date (Knoxville: University of Tennessee Press, 1967–   ), 10:349–52; Gideon Welles, *The Diary of Gideon Welles*, with an introduction by John T. Morse, Jr., 3 vols. (Boston: Houghton Mifflin Company, 1911), 2:473–4.

22. Fairman, *Reconstruction and Reunion, 1864–88: Part One*, 145–6, 199.

23. Simpson, *Let Us Have Peace*, 135–6. Graf et al., *Papers of Andrew Johnson*, 10:397, confuses the relationship between the April 9 circular and General Orders, No. 26.

24. Nieman, *To Set the Law in Motion*, 124; Grant to Stanton, May 15, 16, 1866, in Simon et al., *Papers of Ulysses S. Grant*, 16:196–7, 199.

25. Nieman, *To Set the Law in Motion*, 118–21; Howard to Grant, July 3, 1866, in Simon et al., *Papers of Ulysses S. Grant*, 16:228–9; Mrs. L. E. Potts to Johnson, June [20?], 1866, and Grant's endorsement of July 6, 1866, Sheridan Papers, Library of Congress, Washington, D.C. (Graf et al., *Papers of Andrew Johnson*, 10:602–3, suggests June 20 as the date of the letter); General Orders, No. 44, July 6, 1866, in Simon et al., *Papers of Ulysses S. Grant*, 16:228.

26. Grant to Thomas, July 6, 1866, and annotation, in Simon et al., *Papers of Ulysses S. Grant*, 16:230–1.

27. Grant to Stanton, July 7, 1866, and annotation, in ibid., 16:233–6.

28. McPherson, *Political History*, 149–51.

29. Ibid.

30. Simpson, *Let Us Have Peace*, 143.

31. Ibid., 138–9; Speed to Johnson, July 13, 1866, in Graf et al., *Papers of Andrew Johnson*, 10:688–9.

32. Simpson, *Let Us Have Peace*, 145–6.

33. Grant to Stanton, Nov. 22, 1866, in Simon et al., *Papers of Ulysses S. Grant*, 16:389–90; Ord to Grant, Nov. 16, 1866, Jan. 12, 1867, in ibid., 16:399–401, 403–4.

34. Fairman, *Reconstruction and Reunion, 1864–88: Part One*, 214–5, 222, 232–3; Robert J. Kaczorowski, *The Politics of Judicial Interpretation: The Federal Courts, Department of Justice and Civil Rights, 1866–1876* (New York: Oceana Publications, 1985), 42–3; Simpson, *Let Us Have Peace*, 167.

35. Nieman, *To Set the Law in Motion*, 197–9; McPherson, *Political History*, 168–70.

36. Nieman, *To Set the Law in Motion*, 199–204; George K. Leet to Oliver O. Howard, June 8, 1867 (endorsement on Howard to Grant, June 3, 1867), in Simon et al., *Papers of Ulysses S. Grant*, 17:451–2.

37. Grant to Edward O. C. Ord, July 30, 1867, in Simon et al., *Papers of Ulysses S. Grant*, 17:246; Simpson, *Let Us Have Peace*, 302 (n.38), 247.

38. Grant to Stanton, May 30, 1866, July 31, 1866; endorsements of July 30 and Sept. 24, 1866, in Simon et al., *Papers of Ulysses S. Grant*, 16:518, 271, 532, 305.

2

Andrew Johnson and the Freedmen's Bureau

Hans L. Trefousse

ANDREW JOHNSON'S HOSTILITY to the Freedmen's Bureau has long been recognized; leading historians—LaWanda and John H. Cox, Donald G. Nieman, Paul A. Cimbala, and William S. McFeely, to mention but a few—have all commented on it.[1] What is less well documented, however, is the reason why the president chose the Bureau to break with the Republican/Union Party by vetoing a bill for its continuance that was prepared by Senator Lyman Trumbull. Trumbull was a leading Republican moderate, with whom Johnson otherwise well might have made common cause against the radical Republicans. A minority even within their own party, the radicals could hardly have succeeded had not Johnson totally alienated the moderates. His break with the organization that elected him was one of the crucial decisions of his administration, for whatever else may be said about him, he was not a passive president who merely reacted to pressure. He carefully planned his policies, and his dealings with the Freedmen's Bureau are examples.

In order to examine Johnson's action, it is first necessary to recall the history of the Freedmen's Bureau, or, as it was officially called, the Bureau of Refugees, Freedmen, and Abandoned Lands. Congress established the Bureau during the last months of Abraham Lincoln's administration and placed it in the War Department for the duration of the conflict and for one year thereafter, "for the supervision and management of all abandoned lands, and the control of all subjects relating to refugees and freedmen from rebel States, or from any district of country within the territory embraced in the operations of the army, under rules approved by the President." With a commissioner paid $3,000 a year and an assistant commissioner for each of the insurgent states, the Bureau was authorized to issue provisions, clothing, and fuel, as well as to provide temporary shelter for loyal refugees and freedmen. In addition, it was to set apart for their use abandoned lands within these states, or such lands to which the United States had acquired title, to be assigned to loyal refugees and freedmen in plots of not more than forty acres at an annual rent at 6 percent of its value for three years, at the end of which the occupants might buy them.[2] Lincoln had decided to appoint General Oliver O. Howard commissioner, but before the president could confer the office, he was assassinated; it fell to his successor, Andrew Johnson, to do so.[3]

Howard was a logical choice. A distinguished Civil War commander who had lost one arm at the Battle of Fair Oaks, the general, known for his piety, was called "the Christian soldier." Sympathetic toward the freedmen, he conscientiously sought to ease their transition from slavery to freedom. On July 28, 1865, in order to carry out the Bureau's functions, he issued Circular 13, which directed the assistant commissioners to set aside lands under their control and begin dividing them among the freedmen. Although Johnson already had issued his proclamation granting amnesty and pardon to all but leading ex-Confederates on May 29, the July circular specified that the proclamation did not affect the lands in question.[4]

But Howard had failed to obtain the president's approval for his circular. During the first part of July, Johnson was ill and barely able to take care of his business; as time went on, however, he became aware of the fact that the Bureau was pursuing policies not at all to his liking. Southern born and southern bred, a former slaveholder himself but of poor white origin, he had become popular in the North as the only senator from a seceding state who remained loyal. In so doing, he well represented the feelings of his home district in eastern Tennessee, where a majority had voted against secession,[5] but he also shared his neighbors' racist views and considered the blacks inferior. In 1844, during debates in the House of Representatives about the Gag Rule, Johnson demanded to know whether the foes of slavery were willing to turn loose upon the country more than two million Negroes to "become a terror and a burden to society, producing disaffection between them and their former masters." He maintained that this would finally result in a racial war and the extirpation of the blacks. "If one portion of the country were to be the masters and the others menials," he continued, "he had no hesitancy in bringing his mind to a conclusion on the subject, believing, as he did, that the black race of Africa were inferior to the white man in point of intellect—better calculated in physical structure to undergo drudgery and hardship—standing as they do, many degrees lower in the scale of gradation that expresses the relative relation between God and all that He has created than the white man." The laws must distinguish between white and black, or they would "place every spay-footed, bandy-shanked, hump-backed, thick-lipped, flat-nosed, woolley-headed, ebon-colored negro in the country upon an equality with the poor white man."[6]

As military governor of Tennessee in 1863, Johnson had endorsed a policy of emancipation, which he thought was necessary for winning the war. But he never changed his racial views. To be sure, during the 1864 campaign for the vice presidency, he addressed a number of freedmen in Nashville and agreed to be their Moses to lead them to freedom,[7] but when he became president, he strove to keep the South a "white man's country." Although he did not say so in so many words, his actions were ample proof of his intentions. On May 9, Johnson recognized the "Restored Government of Virginia," headed by Francis Pierpont, which did not provide for black suffrage. On May 29, he promulgated a Proclamation of Pardon and Amnesty and coupled it with his North Carolina Proclamation, in which he appointed a provisional governor whom he asked to convene a convention elected by the voters of 1861, thus relying on white suffrage for Reconstruction. In the days that followed, he published similar proclamations for the remaining southern states—South Carolina, Georgia, Florida, Alabama, Mississippi, and Texas—thus again restricting the suffrage to whites. In August, however, he did advise his own appointee as governor of Mississippi, William L. Sharkey, that it would be wise if his convention enfranchised a few literate blacks and those with property. Such action would not affect many, Johnson reasoned, but it would assuage the radicals "who are wild on the subject." Nevertheless, he neither insisted on this step nor was committed to it as a matter of policy. That Johnson did not oppose the black codes, which virtually remanded the freedmen to slavery, passed by the states that he sought to reconstruct gave ample proof of his indifference to the fate of the blacks.[8]

Under these circumstances, Johnson could not fully sympathize with the purposes of the Freedmen's Bureau. When he heard from a person calling himself William T. Moore that the Bureau had taken nearly half the property in Vicksburg, Mississippi, so that the local citizens were greatly inconvenienced, Johnson sent orders to Howard to stop such practices, in spite of the fact that he had been informed that no one by that name lived in the city. He also had information of the same type from New Orleans and again ordered a halt. In fact, he wrote to General George H. Thomas that the agency was assuming unwarranted powers in Tennessee. He feared that the operations of Treasury agents and the Freedmen's Bureau were creating great prejudice against the government, he apprised the general, and he thought that their abuses must be corrected. General James B. Steedman, the conservative commander of the Department of Georgia, confirmed the president's fears when he warned Johnson that some radical officers of the Bureau were causing nothing but trouble, although he had corrected some of their faults. "Your course in reference to the Freedmen's Bureau as far as understood is approved," Johnson wired to him. "I hope the Bureau will move clearly in the limits prescribed by law."[9]

By the end of July, it had become clear to the president that he could hardly disregard the growing opposition to his Reconstruction policies. He had received a nineteen-page missive from Robert Dale Owen, the British reformer's son, criticizing his procedure.[10] In June, a number of radicals had arrived in Washington to plead with Johnson to change his program. Senator Benjamin F. Wade of Ohio, in particular, sought to convert him to more radical views and then complained to Secretary of the Navy Gideon Welles about Johnson's policies.[11] Thaddeus Stevens, the radical leader of the House, also came to the capital in order to influence the administration, and, having missed the president, on July 6 wrote him very plainly: "I am sure you will pardon me for speaking to you with a candor to which men in high places are seldom accustomed. Among all the leading Union men of the North with whom I have intercourse I do not find one who approves of your policy. They believe that 'restoration' as announced by you will greatly injure the country. Can you not hold your hand and wait the action of Congress and in the meantime govern them by military rulers? Profuse pardoning will also greatly embarrass Congress if they should wish to make the enemy pay the expenses of the war or part of it."[12] Carl Schurz, the German-American immigrant leader, also asked him to modify his proclamation, particularly in regard to South Carolina.[13] Such requests could hardly have left Johnson in doubt about the Radical Republicans' opposition to his schemes. When, at the same time, he received complaints from his supporters in the South that the Freedmen's Bureau favored the radicals, his allegedly initial friendly attitude toward the agency changed and he ordered the withdrawal of Circular 13.[14]

Bureau Commissioner Howard at first sought merely to modify the circular, but the president insisted on a complete withdrawal. Consequently, on September 12, Howard replaced the earlier circular with Circular 15, ordering that no land was to be considered confiscated until it had been legally condemned. If not so condemned, the property was to be restored to the original owners, and those pardoned by the president were eligible to recover their property. The result was that the Bureau lost the income from the lands in question and the freedpeople were deprived of the lands they had begun to cultivate after the harvest was in, especially as Johnson had already rescinded a previous order turning over to the Bureau all tax funds collected for the benefit of refugees and freedmen or accruing from abandoned lands or property set aside for their use. As historian Willie Lee Rose so well put it, "Revolutions do go backward."[15]

This was not all. Influenced by reports from his supporters against the allegedly radical assistant commissioners, Johnson began to remove these Bureau officials, as well, starting with Thomas W. Conway in Louisiana and eventually extending even to Rufus Saxton, the antislavery general who had long been active in South Carolina. Johnson approved of the Bureau's temporary judicial powers but only as a preparation for the reestablishment of regular courts, part of his own policy.[16]

In the meantime, Johnson's prejudices were reinforced by reports of the alleged misdeeds of the Bureau and its agents. One Tennessean complained that it was "giving more trouble than all other things together"; another, of its "intolerable oppressions"; a Mississippian, of its being "a curse to blacks and whites" alike; and a Louisianan, of its giving trouble and causing vexation in his state. These reports did not improve Johnson's assessment of the agency by the time Congress met in December. He was already so hostile to the Bureau that he was bound to interfere with it further.[17]

The events of December 1865 were hardly calculated to change his mind. Not only did Congress refuse to call the names of the delegates-elect from the South, even those undoubtedly loyal, but it established a Joint Committee of Fifteen on Reconstruction, to which all matters pertaining to the subject were to be conferred, thus clearly putting a halt to Johnson's own policy. General Schurz submitted a report entirely hostile to his program, which Johnson countered with one from General Ulysses S. Grant, who wrote favorably about the president's scheme and even reflected his prejudices against the Bureau. Although he did not give the organization's operations the attention that he would have given it had more time been at his disposal, the general asserted, he had nevertheless found that its affairs in some states had not been conducted with good judgment or economy. Holding it responsible for spreading among the blacks the notion that they were to receive land, an idea that made them unwilling to sign contracts, he advised that the Bureau be completely merged with the army. It was what Johnson wanted to hear, but Congress was not convinced.[18]

The next two months constituted a period crucial to the president's relation with the legislature. The majority of the Republican party was not radical; divided among radicals, moderates, and conservatives, most Republicans were perfectly willing to cooperate with the executive, at least up to a point. Then Senator Lyman Trumbull of Illinois, the moderate head of the Judiciary Committee, drew up a new Freedmen's Bureau bill, a measure providing for the continuation of the Bureau by removing the time limit of the old law and extending its jurisdiction over freedmen and refugees in all states. Giving the president the right to appoint twelve assistant commissioners, it appropriated the necessary funds for their salaries. In addition, it authorized the Bureau to divide the lands along the coast and rivers south of Charleston set aside by William T. Sherman's Special Field Orders, No. 15, into forty acres per freedman or refugee, and mandated the secretary of war to provide food, shelter, and clothing for suffering recipients.[19]

Trumbull, who had consulted with Howard while framing the measure, believed it would receive the president's assent.[20] Johnson was to disappoint him. Johnson, however, was to disappoint him. Seeking guidance from advisers who sympathized with him, he hardly retained an open mind on the Bureau issue. One of those who influenced him was General Joseph S. Fullerton, a conservative who had served on Howard's staff and had been sent to Louisiana to investigate complaints against the Bureau. Upon Johnson's inquiry about the general's opinion of the pending bill, Fullerton gave a detailed, scathing answer. He called the legislation unnecessary and class-based. Furthermore, he thought it likely to render the freedmen dependent upon the government. Inveighing against the operations of the Bureau, he maintained that there were no more loyal refugees other than blacks, that the bill would set up a tremendous bureaucracy, and that its expense would be prohibitive. In addition, he labeled the provisions affecting Sherman's land order illegal and concluded that it would be much better for the army to take over directly.[21]

Another adverse opinion came from former Attorney General Edward Bates. A Missouri conservative, Bates had long served in Lincoln's cabinet. Decrying the allegedly illegal schemes of the radicals and castigating their attacks on the president, he cautioned Johnson that both Houses had passed a bill, the Freedmen's Bureau Bill, requiring him "in flat contradiction of your constitutional duty" to extend military jurisdiction over all officers of the Bureau with authority to hear cases involving Negroes, mulattoes, freedmen, refugees, and other persons who are discriminated against. "I shall not weary you, sir," he added, "with comments upon these legislative monstrosities. But I cannot forbear to remark that the faction which now domineers over the two houses of Congress, is itself, not only utterly regardless of the constitution, but is, apparently, determined to force you to be an accomplice in their crime."[22]

Although Johnson did not need any more reasons to veto the bill, he heard other objections. Thomas F. Bramlette, the governor of Kentucky, recalling the state's loyalty during the war, pointed out that the Bureau had no legal existence in Kentucky. He called it a "Pandora's Box" and a "source of evil and only evil" and expressed particular resentment at the idea of placing northern overseers over the government and people of the former slave states.[23] When the president finally brought up the question of signing the bill in the cabinet, he found Secretary of the Navy Welles, Secretary of State William H. Seward, Secretary of the Treasury Hugh McCulloch, and Postmaster General William Dennison in favor of a veto, on which, in any case, he already had decided, whereas Secretary of War Edwin M. Stanton, Secretary of the Interior James Harlan, and Attorney

General James Speed expressed reservations. His mind was made up, and on February 19, he sent his veto to Congress.[24]

His message fully expressed his disdain for the agency. Calling the bill unnecessary because the existing measure had not yet expired, he voiced objections to the proposed extension of military jurisdiction over freedmen to all parts of the United States, the provisions for trials without a jury, and the establishment of extraordinary tribunals justified in time of war but not while the country was at peace. Finding the creation of asylums and schools for freedmen totally without precedent, he pointed out that the bill entailed vast patronage powers and incurred considerable expense. Moreover, he considered the confiscation of estates a violation of the Fifth Amendment. He even deprecated the vast powers that the measure conferred on the executive. Then came the most telling of his arguments: the questionable nature of legislation affecting states that were not represented in Congress. Did not the Constitution clearly entitle them to two members in the Senate and appropriate representation in the House?[25]

Although the veto was sustained by Congress, it created an almost unbridgeable rift between the party and the president, especially as he also objected to Trumbull's other measure, a civil rights bill, that Congress passed by overriding Johnson's veto.[26] Trumbull, who had misread Johnson, was particularly annoyed. Expressing the utmost surprise at the president's opposition, he proceeded to refute the veto message of the Freedmen's Bureau bill point by point. The legislation had been passed to comply with Johnson's own injunction to "best fulfill our duties as legislators by according equal and exact justice to all men," the senator recalled. It was not true that the measure was superfluous, as the original bill would expire in May. Nor did it extend military justice all over the United States. It merely covered the agents of the Freedmen's Bureau, who were already subject to military jurisdiction, which would discontinue anyway as soon as the president ceased to maintain it in eleven states. "Sir," he asked, "if I may be permitted to ask a question of the president of the United States, I would inquire, if you cannot reconcile a system of military jurisdiction of this kind with the words of the Constitution, why have you been exercising it?" The proposed measure was not permanent, and if no asylums had ever been established before, the country had never been in a condition analogous to the present. As for the Sherman lands, they had not been taken away from anyone because they were already in the possession of the government. All in all, the Thirteenth Amendment gave ample enforcement powers to Congress, and if Johnson objected to the absence of the southern states, had they not also been unrepresented during the war and was therefore all wartime legislation illegal? It was an unanswerable argument.[27]

Democratic and conservative newspapers hailed the veto message. "All Hail," wrote the *Wayne City (Ohio) Democrat.* "Great and Glorious! Great Victory for the White Man. Rejoice, White Man, Rejoice! The Hour of Your Deliverance Has Come." The *Boston Post* praised the president for having been able to rise above all party strife, the *New York World* agreed, and the *Washington National Intelligencer* thought the veto showed evidence of Johnson's true convictions of public duty.[28]

Republican journals, however, saw things differently and wrote scathing comments. "Since the closing of the war and the horror of the assassination no event has created such profound sensation as the formal act by which the President has severed himself from the loyal party and united with its enemies, North and South, before the Union is yet restored or the war fully ended," wrote the *Chicago Tribune.* The *St. Louis Democrat* charged the executive with having broken with the loyal people of the country. Commenting that the president could have confined himself to vetoing certain items, it insisted that, by objecting in general, he placed himself, "unfortunately both for himself and the country," in his present relation of antagonism with a majority in both houses of Congress. His denunciation three days later in an impromptu speech of such radical members of Congress as Thaddeus Stevens and Charles Sumner, whom he compared to the traitorous leaders of the rebellion, did not particularly help to smooth things over.[29]

Thus the president had made the Freedmen's Bureau and the attempt to prolong and extend it the focal issue between himself and Congress or, at any rate, the issue about which he was willing to break with the majority of the party. No doubt he felt encouraged by continuing reports about the Bureau's alleged misdeeds. A Tennessee correspondent, asserting that because of his complaints to Johnson he had drawn the agency's anger upon himself, labeled it "a perfect money machine." A. O. P. Nicholson, the famous Tennessee

Democrat, considered it "a useless institution," and a correspondent from Kentucky accused it of being "the worst of tyrants."[30] And the president was unwilling to let up his attack against it. When, on April 2, he issued a proclamation that the rebellion had ended everywhere except in Texas, he asserted in the preamble that "standing armies, military occupation, martial law, military tribunals, and the suspension of the writ of habeas corpus" ought not to be allowed in time of peace. This was clearly a reference to the activities of the Bureau. Lest anyone remain in doubt about his true feelings, on April 12, in an interview with the *London Times,* he "enlarged with considerable detail upon the operations of the Freedmen's Bureau." Its machinery was now being used to convey Negroes from the North to the South by the very men who asserted that blacks were not safe in the former Confederacy and who wanted labor for their lands, he charged. As he saw it, this amounted to a new form of slavery, though conducted by abolitionists. As the reporter concluded in an understatement, Johnson considered the administration of the Bureau "not all that could be desired."[31] Howard was so annoyed that he considered resigning but was persuaded by friends to stay on, even though Johnson soon issued orders denying commanders the right to convene military commissions, orders that destroyed an important part of the Bureau's judicial system.[32]

The president was far from finished. Commissioning his firm supporters, Generals Fullerton and Steedman, to set out upon a tour of inspection of the Bureau, he soon obtained what he wanted. In their report of May 8, the two generals, after visiting only two states, wrote that in Virginia, the freedmen to whom subsistence was being furnished could undoubtedly earn a living for themselves if removed to localities in need of labor. Wherever there were good agents, tolerable conditions prevailed, but in North Carolina, particularly, the investigators insisted, they had uncovered corrupt officials who were using the Bureau for their profit.[33]

After proceeding further, General Steedman, writing on behalf of himself and his colleague, continued his negative reports. He informed Johnson that in Mississippi "the Bureau officers, with very few exceptions, constitute a radical close[d] corporation, devoted to the defeat of the policy of your administration. In Virginia, they were all Radicals. In North Carolina, all we met but one . . . was of the same stripe—South Carolina the same as the other two States." Admitting that the officers in Georgia and Florida were the president's friends, he concluded that General Wager T. Swayne in Alabama was a man of ability and a good officer, "but as fierce a Radical as Thad. Stevens himself." It was precisely what Johnson had long believed and wanted to hear.[34]

In spite of all this activity, the president was unable to prevent Congress from passing another Freedmen's Bureau bill. Extending the Bureau's existence for two years, it provided for salaries for subordinate officials and the proper disposition of lands leased to blacks. Johnson naturally vetoed this measure. Asserting that he would not repeat his well-founded objections to its predecessor, he nevertheless renewed his argument that, peace having been restored, the legislation was unnecessary. He insisted that this was especially true in view of the fact that the Civil Rights Act now afforded ample protection for the freedpeople. Moreover, making use of the Fullerton-Steedman Report, he asserted that many agents used the Bureau for their own pecuniary advantage and, instead of helping the freedmen, exploited them. This time Congress experienced no difficulty in overriding the veto.[35]

Johnson, however, did not give up. In an interview with Paschal B. Randolph, a physician interested in black education, he made it clear that he thought whatever good the agency had done had been overbalanced by the unrecorded evils resulting from its action. Maintaining that he was not the freedpeople's enemy, he concluded, "The question proposed to be solved by the Freedmen's Bureau can only be harmoniously settled by the Southern man and the freedman. They alone can do it, and this without any direct interference of the Federal Government."[36] And when James Gordon Bennett, Jr., asked him if he wanted the Steedman findings printed in the *New York Herald*, Johnson quickly gave his assent. On August 22, Howard sought to contradict the report, but his effort was in vain.[37] Johnson even saw to it that another report, one rendered by General Gordon Granger, whom he also had sent on an inspection tour of the Bureau, was published on August 28. It too contained the usual charges against the agency. "Agents of the Freedmen's Bureau," the general wrote, "stepped between the planter and the laborer, stirring up strife, perpetuating antagonism, and often adding their quota of extortion and oppression."[38]

By this time, the congressional campaign of 1866 was in full swing.

In August, Johnson had called together a Unionist convention in Philadelphia, and, at the end of the month, he set out on his notorious "swing around the circle" to assist in the laying of a cornerstone for Stephen A. Douglas's monument in Chicago. Delivering speeches at various stops, he again lambasted the Bureau. In Cleveland, he said that before the Civil War, there were 4,000,000 slaves held by some 340,000 people who paid their expenses and worked them; now the Freedmen's Bureau proposed to take charge of these 4,000,000, at an expense of about $12,000,000 a year. And, in St. Louis, he charged that the Bureau was "a simple proposition to transfer 4,000,000 slaves in the United States to a new set of task masters."[39]

The president showed his opposition to the Bureau in other ways. Making use of the Supreme Court's decision in *ex parte Milligan*, which declared military tribunals unconstitutional when the civil courts were open, he interfered with the Bureau's judicial functions and refused to approve further organization of Bureau courts.[40] Finally, in 1867 he considered relieving Howard, and in the winter of 1867–1868 he replaced a number of radical commissioners with more conservative successors.[41]

Thus Johnson impeded the success of the Freedmen's Bureau. He curtailed its ability to redistribute land and undercut its efforts to improve the freedmen's lives and change the racial mores of the nation. As long as the dominant race held in contempt and even in hatred the subordinate one, there was small hope for equality of opportunity. That the president did not help the Bureau in this respect is evident. Although the agency did succeed in providing relief to the freedpeople, protecting them temporarily in maintaining their civil rights, and establishing schools and colleges for them, its overall activities were hampered by Johnson almost from the very beginning.[42]

What remains to be established is why Johnson, who might easily have made common cause with the moderate Republicans, refused to do so and made the Freedmen's Bureau bill the issue upon which he decided to break with the party. After all, the radicals, his principal opponents, never constituted a majority within the organization, and collaboration with the moderates might have made it possible for the president to carry out part of his program and retain the loyalty of the party in preparation for his 1868 electoral campaign.

The answer to this question must be sought in his deep-seated beliefs. First and foremost, he was a strong advocate of states' rights.
He always had been a Democrat; states' rights constituted a cardinal
principle of the Jeffersonians and Jacksonians, and on his way to
Washington as vice president–elect, he said he was convinced that it
was only through the Democratic Party that the Union could be fully
restored.[43] In July 1861, he was the sponsor of the Senate resolution
that stated that the war was being fought merely to maintain the
supremacy of the Constitution with all the dignity, equality, and
rights of the several states unimpaired, and that as soon as these
objects were accomplished, the war ought to cease.[44] Although he
had since accepted the necessity of emancipation, he had never wa-
vered from the main objective of this original premise. As he pointed
out in his first annual message, "all pretended acts of secession were,
from the beginning, null and void. . . . The States attempting to
secede placed themselves in a condition where their vitality was
impaired, but not extinguished—their functions suspended, but not
destroyed."[45] In keeping with his convictions, he even had failed to
insist upon minimal conditions suggested to the states that he had
begun to restore—the ratification of the Thirteenth Amendment,
the nullification of the secession ordinances, and the repudiation of
the Confederate debt.[46] Moreover, in his veto of the Freedmen's
Bureau bill, he again clearly stated his firm belief that the seceded
states were full members of the Union. When, in December 1865,
Congress refused to seat the southern members-elect and created
its Joint Committee of Fifteen on Reconstruction, it had openly re-
pudiated these theories; Johnson could hardly forget that William
Pitt Fessenden, a leading moderate, had become the committee's
chairman. In view of the fact that the moderates were willing to
keep the states out until certain conditions had been met, the president could not see any common ground between himself and these
potential allies.[47]

     Another reason for his opposition, and his choosing the Freed-
men's Bureau bill to make the break, was his continued determination to keep power in the hands of the southern whites.
Notwithstanding all his professions of concern for the freedpeople,
he held to his bitterly racist beliefs. When, in February 1866, Frederick Douglass and a black delegation pleaded with him to do something for black suffrage, he not only refused, but afterward said to

his secretary, "Those d—d sons of b—s thought they had mc in a trap. I know that d—d Douglass; he's just like any nigger, & would sooner cut a white man's throat than not." Thus his Philadelphia correspondent Richard Vaux was not wrong when he wrote to him, "The Democratic party of the United States will aid and support you in your present trial, encourage you, defend you, sustain you for so soon as the contest begins, you, with it, are alike devoted to the Constitution, the equal rights of the people, and this government as the white man's system of republican liberty."[48] That Johnson retained his prejudice throughout his presidency impressed even his private secretary, William G. Moore, who wrote in 1868, "The President has at times exhibited morbid distress and feeling against the negroes. Yesterday noon and this morning a dozen stout negroes were hauling a heavy stone roller over grass and walks of the grounds, around the garden house. He at once wanted to know if all the white men had been discharged, and as I could no more than tell him I would make inquiry, he asked his doorkeeper if the white men were not yet employed about the building and grounds."[49]

In view of this attitude, he could neither collaborate with the moderates' limited concern for black rights nor give his assent to the Freedmen's Bureau bill. And it was not surprising that he chose this measure to make his position clear. The legislation not only seemed to interfere with states' rights but also to create special support for the freed slaves. His opposition to the Bureau thus can be easily explained. Its effects were unfortunate for the party, for Reconstruction, for the country, and for the future of race relations in America.

NOTES

1. John H. Cox and LaWanda Cox, "General O. O. Howard and the 'Misrepresented Burcau,'" *Journal of Southern History* 19 (Nov. 1953): 435–6; Donald G. Nieman, "Andrew Johnson, the Freedmen's Bureau, and the Problem of Equal Rights, 1865–1866," *Journal of Southern History* 44 (Aug. 1978): 399–420; Paul A. Cimbala, "The Freedmen's Bureau, the Freedmen, and Sherman's Grant in Reconstruction Georgia, 1865–1866," *Journal of Southern History* 55 (Nov. 1989): 607, 608; William S. McFeely, *Yankee Stepfather: General O. O. Howard and the Freedmen* (New Haven: Yale University Press, 1968), 110–7.

2. Edward McPherson, *The Political History of the United States during the Great Rebellion 1860–1865* (Washington: Philip & Solomons, 1865), 594–5.

3. Oliver Otis Howard, *Autobiography of Oliver Otis Howard, Major General United States Army*, 2 vols. (New York: Baker & Taylor, 1907), 2:206ff.

4. Ibid., 234–5; George R. Bentley, *A History of the Freedmen's Bureau* (Philadelphia: University of Pennsylvania Press, 1955), 93.

5. Hans L. Trefousse, *Andrew Johnson: A Biography* (New York: W. W. Norton, 1989), 223, 17–151.

6. *Congressional Globe*, 28th Cong., 1st sess., 95–8.

7. Trefousse, *Andrew Johnson*, 167–9, 183.

8. Edward McPherson, *The Political History of the United States of America during the Period of Reconstruction* (Washington, D.C.: Philip & Solomons, 1871), 8, 9–12, 19–20, 29–44; LaWanda Cox and John H. Cox, *Politics, Principle, and Prejudice 1865–1866: The Dilemma of Reconstruction America* (New York: Free Press of Glencoe, 1963), 156–8.

9. LeRoy P. Graf et al., eds., *The Papers of Andrew Johnson*, 15 vols. to date (Knoxville: University of Tennessee Press, 1967–), 8:536–7, 445, 585, 600–1, 648.

10. Robert Dale Owen to A. Johnson, June 21, 1865, Andrew Johnson Papers, Library of Congress, Washington, D.C.

11. Howard K. Beale, ed., *The Diary of Gideon Welles*, 3 vols. (New York: W. W. Norton, 1960), 2:325.

12. Graf et al., *Papers of Andrew Johnson*, 8:365.

13. Frederick Bancroft, ed., *Speeches, Correspondence, and Political Papers of Carl Schurz*, 6 vols. (New York: G. P. Putnam's Sons, 1913), 1:260–3.

14. Graf et al., *Papers of Andrew Johnson*, 8:445; Howard, *Autobiography*, 2:224, 227.

15. Howard, *Autobiography*, 2:234–5, 237; Graf et al., *Papers of Andrew Johnson*, 9:39; McPherson, *Political History*, 12; Bentley, *History of Freedmen's Bureau*, 95–6; Willie Lee Rose, *Rehearsal for Reconstruction: The Port Royal Experiment* (Indianapolis: Bobbs-Merrill, 1964), 378.

16. Howard A. White, *The Freedmen's Bureau in Louisiana* (Baton Rouge: Louisiana State University Press, 1970), 21; Bentley, *History of Freedmen's Bureau*, 107; Nieman, "Andrew Johnson," 402.

17. Graf et al., *Papers of Andrew Johnson*, 9:28, 50, 107, 126.

18. Bancroft, *Speeches of Carl Schurz*, 1:279–374; Brooks D. Simpson, LeRoy P. Graf, and John Muldowny, eds., *Advice after Appomatox: Letters to Andrew Johnson, 1865–1866* (Knoxville: University of Tennessee Press, 1987), 213–4.

19. McPherson, *Political History during . . . Reconstruction*, 72–4.

20. Howard, *Autobiography*, 2:280; Mark Krug, *Lyman Trumbull, Conservative Radical* (New York: A. S. Barnes & Co., 1965), 238.

21. Graf et al., *Papers of Andrew Johnson*, 10:64–9.

22. Ibid., 70–3.

23. Ibid., 83–5.

24. Beale, *Diary of Gideon Welles*, 2:434–5; John H. Cox and LaWanda Cox, "Andrew Johnson and His Ghost Writers: An Analysis of the Freedmen's Bureau and Civil Rights Veto Messages," *Mississippi Valley Historical Review* 48 (Dec. 1961): 460–79.

25. James D. Richardson, comp., *A Compilation of the Messages and Papers of the Presidents, 1789–1907*, 9 vols., (Washington, D.C.: Bureau of National Literature and Art, 1907), 6:398–405.

26. McPherson, *Political History during . . . Reconstruction*, 74–80.

27. *Congressional Globe*, 39th Cong., 1st sess., 936–43.

28. *Wayne City (Ohio) Democrat* and *Boston Post*, in Andrew Johnson Papers, series 2, 11; *New York World*, Feb. 20, 21, 1866; *Washington National Intelligencer*, Feb. 24, 1866.

29. *Chicago Tribune*, Feb. 21, 1866; *St. Louis Democrat*, Feb. 21, 1866; *New York Herald*, Feb. 23, 1866; Thomas Ewing, Sr., to Ellen Sherman, Feb. 22, 1866, Thomas Ewing Papers, Library of Congress, Washington, D.C. Further comments, both friendly and hostile, can be found in the Andrew Johnson Papers, series 2, 11.

30. Graf et al., *Papers of Andrew Johnson*, 10:142, 193, 250.

31. Richardson, *Messages and Papers of Presidents*, 6:429–32; Graf et al., *Papers of Andrew Johnson*, 10:406–9.

32. H. M. Turner to J. E. Bryant, Apr. 12, 1866, John Emory Bryant Papers, Duke University Library, Durham, N.C.; Donald G. Nieman, *To Set the Law in Motion: The Freedmen's Bureau and the Legal Rights of Blacks, 1865–1868* (Millwood, N.Y.: KTO Press, 1979), 115–7.

33. U. S. House, *Executive Documents*, 39th Cong., 1st sess., no. 120, 63–72.

34. Graf et al., *Papers of Andrew Johnson*, 10:627–8.

35. McPherson, *Political History during . . . Reconstruction*, 147–51.

36. Graf et al., *Papers of Andrew Johnson*, 10:710–3.

37. Ibid., 11:43, 108–17.

38. Ibid., 127–30; *New York Herald*, Aug. 28, 1866.

39. Trefousse, *Andrew Johnson*, 256–58, 261ff.; Graf et al., *Papers of Andrew Johnson*, 11:178–9, 195–6.

40. Bentley, *History of Freedmen's Bureau*, 153; Nieman, *To Set the Law in Motion*, 144ff. The main case in question was the Watkins case in December 1866. Dr. James L. Watkins, a Virginian who had shot a black, was acquitted, and when General John M. Schofield held him for military trial, Johnson relied on the Milligan decision to release him.

41. Beale, *Diary of Gideon Welles*, 3:142; Bentley, *History of Freedmen's Bureau*, 196.

42. Bentley, *History of Freedmen's Bureau*, 214.

43. Warner Bateman to John Sherman, Mar. 28, 1866, John Sherman Papers, Library of Congress.

44. McPherson, *Political History of the United States during the Great Rebellion*, 286.

45. Richardson, *Messages and Papers of the Presidents*, 6:357.

46. Albert Castel, *The Presidency of Andrew Johnson* (Lawrence: Regents Press of Kansas, 1979), 44; Trefousse, *Andrew Johnson*, 229.

47. Benjamin F. Kendrick, *The Journal of the Joint Committee of Fifteen on Reconstruction, 39th Congress, 1865–1867* (New York: Columbia University Press, 1914), 60–1; James G. Blaine, *Twenty Years in Congress*, 2 vols. (Norwich, Conn.: Henry Bill Publishing Co., 1884) 2:127, 140–1.

48. Philip Riply to Manton Marble, Feb. 8, 1866, Manton Marble Papers, Library of Congress, Washington, D.C.; Graf et al., *Papers of Andrew Johnson*, 9:546.

49. W. G. Moore Diary, April 9, 1868, Andrew Johnson Papers.

3

Emancipation and Military Pacification: The Freedmen's Bureau and Social Control in Alabama

Michael W. Fitzgerald

As THE FIRST MAJOR FEDERAL WELFARE AGENCY in American history, the Freedmen's Bureau of Reconstruction has generated a good deal of controversy. The modern scholarship often presents a critical interpretation of this effort to mediate the social consequences of emancipation. Since the 1960s, many historians have depicted the Bureau as an agent of social control that pressed northern priorities and legalisms on the freedmen.[1] Scholars have been particularly skeptical of the Bureau's efforts to oversee the transition from slavery on the plantations. As Leon F. Litwack concluded, the Bureau had been "in a position to effect significant changes in labor relations, particularly during the chaotic aftermath of emancipation."[2] Such critiques often depict the Bureau as operating autonomously and disregard the severe practical constraints it faced during the period following Confederate surrender.

The situation in postwar Alabama illustrates these issues well. In the literature on Reconstruction, Alabama often typifies the Bureau's most repressive characteristics. Longtime Assistant Commissioner Wager T. Swayne comes in for particular criticism.[3] Because the Bureau's initial labor policies were often authoritarian, it is difficult to fault this view. Still, the situation seems more complex in view of the Radical Republican politics of Swayne and the Bureau leadership.[4] To understand fully the issues of freedom and social control, in Alabama and elsewhere, one must examine the choices available during the critical weeks after Appomattox. Given the exigencies of military conquest and occupation, putting the ex-slave back to work under free labor became the army's obvious goal. The Bureau, as a branch of the army, fell heir to this priority, but social order became less urgent once pacification was complete. Chronology thus appears as the crucial element in understanding Bureau policy, for the organization became more supportive of the freedpeople over time.

Federal military responsibility for Alabama's ex-slaves developed first in the northern portion of the state. Federal occupation of the Tennessee Valley in early 1862 eroded slavery even before formal emancipation. Refugee camps on confiscated plantations housed thousands of contrabands.[5] Vigorous army recruiting gave male slaves an obvious means toward liberty. Facing ruin by 1864, planters in the region "manifested quite a disposition to commence work," but to resume production they had to acknowledge emancipation and pay their workers.[6] Even without clear military direction, a gradual transition to free labor occurred in the Tennessee Valley, with some freedpeople renting lands independently.[7] Although the broad social issues raised by emancipation were similar everywhere in Alabama, the northern section had a unique wartime experience. There, the war's end prompted little additional disorder, but the situation farther south would prove quite different.

The great plantation region of central and southern Alabama escaped direct contact with invading armies until the spring of 1865. In early April, just as Confederate General Robert E. Lee's army was surrendering at Appomattox, Union General James H. Wilson's raid was spreading desolation throughout the cotton belt. In the words of one soldier, the progress of his comrades could be "traced plainly by the smoke."[8] Federal forces torched Selma and damaged Montgomery, before heading east into Georgia. Conflict continued at a diminishing level for weeks, until the final surrender of General Richard Taylor's command on May 8. Even then, as outlying Confederate units disbanded, it was unclear that the war was actually over or what peace would mean. One Union officer found planters asking him for help in retrieving runaways as late as May.[9] Given the gradual cessation of hostilities, Federal authorities initially confronted the liberation process as part of pacification. Compliance with emancipation was one critical indication that resistance had ended, that southerners accepted the situation.

Restoring order under the circumstances was no small task, for the collapse of Confederate authority bred havoc. A Confederate commander actually requested that the Union troops hurry to occupy Demopolis, for fear that his disintegrating command could no longer prevent looting.[10] The advance of Federal forces also spread social disorder. General E. R. S. Canby's occupation forces, arriving late in April from Mobile, were less destructive than Wilson's raiders, but they supplied themselves from civilian resources for weeks. Union troops sought the aid of slaves in finding food and other valuables and often invited them to share in the booty. Treasury agents searching out Confederate cotton often employed the same means, as did the thousands of avaricious stragglers following the Union army. As one soldier wrote, "there is any amount of thieving going on around here."[11] In the weeks after surrender, reports of violence also proliferated.

As they occupied the cotton belt, the soldiers encountered a jubilant black population. Troops heading up the Alabama River saw that "the Negro men & women was waving their hats and wight hankerchieves and welcoming the Yankies."[12] Many shouted and danced for joy, General C. C. Andrews noted in his diary.[13] Appreciating the warm welcome, the soldiers contrasted it with the sullen response of the white population. At Montgomery, a soldier found that "not a single person except the blacks manifested any sympathy or friendship."[14] The belated news of Abraham Lincoln's assassination highlighted the issue of loyalty, and Federal troops frequently demonstrated an initial preference for the freedpeople. One Union camp celebrated the capture of Jefferson Davis by illuminating a caricature of "the Traitor President" with a rope around his neck and placing the rope in the hands of "an over-grown negro woman clad in expensive crinoline."[15] Whatever the dubious racial politics such images displayed, these soldiers demonstrated no eagerness to oppress blacks. At the least, soldiers confirmed the news that African Americans were free and could leave the plantations if they wanted, a message that their superiors increasingly wished to temper. As one officer observed, the soldiers spread "absurd stories" about what freedom meant.[16]

Wherever they went, Union forces encountered multitudes of African Americans seeking their freedom. In Selma, for example, they were "coming in by the 100 to see the Yanks and there was a detail to gather them up."[17] Refugees sought the safety of camps and cities, and each day's new arrivals brought fresh tales of abuse. Federal forces outside Montgomery were astonished when women came into camp with their ears cut off, this as a warning to those who sought Union protection.[18] The complaints had substance, for even after the last Confederate bands surrendered, the byways teemed with bitter Confederate soldiers returning home.

The Union forces immediately encountered pressing issues of social adjustment. One occupier expected they would act "as a sort of police force to keep order," while the people settled into "the new state of society."[19] In practice, Union troops would oversee the immediate aftermath of slavery, being present by the thousands during the crucial period. The concern with military security meant that weeks before the Freedmen's Bureau was organized, decisions were being made. Once the moment of celebration passed and the victorious soldiers became impatient to go home, their attitudes toward the freedpeople camped on their doorsteps hardened. As the liberation process appeared increasingly intractable, authoritarian solutions suggested themselves to military minds.

Whatever the intentions of Union troops, the overriding priority of restoring order shaped the transition to free labor. In practice, this necessity often worked against the freedmen. Most wealthy planters still feared arrest as traitors or confiscation of their property, either of which was still a live prospect for some time after Appomattox. Under the circumstances, the elite generally conciliated military authorities. In Montgomery, for example, Union officers were inundated with dinner invitations from local grandees. Because few white Alabamians were foolhardy enough to abuse freedpeople near the Union presence, the black population presented the more obvious difficulties. In the towns and camps, the flood of in-migration overwhelmed authorities, who were troubled by the prevalence of illness in the refugee camps. In Selma, one official counted sixty-five deaths among freedmen in two months.[20] Union officials had every motive to discourage people from entering the cities.

In the surrounding countryside, the emancipation process disrupted agricultural production during the plowing season. As one Union soldier mused in late May, everything was unsettled and nobody knew their status. While this lasted, there would be "no business, no labor, no crops planted." He feared widespread starvation and compared the task ahead with that of the war just ended.[21] But the army's presence itself often undermined food production. As one planter observed, "the passing through of Federal Cavalry" excited the blacks, while the establishment of garrisons "continued to demoralize them."[22] The planters' complaint was that many ex-slaves had ceased work but expected to be fed. If the Union accounts can be believed, these complaints had considerable validity, and they suggested grim possibilities. Especially in war-ravaged areas, dispirited planters might well abandon the year's crop as hopeless and cease feeding the hands. The consequence could be famine, turmoil, or huge numbers of homeless freedpeople dependent on the government for food. Such nightmare scenarios, from this distance, are difficult to evaluate, but authorities on the scene took the possibilities seriously.

These jitters aside, northern soldiers were culturally predisposed to urge the dignity and necessity of manual labor on the freedpeople.[23] Most northerners accepted that slavery had undermined the moral fiber of the African-American population, and they believed that they must instruct them in the duties of life as freedmen. Whatever the justification for this view, Federal officers invoked negative stereotypes about black laziness, despite the extraordinary circumstances. Temporary idleness by the ex-slaves looked ominous. A sort of "tough love" mentality took hold, as even sympathetic Federal officers concluded that the overriding demand was to get the hands back to work. Federal soldiers were disposed to preach to the freedpeople, and the triumph of Union arms did nothing to undermine their self-esteem.

The soldiers' practical and ideological priorities contrasted starkly with those of the freedpeople. For many ex-slaves, it seemed counterintuitive that emancipation would bring little immediate change in their lives. Refugees in Demopolis, for example, assumed that "working for ole Master on the plantation was played out."[24] Officers blamed such notions on loose talk by passing Union troops, but freedpeople had strong practical motivations for seeking dramatic change, especially by departing the plantations. They left to reunite families, flee abuse, or return to old neighborhoods; many sought guarantees against the possibility of reenslavement, a fear that seemed plausible.[25] Some, particularly women and children, left plantations after having been expelled. However pressing the cause, Union soldiers tended to see their preferences as subordinate to martial order. Only the most obviously abused or needy freedpeople could count on a sympathetic reception.

Freedmen departing the plantations often left because of a realistic sense of what the planters had in mind. Away from cities and outposts, planters tried to keep the northern influence at a distance. Some isolated planters hoped to keep their slaves a while yet or else maintain some of their social authority intact. In early June, for example, the passage of Union forces near the Alabama River allowed some enterprising freedpeople to sell them eggs and chickens. This moved one planter to wholesale whippings in order to demonstrate who was the "boss of the plantation." The freedpeople fled to the army, which sent them off to Selma on the planter's appropriated mules. The planter thereupon expelled his remaining hands before the freedmen's agents could force him to sign contracts. The corn crop was nearly finished, and once northerners tampered with his laborers, the planter concluded they were not worth keeping.[26]

The Union soldiers knew that ex-masters frequently kept isolated freedpeople in a state of twilight slavery. The soldiers intervened when they could. In Greene County, off the track of the Union army, one planter's agent called his hands together. He told them that the army had emancipated them and they were "likely to be free legally in time." In the meantime, he suggested that they keep working while the situation sorted itself out. This they did until around June 1, 1865, when "abolition preachers" arrived to tell them they were "all free." The hands then ceased work, refused to sign a contract, and demanded the overseer be fired. The agent reluctantly called on the army to get them under contract and back to work.[27] The wider point is crucial: the army had a dual role, dependent in large part on the ex-masters' behavior. Planters often called on Union soldiers for protection or to get laborers back to work, which army officials saw as a positive sign. Union officers projected the emancipation policy into the countryside, often with zeal, while exerting themselves to minimize its disruptive effects.

Overseeing emancipation required a balancing act that taxed the most enthusiastic of the Union liberators. In mid-May, Chaplain Henry N. Herrick became "sort of extemporized Supt. of Freedmen" at Demopolis. Demonstrating humanitarian convictions, Herrick wrote that it would "make your blood boil, to see & hear what I do" about slavery. Despite his evident sympathies, he was no sentimental admirer of the freedpeople. A Baptist minister, he felt obliged to preach to them on their moral shortcomings. He denounced the practice of casual marriage and divorce, telling them that it was "the prevailing sin of the colored race." He thought they responded well to the harsh lecture and concluded, "they will take anything from me."[28]

After the Confederates surrendered, Herrick spent much of his time reassuring freedpeople that they were truly free. He pressed them to "return to their plantations & go quietly at work." Feeding hundreds of refugees in town, he told freedmen that he could not provide for more. Herrick soon found that the planters were "anxious to have me come & see them." He rode into the countryside at their request, often in their buggies, and induced the freedpeople to sign contracts. On these trips, he frequently stayed at the homes of the "humbled nabobs," who treated him superbly. Despite the hospitality, Herrick found the position difficult as he labored far into the night on paperwork. He concluded, after arresting several landowners for whippings, that severe measures would be required. Emancipation would not be an easy process. Concerned for his health, he requested reassignment after a mere two weeks on the job.[29]

Herrick's military colleagues demonstrated even less patience, and the freedmen generally suffered for it. Herrick had opposed the notion of a pass system, but the planters prevailed upon his commanding officer for more vigorous measures. By the end of June, one planter reported that perfect order had been restored, with guards stationed on the roads to arrest blacks without passes. The Federals had "used persuasion & finally (in the last few days) their bayonets to make the negroes enter into contracts with their former masters & return to their work."[30] Whatever the animus behind these comments—planters being eager to puncture the northerners' humanitarian pretensions—one suspects the description had some basis in fact. One general in the interior told a planter to strap his hands "like hell" and make them work.[31]

The problem of social order tended to be most acute in the urban centers, and occupied Mobile typified the harsher features of the army's presence. For weeks after capturing the city, Union commanders prepared for a Confederate counteroffensive. On May 1, the army ordered all unemployed men to report for work on the fortifications or face arrest.[32] The army issued certificates of employment, so that jobless blacks "could be easily found and 'pressed.' "[33] No rations would be issued either, except in exchange for labor. Such measures proved effective. One Mobile woman wrote that "the negroes are kept in order not a loiterer is to be seen." The freedmen were all employed, she said, and work houses were even going to be established for the women.[34] Forcible labor recruitment blended easily into vigorous measures against vagrants, even after any military necessity passed. The city was swollen with thousands of refugees, which encouraged harsh policies. Late in May, the army ordered the arrest of all persons without visible means of support, who would be "formed into gangs and worked under guard in cleaning the streets of the city."[35] Even blacks with employment papers received continual harassment.[36] These practices continued into the coming months, as the recalcitrant city officials encouraged racist behavior. Local Freedmen's Bureau agents frequently investigated reports of abuse by soldiers.[37]

The situation proved little better around Montgomery, where army guards patrolled the plantations of absent planters. The guards were "acting the part of the overseers over the negroes that remain."[38] In the city, post commander Charles Turner was impressed with the welcome he received from the white citizens as they plied him with social invitations and strawberry shortcake. He increasingly saw the army's role as protecting planters from black violence. "I tell you," he wrote his wife, "if the army was taken away from here now there would be a slaughter." Turner agreed with the white citizens that there would be "endless trouble" if the government didn't keep "some sort of stringent control" over the freedmen. He considered a great many of the blacks "worthless vagabonds" who wouldn't labor as long as they could get anything to eat. He anticipated, however, that the authorities would soon have them back to work.[39]

One would not want to overstate the point, for the Union army acted both as liberator and as an agent of social control. The military enforced emancipation, and it fed and housed thousands of black refugees. The intentions of the Union soldiers toward the freedpeople were often sympathetic. The difficulty was that the positive influence in the countryside tended to be indirect and tenuous, whereas the repressive features of the army's presence were overt. The planters near at hand behaved themselves, whereas the freed-people seemingly acted up; in the hinterland, the situation reversed itself, but this made less impression on the military authorities. In areas of effective Union control, the process of emancipation disrupted agricultural production, as the emboldened African-American population demanded real freedom and often a temporary cessation of labor. This prompted the soldiers and officers to intervene, and they collaborated with the planters to induce the freedpeople to resume work. As the army in the field relinquished oversight of the ex-slaves, its successors would operate under the broad outlines of army precedent.

Organized efforts to deal with the freedpeople began only some weeks after Taylor's surrender. In mid-May, General Canby brought most of Alabama under the "general provisions" of the labor code of occupied Louisiana. All ex-slaves would sign written labor contracts or register themselves as unemployed with the government, which would put them to work. Contracts lasting through the end of the year would provide laborers with lodging, food, and medical attendance. Bureau agents were to approve all contracts. Care was to be taken not "to disturb abruptly the connections now existing," and workers were urged to stay put if not abused.[40] The upshot was that the wartime Louisiana labor code, widely criticized as authoritarian, now became the model for Alabama in peacetime.

Canby assigned Thomas W. Conway, the person in charge of freedmen's affairs in the Gulf area, with temporary oversight throughout most of Alabama. The assumption was that the newly created Freedmen's Bureau would soon take charge. Conway's orders instructed him to "secure the growing crops, and avert the danger of scarcity and famine."[41] Unemployed freedpeople were to be registered with the government and provided with labor. Conway clearly agreed with the priorities of his instructions. Although he wasted little sympathy on the planters, he brought from his experience in wartime Louisiana an emphasis on prodding the freedpeople to work. Mincing no words, he directed one subordinate: "Hire them [freedmen] out! Cut wood! Do anything to avoid a state of idleness."[42]

Mindful of the transient nature of his responsibility, Conway avoided dramatic initiatives. Still, his choice of officers and their instructions exercised a lingering influence even after the Freedmen's Bureau became operational. In late May, Conway traveled into the interior and appointed subordinate officials in Mobile, Selma, Demopolis, and Montgomery. All four men had served in the U.S. Colored Infantry. Conway chose them because their hearts were in the work. Despite their sympathies, Conway's officers understood "that idleness would be considered a crime and could not be tolerated."[43] Their intervention bolstered the tottering plantation system at a crucial moment; although they discouraged fraud and violence by planters, their efforts likely weakened the negotiating position of the freedpeople as well.

The experience of C. W. Buckley in Montgomery illustrates the conflicting pressures these officials faced. Buckley, a chaplain who had worked with contrabands, thoroughly identified with the freedpeople.[44] He would cause the Bureau some embarrassment when his statements in favor of confiscation and equal suffrage reached the press. Still, believing that "society never existed in such a chaotic state as here," his evident priority was to "bring good order out of such confusion."[45] With 3,200 displaced people in his camp, Buckley discouraged refugees by a "persistent and unyielding determination to make every Negro remain on the plantation," and he added that his pass system had cleared the city of idlers.[46] Passes were demanded of blacks for months, thus forcing all in transit to show evidence of employment or face arrest.[47] Conway approved this policy and assured Buckley that "vagrants can be employed on the public works or on the streets as you mention."[48] As for the plantation hands, Buckley thought them excessively distrustful of their ex-masters; planters made hundreds of applications for military removal of recalcitrant freedmen. He responded by furnishing guards and noted that "their presence restored order at once." Buckley soon expressed satisfaction at his progress, despite his awareness that many hands were working for nothing more than food.[49]

At Selma, things developed similarly. Chaplain S. S. Gardner had the same political profile as his colleague. Gardner feared "literal reenslavement" were the army removed, but his actions were double-edged.[50] Wilson's raid had desolated the vicinity of Selma so badly that most plantations were stripped of both provisions and animals. Ruined planters, he concluded, simply could not pay wages that year. In such cases, Gardner approved labor agreements for nothing more than subsistence, and, like Buckley in Montgomery, he allowed "many contracts" of the sort. Gardner suspected that some planters were feigning poverty, and he insisted on individual inspections. Still, he concluded that many laborers were lucky to be fed.

"Free" labor of this sort implied some coercion, for the ex-slaves were unlikely to honor such contracts with much enthusiasm. Without assurance that the laborers would not leave them at mid-crop, planters would never risk feeding laborers. Gardner thought such concerns justified. In response, he often sent out guards to "maintain proper authority on a place, prevent outrages, and enforce tolerable labor."[51] Heeding complaints about poor work, he decided that "such discipline as would be considered mild and humane under the old plan might be used, especially with the young and thoughtless."[52] Gardner arrived at this policy in consultation with the Federal commander in his vicinity and apparently sanctioned whippings for some weeks. He soon expressed misgivings, but it is striking that he found himself so enmeshed with the practices of the old order.[53]

Buckley, Gardner, and even Conway would become Radical Republican leaders in the coming years. Conway would organize Union Leagues across the South, Buckley would go to Congress, and the unfortunate Gardner would be nearly murdered by terrorists.[54] Such evidence of commitment suggests benign intent, yet all three implemented policies with regressive racial implications. They seem to have perceived little choice. The flood of refugees, combined with the widespread cessation of labor, made the restoration of plantation production a pressing issue. The priority of social order and precedents established under martial necessity overrode other considerations. Immediate problems pushed such men into the arms of minimally cooperative planters. The result was a spartan labor policy that anticipated the black codes passed soon thereafter under civil authority.

In sum, the situation had jelled by late July 1865, when the Freedmen's Bureau became operational under stable leadership. Assistant Commissioner Swayne would head the agency in Alabama for most of its existence. General Swayne is widely depicted in the modern literature on Reconstruction as conservative, "more pro-planter" than most of his peers.[55] One historian accused him of pursuing policies often "fatal to the interests of the freedmen."[56] These criticisms seem overstated, for the army already had determined the basic direction of government labor policy. As Swayne put it, he found "the contract system established here, practically and in orders."[57]

The new assistant commissioner did share the reigning priorities. As one striking recommendation averred, Swayne had "no prejudice in favor of the negro as such."[58] Swayne had earnest Protestant convictions, which inclined him to the moral preachments so common among Union officers. He urged employers to see that their laborers were legally wed, and he regretted that circumstances precluded prosecutions for bigamy or adultery. He initially countenanced discriminatory laws prohibiting the sale of liquor because blacks were "at present an unsettled, numerous and excited people."[59] Fearful of disorder, Swayne discouraged talk of land redistribution and asked for an augmented force in October to discourage any uprising.[60] Swayne's first weeks in Alabama demonstrated an initial wariness of the freedpeople's behavior.

Swayne's labor code, General Orders, No. 12, mostly ratified the military guidelines. Swayne's regulations abandoned the previous provisions for a pass system and provided laborers a lien on the growing crop. The code implicitly banned whipping, an understanding that was soon made explicit. No wage was specified, and the Bureau would coerce no freedman to sign agreements, but Swayne wanted freedpeople to "understand the binding force of a contract."[61] For those laborers who missed more than one day's work without cause, the employer could go to Bureau agents and charge the laborer as a vagrant, who, if found guilty, would be handed over to civil officials for road work. Swayne subsequently found the rigor of his regulations a bit embarrassing. He described his labor code as a "makeshift" of little practical significance because most freedpeople already had made their contracts for the year.[62]

Swayne's labor policies suggested an initial tendency to accommodate the white power structure. Despite antislavery antecedents, his patrician social background allowed him to move comfortably within Alabama's political elite. Whatever his initial racial views, objective constraints pushed him to conciliate the civil leadership. On his arrival in Alabama, Swayne was alarmed to discover his office squeezed for cash. The Freedmen's Bureau was "not only organized on an expensive basis, and utterly without revenues, but also largely in debt."[63] Conway had scattered unpaid bills in his wake, though he did eventually loan Swayne funds to set up his Bureau.[64] The ongoing problem was that the agency depended on the proceeds of confiscated property, but most of Alabama was occupied so late that Swayne discerned "no prospect of confiscated lands."[65] What Confederate property did exist would be sold and the revenue diverted elsewhere. Swayne thus faced daunting problems when he was given the responsibility to protect 450,000 freedpeople with his "four feeble agencies."[66]

Seeking an innovative solution, Swayne approached Alabama's newly installed provisional governor, Lewis E. Parsons, with an offer of cooperation. Swayne would refrain from establishing separate Bureau courts, as had been done elsewhere, in exchange for civilian assistance. Swayne issued General Orders, No. 7, which appointed all civil magistrates as ex-officio Bureau agents if they accepted black testimony, whereupon Parsons recommended they comply. Swayne thought the policy would prove "permanent, cheap, and an educator of public sentiment."[67] General O. O. Howard sanctioned the decision and observed that Swayne was "so crippled by want of adequate means" that he had little choice.[68]

Alabama's civil leaders were well pleased. In one Tennessee Valley area, officeholders were actually "anxious for an agent to be appointed."[69] On the other hand, Swayne's decision loosed a volley of criticism from northern abolitionists, Republican leaders, and even some Bureau officials.[70] The fears proved well founded, for most civil agents did little more than approve contracts for a fee and occasionally help to resolve payment disputes. The social pressure on Bureau agents who actually tried to protect the freedpeople was intense. For example, when a Tennessee Valley agent disapproved a labor contract, local opinion turned on him. Two aggrieved planters, one of them his own brother-in-law, insisted that he resign. When the agent refused, rumors flew about his misconduct. "He is said to be popular among the negroes, but detested by his fellow citizens," a nearby planter wrote.[71] Civil magistrates would seldom cross their planter neighbors.

From several locations came reports of coerced contracts "much to the disadvantage of the colored people," as Tennessee Assistant Commissioner Clinton B. Fisk observed.[72] In the hinterland, away from effective oversight, magistrates still excluded black testimony and pervasive complaints of oppression occurred. For instance, one civilian agent tied up "darkies by the thumbs," according to an appreciative planter.[73] Chastened by such examples, the assistant commissioner reconsidered "the general plan of co-operation on which this office has been conducted."[74] Swayne revoked or threatened to revoke the jurisdiction of civilian agents in several cities and established Bureau courts where problems had occurred.

Swayne found the contract system working equally badly, with many freedpeople unable to collect their wages. Before the rest of his Bureau colleagues, Swayne concluded that his labor code undermined the freedpeople's bargaining position, especially because it combined with unfavorable debt relief and lien laws.[75] Once their expectation of land redistribution passed, freedmen would be best governed by the same compulsions as everybody else. In January 1866, after some "maturity of reflection," Swayne suggested scrapping the whole contract system. In the North, a laborer could "quit without having to account to anybody. This is more and better than all laws."[76] The freedpeople were working well, and the prevailing labor shortage guaranteed them some leverage, whereas annual contracts, in practice, offered no protection before Alabama's courts. By early 1866, Swayne essentially stopped promoting annual contracts and apparently allowed individual agents to formulate policy.[77] Some subordinates still thought contracts useful, and Swayne's faith in the free market might have been too great, but his actions certainly reflect an awareness of the existing problems. Unlike the planters, Swayne was willing that blacks rent land independently, rather than working as hired laborers.[78] Here, too, Swayne anticipated Bureau policy, which grew increasingly supportive of tenant farming as a milestone toward proprietorship.

Swayne's disillusionment notwithstanding, his early conciliatory policies provided one real benefit: he gained influence with the state's moderate political leadership, which he exploited with vigor. Under Provisional Governor Parsons, from August to December 1865, Alabama's political leaders avoided confrontation with the military. Parsons termed Swayne's administration "eminently satisfactory," and Swayne thought that "from the very first, the Provisional Governor entered heartily into the work of the Bureau."[79] Parsons lobbied the president to place the entire state under Swayne's control, the northern portion having been administered separately, and Parsons also asked the president to provide more secure funding for Swayne's Bureau. Both requests succeeded, and Swayne's reputation for moderation proved durable in Washington, thus allowing him to minimize the scrutiny other Bureau personnel received.

Swayne's initiatives proved only temporarily effective in the political realm, and his conciliatory policies came at a cost. At Governor Parsons's urgent request, Swayne accompanied him to Washington to support Alabama's request for recognition under the president's Reconstruction plan. Swayne thus smoothed the way for readmission in December and a partial eclipse of his own military authority.[80] The newly elected legislature presented Swayne with a serious problem. With presidential recognition secured, the lawmakers saw little need for further concessions. Rumors of land redistribution suggested trouble at Christmastime, and planter opinion demanded repressive measures, regardless of the political consequences. Several severe bills passed, including the wholesale reenactment of the antebellum free Negro code, which Swayne termed reenactment of slavery. Swayne helped to persuade Governor Robert M. Patton to veto several of the offensive bills. The black codes adopted were less ferocious than those of neighboring states, and Swayne thought his intervention had "a great deal to do with the suppression of such measures."[81]

By the spring of 1866, Swayne concluded that conciliation had failed. The contract system worked badly, while civil officials were oppressing the freedpeople under his sanction. Swayne was horrified when the legislature reactivated the state militia and requested the removal of Federal troops. The end of martial law prompted violence against freedmen, and he had yet to see his first white person convicted and adequately punished. Even his recent legislative successes had been accompanied by "a marked increase in political animosity."[82] This partly reflected the national political polarization between Congress and President Johnson, and Swayne had little doubt of his Republican loyalties.

Swayne determined upon a more aggressive policy to protect the freedpeople from violence and fraud. In April, he formally discontinued use of state judicial officers as agents of the Bureau.[83] Now having sufficient revenue, Swayne superseded them with paid employees, mostly Union officers who were more amenable to his direction. He also tried to ban use of the chain gang, on the grounds that civil officials used it in discriminatory fashion.[84] This activity did not go unnoticed. As one functionary observed, "the papers generally" had become "unusually severe on the Bureau."[85] Swayne's estrangement from conservative Alabama opinion proved permanent. By the summer of 1866, one visiting Bureau official characterized him as "radical as Thad Stevens himself."[86]

Over the remainder of his service with the Bureau, Swayne became an increasingly ardent proponent of civil rights. He supported black education with enthusiasm and even used financial means of dubious legality to do so. Swayne lobbied the legislature to ratify the pending Fourteenth Amendment, which set forth the rights of all persons born or naturalized in the United States, and, when that failed, he backed Military Reconstruction. In early 1867, he urged the government to arm black militias so that freedmen could defend themselves. Obviously, he had overcome his initial distrust of their behavior. With black suffrage, Swayne used his agency to create the Republican Party and became almost single-handedly responsible for its rapid organization throughout the state. His political activities eventually resulted in his removal by President Johnson in late 1867.[87]

Even this brief description of the subsequent history of Swayne's Bureau suggests the larger point: the more repressive Bureau policies occurred early on, when the military precedents were fresh. Almost inevitably, the conquering soldiers' first priority proved to be restoring order, and the ex-slaves' behavior troubled them. Given the Bureau's subordination to military authority, authoritarian solutions to short-term problems exercised a lingering influence. In Swayne's case, specifically, circumstances pushed him toward conciliation with conservative white opinion. When the situation changed and when he acquired some revenue, he moved as aggressively as could be expected to protect the freedpeople. In particular, it is difficult to see him as the architect of repressive Bureau labor policies, given how quickly he abandoned them.

Beyond the specifics of Swayne's role, the broader issue involves the politics of military pacification. Given the necessities of occupation, one wonders in context how much better the army could have done in the weeks after Appomattox. The soldiers wanted to go home—this was the urgent reality—and the planters they encountered seldom challenged Union authority. The movement of the freedpeople to refugee camps and the temporary abandonment of labor by some presented more pressing difficulties. These practical problems combined with negative racial stereotypes to yield harsh labor policies. The outcome of occupation was unfortunate, though it may well have been inevitable. Still, the army's mixture of liberation and racial repression was its legacy to both the Freedmen's Bureau and the direction of southern society.

NOTES

1. For example, see William S. McFeely, *Yankee Stepfather: General O. O. Howard and the Freedmen* (New Haven: Yale University Press, 1968), 5; and Louis S. Gerteis, *From Contraband to Freedman: Federal Policy Toward Southern Blacks, 1861–1865* (Westport, Conn.: Greenwood Press, 1973), 183–92.

2. Leon F. Litwack, *Been in the Storm So Long: The Aftermath of Slavery* (New York: Alfred A. Knopf, 1979), 386.

3. McFeely, *Yankee Stepfather*, 78–9; Jonathan M. Wiener, *Social Origins of the New South: Alabama, 1860–1885* (Baton Rouge: Louisiana State University Press, 1978), 51; Kenneth B. White, "Wager Swayne, Racist or Realist?" *Alabama Review* 31 (Apr. 1978): 106, 109.

4. Michael W. Fitzgerald, *The Union League Movement in the Deep South: Politics and Social Change during Reconstruction* (Baton Rouge: Louisiana State University Press, 1989); Michael W. Fitzgerald, "Wager Swayne, the Freedmen's Bureau, and the Politics of Reconstruction in Alabama," *Alabama Review* 48 (July 1995): 188–218.

5. Ira Berlin et al., eds., *Freedom: A Documentary History of Emancipation, 1861–1867*, ser. 1, vol. 2, *The Wartime Genesis of Free Labor: The Upper South* (Cambridge, England: Cambridge University Press, 1993), 384.

6. Ibid., 475.

7. U. S. House, *Reports*, 39th Congress, 1st sess., vol. 2, no. 30, 30.

8. Alva C. Griest, "Three Years in Dixie," Apr. 11, 1865 (typescript of journal), Indiana Historical Society, Indianapolis.

9. Henry N. Herrick to Wife, May 18, 1865, Herrick Family Papers, Minnesota Historical Society, St. Paul, Minn.

10. S. Jones to "Officer in Command at Selma of U. S. Forces," [May 1865], Confederate States of America, Reports at Demopolis, Chicago Historical Society, Chicago, Ill.

11. Cornelius Corwin Diary, May 15, 1865, Indiana Historical Society, Indianapolis.

12. John W. Schlagle Diary, Apr. 24, 1865, Indiana Historical Society, Indianapolis.

13. C. C. Andrews Diary, Apr. 24, 1865, Minnesota Historical Society, St. Paul, Minn.

14. Jonathan Merriam to Wife, Apr. 27, 1865, Jonathan Merriam Papers, Illinois State Historical Society, Springfield.

15. Benjamin R. Hieronymous Diary, May 16, 1865, Illinois State Historical Society, Springfield.

16. S. S. Gardner to Thomas Conway, June 12, 1865, in Thomas W. Conway, *The Freedmen of Louisiana: Final Report of the Bureau of Free Labor, Department of the Gulf* (New Orleans: Times Book and Job Office, 1865), 34.

17. John W. Schlagle Diary, May 5, 1865.

18. Robert Ridge Diary, May 15, 1865, Illinois State Historical Society, Springfield.

19. H. N. Herrick to Wife, May 9, 1865, Herrick Family Papers.

20. S. S. Gardner to T. W. Conway, July 3, 1865, reel 15, Registers and Letters Received by the Commissioner of the Bureau of Refugees, Freedmen, and Abandoned Lands, National Archives Microfilm Publication M752 (hereinafter cited as [LR]BRFAL [M752]).

21. "Mitchell" to "Friend Munn," May 29, 1865, Griggs-Mitchell Papers, Chicago Historical Society, Chicago, Ill.

22. J. A. Wemyss to Henry Watson, July 14, 1865, Watson Papers, Duke University Library, Durham, N.C.

23. For northerners' ambiguous attitudes toward manual work, see Jonathan A. Glickstein, *Concepts of Free Labor in Antebellum America* (New Haven: Yale University Press, 1991).

24. Henry N. Herrick Diary, May 15, 1865, Herrick Family Papers.

25. There is a vast literature on this topic, but the classic account is Litwack, *Been in the Storm So Long*.

26. Lemuel Burke Diary (typescript) June 7, 8, 1865, Illinois State Historical Society, Springfield.

27. John H. Parrish to Henry Watson, July 30, 1865; J. A. Wemyss to Henry Watson, July 14, 1865, Watson Papers.

28. H. N. Herrick to Anne Herrick, May 18, 29, 1865, Herrick Family Papers.

29. Henry N. Herrick Diary, May 15, 1865; H. N. Herrick to Anne Herrick, June 3, 22, 26, 1865, Herrick Family Papers.

30. James (?) to Sis Cattie, June 30, 1865, Creagh Family Papers, Southern Historical Collection, University of North Carolina at Chapel Hill.

31. D. W. Whittle to O. O. Howard, June 8, 1865, reel 18 (LR)BRFAL (M752).

32. *The War of the Rebellion: A Compilation of the Official Records of the Union*

and Confederate Armies, 70 vols. in 128 (Washington, D.C.: Government Printing Office, 1880–1901), ser. 1, vol. 49, pt. 2, 560 (hereinafter cited as *Official Records*).

33. George Harmont to T. W. Conway, May 30, 1865, vol. 108, Letters Sent, Mobile Subassistant Commissioner, Records of the Field Offices of the Bureau of Refugees, Freedmen, and Abandoned Lands, Record Groups 105, National Archives, Washington, D.C. (hereinafter cited as BRFAL-Al)

34. Martha V. Schroeder to G. Schroeder, Apr. 1865, H. A. Schroeder Papers, City of Mobile Museum, Mobile, Alabama.

35. F. W. Emery to E. S. Dennis, May 25, 1865, *Official Records*, ser. 1, vol. 49, pt. 2, 907.

36. G. Harmont to. Col. T. Kinney, July 27, 1865, vol. 108, Letters Sent, Mobile Subassistant Commissioner, BRFAL-Al.

37. Henry Crocheron et al. to Wager Swayne, Nov. 24, 1865, reel 5, Records of the Assistant Commissioner for the State of Alabama, Bureau of Refugees, Freedmen, and Abandoned Lands, National Archives Microfilm Publication M809 (hereinafter cited as BRFAL-Al [M809]).

38. Lemuel Burke Diary (typescript), May 14, 1865.

39. Charles Turner to Wife, May 28, June 7, 1865, Charles Turner Papers, Illinois State Historical Society, Springfield.

40. The code in question was that of General Orders, No. 13, issued by the Treasury Department on February 1, 1865. Canby's instructions freely adapted its provisions (Ira Berlin et al., eds., *Freedom: A Documentary History of Emancipation, 1861–1867*, ser. 1, vol. 3, *The Wartime Genesis of Free Labor: The Lower South* [Cambridge, England: Cambridge University Press, 1990], 587).

41. Conway, *Freedmen of Louisiana*, 24–5.

42. T. W. Conway to Gardner, June 20, 1865, reel 1, Records of the Assistant Commissioner for the State of Louisiana, Bureau of Refugees, Freedmen, and Abandoned Lands, National Archives Microfilm Publication M1027 (hereinafter cited as BRFAL-La [M1027]).

43. Conway, *Freedmen of Louisiana*, 25.

44. C. W. Buckley to Carl Schurz, Aug. 19, 1865, in Philip S. Foner and Ronald L. Lewis, eds., *The Black Worker: A Documentary History from Colonial Times to the Present*, vol. 1: *The Black Worker to 1869* (Philadelphia: Temple University Press, 1978), 321.

45. C. W. Buckley to T. W. Conway, June 1, 1865, in Conway, *Freedmen of Louisiana*, 28.

46. C. W. Buckley to T. W. Conway, June 11, 1865, reel 14, (LR)BRFAL (M752).

47. C. W. Buckley to C. Cadle, Oct. 7, 1865, reel 5, BRFAL-Al (M809).

48. T. W. Conway to C. W. Buckley, July 14, 1865, reel 1, BRFAL-La (M1027).

49. C. W. Buckley to T. W. Conway, June 1, 1865, in Conway, *Freedmen of Louisiana*, 32.

50. S. S. Gardner to O. O. Howard, July 25, 1865, reel 15, (LR)BRFAL (M752).

51. S. S. Gardner to T. W. Conway, July 3, 1865, reel 15, (LR)BRFAL (M752).

52. S. S. Gardner to T. W. Conway, June 12, 1865, in Conway, *Freedmen of Louisiana*, 33.

53. S. S. Gardner to T. W. Conway, July 3, 1865, reel 15, (LR)BRFAL (M752)

54. Fitzgerald, *Union League Movement*, 87, 124–5, 241.

55. Wiener, *Social Origins of the New South*, 51; McFeely, *Yankee Stepfather*, 77–78.

56. White, "Wager Swayne," 106, 109. Elizabeth Bethel's study "The Freedmen's Bureau in Alabama," *Journal of Southern History* 14 (Feb. 1948): 49–92, though dated, is reasonably judicious on Swayne's role in state politics.

57. W. Swayne to O. O. Howard, Jan. 31, 1866, in U.S. Senate, *Executive Documents*, 39th Cong., 1st sess., no. 27, 59.

58. J. R. Shipherd to President Andrew Johnson, Oct. 14, 1865, (LR)-BRFAL (M752). See also W. Swayne to O. O. Howard, May 15, 1865, reel 17, (LR)BRFAL (M752); W. Swayne to G. Dodge, Apr. 17, 1865, Grenville Dodge papers, State Historical Society of Iowa, Des Moines.

59. W. Swayne to G. D. Robinson, Sept. 13, 1865, reel 1, BRFAL-Al (M809)

60. Circular No. 1, Sept. 7, 1865, reel 17; W. Swayne to Woods, Sept. 23, 1865, reel 1, BRFAL-Al (M809).

61. General Orders, No. 12, Aug. 30, 1865, reel 17, BRFAL-Al (M809).

62. W. Swayne, "Annual Report," Oct. 31, 1866, in U.S. Senate, *Executive Documents*, 39th Cong. 1st sess., no. 6, 6.

63. W. Swayne to T. W. Conway Aug. 22, 1865, reel 1, BRFAL-Al (M809).

64. W. Swayne to T. W. Conway, July 21, 1865; Robert B. Holly to T. W. Conway, Sept. 13, 1865, reel 1 BRFAL-La (M1027)

65. W. Swayne to O. O. Howard, Oct. 2, 1865, reel 19, (LR)BRFAL (M752).

66. W. Swayne to O. O. Howard, Aug. 21, 1865, reel 17, (LR)BRFAL (M752).

67. W. Swayne to J. S. Fullerton, June 13, 1866, reel 1, BRFAL-Al (M809).

68. O. O. Howard to E. M. Stanton, Nov. 1, 1866, U. S. House, *Executive Documents*, 39th Cong, 2nd sess., no. 1, 741, 708.

69. R. J. Hinton to T. W. Clarke, Sept. 18, 1865, reel 26, Select Records of the Tennessee Field Offices, Bureau of Refugees, Freedmen and Abandoned Lands, National Archives Microfilm Publication T142.

70. Oliver Otis Howard, *Autobiography of Oliver Otis Howard, Major General, United States Army*, 2 vols. (New York: Baker & Taylor, 1907), 2:253–4.

71. J. W. S. Donnell to Maria Donnell, Oct. 19, 1865, James Webb Smith Donnell Papers, Tennessee State Library and Archives, Nashville.

72. C. B. Fisk to O. O. Howard, Sept. 2, 1865, reel 14, (LR)BRFAL (M752).

73. W. H. Tayloe to H. A. Tayloe, Oct. 25, 1865, Tayloe Papers, Virginia Historical Society, Richmond, in Kenneth M. Stampp, ed., *Records of the Antebellum Southern Plantations*, reel 22, series M, part 1.

74. W. Swayne to O. O. Howard, Dec. 5, 1865, reel 19, (LR)BRFAL (M752).

75. As cited in Donald G. Nieman, *To Set the Law in Motion: The Freedmen's Bureau and the Legal Rights of Blacks, 1865–1868* (Millwood, N.Y.: KTO Press, 1979), 157.

76. W. Swayne to O. O. Howard, Jan. 31, 1865, U.S. Senate, *Executive Documents*, 39th Cong., 1st sess., no. 27, 60.

77. W. Swayne, "Annual Report," Oct. 31, 1866, U.S. Senate, *Executive Documents*, 39th Cong., 1st sess., no. 6, 6. For a different interpretation of Swayne's policy, see White, "Wager Swayne: Racist or Realist?" 103–105. It seems inconsistent to criticize Swayne both for approving the labor codes and then for abandoning them.

78. W. Swayne to O. O. Howard, Sept. 11, 1865, reel 17, (LR)BRFAL (M752).

79. L. Parsons to President A. Johnson, Sept. 28, 1865, reel 23, (LR)-BRFAL (M752); W. Swayne to T. M. Owen, Jan. 7, 1902, Swayne Manuscripts; W. Swayne to L. Parsons, July 31, 1865, Governor Parsons Papers, Alabama Department of Archives and History, Montgomery; W. Swayne to J. S. Fullerton, June 13, 1866, reel 1, (LR)BRFAL (M809).

80. C. B. Fisk to O. O. Howard, Oct. 7, 1865, reel 21, (LR)BRFAL (M752); Swayne, "Annual Report," 5.

81. Walter Lynwood Fleming, *Civil War and Reconstruction in Alabama* (New York: Macmillan, 1905), 383.

82. U. S. House, *Reports*, 39th Cong., 1st sess., vol. 2, no. 30, 138.

83. O. D. Kinsman to H. Leverett, April 30, 1866, reel 1, BRFAL-Al (M809).

84. C. Cadle to S. S. Gardner, April 24, 1866, reel 1, BRFAL-Al (M809).

85. O. D. Kinsman to W. Swayne, March 1, 1866, reel 1, BRFAL-Al (M809).

86. W. Swayne to Gen. C. R. Woods, Feb. 27, 1866, reel 1, BRFAL-Al (M809).

87. Fitzgerald, "Wager Swayne."

4

"One of the Most Appreciated Labors of the Bureau": The Freedmen's Bureau and the Southern Homestead Act

Michael L. Lanza

ON JUNE 21, 1866, President Andrew Johnson signed the Southern Homestead Act. It opened up 46 million acres of public lands in Alabama, Arkansas, Florida, Louisiana, and Mississippi to actual settlement and specified that applicants could not be discriminated against on the basis of color. The law thus sits squarely at the core of the era's crucial issues concerning land and labor. Questions of land ownership, freedmen's rights, and punishment of Confederates commingled with nineteenth-century assumptions about agrarianism, private property, and the Protestant work ethic.

Freedpeople believed that control of their own land and labor would provide them with the foundation necessary for controlling their own lives and providing for themselves and their families. These assumptions were at the heart of the free labor ideology, part of which emphasized independence founded on land ownership. Another strain emphasized the complementary interests of capital and labor. The realities of freedom demonstrated the conflicts in these two strains: the expectations of white and black, employer and employee, were generally antithetical. The failure of the Southern Homestead Act can be blamed primarily on the power struggle to control the South's land and labor resources. That struggle was simply not one of capital against labor or the haves against the havenots; at its heart was the issue of race and the history of the inequality of capital and labor that permeated southern history.[1]

The Southern Homestead Act supplemented the Homestead Act of 1862, the apotheosis of the Republican Party's free-soil ideology. The 1862 law gave citizens 160 acres of land free upon payment of a $10 registration fee. The homesteader had to settle on the land and make improvements on it for five years before receiving title. The law excluded all persons who had borne arms against the United States and required an oath of future loyalty.[2] The Southern Homestead Act made several crucial changes. Most significantly, the southern public lands could be acquired only through homesteading, that is to say, a person could not pay for them outright. This restriction was repealed in 1876. The law reduced, for two years, the maximum homestead to eighty acres. Significantly, Congress retained the ban on ex-Confederates' acquiring land, but only for six months. After January 1, 1867, all people, white and black, loyal and Confederate, could homestead. The brief window of six months, when loyal whites and blacks had first access to the lands, was not meant to give these groups a head start. Rather, freedmen had contracted their labor for the year, and Congress did not want them to break their contracts or to entice them from the cotton fields. As one senator put it, the restrictions on former Confederates should remain "until the time when the freedmen will be in a position to avail themselves of the benefit of this law."[3] Practically speaking, the six-month period was meaningless to most freedpeople.

While the law was still being shaped in the House committee, George W. Julian, the energy behind the legislation, added a provision that remained with the bill throughout debate and became a piece of the final legislation: "No distinction or discrimination shall be made in the construction or execution of this act on account of race or color." This was the first time that any legislation included such a stipulation.[4]

Julian's addition of this clause confirmed, by law, that black people had a right to own land. He explained: "In consequence of the Dred Scott decision, and the power of latterday Democracy in debauching the public sentiment of the country, it is not generally understood that black men have any rights in relation to the public domain of the country. . . . I believe it is now unknown to multitudes of white men, even in the northern States, that colored men have any rights under the homestead law [of 1862]. We ought to make that fact known to black and white, so that the multitudes of landless people may understand what are their rights of acquiring land."[5] Julian's provision reinforced a ruling made by the Commissioner of the General Land Office. In mid-1865, he noted that "the [1862] Homestead Law makes no difference in color among those who are proffered its benefits. Whoever shall be able to make the affidavit [about past and future loyalty] required by the act will be entitled to enter a homestead."[6]

Although the disposition of federal lands came under the jurisdiction of the General Land Office, the Freedmen's Bureau took an early and sustained interest because of its charge to oversee all things pertaining to freedpeople in the South. The Bureau had some experience with land matters before the Southern Homestead Act passed because of its responsibility for confiscated and abandoned lands. Yet those lands passed rapidly out of the control of the Bureau as Andrew Johnson issued pardons to Confederate owners and restored their lands to them. Johnson was an early and consistent supporter of homestead legislation but opposed any confiscation measures or a role for the Freedmen's Bureau in land matters.

The Bureau was limited from the beginning in what it could do for freedmen and refugees. Congress conceived of it as a temporary measure and provided no funding for the first year. Beyond that, the agency was limited by the views of those who ran it, both at headquarters and in the states. Bureau Commissioner Oliver Otis Howard and his assistant commissioners shared assumptions about land and labor in the South; those assumptions were complex and often led in contradictory directions. Many agents were committed to providing assistance to the former slaves and assisted them in every way to acquire land of their own, particularly when they were confident that the ex-slaves would be successful. Other agents believed tenaciously that the economic resources of the region should remain in the hands of the current landholders, and that the freed population should continue to serve as laborers. The records of the Freedmen's Bureau are filled with documents attesting to the paramount importance that agents gave to honoring labor contracts. Agents encouraged freedpeople to acquire land if they believed the freedpeople could hold onto it but, at the same time, insisted that they observe the terms of their labor contracts.

The Freedmen's Bureau reacted quickly to the passage of the Southern Homestead Act. In less than two weeks, Howard issued his Circular No. 7. It did more than inform. After stating the details of the legislation, the circular instructed the assistant commissioners to move quickly, for the remaining six months of the year provided unparalleled opportunities for freedpeople to obtain land. Howard believed that this law was the realization of a government promise, for he commented that settlement on public lands would likely "secure" homesteaders "from any interference likely to occur." The commissioner was probably referring to Johnson's pardoning policies, whereby confiscated lands were returned to their owners despite Howard's earlier efforts to retain them.

Before giving the locations of the land offices, Howard made one last request for positive action: "Information of the location and quality of lands, the manner of entry, the advantage of this offer of the Government, the increased security, and many reasons for companies of these people entering lands lying contiguous, shall be collected and presented in the strongest manner."[7]

A week after issuing the circular, Howard wrote the assistant commissioners in the five southern public land states. He touched on the Bureau's assumptions concerning the promises of land ownership when he wrote, "There is no reason why the poor whites and freedmen of the South cannot take advantage of the present homestead law, and enter a career of prosperity, that will secure them fortunes, elevate them socially and morally, add to the general prosperity of the country, and settle the many vexed questions that are now arising." Realities would prove Howard wrong.

The commissioner went on to instruct his subordinates to "resort to every means in your power to spread the information this Circular contains." He authorized the employment of civil agents to assist them in collecting maps of the public lands, ascertaining their quality and location, and answering all questions. These "locating agents" would prove crucial during the early months. Howard concluded by urging his assistant commissioners to move quickly to take "such action as will make the Bureau an efficient agent in settling the public lands, and securing homes to the poor whites and blacks."[8]

Howard was also concerned about those who might want to homestead but who lived in a state with no public lands. About two weeks after he issued his circular, he wrote Assistant Commissioner J. W. Sprague in Arkansas and instructed him to furnish information about the public lands in his state so that it could be transmitted to assistant commissioners in states without public lands. He asked Sprague to include the number of acres, location, some information about the quality and the means of reaching the land, and any other information that might prove useful.[9]

Freedpeople knew about the free lands and made early inquiries. Land officers reported the deluge of requests for land shortly after the passage of the act. Land office register William Carruth of Washington, Arkansas, reported in September that freedpeople were "anxious (many of them) to purchase a homestead for actual settlement, and applications from them are hourly made at this office." That same month, the U.S. Attorney in southern Mississippi reported that freedpeople were inquiring daily about public land in southeastern Mississippi.[10]

Howard understood that poor whites and blacks faced tremendous obstacles in trying to acquire their own homes. To assist those who did not have the means to do so, Howard authorized transportation and subsistence for one month.[11] The Bureau advised that groups of freedpeople should appoint representatives to travel to the land office to make applications for the group, for transportation and subsistence would only be provided to "such as may have located," that is, to those who already had filed their homestead claims.[12] Bureau agents and freedpersons soon noticed that one month's subsistence was often inadequate and that only freedpeople already successful could, in reality, take advantage of the law.

Enormous obstacles lay in the path of those freedpersons who wished to acquire their own land under the Southern Homestead Act. One of the severest problems was the opposition of white people to land ownership by blacks—not only because of the perceived labor shortage that would result if black people withdrew their labor from the plantations but also because of their ideas of white supremacy. Many white people just could not visualize black people in positions of independence.

Other problems appeared in the execution of the law, the quality of the land, and the assumptions underpinning the homestead principle. President Johnson did not appoint land officers and thus reopen the southern land offices until after the six-month restrictive period expired. Fraud was rampant, from the land officers themselves, to the homesteaders, who swore false oaths about the settlement and cultivation provisions. Moreover, timber companies began moving to the South to exploit the rich, virgin stands as midwestern timber was depleted. Their agents had to file dummy homestead claims because the law did not allow cash purchases nor did it allow acquisition of land for any reason other than homesteading. Much of the best land was off limits to homesteaders because it had been reserved earlier for railroad grants or military reservations. Many homesteaders did not discover this fact until they had already settled on the land, only to be told to move on. Poor records and the lack of surveys explain part of the reason for the confusion. Much of the remaining available land was either worthless for homesteading or not worth the cost, in time and labor, to clear it and try to make it productive.[13]

A look at homesteading activities in each of the five public land states illustrates these problems and the various ways that the Freedmen's Bureau agents responded to situations as they arose. Though there are patterns from state to state, there is no clear-cut evidence that agents followed consistent policies that came from higher up.

Freedpeople demonstrated an early interest in homesteading Alabama's 6.7 million acres. Joseph R. Putnam, who had commanded a black regiment during the war, reported that many freedpeople made frequent inquiries about homesteads in north Alabama. He tried to assist them by providing information, but he believed that "unless special means" were employed, most of them would not be able to take advantage of the law; they either could not locate vacant lands or procure them if they did. Moreover, the Bureau agent in the area "is practically a non resident, having moved to Mississippi recently & seldom visits this place." Having in mind Howard's circular authorizing the appointment of special agents, Putnam recommended himself to assist the freedpeople.[14]

Alabama's assistant commissioner, Wager T. Swayne, reported that much of the land in that state was rich in minerals and "well timbered," but land already cleared would be more productive for raising cotton. Freedmen had been making many inquiries about the new law, but "few considered its provisions advantageous." Swayne took steps to disseminate information about the legislation and to assist the freedpeople in their efforts. He predicted that more of them would apply for land "when their annual contracts have expired."[15]

Arkansas provides evidence of a Bureau agent hard at work to help freedpeople obtain land and the hoops through which the freedpeople would have to jump to acquire it. Assistant Commissioner John W. Sprague found three-fourths of the nine million acres available in Arkansas to be worthless. The land officers were willing to help the freedpeople, but their records were faulty, having "not been *posted* for *Twenty years* or more." Under the authority granted him by Howard's Circular No. 7, Sprague employed Dr. W. W. Granger as a surveyor in order to determine the location of the public lands and to assist freedpeople and others in locating them. Sprague also pointed to one of the harshest realities: "[N]early all the Freedmen who have the means or disposition to secure Homesteads are either under Contract to labor or are engaged with their crops until about the 1st of Jany next when the exclusive benefit of the Homestead law to the *union* and *Freedmen* will expire[.]" Sprague believed that this provision of the law should be extended for at least another year.[16]

Many freedpeople who wanted public lands in Arkansas came from other states, particularly Georgia. G. L. Eberhart, the Georgia Bureau's superintendent of education, endorsed the migration of large numbers of former slaves to Arkansas because they were "cruelly treated" and "can remain in Georgia no longer." They wished to emigrate "where they can purchase Govt. lands and escape the cupidity and persecution of the late masters." Eberhart argued that by getting rid of blacks who wanted to leave, he could create a greater demand for the labor of those who remained, which would lead whites to offer better wages and treatment: "If we could take a few hundred families out of this State within the next 6 months it would I think produce a very wholesome influence upon the whites and upon the condition of those freedmen who remain."[17]

Yet, their arrival in Arkansas was not likely to engender a welcome reception. The state's newly appointed assistant commissioner, General E. O. C. Ord, wrote Davis Tillson, his counterpart in Georgia, that "there is only a small portion of any of the State where the immigration of Freedmen would be looked upon with favor. . . . I do not wish to discourage immigration but think it right that Freedmen coming here should be informed they must not expect to be received with cordiality." Still, Ord promised to provide them protection, offered Granger's services as surveyor, and agreed to furnish transportation and subsistence to any who might need it.[18]

In late November, Robert McWhorter of Greene County, Georgia, applied for transportation only, not rations, to go to Arkansas with thirteen other heads of family, about 190 people in all. He wanted to act quickly because his neighbors' contracts were about to expire and "they will be without the means of subsistence." Assistant Commissioner Tillson forwarded McWhorter's request to Howard, but Washington turned him down. The freedmen were not dependent on the government for support, and "[b]esides, there is no evidence that they would not become a charge upon the Gov't on arriving in Arkansas, should transportation be granted." In order for them to receive the transportation expenses to another state, the freedmen would first have to make contracts for their labor or prove they had a stake.[19]

That some agents were more interested in keeping the freedpeople at work than in allowing them to acquire their own land is evident in another case from Georgia. Agent James Davison, also from Greene County, feared that so many freedmen were interested in going to Arkansas to acquire their own land that a labor shortage would certainly occur in Georgia. This fear did not prevent Davison from requesting transportation to Panola County, Mississippi, for two freedmen hired by two citizens of Greene County to work on a plantation they had acquired there. As long as freedmen had work lined up on someone else's land, some Bureau agents would assist them to get there.[20]

Assistant Commissioner Tillson willingly helped freedpeople in Georgia to emigrate to a public land state. But he would assist only those who were "so situated as to make it probable they would succeed." His opinions of the former slaves were not sanguine; he believed they were "[u]naccustomed and incompetent, with few exceptions, to foresee their wants or make suitable provision for the future." Because they have an "almost universal desire to possess land," many would attempt to homestead without the wherewithal to support themselves until they produced a crop. They would "thereby bring upon themselves and families inevitable suffering, turning the intended bounty of the Government into a curse."[21]

A great deal of evidence suggests that representatives of two groups of freedpeople came from Georgia to the area around Fort Smith, Arkansas, in order to acquire homesteads. One group represented 150 families, the other 18 families. Leading the party of 18 families from Dougherty County were Samuel Brown and Squire Sherman, to whom Granger showed land in late February and early March 1867. Granger reported that they had run out of money after six days, and, if they were not provided assistance, they would have to end their efforts at locating homesteads for their fellow Georgians. Abraham Colby represented the larger group from Greene County; he selected lands for them in the Clarksville land district. The land office at Clarksville was apparently closed, however, for General Ord pleaded with General Howard to use his influence to open the office. It seems that this group eventually located lands in Sebastian County that were heavily timbered with access to "good water." Bureau agent Charles Banzhaf believed that "[t]he soil will compare favorably with any in the State."[22]

The delegates from both colonies found themselves having to call on Granger in Little Rock because of another difficulty—George W. Denison, the register of the land office at Little Rock. By strictly interpreting a section of the Homestead Act, Denison impeded homesteaders from out of state. The law allowed prospective homesteaders to swear the required oaths before the clerk of court in the county in which they resided. Denison would not accept the oaths if they were sworn out of the state or even out of the district where the land was located.

Granger was palpably angry at the register's interpretation and made several efforts to alert the proper officials. He expressed faith that these were "a thrifty industrious community of Freedmen, whose settlement of lands . . . will add much to the material development of the country, and also carry out, in a measure, the spirit and aim of the 'Homestead Law.' " Granger explained that the colonists could not afford to come from Georgia as a group and wait while the lands were selected and surveyed. Their agents would come first to Arkansas to select land. The rest would make their affidavits where they lived, carry out their obligations in Georgia, then come to Arkansas, and support themselves with what they had saved while they cleared their new lands. Granger also believed that the time for actually moving onto the lands should be extended until Christmas 1867 (the law required homesteaders to move onto their lands within six months of making an entry) so the colonists could fulfill their labor contracts.[23]

On April 1, at the request of Ord, Granger made a full report of the problems inherent in the law and its interpretation and made recommendations for their amelioration. He pointed to the requirement of settling on the land within six months of making the entry, the *"want of a provision"* by which applicants from another state could make their affidavits in their home state, the closed land offices (Little Rock was the only one open), and the lack of some arrangement for surveying the lands prior to selection of a plot. Granger had been complaining about this last problem for some months. Because of lack of help, he surveyed the lands only when prospective homesteaders came to select them and helped him to complete the surveys. They often discovered that the land was poor or already claimed by someone else.[24]

Granger believed that were the lands surveyed in advance, the number of homestead applications by freedpeople would increase. The problem was especially troublesome at the beginning of the year, "in the interval between the expiration of the old contract, and the beginning of new ones." During this brief time, the freedman, "with his little savings available," could make prompt selections of land if it had already been surveyed. But obstacles got in the way. Because of delays caused by the need to have the lands surveyed, and because many freedmen "are afraid of missing a good engagement for the year," they do not attempt to homestead but "return to the plantations." Those who decided to wait often spent their small savings until, late in the year, they found a legitimate homestead. But then they did not have the means to begin a new life and were disadvantaged for a year or two.

Granger took the initiative in trying to locate the public lands; by early May, he was beginning to prepare maps showing their amount and quality. By early June, he had examined the records of 427 townships and found about 1.5 million acres subject to entry. Of this number, he recommended about 450,000 acres for settlement.[25]

In surveying and mapping the lands, Granger discovered that not all the vacant lands were public lands; some had been given to the railroads for construction, and others were swamplands that had been given to the state. Often, homesteaders were adversely affected because they had unknowingly settled on land that had been reserved for other purposes. In one case, for example, a family paid several hundred dollars for improvements already made on the land they claimed and then spent a year clearing, fencing, and cultivating thirty-five acres. The plot turned out to be on land claimed by a railroad and was a mile and a half from the land that the homesteader thought he was getting. Granger concluded that "whether cupidity or ignorance leads to the misinformation," the freedman "who labors on it and buys improvements, or makes them, on what he mistakenly supposes to be public land, is always victimized & generally demoralized by the result." The land office records contain countless examples of hardships caused because homesteaders settled on these so-called reserve lands.[26]

The Freedmen's Bureau's efforts, particularly those of W. W. Granger, provided the opportunity for several freedpeople to get land in Arkansas during the first year that the Southern Homestead Act was in operation—despite the hardships, frustrations, and confusions that Granger detailed. In his annual report for the year ending September 30, 1867, Granger wrote that he had surveyed 243 tracts and had rejected 100 as unfit for settlement. Of the 143 that were suitable, freedmen entered 116 of them. The report mentioned the poor condition of the Little Rock land office records because of their neglect during the war, but it concluded on an optimistic note: "I am able to repeat that most of those who entered Homesteads in time to do so, have made gratifying progress in their improvement, and towards that personal independence which nothing assures better than land ownership. With favorable opportunities, their interest in the subject, and the number of entries made, will doubtless continue to increase."[27]

Many of the same themes sounded in Arkansas repeated themselves in Florida. Freedpeople desired their own land; labor contracts often interfered with their getting it; land quality was uncertain; poor records and closed land offices hindered settlement; land officers were often corrupt; and the Freedmen's Bureau did what it could, with limited resources and against tremendous odds, to assist former slaves to begin a new life. Florida was different, though, from the other four southern public land states in several respects. For one, it had more federal land than any other, 19 million acres representing 51 percent of Florida's land, about twice as much as second-ranked Arkansas. Of the 19 million acres, about 11 million had not been surveyed and were therefore off limits for homesteading until surveys were completed. In Arkansas, all the lands had been officially surveyed, although the appointment of Granger as a surveyor for the Freedmen's Bureau demonstrates that much work was yet to be done. Florida did not get an official surveyor general until President Ulysses S. Grant appointed Marcellus L. Stearns in the spring of 1869.[28]

Assistant Commissioner John G. Foster believed that much of the land in Florida was poor; he questioned whether "it will ever be a benefit to the colored people." In recognizing the reality of beginning a new life, he argued that freedpeople would need a year's provisions to start, not the one-month subsistence that the Bureau promised, and some agricultural implements, which the Bureau would not furnish. Still, Foster concluded that despite the problems and the seeming inevitability of failure, from "a political point of view the law is very important, as it will enable the colored people to become landowners and independent producers," and he promised to do what he could to help them, "even at the risk of having to support some that may utterly fail in their efforts to produce enough for their support."[29]

As in other states, freedpeople in Florida showed an early interest in acquiring lands under the Southern Homestead Act. The Freedmen's Bureau actively alerted them to their opportunities. By the fall of 1866, Subassistant Commissioner F. E. Grossman in Lake City found "a strong disposition on the part of the freedmen to avail themselves" of the law. Several freedpeople already had entered land in his district, and he believed that many more would but for the fact that they could not determine the location of government land. Grossman asked Dr. A. B. Stonelake, the register of the land office at Tallahassee, for maps for which "the freedmen readily pay the required charge" of $5.00 for each one.[30]

In early September 1866, word also came from Subassistant Commissioner T. Seymour in Pensacola that a large group of about 325 families wished to establish a community on the public lands, and he was supplying them with transportation costs to go to Tallahassee to get the necessary information to locate. Agent Jacob Remley reported from Marion County in late September that "a large number of the Freedmen will avail themselves of the provisions of the Homestead Law—Many more than I a month ago anticipated." Assistant Commissioner Foster, in his report to Howard in October, told the commissioner that freedpeople had entered 32,000 acres since the opening of the Tallahassee land office in late August, and Register Stonelake reported that freedpeople had made 279 entries in October. Foster wrote that a "large settlement" would be made soon "at New Smyrna, on the upper St. John's River, on the Suwannee River, and on the Manatee River and its tributaries."[31]

Along with the great desire of freedpeople to homestead came opposition to black homesteaders. Foster reported in September 1866, "In some localities combinations have been formed to resist the settlement of the negroes, and to drive them off." He was preparing to suppress these "combinations" and to enforce the law.[32]

In early September 1866, freedman Thomas Harley and nine others set out from Tallahassee for Lafayette County, Florida, to locate land under the Southern Homestead Act. They were stopped at Moseley's Ferry and informed that white people had banded together to prevent them from claiming lands. They headed on to Lafayette County, where Jim Jones informed them that a group of twenty-five white people, with twenty-five more expected, intended to prevent them from settling there. Jones also told them that the bodies of three black men had been found in the Suwannee River and the sheriff was confiscating arms found in the possession of the freedmen. The men decided not to homestead and returned to Tallahassee.[33]

Coley Mayner, a freedman in Leon County, Florida, tried to homestead on some land on the Ochlockonee River, about twenty miles from Tallahassee. When he arrived, he was met by a group of white people who were unwilling to help him or to provide him with any information. One of them told Mayner, "We are not whipped yet nor gone back into the Union, so they have no right to sell the land to you it belongs to the Territory." Someone else told Mayner that "if the negroes settle around here," their white neighbors would begin stocking up on ammunition to be used against them.[34]

A small force under Lieutenant S. Smith was sent to the region to notify the inhabitants that any opposition to homesteading by freedmen would be "punished with the severest penalties of Military law." Lieutenant Smith interviewed the man who had not "gone back into the Union" and discovered that now he was a good Union man. Smith could not find anyone willing to admit that white people had been trying to interfere with the black homesteaders; in fact, even the freedmen would not attest to it. Smith concluded his report by observing that plantation owners in the area "will do all in their power to keep [land] out of the hands of the Freedmen. Although they will probably commit no overt act as long as there is a show of Military force in the state."[35]

Stearns, by then subassistant commissioner for Gadsden, Liberty, and Calhoun Counties, confirmed that his district also held strong views about land ownership by the blacks. "They are opposed at every point and it is demanded of them first to employ a land surveyor & establish the exact boundries [sic] of their land before allowed to occupy the land and then the adjacent land holders refuse to join fences with them &c. causing them much trouble. Some have entered land already occupied by parties who peremptorily refuse to give up the possession."[36]

One of the most eloquent pleas from freedpeople concerning their plight in Florida and their difficulties in obtaining their own land came from a group from Jacksonville who had gathered together in the rain on January 1, 1867, to celebrate the fourth "anniversary day of our independence." The petition, sent to Congress, was written by Jonathan Cory, Jr., a Presbyterian teacher in the freedmen schools, who was active in finding homes for refugees and freedmen.

The memorial began with a series of "thank yous": for the Emancipation Proclamation, the Freedmen's Bureau, the Thirteenth Amendment, legislation in behalf of the freedmen's welfare, and teachers and books. The petitioners then recounted the treatment received at the hands of their white neighbors, who had cheated them of their wages; assaulted them; ravished their wives and daughters; shot and killed them, with their murderers walking free; and kept them ignorant and homeless.

These freedmen reminded Congress that the slaves answered the call for assistance to the Union, and they took credit for the Union victory. They did not blame the Congress for the wrongs inflicted upon them, but they did not see any bright prospects for the future, either. Then they expressed directly what they wanted: "We humbly pray your honorable bodies to provide for our race such transportation, rations, building materials, tents, surgeons, & surveyors, as will enable us to enter the United States homesteads, and such legislation as will secure among ourselves honesty, industry and frugality, and deliver us from the fear of all who maliciously hate and persecute us, so that none can say in coming time, 'the people of the United States are unjust.' "

Commissioner Howard saw this remarkable document and forwarded it to Representative Thomas D. Eliot, an early supporter of the Southern Homestead Act. The commissioner was deeply moved by what he read. He did not know how relief could be provided in any general way without incurring tremendous expenses, "yet I am oppressed beyond measure, with the cry of the poor," and if anything could be done for these "poor settlers, no one will be more grateful than your Humble Servant."[37]

The failed colony at New Smyrna provides the best-documented example of freedpeople trying to take advantage of the Southern Homestead Act.[38] In broad outline, Ralph Ely, a former Bureau agent in South Carolina, whom Eric Foner has called "wholly unfit for the job,"[39] organized a colony of about 1,200 freedpeople to go from Charleston to Florida to homestead. He collected about six hundred dollars in fees from them and sent the money to Register Stonelake at Tallahassee, who penciled in the entries on the books. Unfortunately, New Smyrna, Volusia County, was in the St. Augustine district, which had not been reopened, so lands could not be officially taken there. When Ely demanded a refund of the money, Stonelake refused. He argued that the freedpeople had paid the fees with the intent of homesteading. Apparently, the fees were legal but the applications were not.[40]

The colonists were destitute when they arrived in Florida near the end of January 1867. They had been given only a partial month's subsistence and were starving, and, in the view of one Bureau agent, the land was worthless and would not provide enough sustenance to make a living. Assistant Commissioner Sprague sent a special agent to investigate in February. He reported that about three-fourths of those who had come to Florida out of harsh necessity already had contracted their labor with planters from nearby counties. In his monthly report to Howard, Sprague confessed that "[t]he establishment of the Colony is a failure."[41]

The fullest accounting of the misbegotten colony comes from W. J. Purman, special agent for the Bureau, appointed by Sprague to investigate the New Smyrna catastrophe. His report of March 20,

1867, provides a rare glimpse into the lives of about 1,200 freedpeople as they set out to begin homes of their own.

When the group landed in Florida, "they found no shelter but palmetto trees, no prospects but hard labor, no certainties but hardships and privations, no homesteads surveyed and ready for them, no town or inhabitants from whom to expect assistance, and no source from which to receive their daily subsistence for which they were already anxious and stinted." Most of them responded eagerly to offers to contract their labor to nearby planters to keep from starving, but about 250 men, women, and children remained on their own.

Their greatest need was provisions, though no general suffering had yet occurred. Purman found three barrels of pork and one barrel of beans still remaining of the rations provided by the Bureau, and he distributed these to the most needy. He discovered that the settlers were living on roots, vegetables, fish, and small game. A few freedpeople worked at a nearby sawmill. Others had to walk fifty or sixty miles to seek employment because the area was so sparsely populated.

The freedpeople had not raised much corn, and they had no implements, except the hoe, and no livestock. Purman worried that "when human maintenance falls upon such precarious resources, hope may well turn into despair, life become a burthen, and all feelings of civilization descend into a species of barbarism." Yet, the settlers wanted to remain if possible. "Their desire to possess land or a home of their own, is very strong. They have a point of pride, not to return, under any circumstances, to South Carolina, in case of the final failure of their colony." He then cast his blame, asserting that this was "a schem[e] either so blind or heartless that no ordinary judgment of conscience could conceive and execute it."[42]

Blame for the failure of the New Smyrna colony can be spread around easily, and Special Agent Purman was particularly incensed with the players who orchestrated this drama. Certainly, former Bureau agent Ralph Ely was at fault; Register A. B. Stonelake of the land office must also share responsibility, for he kept freedpeople's money and misunderstood the fees. The register resigned in September.[43]

In reporting to Howard, Sprague revealed something of his own predilections and assumptions. He took credit for providing assistance. Shortly after the colony arrived, he furnished it with rations and placed a "competent Bureau officer" in charge. But the freedmen began roaming the countryside, depredating the livestock. The Bureau was partially to blame, for "[s]o long as the Government would supply rations, there was little or no disposition to work." Sprague also had hired several civilian surveyors, who helped freedpeople determine the location and quality of the public lands. He was convinced that homesteads would benefit those freedpeople who could get them. Having their own land made them "self-reliant and better qualified to discharge the rights and duties of citizens, as, while adrift, without homes, they are in a great measure within the power of employers and landed proprietors; with Homesteads, they may hire their services, or cultivate their own lands, as best suits their interest."

Sprague told Howard that, as of October 1867, 2,012 homesteads had been entered, and Florida's population had increased since 1860. Part of that increase was due, in Sprague's view, to the emigration of freedpeople from nearby states who "manifest a strong desire for emigration to Florida." He believed Florida was a suitable home for the freedpeople because the climate "suits them as well as Africa, and is much better adapted to the negro than the white man. A warm humid climate, though unhealthy for the Anglo-Saxon, precisely suits the negro."

Sprague had strong views about the primary people under his charge, and the Bureau actions in Florida, despite some notable exceptions, undoubtedly reflected its leader's philosophy. Sprague was utterly convinced of the baseness of black people: "His gross physique, degraded intellect, grovelling pursuits, habitual slothfulness and licentious habits, tend to make him a terror in society, which can only be governed by stringent laws faithfully administered."[44] Sprague remained assistant commissioner in Florida for almost two years.

The experience of freedpeople trying to acquire their own land, and the Bureau's attempts to assist them varied in Florida from the other states only in the amount of land available for homesteading. The quality of the lands, capabilities of the land officers, disposition of the Bureau agents, and the resources of the freedpeople themselves determined success or failure. As in other states, Louisiana's early assistant commissioners were solicitous of the needs of the freedpeople and did what they could to assist them. Absalom Baird held that post when the Southern Homestead Act was passed and took quick action soon after Howard issued his Circular No. 7. On July 25, 1866, Baird issued his own Circular No. 7, in which he announced the appointment of J. J. Saville as special locating agent and insisted on the urgency of making early application before the January 1, 1867, deadline opened the state's 6 million acres to ex-Confederates. In a few weeks, Baird issued his Circular No. 8, in which he gave instructions to guide freedpeople as they proceeded to obtain lands. He encouraged them to settle in groups of ten families, "that they may assist each other in cultivating their farms and support schools and churches." He assumed, like others, that only freedpeople with some means would be successful. Each group of ten families, therefore, should have two wagons and teams, and each family should have a horse or mule, in addition to farming implements. So that freedpeople would not have to break their labor contracts to look for land, Baird had appointed Saville to select lands for them. He instructed those who wished homesteads to inform the nearest agent of the Bureau of their names and residences, whether or not they were under contract, and what resources they had to sustain them. This information would be sent to Saville, and "as soon as Freedmen can move without violating existing contracts, lands will be procured for them."[45]

Saville was eager to execute his duties, and he seemed to be untiring in his efforts. By January 1867, he had located homesteads for eighty-seven freedpeople, seventy-three white refugees, and fourteen soldiers, but because the New Orleans land office was closed, only seven of these had filed their applications. The closed office was only one of the problems that homesteaders encountered. White opposition deterred them. In February 1867, freedpeople near Opelousas had trouble when they tried to enter homesteads and were driven off "by a lawless band." The Freedmen's Bureau agent who had heard the report volunteered to proceed to the area and investigate the matter himself. But he acknowledged the dangers, not only against freedpeople but against the Bureau, when he wrote that he was ready to go at any time, "but I consider, it would be safer to proceed there with an escort."[46]

In addition to white opposition, problems common in the other states plagued Louisiana homesteaders as well. Saville pointed out that the available lands were practically worthless, most of them having failed to sell under the 1856 Graduation Act, which reduced their price to twelve and a half cents an acre. The expenses involved in filing an application exceeded the value of the land. Agent Saville found some valuable land along the right-of-way of the New Orleans, Opelousas, and Great Western Railroad, a strip about forty miles wide. The grant to the railroad had expired in June 1866, but the lands had not yet been returned to the federal government. Congressional inaction delayed these efforts until the summer of 1870. Hundreds of people settled on these lands, but, two years later, they were still waiting for confirmation of their claims. Until the governor prepared a list of those lands, all claims and counterclaims were held in abeyance.[47]

Nothing went smoothly for Saville, and the obstacles he encountered were not unique. Because the New Orleans office was closed throughout most of his appointment, until July 1868, and because it had only one land officer, very few freedpeople actually filed official papers. In addition, John Tully, register at New Orleans, complained that Saville was interfering with his official duties. The register charged Saville with deluding the freedpeople by charging them "exorbitant" fees and by locating them on land not belonging to the federal government. Several freedmen complained about Saville's irregular actions.[48]

Evidence supports the contention that Saville was charging the wrong fees, but this can be blamed on ignorance of the law—surely a trait Saville shared with some land officers. His general actions deserve praise because of his efforts to help freedpeople, the nature of land office business, and his attempts to alert Congress to some of the realities of public land needs in Louisiana, particularly with the railroad forfeitures.

Mississippi homesteaders shared much with those in the other southern states. Many freedpeople could not lay claim to the state's 4.7 million acres during the first six months because of their labor contracts. For example, former slaves at Davis Bend had to wait until the end of 1866 before deciding to seek work elsewhere, and "quite a number are awaiting the return & reports of Deputations Sent out by them to examine the public lands offered for homesteads in this and the neighbouring States, with a view to taking up and Settling on these lands in a body for the mutual protection and benefit of all."[49]

While Davis Bend workers looked outside of the state for their own lands, freedpeople from Georgia inquired about lands in Mississippi. From Augusta came an inquiry to Assistant Commissioner Thomas J. Wood about the quality and location of the government lands. A colony of between fifteen and twenty families was eager to relocate to Mississippi. Wood could not supply the information because the records were so poor.[50]

The Freedmen's Bureau's efforts to assist freedpeople and refugees to acquire homesteads did not last very long because the Bureau itself did not last very long. From the passage of the Southern Homestead Act until about mid-1868, Bureau agents found themselves stymied in every direction. Land offices were closed because one or both of the land officers had not been appointed. Records were abysmal because of neglect during the war and poor bookkeeping afterward. Many land officers, all of them political appointees, were not interested in helping homesteaders. Most of the best lands were in private hands, and most of the remaining lands were either too poor for agriculture or under the control of the states or railroads. Many white people did not want black people as neighbors. Many Bureau agents actively and devotedly assisted freedpeople to acquire their own homes, but many of them, too, were limited by their own racial views or the tenets of the bankrupt free labor ideology.

About 67,600 entries were made under the Southern Homestead Act during its ten-year history. Arkansas had the most (26,173) and Louisiana the least (6,449). In the two years that the Freedmen's Bureau was most active, 5,647 entries were recorded, about 8 percent of the total number. Almost 28,000 entries were patented, that is, homesteaders received title to their lands. That number is inflated because homesteaders could make their final affidavits from five to seven years after their initial entry, so some of the claims counted here could have been made after the Southern Homestead Act was repealed.[51]

How many freedpeople claimed land and were successful in securing their titles? That number is impossible to determine from the General Land Office records, but an estimate, based on statistical sampling, is suggestive. Black people constituted between 20 percent and 25 percent of all applicants, and their success rate was equal to or greater than that of whites.[52]

In the end, the promise of land for the freedpeople was illusory. The federal agency charged with the oversight of the federal lands had many problems in the southern states. The federal agency charged with the care of the freedpeople had limited resources and a limited outlook. But to look at the general without examining the particular leaves much of the heroic efforts of individuals—both freedpeople and Bureau agents—unsung. Let W. W. Granger, the civilian agent of the Bureau in Arkansas, have the final word: "I have the pleasure of believing that the work of putting the freedmen on Homesteads, is not only one of the best, but one of the most appreciated labors of the Bureau in their behalf."[53]

NOTES

1. Leon Litwack, *Been in the Storm So Long: The Aftermath of Slavery* (New York: Alfred A. Knopf, 1979); Ira Berlin et al., eds., *Freedom: A Documentary History of Emancipation*, 4 vols. to date (Cambridge, England: Cambridge University Press, 1982–   ); Ira Berlin et al., *Slaves No More: Three Essays on Emancipation and the Civil War* (Cambridge, England: Cambridge University Press, 1992); Eric Foner, *Reconstruction: America's Unfinished Revolution, 1863–1877* (New York: Harper & Row, 1988). I thank the staff at the Freedmen and Southern Society Project at the University of Maryland, College Park, particularly Leslie Rowland and Susan O'Donovan, for their time, generosity, and hospitality. Also, they and their colleagues, Steven Miller and Stephen West, commented on the manuscript, for which I am most grateful.

2. *The Statutes at Large of the United States, 1789–1873*, 17 vols. (Washington, D.C.: Government Printing Office, 1850–1873), 12:ch. 75.

3. *Congressional Globe*, 39th Cong., 1st sess., 3179.

4. The debate on the Southern Homestead Act can be followed in Michael L. Lanza, *Agrarianism and Reconstruction Politics: The Southern Homestead Act* (Baton Rouge: Louisiana State University Press, 1990), 14–23.

5. *Congressional Globe*, 39th Cong., 1st sess., 716.

6. J. M. Edmunds to W. H. Gleason, May 31, 1865, enclosed in W. H. Hunt to O. O. Howard, Dec. 2, 1865, Letters Rec'd, Washington Hdqrs., Bureau of Refugees, Freedmen, and Abandoned Lands, Record Group 105, National Archives, Washington, D.C. (hereinafter cited as BRFAL) [A63]. (The bracketed alpha-numeric designation refers to the filing system of

the Freedmen and Southern Society Project at the University of Maryland, where these papers were examined.)

7. O. O. Howard, Circular No. 7, July 2, 1866, Printed Circulars and Circular Letters, BRFAL [A10720].

8. O. O. Howard to Assistant Commissioners in Alabama, Mississippi, Arkansas, Louisiana, and Florida, July 9, 1866, Letters Rec'd, Florida Assistant Commissioner, BRFAL [A1141]. See also the same letter, but from Samuel Thomas to the Assistant Commissioners, July 9, 1866, vol. 2, Register of Letters Sent, Washington Hdqrs., BRFAL [A2557].

9. O. O. Howard to J.W. Sprague, July 19, 1866, Letters Rec'd, Arkansas Assistant Commissioner, BRFAL [A2586]. Sprague apparently did not reply to Howard's letter, for there is another letter from Samuel Thomas asking Sprague why he had not answered the commissioner. Thomas to Sprague, Oct. 5, 1866, Letters Rec'd, Arkansas Assistant Commissioner, BRFAL [A2586].

10. W. Carruth to J. Edmunds, Sept. 8, 1866, Division "D," Miscellaneous Letters Received from Private Persons, Land Entrymen, Attorneys, and Other Persons (MLR), G87152; R. Leachman to O. Browning (forwarded to General Land Office), Sept. 18, 1866, MLR, G87396, Bureau of Land Management (General Land Office), Record Group 49, National Archives, Washington, D.C.

11. O. O. Howard to J. C. Robinson, Aug. 22, 1866, vol. 66, Registers of Letters Sent, Washington Hdqrs., BRFAL (A63). Copies of this letter were also sent to the assistant commissioners of South Carolina, Florida, Alabama, Mississippi, and Louisiana.

12. Allan Rutherford to J. T. Chur, Oct. 29, 1866, Annual Reports of Operations Received from Staff and Subordinate Officers, North Carolina Assistant Commissioner, BRFAL [A693]. The ruling from Washington is contained in endorsements on L. Speed and others to G. S. Eberhart, Nov. 27, 1866, Letters Rec'd, Georgia Assistant Commissioner, BRFAL [A125]. Eberhart referred the request to Assistant Commissioner Davis Tillson on Nov. 30. Tillson forwarded it to Howard on Dec. 4; A. P. Ketchum referred it to H. Whittlesey on Dec. 8; quoting an as yet unpublished "Officer's Manual," Whittlesey replied in his endorsement of Dec. 10.

13. All of these problems are documented in Lanza, *Agrarianism and Reconstruction Politics*.

14. J. R. Putnam to W. Swayne, July 16, 1866, Unregistered Letters Rec'd, Alabama Assistant Commissioner, BRFAL [A1748].

15. W. Swayne to O. O. Howard, Oct. 31, 1866, Annual Reports of the Assistant Commissioners, Washington Hdqrs., BRFAL [A1575].

16. J. W. Sprague to O. O. Howard, Oct. 12, 1866, Letters Rec'd, Washington Hdqrs., BRFAL [A2257]. The assistant commissioner's report for

July 1866 shows that Granger was appointed on July 9, Monthly Rosters of Officers and Civilians Employed by the Bureau, Arkansas Assistant Commissioner, BRFAL [A2557]. He was discharged Dec. 31, 1868, "by reason of Bureau discontinued." Station Book of Officers and Civilians on Duty in the District, Arkansas Assistant Commissioner, BRFAL [A2557].

17. G. L. Eberhart to J. W. Alvord, Sept. 22, 1866, Unregistered Letters and Miscellaneous Papers and Reports from State Superintendents of Education, Education Division, Washington Hdqrs., BRFAL [A5856].

18. E. O. C. Ord to D. Tillson, Oct. 31, 1866, Unregistered Letters Rec'd, Georgia Assistant Commissioner, BRFAL [A5440].

19. R. McWhorter, Nov. 29, 1866, vol. 2, Registers of Letters Rec'd, Georgia Assistant Commissioner, BRFAL [A286]; the request was returned to D. Tillson, signed by H. M. Whittlesey, on Jan. 16, 1867, vol. 21, Endorsements Sent, Georgia Assistant Commissioner, BRFAL [A286].

20. J. Davison to D. Tillson, Dec. 6, 1866, Unregistered Letters Rec'd, Georgia Assistant Commissioner, BRFAL [A217]; Davison to Tillson, Dec. 19, 1866, Unregistered Letters Rec'd, Georgia Assistant Commissioner, BRFAL [A217].

21. D. Tillson to O. O. Howard, Nov. 1, 1866, Annual Reports of the Assistant Commissioners, Washington Hdqrs., BRFAL [A5005, filed in folder labeled 5001–5008].

22. W. W. Granger to J. Kirkwood, Feb. 24, 1867, Letters Rec'd, Washington Hdqrs., BRFAL [A2271]; W. W. Granger to J. Tyler, March 2, 1867, Letters Rec'd, Arkansas Assistant Commissioner, BRFAL [A2658]; Charles Banzhaf to E. O. C. Ord, March 4, 1867, Letters Rec'd, Arkansas Assistant Commissioner, BRFAL [A2368]; Charles Banzhaf to E. O. C. Ord, March 12, 1867, Letters Rec'd, Arkansas Assistant Commissioner, BRFAL [A5451]. Paul A. Cimbala has traced the Brown and Sherman group from Wilkes County to Dougherty County, Georgia; see his "A Black Colony in Dougherty County: The Freedmen's Bureau and the Failure of Reconstruction in Southwest Georgia," *Journal of Southwest Georgia History* 4 (fall 1986): 72–89.

23. W. W. Granger to G. Denison, Mar. 19, 1867, Denison to Granger, Mar. 19, 1867, and Granger to J. Tyler, Mar. 20, 1867, Letters Rec'd, Arkansas Assistant Commissioner, BRFAL [A2676]; W. W. Granger to J. E. Bennett, June 29, 1867, Letters Rec'd, Washington Hdqrs., BRFAL [A2271].

24. W. W. Granger to J. Tyler, Apr. 1, 1867, Letters Rec'd, Arkansas Assistant Commissioner, BRFAL [A2267].

25. W. W. Granger to J. Tyler, Apr. 19, 1867, Letters Rec'd, Arkansas Assistant Commissioner, BRFAL [A2267]; Granger to Acting Assistant Adjutant General, May 3, 1867, Letters Rec'd, Arkansas Assistant Commissioner, BRFAL [A2385]; Granger to J. E. Bennett, June 4, 1867, Letters Rec'd, Arkansas Assistant Commissioner, BRFAL [A2389].

26. W. W. Granger to J. E. Bennett, July 1, 1867, and Granger to Bennett, Aug. 1, 1867, Letters Rec'd, Arkansas Assistant Commissioner, BRFAL [A2267]. For more on the reserved lands, see Lanza, *Agrarianism and Reconstruction Politics*, ch. 5.

27. C. H. Smith to O. O. Howard, Oct. 22, 1867, Annual Reports of the Assistant Commissioners, Washington Hdqrs., BRFAL [A2280]. The part of the report dealing with homesteads is an extract from Granger's report.

28. U.S. Congress, House, Land Commissioner James Edmunds to Congressman Julian, 39th Congress, 1st sess., Feb. 7, 1866, *Congressional Globe*, 715; U.S. Department of Interior, General Land Office, *Report of the Commissioner of the General Land Office, 1866*, Table 1, 57. Appointments Division, Florida, Records of the Secretary of the Interior, Record Group 48, National Archives, Washington, D.C.

29. J. G. Foster to O. O. Howard, Aug. 10, 1866, Letters Rec'd, Washington Hdqrs., BRFAL [A1491].

30. F. E. Grossman to S. L. McHenry, Sept. 1, 1866, Letters Rec'd, Florida Assistant Commissioner, BRFAL [A1098].

31. T. Seymour to Assistant Adjutant General, Sept. 1, 1866, enclosed in Foster's report to Howard, Oct. 8, 1866, Letters Rec'd, Washington Hdqrs., BRFAL [A1484]; Seymour to Acting Assistant Adjutant General, Oct. 29, 1866, Letters Rec'd, Florida Assistant Commissioner, BRFAL [A1415]; J. A. Remley to C. Mundee, Sept. 30, 1866, Letters Rec'd,, Florida Assistant Commissioner, BRFAL [A1279]; J. G. Foster to O. O. Howard, Oct. 1866, Letters Rec'd, Washington Hdqrs., BRFAL [A1486]; A. B. Stonelake to Foster, Nov. 8, 1866, Letters Rec'd, Florida Assistant Commissioner, BRFAL [A1414].

32. J. G. Foster to G. S. Hartsuff, Sept. 20, 1866, Letters Rec'd, Department of the Gulf, Records of United States Army Continental Commands, 1821–1920, Record Group 393, Pt. 1, National Archives, Washington, D.C. (C589).

33. Affidavit of Thomas Harley and nine others, sworn before J. F. Denniston, Sept. 17, 1866, Letters Rec'd, Florida Assistant Commissioner, BRFAL [A1147].

34. Affidavit of Coley Mayner, sworn before J. F. Denniston, Sept. 22, 1866, Letters Rec'd, Florida Assistant Commissioner, BRFAL [A1285].

35. S. Smith to J. H. Lyman, Sept. 24, 1866, Letters Rec'd, Florida Assistant Commissioner, BRFAL [A1296].

36. M. L. Stearns to E. C. Woodruff, Dec. 31, 1866, Letters Rec'd, Florida Assistant Commissioner, BRFAL [A1403]. This is the same Marcellus Stearns that Grant would appoint surveyor general of Florida, and who would serve as Florida's last Republican governor during Reconstruction (1874–1877).

37. J. Cory, Jr., to S. Colfax, Jan. 2, 1867, enclosing petition of freedmen of Jacksonville and vicinity to Congress, Jan. 1, 1867, and O. O. Howard to T. D. Eliot, Jan. 21, 1867, 39AH11.1, House Committee on Freedmen's Affairs, Petitions and Memorials, ser. 493, 39th Cong., Records of the United States House of Representatives, Record Group 233, National Archives, Washington, D.C. [D5].

38. Several accounts of this failed attempt at colonization exist, so the details are not important here. See Joe M. Richardson, *The Negro in the Reconstruction of Florida, 1865–1877* (Tallahassee: Florida State University Press, 1965), 74–75; Claude F. Oubre, *Forty Acres and a Mule* (Baton Rouge: Louisiana State University Press, 1978), 143–47; Lanza, *Agrarianism and Reconstruction Politics*, 48–50.

39. Foner, *Reconstruction*, 143.

40. Apparently, Stonelake was also overcharging. The Southern Homestead Act lowered to $5 the $10 entry fee of the 1862 Homestead Act and made it payable when the patent was issued rather than at the time of entry. Commissions for the land officers remained at 2 percent. Stonelake charged $5 plus $2 in officers' fees. Part of this mistake, Stonelake claimed, was due to a misunderstanding on the part of Howard, who in his Circular No. 7, informed his subordinates that the fee for entering homesteads was $5 at the time of entry. Stonelake also collected money to provide freedmen with maps and surveys, though he claimed to have discussed the appointment of surveyors with General Howard. See Stonelake to Sprague, Mar. 11, 1867, Letters Rec'd, Florida Assistant Commissioner, BRFAL [A1410].

41. R. B. Patterson to J. M. J. Sanno, Jan. 31, 1867, Letters Rec'd, District of Florida, RG 393, Pt. 1 [C357]; R. Ely to E. C. Woodruff, Feb. 4, 1867, Letters Rec'd, Florida Assistant Commissioner, BRFAL [A1347]; C. F. Hopkins to Sprague, Feb. 27, 1867, Letters Rec'd, Florida Assistant Commissioner, BRFAL [A1367]; Sprague to Howard, Feb. 28, 1867, Letters Rec'd, Washington Hdqrs., BRFAL [A1498].

42. W. J. Purman to E. C. Woodruff, Mar. 20, 1867 (forwarded to Howard by Sprague), Letters Rec'd, Washington Hdqrs., BRFAL [A1522]; Purman to Woodruff, Apr. 13, 1867, Letters Rec'd, Florida Assistant Commissioner, BRFAL [A1390].

43. For another example of Stonelake's problems with fees, which resulted in preventing freedpeople from getting land, see T. Seymour to Acting Assistant Adjutant General, April 19, 1867, with endorsements, Letters Rec'd, District of Florida, RG 393, Pt. 1 [C352].

44. J. T. Sprague to O. O. Howard, Oct. 1, 1867, Annual Reports of the Assistant Commissioners, Washington Hdqrs., BRFAL [A1485a].

45. Circular No. 7, July 25, 1866, and Circular No. 8, Aug. 10, 1866,

vol. 27, Scrapbook of Orders and Circulars Received and Issued, Louisiana Assistant Commissioner, BRFAL [A11019].

46. M. Armien to W. H. Sterling, Feb. 5, 1867, Letters Rec'd, Louisiana Assistant Commissioner, BRFAL [A8600].

47. J. J. Saville to W. H. Sterling, Jan. 28, 1867, Letters Rec'd, Washington Hdqrs., BRFAL [A2551]; H.R. 2359, *Congressional Globe*, 41st Cong., 2nd sess., 5128, 5314, 5657; Thomas T. Tolson to G. W. Julian, Feb. 6, 1872, in MLR, I82377, RG 49; Andrew Hero to Commissioner, General Land Office, Feb. 15, 1873, in MLR, K36068, RG 49.

48. John Tully to J. Wilson, Oct. 31, 1866, enclosed in MLR, G89540, RG 49; see also Oubre, *Forty Acres*, 120.

49. W. L. Ryan to A. W. Preston, Dec. 1, 1866, Registered Letters Rec'd, Mississippi Assistant Commissioner, BRFAL [A9165].

50. W. F. White to Assistant Commissioner of Mississippi, Dec. 25, 1866, filed as Jan. 17, 1867, Unregistered Letters Rec'd, Augusta, Georgia, Subassistant Commissioner, BRFAL [A173].

51. Record of the Disposal of Public Lands under the Homestead Laws, Division "M," RG 49. See also Lanza, *Agrarianism and Reconstruction Politics*, App. B.

52. For the sample, along with caveats, see Lanza, *Agrarianism and Reconstruction Politics*, 88–90, App. B.

53. W. W. Granger to J. E. Bennett, June 4, 1867, Letters Rec'd, Arkansas Assistant Commissioner, BRFAL [A2389].

5

The Personnel of the Freedmen's Bureau in Arkansas

Randy Finley

LOCAL AGENTS of the Freedmen's Bureau in Arkansas entered their offices with varied pasts and diverse ideologies. Some agents did anything necessary to impress their superiors to maintain their positions in an army that had slashed personnel at the end of the Civil War, whereas others held deep-seated sympathies or antipathies toward blacks. As some agents tentatively brokered new relationships with freedpeople and planters, others helped planters to regain power. Some agents actively pursued a radical agenda and hoped to transform Arkansas, but other more conservative agents did little and wished only to maintain order and restore a black workforce to the cotton fields. Many agents embraced a pragmatism that recognized the Bureau as a temporary agency, and they acknowledged that it could address only the most fundamental conflicts between newly freed blacks and whites. To capture the complexity, confusion, promise, and disillusionment that was Reconstruction in Arkansas, as elsewhere, it is essential to focus on the role of local Bureau agents. By examining closely the beliefs and behavior of agents in one setting, it becomes possible to untangle the motivations that fueled their behavior toward the conquered Confederates and the emancipated blacks in Arkansas and to suggest how their experiences reflected those of others across the South.

Bureau Chief General Oliver Otis Howard recalled that "Arkansas was a difficult state to reconstruct, and progress, especially in the line of justice, was slow enough." The physical distance from Washington, D.C.; the still frontier-like conditions of much of the state;

and the limited number of Bureau agents and troops in the state compounded the problems facing the Bureau. Arkansas roads, never that good before the war, lay in even greater disrepair after four years of neglect. Constant lowland flooding in areas in which freedmen were concentrated often disrupted and hampered the Bureau's work, as it did any rebuilding of the local economy. It remained to be seen in 1865 if Howard's dream of empowering Arkansas's 110,000 blacks could be realized.[1]

In each state where the Bureau labored to bring a new birth of freedom to southern blacks and whites, assistant commissioners supervised state Bureau personnel. The three individuals chosen to be assistant commissioners for Arkansas between 1865 and 1869 reported directly to General Howard in creating and monitoring the Bureau's work. Each of the three hailed from the North, had led troops during the Civil War, and had cultivated contacts in the army leadership to receive their appointments. The first agent appointed for Arkansas was New York native John W. Sprague, who had been trained at the Rensselaer Polytechnic Institute and had managed several businesses before joining the 7th Ohio Volunteers in 1861. Sprague became a brevet major general in March 1865 and won the Medal of Honor for his Civil War heroism. At war's end, Secretary of State Edwin Stanton recommended Sprague for the Arkansas post.[2]

Sprague faced the obstacles of creating the Freedmen's Bureau bureaucracy in Arkansas. His ideology and activism crucially shaped the attitude and policy of the Bureau toward freedpeople, white loyalists, and Confederate sympathizers. Like so many white Americans, he displayed an ambivalence toward blacks that often hampered the Bureau's mission. At his worst, he wrote a Chicago editor that he had nearly concluded that it might be better to let freedmen "perish from the earth." At other, less despairing moments, however, he reminded local agents that blacks had to be treated as "white free men and in no other way." He repeatedly cautioned his subordinates against controlling the freedpeople too much and warned Bureau agents that "they are in no sense the *masters* or *overseers* of the freed people. All are free." "Make sure your civilians know," he admonished local officials, "that they are not the Negroes' master."[3]

Sprague viewed the Freedmen's Bureau as a temporary expedient to boost black freedom in the South. Economic power rather than

government agency, Sprague believed, was the surest route to freedom. As a result, Sprague urged Arkansas freedmen to work hard and
become self-reliant. Fearful that southern whites would attempt to
resurrect slavery "under some new name," he sought to counter this
by demonstrating to both blacks and whites exactly what "a free
laborer is."[4]

Ironically, the implementation of his free-labor ideology often
provided much needed field hands for planters. In the spring of
1866, Sprague boasted to General Howard, that "the Bureau has
caused the Negroes to work cheerfully and well and that *more than
double the cotton* will be raised this year than would have been without
the Bureau." Promising Pine Bluff planter S. R. Cockrell a "stable"
labor force for the 1866 cotton crop, Sprague, perhaps unwittingly,
helped planters slowly to reclaim their power. The promise of "forty
acres and a mule" never captured Sprague's imagination. As early as
November 1865, he insisted that an abandoned Monticello County
plantation would not be needed by the Bureau; four months later,
he recommended that plantations should be returned to their owners for the benefit of black and white alike. From the beginning,
Bureau Chief Sprague tried to harness Arkansas blacks to the plantation system that had produced so much cotton during the years before the war.[5]

Although Sprague hoped to restore a reconstructed Arkansas
where the majority of blacks still planted and picked cotton most of
the time, he did not countenance a return to chattel slavery. Even if
his faulty economic analysis allowed planters to regain substantial
control, he defended black rights in other areas. Sprague insisted
that a freedman's right to protect himself by carrying arms was inviolable and had to be secured by the Bureau. He ordered the distribution of food and clothing to indigent freedmen during the winter of
1865–1866. He recognized the need for someone to replace planters
as health care providers for freedmen, and he urged local agents to
demand that medical provisions be included in contracts between
freedmen and their employers. Sprague also implored northern philanthropic agencies to aid freedpeople. A typical letter in August
1865 addressed the suffering that confronted Arkansans. "Very many
both white and blacks," he warned Mrs. H. N. Cobb of the Chicago-
based American Missionary Commission, "will perish next winter if
timely aid is not extended. . . . *Now food and clothing* are needed."[6]

In addition to his attempts to alleviate the physical suffering of destitute freedmen, Sprague promoted schools as a means of encouraging black self-reliance. Recognizing that freedmen craved to learn to read and write, he also wanted schools to inculcate moral virtues that would control an otherwise "fearfully disturbing element" in the population. Convinced that schools made blacks "contented and cheerful" and thereby promoted "the material interest of the employer," Sprague desired schools for social control as much as for the benefit of freedpersons.[7]

Churches also provided social control in the world envisioned by Sprague. Insisting that freedmen's moral character was "in great need of elevation," he encouraged the marriage of partners of the same race, but detested interracial marriages, which he declared "illegal and nul." To bolster monogamous relations, Sprague instructed a local agent to seek indictments for adultery from a county grand jury and recommend that if local officials balked, then "severe punishment" should be inflicted upon the guilty parties by the Bureau agent. Abuse of alcohol by blacks also worried Sprague; he sanctioned stiff penalties for anyone selling freedmen alcohol without Bureau approval.[8]

Sprague expected black preachers to help him extol monogamy and temperance. As a rule, he urged local agents to let white and black congregations judge a preacher's integrity and doctrinal correctness for themselves, but his paternalism occasionally overcame his commitment to black self-rule, as when he forced the expulsion of a Methodist Episcopal minister for "licentiousness."[9]

Although, in many cases, Sprague favored black independence, his underlying paternalism often thwarted black freedom. Abstractly, he said he believed blacks could and should take care of themselves, but his actions belied his theory because he often tried to shape black attitudes and behavior. He, along with many other Bureau agents, often saw blacks as problems and not as people.

Sprague's successor, Brevet Major General Edward O. C. Ord, was as paternalistic as Sprague. Born in Maryland in 1818 and educated at West Point, Ord joined the Army in 1839. He fought in the Seminole War, and he helped to capture John Brown at Harper's Ferry in 1859. During the Civil War, he was severely wounded in skirmishes at Hatchie, Mississippi, and Fort Harrison, Virginia. After their

Freedmen's Bureau tenures, both Sprague and Ord successfully engaged in western railroad ventures.[10]

Ord's limited stint of six months (October 1866–March 1867) restricted his influence on the Freedmen's Bureau in Arkansas, but while he headed the agency, he actively pursued a paternalistic policy that attempted to aid both freedmen and planters. He praised freedmen for better understanding the mechanics of contract labor with each passing day. He insisted to Ashley County planters that they and freedmen were "mutually dependent upon each other and united by a common interest." In Ord's assessment, lower-class whites created most of the region's problems because they asserted that if blacks did not labor on plantations then the land would be divided among themselves. "Bitter feelings," Ord wrote to General Ulysses S. Grant, "grow up between the blacks and low class of whites in this state."[12]

To offset lower-class white animosity, Ord creatively intervened for the freedpeople. He monitored black mortality and demanded a new head surgeon who would be "familiar with the peculiar habits and diseases of freedmen." Unlike his predecessor, General Ord believed land ownership by blacks would substantially improve their chances of realizing their freedom. He assigned a special surveyor, W. W. Granger, to locate Arkansas land that had been opened up under the Southern Homestead Act of 1866 and to proselytize blacks in urban areas concerning land availability. In a typical letter to a black in Augusta, Georgia, Ord warned of the prejudice and hostility in Arkansas, but he nonetheless encouraged the blacks' movement westward.[12]

But regardless of Ord's intentions to help freedmen get their forty acres and a mule, his brief tenure in Arkansas meant only that his successor, Brevet Major General Charles H. Smith, would fulfill or extinguish that dream. Smith supervised the Bureau during its last two years of existence in Arkansas (March 1867–May 1869).

The Maine-born Smith also came to the Bureau from the army. He had fought at Second Bull Run, Antietam, Fredericksburg, and Gettysburg. He was awarded the Medal of Honor after receiving wounds at the Battle of St. Mary's Church in June 1864. What distinguished Smith's military career, however, was his command of the 28th U.S. Colored Infantry. Smith came to his Bureau office with more firsthand experience in dealing with African Americans than did any of his Bureau predecessors.[13]

Assuming command in the spring of 1867, Smith recognized that "freedmen in many places are still freedmen, not free men. The white man still arrogates the rights and powers of mastery while the freedman half acknowledges them." To facilitate the metamorphosis from freedman to free man, Smith personally toured regions as distant as southwestern Arkansas to discover for himself how freedpeople actually lived. And what he discovered—"entire counties bankrupt" and a pervasive and "gloomy foreboding"—dismayed him. Smith not only familiarized himself with all areas of his jurisdiction, but he also closely monitored local Bureau agents. An agent in Fort Smith, for example, was slowly edged out of his position when he "opposed any political advancement of the freedmen." Smith also was an innovative bureaucrat. As freedmen's larders became empty during the early spring of 1867, he channeled large amounts of corn and meal to areas with the densest black populations before the actual reports requesting such aid arrived in his office.[14]

Although Smith often worked diligently on behalf of Arkansas freedmen, the old compulsion to favor the planter class was equally revealed in his actions. Smith transported freedmen with Bureau funds from one area of Arkansas to another at the behest of favored planters. During the frigid winter of 1868, he refused to establish soup houses in small towns for fear that this would entice freedmen from the plantations where the planters needed them. Praising freedmen for selecting employers and abiding by their contracts better than they had done during their first years of freedom, he urged southwestern Arkansas freedmen to work an additional year at their present locations before attempting to acquire their own farms. In many cases, Smith became a planter proxy and helped to tie freedmen to a life of servitude and debt.[15]

But it was never a simple matter of being either pro-planter or pro-freedmen. Smith seems to have been more interested in arranging some kind of *modus vivendi* so that both he and the army, now a greater presence under Military Reconstruction than under Presidential Reconstruction, could leave. Pragmatism primarily guided his actions, but the hysteria and violence unleashed as Radical Reconstruction authorized a new constitution for Arkansas and black male enfranchisement prohibited the possibility of compromise. Describing conditions in Arkansas as a "reign of terror," Smith reported to his superiors in the spring of 1868 that "just at this time we are holding our breath in suspense." A leading historian of Reconstruction violence, Allen Trelease, estimates that more than two hundred Arkansans were murdered on the eve of the 1868 presidential election. When the Ku Klux Klan began to burn black churches and to beat and to murder black and white activists who urged blacks to vote, to go to school, or to build their own churches, Smith responded swiftly in defense of freedmen. Demanding that martial law be established throughout Arkansas, he personally did all in his power to quell the violence by stationing troops in twenty-four different areas in Arkansas. This military aid, coupled with the self-defense militias established by blacks, forced the Klan and other such hooligans to lose their grip on Arkansas quicker than in most other southern states.[16]

Assistant commissioners set the tone for the Bureau's work in Arkansas. Over the years, seventy-nine local agents—thirty-six civilians and forty-three army officers—took orders from these three assistant commissioners. Agents were appointed to thirty-six locales and were primarily centered in thirty towns south, east, and west of Little Rock, the state's capital located in the center of the state. The heaviest concentrations of black population and proximity to cotton plantations and major rivers determined the location of a Bureau office. Compared to Freedmen's Bureaus in other states, the personnel in Arkansas consisted of far more civilians than military personnel. In North Carolina, South Carolina, Virginia, Louisiana, and Texas, military personnel predominated.[17]

Assignments to the Freedmen's Bureau prompted fierce intra-army competition. Applicants used European backgrounds, pre–Civil War experiences, and Civil War heroism to bolster their chances for appointment. Contacts were honed. One successful applicant's wife reminded officials of her ties to General Grant, and another appointee included in his application a letter of recommendation from Abraham Lincoln.[18]

Only biographical shards of the pre-Bureau careers of agents can be discovered. In a sample of twenty-five agents, thirteen were northern-born, six were southern-born, three were native Arkansans, and three had originally come from Europe. Middle-class professions predominated among civilian Bureau agents and included physicians, lawyers, merchants, druggists, and, inexplicably, an overseer and a former Confederate officer. Several agents had suffered severe wounds in the Civil War, and one had endured chronic diarrhea since 1863. Agents entered their offices from diverse backgrounds, but most important was the cultural baggage they brought with them into their positions.[19]

Bureau agents entered their posts with complex personalities and agendas. A southwestern agent, Volney Voltaire Smith, recognized that every agent "has had different ideas as to the manner in which the duties devolving on him should be discharged." But the major challenge every agent fundamentally addressed was tellingly phrased by Indiana-born Monticello Bureau agent E. G. Barker: "Our offices are crowded from morning til night with citizens asking what is required of them to do with their 'niggers.' " Agents' racial attitudes and ideologies—ranging from humanitarianism and paternalism to overt racism—critically shaped the workings of the Bureau in Arkansas. Equally important to an understanding of an agent's role in Reconstruction was to what degree he actively forced his racial ideology upon freedmen, planters, and yeomen whites. By studying agents' racial attitudes, coupled with their degree of activism in attempting to realize their racial notions, a clearer understanding of the Freedmen's Bureau in Arkansas emerges.[20]

Although an openly racist Bureau agent would seemingly be excluded from the Bureau, Chicot County's Thomas Hunnicutt, a Virginia-born overseer, stayed in office seven months in the densely black-populated southeastern county. His racism irreparably damaged the Bureau's image among freedpeople and whites. Often forcing blacks to move to plantations where planters had bribed him to furnish black laborers, he also supplemented his income with blackmail payments from both whites and blacks. Believing that white men had a natural right to have sex with black women whenever they wished, he transformed his Bureau office into a brothel as he forced freedwomen to perform sexual acts before he helped them find lost family members or gain contractual pledges. Although relieved within seven months, Hunnicutt's improprieties left freedmen leery of the Freedmen's Bureau. It is most likely that memories of Hunnicutt caused James W. Mason, the Chicot County black delegate to the 1867 Constitutional Convention, to propose that the

Freedmen's Bureau be extended only if "more honest and efficient agents" were procured.[21]

Hunnicutt was the most openly racist of Arkansas's seventy-nine Bureau agents, but other agents barely contained their contempt for the very people they were supposed to help. "I cannot help remarking," Jacksonport agent William Tisdale observed, "that these people [freedmen] as a general thing are both shiftless and lazy, preferring rather to beg subsistence from the government than earn it by honest toil." He believed their "crude notions of manhood and freedom" frittered away his hours with "trivial complaints." Freedpeople demonstrated to Tisdale "little regard for the future," and his major intervention in his three-month tenure at Jacksonport was to force black males under the age of forty-five to work twelve days per year as their road tax assessment.[22]

William Dawes of Pine Bluff equally belittled Arkansas freedpeople and seldom acted in their behalf. Convinced that most blacks were "trifling and indolent," he was certain that "promiscuous cohabitation is the universal custom" among blacks and that "the most deplorable state of morals exists throughout my entire district." Black churches proved worthless in uplifting African Americans, according to Dawes, because they were "controlled by preachers and exhorters as ignorant as the hearers themselves." He believed freedmen quickly relapsed "into those heathenish customs and rules which are practiced in the land [from] which they came."[23]

Mostly, however, Dawes yearned to keep things quiet. Remembering recent race riots, Dawes swore that he wanted no "Memphis or New Orleans job on my hands." He advised blacks "to stay at their houses and not collect in squads in the streets." "I refrain from all political considerations," he naively insisted, unaware that his silence and apathy became very powerful acts in the revolutionary milieu of Reconstruction. Even sadder is that he urged blacks to mimic his quietism and to abstain from all political activity. Dawes was an agent who coupled racism with a stifling conservatism that extolled passivity and acquiesced in the resurrection of antebellum hierarchies and racism in what was supposedly a new day for freedpeople.[24]

Other Bureau agents hindered freedmen just as much with their affinity to the planter class and white race. Arkansas County agent Captain William Stuart observed that "the negro is full of the idea of controlling his own time and of being a planter," but he thought such sentiment nonsensical and desired to keep freedmen controlled by white planters. He initially ordered planters to give freedmen a share of the 1865 crop that they helped to produce, but later, in the same order, he amended that command and recommended that planters at least give their laborers fifteen-days' rations. When planters accused freedmen of stealing crops and livestock, Stuart confiscated blacks' firearms. The fact that he could not see the need for blacks to have guns as a means of self-defense revealed his planter sympathies and indifference to black freedom.[25]

German-born, New York native Captain Fred Thibaut also seemed more concerned with protecting planters than freedmen. Thibaut lamented the work that planters lost when freedpeople attended political speeches and rallies during the fall of 1867. He forbade freedmen to use their school for political rallies or for any other meetings. Abstaining from voter registration drives, he compelled blacks to broadcast word of approaching elections themselves. By the fall of 1868, he was overjoyed that planters were taking better care of *their* freedmen.[26]

Among the agents who aspired to become planters, few equaled Sebastian Geisreiter. Born in Bavaria in 1840, Geisreiter moved with his parents to New York City in 1854. Working in New York City as a salesman and bookkeeper until 1857, he joined that innumerable caravan seeking gold or silver westward. Discovering no El Dorado, he joined the 2nd Minnesota Cavalry during the Civil War and battled Indians on the Great Plains. At war's end, he was transferred to Arkansas, where he served as Bureau agent in four different locales. He found Pine Bluff most to his liking and cultivated contacts that culminated in his 1877 marriage into a prominent Pine Bluff family. At his death, he had become one of the wealthiest planters of southern Arkansas. He exemplified the "man-on-the-make," so important to Americans during the Gilded Age.[27]

His actions as a Bureau agent clearly revealed his dedication to self-promotion and aggrandizement at the expense of the freedmen. "There is always room for apology on behalf of the negroes," Geisreiter assured his superior, "but the patience of the agent is at times sorely tried." To placate planters, he forced freedpeople to work on Saturdays. When planters feared a Christmas insurrection by freedpeople, he met with blacks to urge their passivity. Instead of promising to protect an Osceola schoolteacher who wanted to establish a school for freedmen, he instead strongly urged him to stay away. During the critical elections of 1867, he believed that freedmen "were getting rather overzealous in attending barbecues and other political meetings . . . to the detriment of their crops." Criticizing the Reverend George Rutherford for devoting his time to political matters, he did not, or could not, deter planters and Klansmen from intimidating the freedmen in order to prevent their political participation. With every word and deed, Geisreiter avoided offending the Jefferson County elite. When he left the Bureau, these planters whom he had courted did not forget him. He eventually joined them as one of the economic elite of southern Arkansas. His Bureau tenure had been but a rung on the ladder of success for him; alas, he had forgotten the people he was supposed to help.[28]

Agents who actively helped blacks to gain a semblance of freedom were as few as the overtly racist or pro-planter Bureau agent. Christian humanitarianism primarily motivated Chicot County agent George Benson. Disparagingly called a "Negro worshipper" by *Chicot Press* editor Philip Gatewood, Benson incessantly talked to freedmen of kind acts, good deeds, and hard work. He further disseminated this gospel by establishing a Sunday school class in his office, where he and his wife inculcated bourgeois virtue among freedpeople. Understanding that economic justice was crucial for black freedom, he audited planters' ledgers line by line and often deleted items or reduced prices charged to freedmen's accounts. In the election furor of 1867 and 1868, he often exhorted audiences to register and to vote. When anti-black animus turned violent, he immediately requested troops to protect the civil and political rights of blacks. Believing he was performing Christian acts of charity in his Bureau role, Benson exemplified the agent who championed African Americans.[29]

Although Christian humanitarianism did not motivate Hiram Willis, he nonetheless assisted Arkansas's freedpeople. Willis labored in southwestern Arkansas, where he thought local whites "had no respect for God, man, or devil, and the most utter contempt for anything that is blue or connected with the Freedmen's Bureau." Willis persistently tried to realize the radical agenda of Reconstruction. Nothing grated local whites more than his inclusion of a clause in contracts requiring black children to be treated "as fully as if they were white children."[30]

The New Yorker Willis responded to local blacks' demands for schools by insistently urging his superiors to fund schools and send teachers to southwestern Arkansas. He requested northern teachers because freedmen "desire to learn Northern principles." Not content that others teach freedmen, he often conducted civics classes to explain the American political process.[31]

Willis's intervention in the Arkansas economy on behalf of freedpeople angered as many whites as did his social agenda. He spent hours discussing with freedmen the advantages and disadvantages of various labor schemes. He also vexed local planters by explaining to blacks how to get a homestead. Like many other Bureau agents, Willis carefully audited, item by item, the planters' claims of freedmen's purchases. In one instance, he angrily slashed the charges by 50 percent. In another case, he reduced a freedman's debt from $130 to $34.20. In late 1867, sensing that planters had advanced more to freedmen than their crops were going to bring in, Willis postponed repayment to the planters until after the next year's crop.[32]

Pursuit of radical social aims and of economic opportunity for blacks outraged and angered many whites. Murder, whipping, and arson escalated as whites resisted the new order that Willis tried to impose. "The civil courts are of no account here. . . . The sheriffs dare not to undertake to enforce their duties from fear of the mob law," he noted. As violence spiraled, several assassination attempts on Willis failed to stymie his efforts. "The soldiers and myself," he recounted, "met with no accident although the bullets whistled pretty close to us." On October 24, 1868, a bullet found its mark as a member of the Barker gang, a local group of desperadoes who hid in the wilderness and swamps of southwestern Arkansas, southeastern Oklahoma, and northeastern Texas, murdered Willis. Bureau agents supported blacks at their own risk.[33]

Albert Coats, southwestern Arkansas Bureau agent, also facilitated blacks' freedom. Born in Ohio where schools were far more plentiful than in Arkansas, he urged the Bureau to fund schools for the "mental and moral" training of freedpeople. Coats was the only agent on record to ask for a copy of the Civil Rights Act so that he would know exactly what it guaranteed. He also worried about the deterioration of the freedmen's health because planters no longer provided medical care for blacks, and he urged the Bureau to secure doctors and medicine.[34]

Coats's economic interventionism increasingly irked planters. An order to Colonel Joseph Brand to "stop the shipment of cotton and the disposal of any cotton until further instruction from this office" exemplified how Coats ensured that blacks receive just payment. He infuriated planters even more when he encouraged freedmen to seek their own homesteads and when he requested maps that disclosed available lands. Coats's first priority was the freedmen, not the planters. He believed that the Bureau existed not as a planter surrogate, but rather as an institution to help blacks realize their freedom promised at emancipation.[35]

But good deeds did not go unpunished in Arkansas. During the winter of 1868, planters and their compatriots informed state officials that Coats engaged in "improper conduct with nearly every colored girl he meets." Coats's roommate, H. C. DeWolf, complained the loudest and swore that he had seen Coats in his bed with a "black lady" and that the bed "was badly tumbled and many of the slats had fallen on to the floor." Whether the charges were true is unclear, but Coats was reassigned and replaced by DeWolf, an agent much more pliant to planters' bidding.[36]

One of the most innovative and pro-freedmen agents was A. G. Cunningham of Ashley and Chicot Counties. He constantly monitored planters' behavior and recorded his opinions of them. Several planters "required strict watching," and Cunningham was just the man for the job. He recognized that planters often swindled freedmen by fraudulently inflating debts. To counter this, he urged use of weekly passbooks for freedmen so that he could more accurately supervise the freedpeople's finances. He also lobbied as late as 1868 for plantation confiscation and division among the freedpeople.[37]

Planters were appalled. One Chicot County planter wrote of the situation to state officials: "Poor, ignorant, credulous creatures— they [freedmen] never would have behaved, as they have of themselves. They have been tampered with, and put up to it by others. The Freedmen's Bureau agent, Cunningham, having been in great measure instrumental in getting them in trouble, ought to be compelled to take care of them." Threatened with tar and feathers and worse, Cunningham eventually requested and received troops to maintain order.[38]

Although never supervising a Bureau office, special surveyor Granger helped freedmen as much as any Bureau agent. Granger became an evangelist for the Southern Homestead Act of 1866. Spending much of his time on horseback loaded down with surveying tools, he tirelessly hunted available homesteads. Once boundaries had been located, he hit the road again to tell blacks of the opportunity for farms of their own. He recognized that freedmen who owned their own homesteads displayed "a different, freer spirit," and he addressed local congregations in Little Rock, Pine Bluff, and Helena on the hardships and joys of frontier living. Granger saw the big picture as well as anyone; in a typical address to a Helena audience, he extolled not only homesteads but also schools and savings banks.[39]

Occasionally, southern-born Bureau agents encouraged blacks in their struggles for freedom as well as their northern counterparts. Tennessee-born lawyer E. W. Gantt, Hempstead County Bureau agent, was well versed in the southern way. During the early days of Bureau operation, he worried that freedmen "will be starved, murdered, or forced into a condition more horrible than the worst stages of slavery. I say this sorrowfully of our people, but I know it is but too true. *Their prejudices give very slowly.* Their wrath over defeat would be poured upon the heads of the helpless ones once their slaves." In a public address to area African Americans, his racial attitudes emerge. "Some of you feel," he noted, "that the Freedmen's Bureau is a change of masters for you. That the Superintendents are like so many overseers. This is all wrong. The Bureau wishes to let you alone as much as possible. Its object is simply to protect you until laws and public sentiment gives you all the protection that any other free man has." To help realize this vision, Gantt energetically defended blacks' rights while carefully trying to let blacks do as much as they could for themselves. He prohibited planters from using corporal punishment, demanded that blacks serve on juries, and insisted that freedmen could live wherever they chose.[40]

Alexander Dyer, born in Virginia and a veteran of the Seminole, Mexican, and Civil Wars, was another southerner who recognized that old times had to be forgotten in the South. He judiciously audited planters' contracts with freedmen. In a circular broadcast throughout his jurisdiction, he warned planters that he would prosecute them if they drove freedmen off the land after the crop had been gathered or if they withheld freedmen's wages. In contracts, he insisted that health care, comfortable and healthy living quarters, and time off be stipulated. Considering education "the groundwork of all liberty and freedom," he promoted schools for freedmen. During the frigid December days of 1867, he distributed coats, boots, blankets, and hats found in army storage to indigent freedpeople. Dyer was among a rare minority of southerners who insisted that the Old South had to be abandoned and a new way of living adopted.[41]

Although there were agents with clearly discernible planter or freedmen proclivities, most agents were as ambivalent about African Americans as were most white Americans. Most agents wanted blacks to adopt their own white middle-class values and ideologies. They often ambiguously aided both freedmen and planters. This reflected their uncertainty as to just what southerners, white and black, were and what they wanted them to become. Pragmatism dominated their every action as they hoped to engineer a peaceful ending to the bloody Civil War.

Indiana-born E. G. Barker displayed such ambivalence. Motivated primarily by paternalism, he viewed blacks as "but *children* in their new position and easily led astray." Emancipation "puffed up" blacks "with a false idea of freedom," Barker claimed. He therefore hoped to deflate their new soaring egos with plenty of missives on honesty, industry, and chastity. Believing that black preachers ineffectively taught the gospel that he wanted disseminated, he denounced black religion as "often governed by a wild nervous excitement more than by pure religion." He alone knew what the freedmen really needed—or so his words and actions suggested.[42]

Barker helped planters to regain economic power. He praised Chicot County planter Lycurgus Johnson for using the same hands whom he had used during the prewar years. He castigated freedwomen who were not getting out quite as early in the mornings as they had done under slavery. When Drew County freedmen tried to board Mississippi River steamboats to go north to seek their fortunes elsewhere, Barker feared that planters would lose necessary laborers. He stalled their departure, but state headquarters ordered him to leave them alone.[43]

Barker, however, was no mere planter pawn. He frequently forbade planters to sell a crop until he had investigated freedmen's claims of fraud. In a typical directive, he ordered a Marion planter not to "remove any portion of your present crop or in any manner dispose of it till you have settled with and paid the Freedmen for

their service for the year 1866 and 1867." He demanded that planters cease whipping freedmen and called the practice "a relic of slavery." Amid escalating political turmoil in 1867–1868, he urged blacks
to go about their politics quietly but to vote as they pleased. As
violence increased, he disallowed planters' fines of laborers who
owned guns, and he repeatedly harangued state headquarters with
demands for troops.[44]

Violence posed a major problem for Barker. He believed that "lawlessness of every kind is practiced here and I do not consider either
life or property any safer now than it was during the war." In 1866,
he was shot and seriously wounded. Eventually he had an arm ampu-
tated, but he persevered until buckshot peppered his face, hand,
and wrist in 1868 while he was talking to friends in his home. Having
endured, Barker asked leave to go back home to Indiana.[45]

Northeastern Arkansas agent William Brian also suffered from bi-
furcated vision. At times, he supported local planters, but he sided
with freedmen on other occasions. Brian believed that, "like the
poor whites," freedmen "exhibit a fancied taste for city life and a
laziness for honest labor." Worrying more about cotton picked than
votes cast in 1868, he counseled freedmen "to keep quiet, have little
to say, remain at home, and attend to their own business." When
blacks did not heed his advice and became boisterously political,
the Klan responded with attacks on freedmen's cabins and wounded
several black children. Brian countered with troops. Sensing that
planters practiced "barbarous subterfuge" in settling accounts with
freedmen, he often ordered the local sheriff or planters to "immediately stop moving said cotton." Seeing the constant fraud practiced
by planters to thwart black freedom, he urged blacks to plant subsistence crops and to end their dependence on King Cotton. He also
joined with freedmen in demanding schools as a contractual stipulation and helped to fund planters who erected school buildings on
their plantations. Brian's views on black women were even more ambivalent than his views on black men. On the one hand, he quickly
tried a Jacksonport white man for using "insulting and obscene language" to the teacher and female students of the freedmen's school.
On the other hand, he sarcastically noted that "strange as it may
appear, however, political agitation seems to be confined to the females."[46]

New Yorker Lewis Carhart also seriously misunderstood southern freedpeople. "There is little reasonably to be expected from the adult colored population," he proclaimed. "The *hope* of the race is in the children of the present generation." Carhart assumed black immorality, and he praised Camden blacks for not succumbing to what he thought was their true nature. He helped planters to maintain an adequate labor force by ordering freedmen to choose an employer and to stay with him. He also prohibited blacks from congregating in towns or around military camps. In the world, according to Carhart, a freedman's place was on a plantation, but it was not the plantation of antebellum days. Floggings were out, schools were in, and the black family was united and preserved in nearly every decision rendered by Carhart. He implored blacks to register and to vote, and he established in Magnolia a strong Union League, a pro-Republican organization. Freedmen trusted Carhart and confidently reported to him after a night raid by the Klan because they sensed that he protected them and their newly gained rights.[47]

William McCullough, another New Yorker, also exemplified the ambivalent attitude and behavior that many Bureau agents manifested toward freedmen. To assist planters, McCullough transported many freedmen to areas lacking laborers. When planters complained about freedmen's work absences, he ordered blacks to arrive in fields earlier in the day and banned Saturday hunting and fishing. Instead of procuring plantation farmland for use by blacks, he sent notices to planters to come to his office expeditiously to reclaim their land.[48]

But McCullough drew a line that planters dared not cross in their dealings with freedmen. He warned planter J. W. Harrell that a freedwoman "has a right to go where she pleases and remain as long as she pleases." He also worried that many planters controlled black orphans illegally as late as 1867, and he monitored planters' use of black children with great care. In 1868, when he discovered destitute freedmen, he immediately issued them clothing and food. When a smallpox epidemic ravaged De Vall's Bluff blacks, he dispersed a camp of blacks who lived in unsanitary conditions, commanded soldiers to supervise the washing of clothes by the blacks, and dispensed lime to all black households. Smallpox deaths waned. He constantly sought to establish schools and often recommended that blacks become trustees of their own schools. When the Regulators, a northwestern Arkansas terrorist organization, threatened and beat freedpeople, McCullough investigated and swiftly requested troops. Probably the best testimony to his aid to freedpeople was the local newspaper's vitriolic attitude on his activities as a Freedmen's Bureau agent.[49]

Ohio-born William Colby, the leader of freedmen's education in the Freedmen's Bureau in Arkansas, displayed this maddening ambivalence in his relationship with Arkansas blacks. As superintendent of education in Arkansas, he longed to remake Arkansas into another Massachusetts. "The school and building," he glowingly described a new Pine Bluff facility, "would do credit to a New England village." Few schools preceded Colby in Arkansas, and he lamented that "30% of white voters registered and 50% of the entire population are unable to write their names."[50]

Colby labored diligently to fund school buildings and to pay teachers to journey to Arkansas. By 1866, 1,655 blacks were enrolled in state institutions. Schools emphasized fundamental literacy skills and a values system that inculcated bourgeois behavior in freedpeople. Colby constantly clamored for "moral improvement." He insisted that temperance training was as important as reading and writing. As the elections of 1867 and 1868 approached, he established a traveling lecturer who extolled citizenship duties.[51]

Interminably berating Arkansas teachers, Colby deeply regretted "that a better sort of teachers are not in the field." He discovered some teachers hired in 1867 "incapable of instructing in any branches correctly." "Some native teachers," he mused, "should themselves be attending a good primary school." At his most piqued, Colby vehemently swore, "The school moneys are worse than thrown away upon unqualified and unworthy teachers."[52]

Black preachers who opposed the establishment of schools (or maybe it was Colby's control of them) also drew Colby's wrath. Colby believed that black ministerial opponents to schools feared that they would lose influence to teachers. Arguing that many black pastors were "a bane both to the church and the school," Colby demanded whole-hearted support for his educational blueprint for Arkansas.[53]

The freedpeople chafed under Colby's pedantic condescension and bourgeois arrogance. In June 1867, they petitioned for his removal because of his "arbitrary and at times insulting conduct, threatening to break up schools, by such retarding the progress of education." Eventually recanting and accepting Colby's educational leadership until the Freedmen's Bureau educational operations ceased in 1870, the petitioners who desired Colby's ouster revealed the ambiguity of Colby's efforts in Arkansas. Blacks and many whites appreciated his labors to establish schools. Many former illiterates could now read and write, thanks to the efforts of William Colby. But they resented his arrogance, his dogmatism, his supercilious-ness, and his desire to remake everyone in his image.[54]

Henry Sweeney, Bureau agent in the Mississippi River port of Helena, best exemplified the agent who was never quite sure what to do with either planters or freedmen. He faced immense and complex problems that confounded any simple consistency in his actions. On one day, he appeared to be supporting the restoration of planter hegemony. On the next day, he appeared to be defending the rights of freedmen. Neither planters nor freedmen could ever safely predict Sweeney's decisions.

Born in Dublin, Ireland, in November 1833, Sweeney trained as a druggist and migrated in 1854 to New York City where he joined the army. Serving as a hospital steward during the years before the attack on Fort Sumter, he saw action at Wilson's Creek, Fort Donelson, Shiloh, and in the march on Atlanta during the Civil War. He was placed in charge of the 60th U.S. Colored Troops in 1864 and gained insights into blacks and their cultures. Fellow officer John Randolph attested that Sweeney was a "well-educated man" and a "thorough soldier." Ironically, *both* Arkansas planters and freedmen agreed and praised Sweeney for his work as a Freedmen's Bureau agent.[55]

At times, Sweeney clearly favored planters in his attitude and Bureau decisions. He often urged freedpeople to abandon town life and to work and live on Mississippi River plantations. In a November 1865 circular addressed to plantation-working blacks, Sweeney emphasized that because "every hour of said time being of the greatest importance in picking and saving a large portion of the crop," blacks had to stay on the plantations until the harvest ended. "No negro will leave the plantation," he ordered, "on which he is employed" without his employer's permission. Freedmen who violated this command were arrested and fined. In September 1865, with no concern for family reunions, Sweeney shipped eighty black Helena orphans to St. Louis, where they were reassigned to various southern destinations as laborers. When planters accused freedmen of stealing river-bottom cotton at night, he required that blacks obtain a permit from his office before they could sell their cotton.[56]

Sweeney interfered in the blacks' social lives, as well as in their economic concerns. He insisted that many black evangelists preached "the most ridiculous nonsense to large gatherings of the people," and he tried to censor their exhortations. When "religious excitement" kept freedmen up until 2 or 3 A.M., "unfitting them for work," he prohibited such meetings. He appears to have used informants to keep black religion under surveillance, for he carefully monitored a black prophet who appeared on a local plantation and proclaimed "that the end of the world would be in a few days" and who was commanded by God to walk on the waters of Old Town Lake.[57]

Although Sweeney often upheld the planter class in its right to control the Arkansas economy, he also, at times, defended black rights and assisted freedmen in their struggles to be free. He consistently favored schools for blacks, whom he helped to establish a literary league with more than 250 members in Helena. He closely monitored black health care and lobbied for improved hospitals. He founded a government-owned wood yard and paid wages to freedmen who wished to forsake the cotton fields. In January 1867, he warned planters that if the murder of freedmen continued, he would send "a force of colored cavalry to remove all the freed people in the county and station colored troops in districts where outrages are committed."[58]

At other times, Sweeney, in his paternalism, attempted to placate both planters and freedmen simultaneously. He often organized public meetings where planters and blacks met together in school or religious ceremonies. He urged planters to accept the Fifteenth Amendment as inevitable and held public forums with planters and freedmen at which he analyzed political issues.[59]

In November 1865, Bureau Commissioner Howard ordered Assistant Commissioner John W. Sprague to investigate accusations that Sweeney was guilty of "drinking, profanity, and being unkind to negroes." When planters and freedmen heard of the ensuing inquiry, they mobilized to support Sweeney. Black elites called a public meeting, and hundreds of blacks gathered in Helena to champion Sweeney. In Helena to reconnoiter the situation, General Sprague discerned that "the most intelligent freedmen there" offered "not a single complaint against Captain Sweeney." Planters John H. Cole and Edward Malloy, among others, lionized Sweeney and climbed aboard the Sweeney bandwagon. A fellow officer, Colonel Max Bentzoni, swore that Sweeney neither drank nor cursed blacks and that "his dealings with the negroes have been fair and just." Sprague found no grounds to dismiss Sweeney, and he retained his position until he resigned in 1867 when he joined a Fenian raiding party in Canada. What is significant is how both planters and freedmen defended Henry Sweeney.[60]

Although it appears that many Bureau agents were motivated by racism or its hybrid, the more complex motive of paternalism drove most agents to an ambivalence that both helped and hindered Arkansas freedmen's drive for freedom during the years immediately after the Civil War. Few Bureau agents brought with them to Arkansas an unalterable vision that they hoped to realize in the state. The few that did found innumerable obstacles, which overwhelmed their vision. Pragmatism subsumed almost all dreams in the complexities of Reconstruction. Most agents rather hoped to fashion some sort of compromise among freedmen, planters, and yeomen whites so that the havoc and disruption resulting from the Civil War would cease. This basic need to foster compromise after such a civil war best explains why most agents behaved so ambivalently toward freedmen. That national policy regarding Reconstruction was also ambivalent hardly helped Arkansas agents, or the Bureau anywhere in the field, to pursue a consistent ideological line. They were primarily, and tragically, more interested in producing any kind of stop-gap, uneasy peace between planters and freedmen than in ensuring justice and equality for Arkansas's 110,000 freedpeople. The personnel of the Freedmen's Bureau in Arkansas helped some blacks, at least, to become more free than they had been under chattel slavery, but they left many other black Arkansans once again under the mastery of the planter class. This compromise would tragically reverberate in southern and African-American history for more than one hundred years.

NOTES

1. Oliver Otis Howard, *Autobiography of Oliver Otis Howard, Major General United States Army*, 2 vols. (New York: Baker & Taylor, 1907), 2:335; L.

Carhart to W. G. Sprague, July 28, 1865, reel 13; H. C. DeWolf to J. S. Bennett, May 31, 1868; R. W. Barnard to S. M. Mills, Sept. 30, 1868, reel 27; H. Sweeney to J. Tyler, Mar. 30, 1867, reel 25; and J. Adair to J. W. Sprague, Apr. 30, 1866, reel 23, all in Records of the Assistant Commissioner for the State of Arkansas, Bureau of Refugees, Freedmen, and Abandoned Lands, National Archives Microfilm Publication M979 (hereinafter cited as BRFAL-Ark [M979]).

2. *The National Cyclopedia of American Biography*, 53 vols. (New York: James T. White and Company, 1897), 5:55.

3. George R. Bentley, *A History of the Freedmen's Bureau* (reprint, New York: Octagon Books, 1970), 58; J. W. Sprague to H. M. Cullen, Apr. 19, 1866, reel 2; J. W. Sprague to E. G. Barker, Jan. 3, 1866, reel 4; J. W. Sprague, Circular No. 17, Jan. 15, 1866, reel 21; and J. W. Sprague to J. M. Bowles, Dec. 16, 1866, reel 2, BRFAL-Ark (M979).

4. J. W. Sprague, Circular, June 20, 1865, and J. W. Sprague to O. O. Howard, June 22 and Aug. 21, 1865, reel 1, BRFAL-Ark (M979).

5. J. W. Sprague to O. O. Howard, Mar. 23 and Apr. 4, 1866, and J. W. Sprague to S. R. Cockrell, Feb. 24, 1866, reel 2; and J. W. Sprague to E. G. Barker, Nov. 25, 1865, reel 4, BRFAL-Ark (M979).

6. J. W. Sprague to O. O. Howard, Nov. 20, 1865, and J. W. Sprague to E. T. Wallace, May 4, 1866, reel 4; J. W. Sprague to O. O. Howard, July 25, 1865, and J. W. Sprague to H. N. Cobb, Aug. 3, 1865, reel 1; J. W. Sprague to J. Riggs, Feb. 3, 1866, reel 2; and J. W. Sprague to N. A. Britten, Nov. 30, 1865, reel 32, BRFAL-Ark (M979).

7. J. W. Sprague to R. W. Trimble, Mar. 26, 1866, reel 2, BRFAL-Ark (M979).

8. J. W. Sprague to O. O. Howard, June 7, 1866, reel 23; J. W. Sprague, Circular, Mar. 31, 1866, reel 12; J. W. Sprague to H. Sweeney, July 3, 1866, reel 4; and J. W. Sprague, Circular, May 23, 1866, reel 21, BRFAL-Ark (M979).

9. J. W. Sprague to L. Carhart, May 4, 1866, reel 2; and J. W. Sprague to O. O. Howard, May 29, 1866, reel 1, BRFAL-Ark (M979).

10. Adjutant General Report: Appointment, Commission, and Personnel Branch Document File, "E. O. C. Ord," National Archives, Washington, D.C.; Dean S. Thomas, *Civil War Commanders* (Arendtsville, Pa.: Thomas Publications, 1986), 38; Mark Mayo Boatner III, *The Civil War Dictionary* (New York: David McKay Co., 1959), 609–10.

11. E. O. C. Ord to O. O. Howard, Feb. 22 and Mar. 15, 1867, reel 1; E. O. C. Ord to S. Hill et al. of Ashley County, Mar. 7, 1867; and E. O. C. Ord to U. S. Grant, Jan. 12, 1867, reel 3, BRFAL-Ark (M979).

12. E. O. C. Ord to O. O. Howard, Oct. 12, 1866; E. O. C. Ord to L. A. Edwards, Feb. 18, 1867; E. O. C. Ord to T. Davis, Oct. 31, 1866; and E. O.

C. Ord to O. O. Howard, July 22 and Mar. 15, 1867, reel 1, BRFAL-Ark (M979).

13. Charles H. Smith, Civil War Pension Files, Records of the Veterans Administration, Record Group 15, National Archives, Washington, D.C.; Torlief S. Holmes, *Horse Soldiers in Blue* (Gaithersburg, Pa.: Butternut Press, 1985), 227–29; Boatner, *Civil War Dictionary*, 769.

14. C. H. Smith to O. O. Howard, Aug. 21 and Dec. 28, 1867, reel 23; and C. H. Smith to O. O. Howard, Apr. 26, 1867, and June 11, 1868, reel 1, BRFAL-Ark (M979).

15. C. H. Smith to O. O. Howard, Jan. 14, 1865 and Feb. 7, 1868, reel 1; and C. H. Smith to O. O. Howard, May 25, 1867, and Feb. 27, 1868, reel 23, BRFAL-Ark (M979).

16. C. H. Smith to O. O. Howard, Mar. 5, 1868; Apr. 20, 1868, reel 1; and C. H. Smith to O. O. Howard, May 25 and June 24, 1868, reel 27, BRFAL-Ark (M979); Allen W. Trelease, *White Terror: The Ku Klux Klan Conspiracy and Southern Reconstruction* (New York: Harper and Row, 1971), 154; Randy Finley, *From Slavery to Uncertain Freedom: The Freedmen's Bureau in Arkansas, 1865–1869* (Fayetteville: University of Arkansas Press, 1996), 160–1.

17. Station Book, 1865–1869, reel 51, BRFAL-Ark (M979); Paul A. Cimbala, "The Terms of Freedom: The Freedmen's Bureau and Reconstruction in Georgia, 1865–1870" (Ph.D. dissertation, Emory University, 1983), 123–4; Martin Abbott, *The Freedmen's Bureau in South Carolina, 1865–1872* (Chapel Hill: University of North Carolina Press, 1967), 23; William L. Richter, *Overreached on All Sides: The Freedmen's Bureau Administrators in Texas, 1865–1868* (College Station: Texas A & M University Press, 1991), 37.

18. Frank Gross and Francis Springer, Civil War Pension Files, Records of the Veterans Administration, Record Group 15, National Archives, Washington, D.C.

19. 1860 Manuscript Census, Arkansas; Station Book, 1865–1869, reel 51, BRFAL-Ark (M979).

20. V. V. Smith to Bennett, July 8, 1867, reel 9, and E. G. Barker to E. B. Sherwin, July 31, 1865, reel 15, BRFAL-Ark (M979).

21. W. Dawes to E. T. Abel, July 27, 1866, reel 10, BRFAL-Ark (M979); *Arkansas Constitutional Convention: Debates and Proceedings, 1868* (Little Rock: J. G. Price, 1868), 433.

22. W. Tisdale to J. W. Sprague, Sept., Oct. 31, and Dec. 18, 1865, reel 32, BRFAL-Ark (M979).

23. W. Dawes to J. Tyler, Nov. 12 and 30, 1866, reel 16, BRFAL-Ark (M979).

24. W. Dawes to E. O. C. Ord, Dec. 31, 1866, reel 10, and W. Dawes to J. Tyler, Nov. 30, 1866, reel 24, BRFAL-Ark (M979).

25. W. Stuart to W. G. Sargent, Oct. 31, 1865, reel 23; and W. Stuart to J. W. Sprague, Aug. 4, 1865, and W. Stuart to E. W. Gantt, Dec. 18, 1865, reel 1, BRFAL-Ark (M979).

26. F. Thibaut to J. Bennett, Oct. 31, 1867, reel 26; W. Colby to F. Thibaut, Oct. 14, 1867, reel 21; and F. Thibaut to J. Bennett, Nov. 1, 1867, and Oct. 1, 1868, reel 16, BRFAL-Ark (M979).

27. Fay Hempstead, *Historical Review of Arkansas*, 3 vols. (Chicago: The Lewis Pub. Co., 1911), 3:1242–44; Fay Hempstead, *Centennial History of Arkansas*, 3 vols. (Chicago: S. J. Clarke Pub. Co., 1922), 2:92–5.

28. S. Geisreiter to J. Bennett, Sept. 30, 1867, Feb. 29, 1868, and May 1, 1868, reel 17; S. Geisreiter to J. Tyler, Mar. 26, 1867, reel 14; S. Geisreiter to J. Bennett, Aug. 31, 1867, reel 16; S. Geisreiter to J. Bennett, Sept. 30, 1867, reel 17; S. Geisreiter to S. M. Mills, Nov. 2, 1868, reel 27, BRFAL-Ark (M979).

29. G. Benson to C. H. Smith, Sept. 12, 1867; G. Benson, Circular, Oct. 3, 1867; G. Benson to C. H. Smith, Aug. 16, 1867; G. Benson to O. Greene, Aug. 19, 1867; and G. Benson, Audit, Nov. 15, 1867, reel 7; and C. H. Smith to G. Benson, Aug. 23, 1867, reel 15, BRFAL-Ark (M979).

30. Quoted in William L. Richter, " 'A Dear Little Job': 2nd Lieutenant Hiram F. Willis, Freedmen's Bureau Agent in Southwestern Arkansas, 1866–1868," *Arkansas Historical Quarterly* 50 (summer 1991): 160; Willis contracts, Sevier County, Jan. 10, 1866, reel 16, BRFAL-Ark (M979).

31. H. Willis to J. Bennett, June 30, 1867, and Jan. 4, 1868, reel 16, BRFAL-Ark.

32. H. Willis to J. Bennett, Oct. 31, 1867, and Jan. 31, 1868, reel 26; and H. Willis to J. Tyler, Feb. 1, 1867, and H. Willis to J. Bennett, Nov. 30, 1867, reel 16, BRFAL-Ark (M979).

33. H. Willis to J. Tyler, Dec. 31, 1866, and Mar. 20, 1867, reel 16; and J. Sprague to Howard, Mar. 5, 1868, reel 1, BRFAL-Ark (M979); Richter, "A Dear Little Job," 197.

34. A. Coats to J. Bennett, Nov 1, 1867; Feb. 7, 1868, reel 20, BRFAL-Ark (M979).

35. A. Coats to J. Brand, Nov. 16, 1867, reel 20; A. Coats to J. Bennett, July 7, 1867, reel 26; and A. Coats to J. Bennett Nov. 7, 1867, Letters Sent, Pine Bluff Agent, reel 20, BRFAL-Ark (M979).

36. H. C. DeWolf to J. Bennett, Feb. 4, 1868, reel 17, BRFAL-Ark (M979).

37. A. G. Cunningham to C. H. Smith, Aug. 1868, reel 8; A. G. Cunningham to J. Bennett, July 1, 1868, reel 27; and Rayner to O. D. Greene, Jan. 10, 1868, reel 17, BRFAL-Ark (M979).

38. Ibid.; A. G. Cunningham to S. M. Mills, Aug. 22, 1868, reel 18; and A. G. Cunningham to C. H. Smith, Aug. 25, 1868, reel 5, BRFAL-Ark (M979).

39. W. W. Granger to J. Bennett, Mar. 6, 1868, and W. W. Granger to S. M. Mills, Oct. 31, 1868, reel 26; W. W. Granger to J. Bennett, July 1, 1868, and W. W. Granger to S. M. Mills, Aug. 31 and Sept. 30, 1868, reel 27; and W. W. Granger to J. Tyler, Feb. 1, 1867, reel 24, BRFAL-Ark (M979).

40. E. W. Gantt to J. Sprague, Dec. 23, Jan. 13, 1865, and E. W. Gantt to W. A. Britton, Dec. 23, 1865, reel 20, BRFAL-Ark (M979).

41. A. Dyer, Circular No. 17, Oct. 2, 1867, and A. Dyer to C. H. Smith, Dec. 23, 1867, reel 11; A. Dyer, Apr. 1867 to July 1868, reel 14; and A. Dyer to J. Sprague, June 8, 1866, reel 23, BRFAL-Ark (M979).

42. E. G. Barker to T. D. Elliott, Jan. 12, 1868, reel 14; E. G. Barker to J. Sprague, Sept. 4, 1865, reel 6; E. G. Barker to J. Bennett, June 15, 1866; E. G. Barker to Taylor, July 21, 1866; and E. G. Barker to J. Sprague, July 31, 1866, reel 15, BRFAL-Ark (M979).

43. Ibid.; E. G. Barker to J. Sprague, Jan. 3, 1866, reel 4, BRFAL-Ark (M979).

44. E. G. Barker, Nov. 30, 1867, Jan. 6, 1868, reel 14; E. G. Barker, May 4, 1866, reel 15; E. G. Barker to S. M. Mills, Sept. 30, 1868, reel 27; and E. G. Barker to R. Moss, Dec. 13, 1867, BRFAL-Ark (M979).

45. E. G. Barker to Reynolds, Jan. 17, 1866, reel 1; and E. G. Barker to Chief Surgeon, Apr. 14, 1866, and E. G. Barker to C. H. Smith, Aug. 14, 1868, reel 15, BRFAL-Ark (M979).

46. W. Brian to C. H. Smith, June 1 and Apr. 30, 1868, reel 27; W. Brian to C. H. Smith, Oct. 31, 1868, reel 26; W. Brian to Jackson County Sheriff, Feb. 1, 1868; W. Brian to S. Thomas, Mar. 10, 1868; W. Brian to W. Colby, June 18, 1867; and W. Brian to T. Y. Scott, Sept. 20, 1867, reel 7, BRFAL-Ark (M979).

47. L. Carhart to J. Sprague, Mar. 26, 1866; L. Carhart to E. B. Sherwin, Aug. 31, 1865; and L. Carhart to J. Sprague, July 19, 1865, reel 23; L. Carhart, Orders, Nov. 23, 1865, and L. Carhart to J. M. Kelson, Feb. 1, 1866, reel 2; L. Carhart to J. Bennett, Aug. 31, 1867, reel 25; and L. Carhart to J. Bennett, Apr. 30, 1868, reel 27, BRFAL-Ark (M979).

48. W. McCullough to J. Sprague, Nov. 13, 1865, and W. McCullough to W. Peters, Nov. 24, 1867, reel 3; and W. McCullough to J. Bennett, Nov. 30, 1867, reel 23, BRFAL-Ark (M979).

49. W. McCullough to J. W. Harrell, Dec. 6, 1865; W. McCullough to E. O. C. Ord, Feb. 20, 1867; W. McCullough to C. H. Smith, May 31 and July 18, 1868; W. McCullough to J. Sprague, May 4, 1866; W. McCullough to E. O. C. Ord, Jan. 4, 1867; and W. McCullough to J. Bennett, Nov. 30, 1867, reel 3; and W. McCullough to J. Sprague, Nov. 30, 1865, reel 23; BRFAL-Ark (M979).

50. Station Book, 1866–1869, reel 51; W. Colby to C. H. Smith, May 1, 1868, reel 28; W. Colby to C. H. Smith July 10, 1868, reel 12; and Educational Statistics, 1865–1869, reel 1, BRFAL-Ark (M979).

51. Ibid.; W. Colby to C. H. Smith, Jan. 1, Feb. 1, 1868, reel 28; and W. Colby to C. H. Smith, May 2, 1867, reel 5, BRFAL-Ark (M979).

52. W. Colby to E. O. C. Ord, Feb. 21, 1867, reel 28; J. W. Alvord to O. O. Howard, Jan. 1, 1867, reel 1; and W. Colby to E. O. C. Ord, Dec. 21, 1866, and W. Colby, Report, July 1, 1870, reel 12, BRFAL-Ark (M979).

53. W. Colby, Report, June 26, 1867, and W. Colby to J. Tyler, Nov. 26, 1866, reel 12; and W. Colby to C. H. Smith, Mar. 1, 1868, reel 28, BRFAL-Ark (M979).

54. W. S. Andrews, Petition, June 14, 1867, and J. Henry to E. O. C. Ord, July 13, 1867, reel 5, BRFAL-Ark (M979).

55. Henry Sweeney, Civil War Pension Files, Records of the Veterans Administration, Record Group 15, National Archives, Washington, D.C .

56. H. Sweeney to J. Sprague, Mar. 31, 1866, reel 23; H. Sweeney, Circular, Nov. 14, 1865, and H. Sweeney to G. Dayton, Sept. 1, 1865, reel 6; H. Sweeney to J. Sprague, Oct. 20, 1866, reel 12; and H. Sweeney, Circular, Nov. 12, 1866, reel 7, BRFAL-Ark (M979).

57. H. Sweeney to J. Sprague, Apr. 20 and Sept. 8, 1866, reel 5; and H. Sweeney to J. Sprague, May 31, 1866, reel 23, BRFAL-Ark (M979).

58. H. Sweeney, Report, Jan. 24, 1865; H. Sweeney, Report, June 30, 1865; and H. Sweeney to E. O. C. Ord, Jan. 24, 1867, reel 6; H. Sweeney to J. Bennett, May 31, 1867, reel 25; and H. Sweeney to W. G. Sargent, Jan. 31, 1865, reel 13; BRFAL-Ark (M979).

59. H. Sweeney to J. Sprague, Nov. 25, 1865, and June 30, 1866, and H. Sweeney, Circular, Nov. 12, 1866, reel 6; and H. Sweeney to J. Taylor, Nov. 20, 1866, reel 12, BRFAL-Ark (M979).

60. O. O. Howard to J. Sprague, Nov. 30, 1865, and M. Bentzoni to J. Sprague, Dec. 24, 1865, reel 5; H. Sweeney to J. Sprague, June 6, 1866, reel 6; J. Sprague to O. O. Howard, Mar. 2, 1866, reel 4; and J. H. Cole and E. Mallory to J. Sprague, July 1, 1866, reel 12, BRFAL-Ark (M979).

6

Architects of a Benevolent Empire: The Relationship between the American Missionary Association and the Freedmen's Bureau in Virginia, 1865–1872

E. Allen Richardson

THE AMERICAN MISSIONARY ASSOCIATION (AMA), one of the oldest and most influential of the antebellum Protestant benevolent societies, was organized in 1846 as a coalition of abolitionist organizations. The AMA became identified with the evangelical visions both of ending slavery and, in the spirit of the Second Great Awakening, of establishing a Christian America. In keeping with this vision following the Civil War, AMA administrators and teachers established more than five hundred schools for blacks and chartered nine historically black colleges drawing on the northern churches that sustained the agency.

The AMA also developed and maintained a lasting relationship with an arm of the federal government, the Bureau of Refugees, Freedmen, and Abandoned Lands, during the short period of the Bureau's existence from 1865 to 1872. This relationship was similar to that of other benevolent societies in its sharing of funds and cooperative endeavors to establish schools for freedpeople. It was also unique, for in no other instance was power so completely integrated between church and state in a complex, symbiotic pattern of dual appointments, mutual agendas, and shared perceptions about the nature of Reconstruction.

The association between the AMA and the Bureau has been interpreted in a number of ways. For example, it has been seen as an expedient mechanism for the realization of the Bureau's emphasis on education and as the product of the close, lasting friendship between AMA executive George Whipple and Bureau Commissioner General Oliver O. Howard.[1] Although both of these interpretations offer some insights into the nature of the relationship, neither is sufficient for understanding the symbiosis of ideological forces that drew the two agencies together. The relationship also has been correctly described as a nexus between northern Republican ideology and abolitionist beliefs that, together, shaped the character of Reconstruction.[2] In actuality, the relationship between the AMA and the Freedmen's Bureau was much more. It evolved from a far broader synthesis of ideologies related to race, reform, and Reconstruction, which also included the tenets of the Tappan wing of Christian abolitionism, free-labor thought, and the evangelical beliefs that evolved from Charles Finney's contribution to the Second Great Awakening. This ideological development had geographical origins in Ohio, where Finney, Oberlin Institute, and free-labor ideology had significant influence on the AMA's organizers. It continued throughout the South between 1861 and 1865 in a variety of federally funded free-labor experiments that frequently involved northern benevolent societies. Finally, during the brief life of the Freedmen's Bureau, it matured as the complex array of ideologies coalesced into a common vision of a reconstructed South, which its federal and ecclesiastical architects were sure would soon create the foundation of a benevolent empire.

The mechanisms that enhanced the relationship included frequent interaction among field staffs (assistant Bureau commissioners and AMA superintendents), dual appointments, and cooperative patterns of management that included the use of combined resources for the construction of schools, mutual consultation in the selection of staff, and joint problem solving. The Bureau's emphasis on education also was intertwined with the AMA. Interagency cooperation began at the top. Whipple and Howard maintained a regular correspondence. Howard was often invited to address AMA meetings; Whipple advised the Bureau concerning a variety of projects. The Bureau and the AMA also coordinated the development of the Freedmen's Savings and Trust Company, a mutual savings bank organized to help former slaves become self-sufficient. The bank became an informal link between the two agencies and frequently employed AMA personnel as officials.

Although such individuals as Howard and Whipple created the relationship between the two agencies on a national level, Bureau assistant commissioners and AMA superintendents continued the pattern in the states. In Virginia, AMA missionaries became Bureau agents. In Georgia, Superintendent of Education Gilbert L. Eberhart explored the possibility of giving AMA agents Bureau status.[3] In Texas, AMA agent George W. Honey was appointed as assistant superintendent of the Freedmen's Bureau. In Chicago, O. O. Howard's brother, Charles, became AMA district secretary while still employed by the Bureau.[4] This pattern of dual appointments, which also was practiced by other benevolent societies, was the most visible in the AMA and therefore was an easy target for criticism. In Georgia, for instance, the appointment of abolitionist Edmund A. Ware as Eberhart's successor was critiqued by other societies because of Ware's close association with the AMA.[5]

Such instances of cooperation between the two agencies were more than the result of bureaucratic alignment or convenience. Rather, they were much more the product of a continuous process of ideological development that influenced both the leadership of the Bureau and the AMA. The ideologies that were part of this process included both Tappanite abolitionism and Finneyite revivalism at Oberlin Institute.

At Oberlin, Finney's interpretation of American evangelism was a significant influence on AMA leaders Lewis Tappan, Whipple, and Michael Strieby. Tappan had led the *Amistad* Committee and, following its victory before the Supreme Court in the famous case freeing the *Amistad* captives, had invested in Oberlin Institute, a school that had since developed a strong abolitionist tradition. Whipple, who became the AMA's first executive secretary, had been both an Oberlin student and professor. Strieby was an Oberlin graduate and Congregational minister who succeeded Whipple. Appointed as AMA corresponding secretary in 1864, Strieby was an active proponent of Finneyite perfectionism, which stressed the complete removal of sin and the subsequent elevated role of the evangelical community.[6] For the AMA leaders, who already were committed to abolitionism, Finney's theology offered not only a way of motivating churches but also of placing abolitionism in a wider theological context. Because of the role of the Finneyite evangelicals, who saw themselves as already saved, the tradition also presented a contradiction. On the one hand, it emphasized economic independence and freedom; on the other hand, it supported paternalism in which the evangelicals understood their roles as missionaries. The missionary tradition that had rapidly developed as part of the Second Great Awakening insisted that such lofty ideals as self-determinism could be achieved only after they had been taught in the classroom and illustrated by the personal example of an elite cadre of religious leaders.

The evangelicals also were informed by free-labor thought, a complex amalgam of ideologies that influenced the Liberty, Free Soil, and Republican Parties. Free-labor beliefs emphasized the value of work in a free-market economy. Drawn from American entrepreneurial tradition and Jacksonian Democratic values, free-labor ideology also had grown from suspicion of monied interests and the rise of a growing middle class with strong beliefs in equality and the mutual ownership of capital. At the same time, much like the evangelical tradition, which also had become paternalistic, free-labor ideology saw the northern business interests as superior but benevolent caretakers of an expanding economic system in the South.[7]

Against this background, adherents of free labor sought to dignify work and to link it not only with human potential but also with the future of the nation. Although it incorporated the Protestant work ethic, the free-labor vision of progress went well beyond that ideology. As historian Eric Foner explains:

> [I]f one's calling were divinely ordained, the implication might be that a man should be content with the same occupation for his entire life, although he should strive to grow rich in it. In a static economy, therefore, the concept of "a calling" may be associated with the idea of a hierarchical social order, with more or less fixed classes. But Republicans rejected this image of society. Their outlook was grounded in the Protestant ethic, but in its emphasis on social mobility and economic growth, it reflected an adaptation of the ethic to the dynamic, expansive, capitalist society of the antebellum North.[8]

A primary architect of free-labor ideology was Cincinnati attorney Salmon P. Chase. As the driving force behind the success of the

Ohio Liberty Party and, following its demise, of the Free Soil Party, Chase, perhaps more than any other person, orchestrated the synthesis of ideologies that became the foundation of the Republican Party. Chase also became the bridge that connected the public and private realms. An untiring advocate of voluntary associations, he supported the work of both the AMA and the American Freedmen's Union Commission, a consortium of associations that he served as president.

In 1862, Chase, then Secretary of the Treasury, initiated the first of a series of free-labor experiments designed as a partnership between the voluntary associations in the North and the federal government. Under Chase's directive and the control of the Department of the Treasury, 195 plantations were appropriated for an initial project in Port Royal, South Carolina.[9] With the help of longtime friend and Methodist minister Mansfield French, Chase was instrumental in the formation of a broad-based coalition of benevolent societies called the National Freedmen's Relief Association (NFRA), which had been organized by the AMA. The NFRA was an attempt to broaden the AMA's ability to encompass a variety of ecclesiastical and secular interests. The project was intended as a demonstration of free-labor ideology and was the first programmatic expression of the shared free-labor and evangelical ideologies. Other examples that soon followed under the direction of the Treasury Department included the emergence of a Bureau of Free Labor, a forerunner of the Freedmen's Bureau.[10]

The shared expression of Christian abolitionism, revivalism, and the ideologies of free labor–free soil thus created a climate not only of reform but of the quest for sustained political action. Moreover, it presented those who saw themselves as supporters of a benevolent empire with a mandate that was fully in keeping with established American principles, thus creating a powerful network of allies in the fight for abolition. Perhaps most important, it further cemented the ties between voluntary associations and the government and resulted in a dialogue between church and state that would influence the creation of the Freedmen's Bureau. A plan for the Bureau had been introduced into the House of Representatives in 1863 and, following extensive lobbying efforts by voluntary associations, finally emerged in 1865 under the auspices of the War Department.

The AMA greeted the formation of the Bureau with unbridled

enthusiasm. *The American Missionary*, the AMA's principal voice, proclaimed:

> The Bureau should have the countenance and support of all Christians and Philanthropists; Government should immediately place in their hands all the abandoned and confiscated lands needful for the accomplishment of their purposes. . . . The Freedmen will become self-supporting. The control of all Freedmen should pass immediately from post and department military commanders, to the Bureau.[11]

The article continued, "Christians must help the government."[12] The AMA's perception of the role of the Bureau reflected its belief that free-labor initiatives were a mechanism through which a Christian America could be realized. For the Bureau, economic development was coterminous with patterns of education that would enable masses of former slaves to become productive members of an industrialized class. Both visions gave license to charity in which capitalist and evangelical leaders perceived a mandate to create substantial change, which they believed would come about through the introduction of Christian principles and education.

Bureau Commissioner Howard was one of the most outspoken advocates of this position. He was a popular speaker at AMA meetings and publicly gave his support for a northern Christian presence in the South. Often employing evangelical rhetoric, Howard urged supporters of the association to "Work . . . while the sun shines. Do what the Government cannot do, send Christian men and women who are not afraid to be hated . . . not afraid to die; send them as teachers and almoners of your contributions and as Christian missionaries."[13]

Popularly dubbed "the Christian general," Howard was an active Congregationalist who had even considered entering the ministry. His commitment to evangelical principles also influenced his appointments. For example, he nominated a Congregational minister, the Reverend John Watson Alvord, as the Bureau's superintendent of education. Alvord's commitment to the evangelical and free-labor ideologies was reflected in his career. Like the AMA executives themselves, he was a product of the Finneyite abolitionist tradition at Oberlin Institute. He served churches in Connecticut and Massachusetts and, in the spirit of free-labor beliefs, had helped blacks in Savannah, Georgia, establish an independent school system.

Under Howard's and Alvord's leadership, the Bureau supported the role of missionary teachers, who were frequently white women recruited from northern churches. Their ranks also came to include some men, a number of African Americans, and spouses of military and Bureau officials. Most of these people were inexperienced or had little formal teaching experience. Despite this lack of training, the leaders of the AMA and other benevolent associations believed that they were an important means of meeting the overwhelming human needs of the freedpeople and, at the same time, of instilling in them the common evangelical and free-labor principles of self-reliance and an appreciation for the value of work.

The missionary teacher tradition was built on the foundation of charity education that had been developed during the first half of the nineteenth century, but it went beyond that by incorporating the Republican emphasis on free labor. Teachers were prepared for this interdependent vision by such texts as Lydia Maria Child's *The Freedmen's Book* (1865), which argued that the freedpeople were expected to reflect Christian virtues, to be industrious and self-supporting, and also to demonstrate their capability of making a profit.[14] Education was understood as a means through which freed slaves could become employable, providing them with the skills necessary to assess the value of contracts, to negotiate with potential employers, and to form a southern counterpart to the expanding northern capitalist economy. These principles had shaped the presence of missionary teachers in the earliest free-labor experiments in Port Royal, South Carolina, in 1862. Their role had ever since remained a practical emphasis in the evangelical and free-labor traditions.

These views about the symbiotic role of religion and education were often shared by Bureau administrators. For example, J. H. Caldwell, Bureau official and educator in Georgia, concluded, "It is one of the most hopeful signs of the times . . . that throughout my entire district, when the benign influences of education and religion have prevailed, the Colored population have been marked for their morality and industry."[15] Although similar sentiments were common in both the Bureau and the AMA, they also degenerated, at times, into outright condemnation of the black community for its failure to adopt northern principles.

The following case study of the relationship between the Bureau and the AMA in Virginia illustrates the way in which free-labor and evangelical thought influenced Bureau educational policies. It also shows how, in a state where the missionary teacher tradition was already well established, the Bureau expanded the tradition and also increasingly relied on the presence of evangelical leaders who were employed as special agents and as Bureau officials. Finally, it demonstrates how, in concert with these actions, the Bureau's assistant commissioner for Virginia, Colonel Orlando Brown, emphasized strict compliance with the free-labor vision before it was finally eroded by Johnsonian Reconstruction.

Brown had been appointed to this position from a post as assistant quartermaster and superintendent of Negro affairs in Norfolk. He served the Bureau as assistant commissioner from June 1865 to May 1866 and from March 1867 to May 1869.[16] Brown had not been Howard's first choice for the position, but the enthusiastic recommendation of Secretary of War Edwin M. Stanton and Brown's previous attempts to provide relief and education to blacks made him a logical choice. Brown also had experience with missionary teachers and, before his appointment to the Bureau, had helped to establish the AMA's presence in the tidewater region of the state.

Brown had also developed a friendship with AMA executive Whipple. This alliance had created a continuing opportunity for Whipple's entry into regional issues in Virginia and had become an efficient mechanism for solving mutual problems. Whipple and Brown had worked together to eliminate sources of controversy that might embarrass both the military and the AMA. In January 1865, for example, they had removed two teachers, Mary Reed and Samuel Walker, who had escalated racial tensions by condemning shared housing arrangements for black and white teachers. Further responding to gossip about an affair between the couple and a general level of discontent about the incident among the teachers, Whipple and Brown acted swiftly and quietly to transfer both instructors out of the state.[17]

By the time of the creation of the Bureau, Brown and Whipple had developed such a close working relationship that, at times, because of Whipple's friendship with Howard, the distinction between the bureaucracies became blurred. Whipple was described as an agent of the Bureau. He even periodically interpreted Howard's wishes to Brown, advised him of the commissioner's activities, and relayed official requests.[18]

This interdependence between the bureaucracies also created

confusion for teachers. The Bureau provided funds for the purchase and construction of schools, and, in return, the benevolent associations were expected to pay teachers' salaries. In keeping with this arrangement, supervision of the teachers was left to AMA superintendents. At times, however, teachers became confused about their relationship with the Bureau. In June 1865, for example, a teacher in Fortress Monroe wrote Brown to request clarification "[am I] to be regarded as in the employ of the Bureau and to look to you for pay, or is my supervision to be more voluntary and nominal with the understanding that I am still in the employ of the A.M. Association and to look to them for my pay?"[19] In succeeding years, this confusion was also increased by changes in the Bureau structure. Originally, Virginia had been divided into ten districts and numerous subdistricts administered by superintendents and assistant superintendents. In 1867, the state was reconfigured into ten subdistricts directed by subassistant commissioners.[20] Two years later, when most Bureau functions in the state had ceased except for the development of schools, the state was again reorganized into eight educational subdistricts. For AMA teachers who had to deal with the association's own administrative structure and the confusion about their accountability, the total system was chaotic and often overwhelming.

Within this complex alignment of administrative machinery, both Brown and Whipple became involved in a system of mutually dependent relationships in which the free-labor and evangelical ideologies continued to shape a common vision of reform. The missionary teachers were perceived as a primary instrument of this reform and were understood to be catalysts for an educational process that would reconstruct southern society. In keeping with this vision of renewal, Bureau officials such as Brown, who often had no formal connections with the evangelical tradition, were frequently sympathetic to the value that it placed on self-determinism, which was in concert with free-labor beliefs. For Brown, this also led to an appreciation of congregational autonomy for blacks. He had complained to Howard, for example, that the black members of a Methodist Episcopal Church in Richmond were prohibited from controlling their own affairs because of the action of white trustees who were appointed by quarterly conferences of the denomination. Instead, he argued, control of the church should be returned to the freed-people.[21]

In addition to his support of the right of blacks to worship as they saw fit, Brown visibly demonstrated his belief in free-labor princi-ples. With the establishment of his office in Richmond in June 1865 and the subsequent appointment of district superintendents, he af-firmed the advisory role of Bureau officials in helping blacks to make contracts, but he staunchly resisted any suggestion that their advice was controlling. As a loyal Bureau official, he opposed the use of charity and supported the ability of blacks to enter into contractual arrangements with employers unhampered by governmental inter-ference. Brown had reminded a district superintendent, Captain A. S. Flagg, of this emphasis, for example, when members of his staff on Virginia's Eastern Shore had attempted to influence contracts suggesting that, "Although it is desirable to prevent trouble it is an inexcusable error, for agents to attempt to force such contracts on freedmen, unless they are vagrants or paupers."[22]

Within this context of strong beliefs in free labor and ongoing support for the work of missionary teachers, Brown recruited persons with a visible commitment to the evangelical and free-labor visions to direct the Bureau's work in education. In 1866, for example, he nominated the Reverend William H. Woodbury as superintendent of schools.[23] One of the earliest AMA teachers sent to Norfolk, Wood-bury had known Brown for several years and had established a school run entirely by blacks. He typified the missionary teacher who not only propagated Christian values, but who also helped the freedpeo-ple to become self-supporting. Known as "Professor Woodbury," he had maintained a close working relationship with both Brown and Whipple and was a frequent traveler between Bureau offices in Rich-mond and AMA headquarters in New York. In his new position, Woodbury continued his earlier association with Brown and main-tained relationships with other officers whom Brown had appointed to Bureau positions. These included Assistant Superintendent of Negro Affairs Frederick S. Tukey, whom Brown had nominated as assistant subassistant commissioner in Bowling Green. Like Brown, Tukey also had an association with the AMA and was committed to the role of missionary teacher. For example, he had corresponded with Whipple in December 1864 to seek a commission for a member of a Methodist Episcopal Church in Portsmouth and to express interest in the association's schools.[24] Because of this background, Woodbury saw Tukey as part of an AMA network for recruiting persons to help manage the association's schools. In January 1865, for instance, Woodbury checked with Tukey about the ability of Samuel W. Taylor as a nominee for the position of assistant superintendent of colored schools.[25] Tukey responded that Taylor was well suited for the position not only because he was an excellent disciplinarian, but also because both he and his wife were biblical scholars and were connected with an evangelical church.

The same pattern of appointment was evident in Woodbury's successor, Ralza Morse Manly, a Methodist minister who became superintendent of education. Manly had a background in both education and religion and was well suited for the position. He had been principal of a grammar school in Vermont, a seminary teacher, and a military chaplain.[26] In addition, he was a member of the American Freedmen's Union Commission, the consortium of benevolent societies once led by free-labor advocate Salmon Chase. Although not an AMA missionary, Manly had developed a strong interest in the role of missionary teachers. In 1864, for example, he had written Whipple about obtaining copies of *The American Missionary* and inquiring about AMA commissions for his wife and daughter, who had both taught in the association's schools since 1863.[27] Following receipt of their commissions, both women taught black soldiers in Manly's regiment.

For Woodbury, Tukey, Manly, and others, AMA commissions were more than a device to secure wages. They were a form of legitimization of the evangelical vision. As Bureau superintendent of education, Manly was to develop this interest as a way of chartering new schools and of attracting the AMA to direct them. In June 1866, for example, Brown nominated Manly as superintendent of the school at Hampton. In a note to Howard suggesting Manly for the position, Brown wrote, "I beg leave to suggest that I be ordered to appoint a committee to investigate the condition of the school and report. I think some *powerful friends* of the colored people would be glad to have the school continued on the present plan."[28] The AMA and the Bureau later developed the Hampton school under the leadership of a retired general, Samuel Chapman Armstrong, who transformed it into a model of the free-labor and evangelical visions.

For Manly and Brown, who had rejected the more radical assumptions of the evangelical tradition in which blacks were understood to have political rights, the missionary teacher was also a safe pursuit. In 1869, for example, they opposed an attempt to create a convention for black political leaders based on their belief that such actions overemphasized their political rights. In taking this position, they supported a faction in the Republican Party led by Henry H. Wells that backed the federal plan for Reconstruction, and they rejected a more radical stance in which the political position of blacks would have been further developed.[29] In keeping with this tack, Manly and Brown used their association with the AMA and the rapid expansion of the missionary teacher tradition to create schools in the state and to avoid involvement with black political candidates. Although this degree of moderation was criticized by black instructors, it was fully compatible with free-labor ideology, which, while opposing slavery, did little to improve the political position of blacks.

Beyond the work of Bureau officials in creating schools, Brown also employed AMA ministers for special assignments as Bureau agents when it was clear that their commitment to education was similar to his own. For example, in 1865, he employed the Reverend Henry Eddy in response to a suggestion by Whipple.[30] Eddy was assigned as a temporary agent to do reconnaissance in an area of the state where the feasibility of developing schools was uncertain. He also was given the more complicated task of determining the level of cooperation that the Bureau could expect from the military.

This role was significant because the Bureau was subject to the wishes of the military as long as the state remained under martial law. Although the Bureau was a quasi-military agency within the War Department, it experienced a level of autonomy from the army that often hampered communication. Unsympathetic military commanders could create difficulty for Bureau administrators who, in keeping with Brown's disposition to create as many new schools as possible, made education a priority.

Eddy's reconnaissance convinced him that a level of cooperation between the Bureau and the military was possible.[31] Still, he had failed to find any buildings that the agency could transform into schools. In addition, he discovered that race relations were far from ideal. He learned that at least five white families refused to acknowledge the free status of their former slaves and that freedpeople were sufficiently suspicious of their former masters to refuse to accept them as schoolteachers. Nevertheless, Eddy was sure that the freed-people wanted education; each black home that he had visited owned a spelling book.[32]

The shared evangelical and free-labor ideologies often supported Bureau activities, but, in some instances, they became a source of resistance to changes in federal policy. This was the case when AMA missionary and Bureau Assistant Subcommissioner Charles Wilder resisted revised policies toward Reconstruction initiated by President Andrew Johnson.

Wilder had been appointed in 1866 following the work of another AMA missionary, Charles Lockwood, who had been sent by the AMA to Fortress Monroe to provide medical care, education, and basic necessities to the hundreds of freedpeople congregated in the former barracks outside Hampton.[33] As a former businessman and member of the AMA's executive committee, Wilder had developed significant influence within the association.

As a dual appointee of the AMA and the military, Wilder also had been given the rank of captain and the designation "Assistant Quartermaster and Superintendent of Negro Affairs." He soon became adept at manipulating the bureaucracies to meet the principles that he understood as important. Foremost was the common evangelical–free-labor belief in self-determinism that undergirded the interest of both bureaucracies in establishing schools. Acting on this conviction, Wilder had developed considerable influence and had attempted to streamline the establishment of schools. He not only suggested locations to the AMA for additional sites but even proposed the names of persons whom he thought would function well as teachers. In December 1864, for example, he had written to the AMA secretaries, "to urge your attention to the suggestion in regard to a man (minister) of the right kind for the New School House soon to be opened (which) will seat 600."[34] Wilder continued that the minister should be able to attract both blacks and whites, and he concluded with a nominee for the secretaries to consider.

As a military officer and Bureau agent, Wilder also had retained his belief in the role of the missionary teacher as the principal means of elevating the social position of the freedpeople. Nevertheless, the paternalism that had become part of both the free-labor and the evangelical positions led him to condemn the black religious experience as inferior to the white Protestant evangelical faith. In January

1865, for example, Wilder wrote AMA Corresponding Secretary Michael Strieby about a minister who "might be a good man to help wean the people from clinging to the ignorant apologies among the colored people who rant about but fail to educate and elevate. He should be thankful enough in getting ministers to attract and interest the people from such preaching as they get."[35]

Ultimately, Wilder's uncompromising support for the free-labor vision, coupled with his evangelical zeal, resulted in his downfall. In August 1865, President Johnson decreed that properties that had been abandoned or confiscated from white southern plantation owners had to be returned. Howard had little choice but to comply, and he issued Circular Order No. 15 on September 12, 1865, to Brown and the other assistant commissioners that mandated their compliance. As a result, Bureau control of land decreased quickly as the remaining properties were returned to their owners with the token provision that blacks be offered small plots by their former masters, who were also encouraged to employ them. Feeling that the Bureau could not be trusted, blacks were outraged. As tensions increased, Brown anticipated violent reactions from freedpersons, who, many alleged, were harboring weapons.[36]

At the heart of the dilemma were the virtual elimination of reasonably priced land for blacks, the suggestion that freedpeople should work for their former masters, and the termination of the free-labor ideology that had been so much a part of the Bureau's identity. Reacting to this change, Wilder attempted to minimize the damage through a process of questioning orders and creating delays to prevent blacks from being forced off the lands they occupied.[37] A year later, because of his increasing resistance to military and Bureau authority, he was court-martialed on charges of malfeasance.[38] Although the specific charges (selling cannon to blacks, permitting freedpeople to take timber from restored land, and speculating in the sale of land) were seemingly unrelated, they represented an attempt by the military to remove a source of resistance to federal policy. Because Virginia remained under martial law, the case sought to challenge disobedience and to reaffirm the military's own superiority over Bureau authority.

Eventually, Wilder was exonerated, but the situation had made it virtually impossible for him to continue in the army. Howard reassigned him to another part of the state. Ironically, Wilder's successor, General Armstrong, was also an ardent supporter of the shared evangelical and free-labor ideologies. Unlike Wilder, who resisted change in Bureau policy, Armstrong constructed an educational empire in which the free-labor and evangelical beliefs could be institutionalized and removed from federal control.

Armstrong was a curious mixture of ideals. As the son of a Congregational missionary in Hilo, Hawaii, he had grown up amid issues of relief. Armstrong's Hawaiian background also had given him a strong sense of the Protestant work ethic and the way that it could be applied to students' manual labor. His parents' school in Hilo had emerged as a manual labor institution much in the character of the Oneida and Oberlin colleges. He also had been fully immersed in evangelical Christianity and, in keeping with the emphasis on missions that continued to be part of the Second Great Awakening, understood his work with blacks in evangelical terms. Yet, as a high-ranking member of the military establishment, he also both understood and advocated the Republican free-labor ideology. Armstrong arrived in Hampton, Virginia, in June 1866. There, he witnessed overwhelming human need in the midst of the deplorable conditions endured by the large numbers of freedpeople at Fortress Monroe. He managed to secure a commission from the AMA as superintendent of schools and also was appointed by the Bureau as agent, with control over ten counties of the Fifth Subdistrict of Virginia.[39] In addition, Armstrong was appointed as Bureau superintendent of schools in the same region.

Armstrong explored the possibility of creating an educational institution with both Bureau and AMA funds. By July 1867, he had shared his plan with Howard and the AMA executive staff.[40] The proposal included an initial construction grant of $2,000 from the Bureau, coupled with a donation of $10,000 secured through the offices of Judge Josiah King, who was the administrator of an estate in Pittsburgh. The money would be used to purchase a 160-acre farm, which included a mansion and a flour mill. These buildings would be converted into a house for the principal and a residence hall, and adjacent hospital barracks at Fortress Monroe would be used as a source of building materials. Armstrong also persuaded the AMA to add $9,000 to an additional Bureau grant of $13,000. The total effort was secured by yet another private donation of $10,000. Thus, within a year of his appointment to the Bureau in 1866, Armstrong had collected $44,000 for a plan in which he would become the principal of a school described as the Hampton Normal and Agricultural Institute.

The AMA executive staff and Armstrong became the primary incorporators of the venture, which distanced the institute from the Bureau. Further, a county charter granted by the Circuit Court of Elizabeth City County on September 21, 1868, named Whipple as the institute's president, AMA staff members Edward Smith and William Whiting as vice president and treasurer,[41] and Armstrong as secretary. The deed to the property was even put in Whipple's name. Subsequent correspondence from General Henry Whittlesey on Howard's staff challenged these arrangements and insisted that the property be deeded to a board of trustees. Whittlesey wrote Armstrong, "To avoid trouble and . . . litigation as the legal title of the lands and the buildings created thereon the Commissioner desires that the AMA and Rev. Whipple transfer all their interest in the land and other property to the Trustees of the Corporation; until such transfer is made he does not feel authorized to transfer the buildings created by the government to the Trustees nor to pay rent therefor."[42] Armstrong subsequently convinced the AMA to make the change.

As a measure of its control of the Hampton project, and as a visible symbol of Armstrong's own beliefs in free labor, the plan also had included the development of a working farm. The property had been known as "Little Scotland" and was now described as the "Whipple Farm." *The American Missionary* described the proposal: "The farm which is embraced in the plan, is under the management of Mr. Francis Richardson . . . [who] has made . . . [it] into a model farm. Mr. Richardson is making daily shipments to the east of strawberries and peas, and will . . . have shiploads of potatoes, cabbages and other products of his former craft."[43]

The Hampton Normal and Agricultural Institute thus became a curious blend of entrepreneurial development and free-labor ideology fused with Armstrong's own evangelical understanding of manual labor and education. Students were compelled to work two days a week, to contribute a portion of their earnings toward their education, and to attend classes. Although Armstrong expected the total endeavor, in the context of free-labor ideology, to be self-sustaining, he was content to accept minor losses while always careful to describe the project publicly as educational. This ideology was only sustained when the project produced a profit. The manual labor plan and free-labor incentive were viable recruiting tools, but they often plunged the school into significant debt. Armstrong repeatedly sought additional funds from the AMA, which began to get weary of the constant drain on its limited resources.

By 1870, the combined manual and free labor visions at Hampton had become the defining features of the institution. Armstrong instituted a monthly publication, *The Southern Workman*, which became the institute's official newspaper and a continuing voice for the utopian vision of the dignity of labor. Retaining his position as the paper's editor, Armstrong sought to sustain a vision of Reconstruction in which the freedpeople would create a new industrial class. Labor was described in idealized terms intimately associated with Christian civilization. Armstrong wrote: "We call the dispensation of labor a curse from the Almighty's hand. . . . It is rather the guardian of virtue and happiness; a pleasant companion, in whose absence we are lonely and ill at ease. It is a law of God's economy that man shall earn his bread by the sweat of his brow, and the breaking of this law brings evil consequences."[44]

The newspaper also espoused principles familiar to supporters of free labor:

> The thing to be done was clear: to train selected Negro youth who should go out and teach and lead their people, first by example, by getting land and homes; to give them not a dollar that they could earn for themselves; to teach respect for labor, to replace stupid drudgery with skilled hands; and to these ends to build an industrial system, for the sake not only of self-support and industrial labor but also for the sake of character.[45]

Thus, while deriving its focus and much of its initial funding from a combined Bureau-AMA commitment to free labor, Armstrong protected the Institute from further federal control by developing it as a religiously based private school in which the AMA held a dominant position on its Board of Trustees. At the same time, he created an administrative structure in which he had ultimate control.

Hampton Institute, the most substantial of the AMA-Bureau schools in Virginia, was developed as a demonstration of the shared evangelical and free-labor ideologies. It also reflected the paternalism recurrent in both ideologies by which northern principles were brought into the South. Although Armstrong vehemently claimed, "An imitation of northern models will not do,"[46] the mission of the institute left little room for the emergence of a unique southern economy.

Yet, despite this contradiction, Hampton Institute and other Bureau schools in Virginia retained their belief in the ability of the evangelical and free-labor ideologies both to renew and to reconstruct the South. This vision was supported by Assistant Commissioner Brown as he recruited Bureau leadership from a cadre of officers who were proponents of African-American education and who had a history of association with the evangelical tradition and the AMA. Under Brown's leadership, the missionary teacher tradition was expanded and sanctioned by the Bureau as an integral part of its understanding of Reconstruction.

The Bureau's work in Virginia thus helped to transform the utopian ideology of evangelical and free labor beliefs into bureaucratic structure. Part of this transformation was the moderation of some of the more radical parts of the Finneyite reforms that had earlier led to expressions of abolitionism in the North. In the climate of Reconstruction, the concern for radical political action was replaced by a measure of societal reform that continued to emphasize individual salvation and perfection in the context of established northern capitalist principles. Together, Bureau officials and AMA missionary teachers planned for what they understood as the benevolent empire, a utopian partnership between church and state. The empire also became a euphemism for a Christian America dominated by the drive for equality and a benign form of government built on the principles of a free and open market. For Bureau officials in Virginia and in other southern states, the AMA, as the largest of the Protestant benevolent societies, remained a formative piece of this architecture. Indeed, the AMA outlasted the Bureau and, through such institutions as Hampton Institute and scores of black schools across the state, kept alive an evangelical and self-help emphasis even after Reconstruction collapsed.

NOTES

1. Ronald E. Butchart, *Northern Schools, Southern Blacks, and Reconstruction: Freedmen's Education, 1862–1875* (Westport, Conn.: Greenwood Press,

1980), examines the role of ecclesiastical societies and the Bureau in developing a relationship based on expediency and the manipulation of power. Joe M. Richardson, *Christian Reconstruction: The American Missionary Association and Southern Blacks, 1861–1890* (Athens: University of Georgia Press, 1986), 76ff., describes the manner in which former Lane seminarian and Freedmen's Bureau General Superintendent of Education John W. Alvord introduced George Whipple to Howard. Richardson's description implies that the resulting friendship had significant influence in shaping the relationship between the Bureau and the Association. Although this assumption is certainly correct and the mediating role of Alvord between the two bureaucracies is important, the cooperation between the two agencies must also be seen as the result of the symbiotic relationship between the ideologies suggested in this chapter.

2. See Jacqueline Jones, *Soldiers of Light and Love: Northern Teachers and Georgia Blacks, 1865–1873* (Chapel Hill: University of North Carolina Press, 1980), 3ff. Jones cites James M. McPherson's argument that abolitionism "survived the war intact and provided both the ideology and fervor that sparked the northern-sponsored education during and after Reconstruction," 4. Although there is little doubt that the abolitionist spirit did indeed sustain the enthusiasm for a northern-style education, the movement also drew inspiration from the Second Great Awakening itself, which infused perceptions about the nature and value of labor.

3. Paul A. Cimbala, *Under the Guardianship of the Nation: The Freedmen's Bureau and the Reconstruction of Georgia, 1865–1870* (Athens: University of Georgia Press, 1997), 124, suggests that Superintendent of Education Ware also recommended that Bureau officers become AMA superintendents. These ideas were never realized, however, perhaps because of the AMA's reluctance to become too involved with the Bureau, which was widely criticized. For an alternative perspective on the use of dual appointments in Georgia, see Jones, *Soldiers of Light and Love*, 96.

4. Richardson, *Christian Reconstruction*, 81.

5. Cimbala, *Under Guardianship of the Nation*, 123.

6. Finney's perfectionist theology is described in his memoirs. See Garth M. Rosell and Richard A. G. Dupuis, eds., *The Memoirs of Charles G. Finney: The Complete Restored Text* (Grand Rapids, Mich.: Zondervan Publishing House, 1989).

7. The best description of free-labor thought is Eric Foner, *Free Soil, Free Labor, Free Men: The Ideology of the Republican Party before the Civil War* (New York: Oxford University Press, 1970; reprint ed., 1995).

8. Ibid., 13.

9. See Willie Lee Rose, *Rehearsal for Reconstruction: The Port Royal Experiment* (Indianapolis: Bobbs-Merrill, 1964; reprint ed., New York: Oxford University Press, 1978).

10. Paul Skeels Peirce, *The Freedmen's Bureau: A Chapter in the History of Reconstruction* (Iowa City: State University of Iowa, 1904; reprint ed., New York: Haskell House Publishers, 1971), 1–33. See also Herman Belz, *A New Birth of Freedom: The Republican Party and Freedmen's Rights, 1861–1866* (Westport, Conn.: Greenwood Press, 1976); and George R. Bentley, *A History of the Freedmen's Bureau* (Philadelphia: University of Pennsylvania Press, 1955; reprint ed., New York: Octagon Books, 1974).

11. *The American Missionary* 9 (July 1865): 147.

12. Ibid.

13. *The American Missionary* 10 (June 1866): 127. Howard's commitment to the evangelical Protestant tradition is described in his autobiography. See Oliver Otis Howard, *Autobiography of Oliver Otis Howard, Major General United States Army*, 2 vols. (New York: Baker & Taylor, 1907).

14. Child's text, originally published by Ticknor and Fields in Boston (1865), is discussed in Robert C. Morris, *Reading, 'Riting and Reconstruction: The Education of Freedmen in the South, 1861–1870* (Chicago: University of Chicago Press, 1981), 181. Morris provides other examples of texts, such as Helen E. Brown, *John Freeman and His Family* (Boston: American Tract Society, 1864), which combines the Republican emphasis on work with Christian virtue. In addition to these sources, the role of charity education is discussed in Butchart, *Northern Schools, Southern Blacks, and Reconstruction*. See also Carl F. Kaestle, *Pillars of the Republic: Common Schools and American Society, 1780–1860* (New York: Hill and Wang, 1983).

15. J. H. Caldwell to J. R. Lewis, Oct. 5, 1867, quoted in Morris, *Reading, 'Riting and Reconstruction*, 211.

16. Introduction, Records of the Assistant Commissioner for the State of Virginia, Bureau of Refugees, Freedmen, and Abandoned Lands, 1865–1869, reel 1. National Archives Microfilm Publications M1048 (hereinafter cited as BRFAL-Va [M1048]), 2.

17. Richardson, *Christian Reconstruction*, 205. See also O. Brown to G. Whipple, Jan. 8, 1865, American Missionary Association Archives, Virginia, Amistad Center, Tulane University, New Orleans, La. (hereinafter cited as AMA-Va).

18. See G. Whipple to O. Brown, Nov. 23, 1865, reel 36, BRFAL-Va (M1048).

19. E. Knowlton to O. Brown, June 29, 1865, reel 36, BRFAL-Va (M1048).

20. Introduction, reel 1, BRFAL-Va (M3777), 2.

21. O. Brown to O. Howard, July 20, 1865, reel 36, BRFAL-Va (M1048).

22. O. Brown to A.S. Flagg, Jan. 5, 1865, reel 1, BRFAL-Va (M1048).

23. O. Brown to O. Howard, June 11, 1865, reel 36, BRFAL-Va (M1048).

24. F. Tukey to G. Whipple, Dec. 9, 1864, AMA-Va.

25. F. Tukey to W. Woodbury, Jan. 20, 1865, AMA-Va.

26. Morris, *Reading, 'Riting and Reconstruction*, 38.

27. R. Manly to G. Whipple, Dec. 5, 1864, AMA-Va. See also R. Manly to G. Whipple, Feb. 27, 1865, AMA-Va.

28. O. Brown to O. Howard, June 11, 1866, reel 2, BRFAL-Va (M1048).

29. Morris, *Reading, 'Riting, and Reconstruction*, 239.

30. G. Whipple to O. Brown, Oct. 28, 1865, reel 36, BRFAL-Va (M1048).

31. H. Eddy to O. Brown, Nov. 29, 1865, reel 36, BRFAL-Va (M1048).

32. Ibid.

33. Lockwood was one of the earliest AMA missionary teachers in Virginia and began relief efforts at Fortress Monroe in 1861. Lockwood also articulated the evangelical–free-labor ideologies and, in frequent correspondence with AMA headquarters in New York, wrote of the training that was necessary to equip blacks to become self-sufficient. Lockwood's correspondence is included in the Virginia collection of the AMA archives at the Amistad Center at Tulane University.

34. C. Wilder to M. Strieby and G. Whipple, Dec. 19, 1864, AMA-Va.

35. C. Wilder to M. Strieby, Jan. 25, 1865, AMA-Va.

36. Robert Francis Engs, *Freedom's First Generation: Black Hampton Virginia, 1861–1890* (Philadelphia: University of Pennsylvania Press, 1979), 101–11.

37. Ibid. See also C. Wilder to O. Brown, Aug. 31, 1865, reel 36, BRFAL-Va (M1048).

38. Engs, *Freedom's First Generation*, 101–11.

39. Armstrong was commissioned by the AMA on Nov. 13, 1867.

40. The plan is described in "The First Report of the Principal," Hampton University Archives. It is also explored in William Hannibal Robinson, "The History of Hampton Institute, 1868–1949" (Ph.D. dissertation, New York University, 1953). See also Edith Armstrong Talbot, *Samuel Chapman Armstrong: A Biographical Study* (New York: Doubleday, Page and Co., 1904).

41. County Charter for the Hampton Normal and Agricultural Institute, Circuit Court of Elizabeth County, Virginia, Sept. 21, 1868, Hampton University Archives, Hampton, Va.

42. H. Whittlesey to S. Armstrong, Feb. 19, 1870, Hampton University Archives.

43. *The American Missionary* 13 (July 1869): 145–6.

44. *The Southern Workman* 3 (March 1874), Hampton University Archives.

45. The Armstrong League of Hampton Workers, *Memories of Old Hampton* (Hampton, Va.: The Institute Press, 1909), 11.

46. Samuel Chapman Armstrong, "Report of the Principal, 1876," Hampton Normal and Agricultural Institute, Hampton University Archives.

7

"Une Chimère": The Freedmen's Bureau in Creole New Orleans

Caryn Cossé Bell

ARRIVING IN NEW ORLEANS from Mobile, Alabama, on November 5, 1865, General O. O. Howard, head of the Freedmen's Bureau, addressed the large, enthusiastic audience that greeted him in the city's Orleans Theatre on Sunday evening. Commissioner Howard's evident sincerity and earnest demeanor impressed his listeners, and the racially mixed gathering applauded approvingly when Howard explained that the central mission of the Freedmen's Bureau "was . . . to relieve the shock [of the freedmen] in passing from slavery to freedom." Still, many of those in attendance, though polite and attentive, deplored the Bureau's recent actions and already had concluded that Howard's agency was no more than "une chimère" (a chimera).[1]

Only five months earlier, the interracial delegation of unionist radicals who accompanied Howard to the stage and introduced him to the audience had founded a political coalition, the Friends of Universal Suffrage. They launched the organization in mid-June after President Andrew Johnson sanctioned the takeover of Louisiana's provisional government by returning Confederates and their conservative allies. Pressing for equality of voting rights, as well as proportional representation in political office holding, the Friends organized a "voluntary election" to coincide with the state's official balloting on November 6. Hoping for a significant voter turnout in a successful parallel electoral campaign, they proposed to win congressional support for a new model of Reconstruction based on universal suffrage.[2]

Not coincidentally, Howard arrived the day before the election. President Johnson, conceiving of the Freedmen's Bureau as a vehicle for advancing his own plan of Reconstruction, had dispatched the commissioner on a carefully scheduled tour of the South with a message designed to win over white conservatives while demoralizing proponents of land reform and black voting rights. Early in his New Orleans address, in keeping with the president's objectives, Howard extinguished hopes for land distribution. Johnson's decision to return confiscated lands to former owners originated, the commissioner explained, in the president's desire for "a complete reconstruction and reconciliation." With those goals in mind, the freedmen must accommodate, Howard insisted, to "any difference between them [the freedmen] and the white people . . . and work for them [the whites] and have the wages they can pay." True, white southerners possessed "a thick crust of prejudice," but through initiative, hard work, and "good conduct . . . all prejudices will be overcome, all differences reconciled, and the land will prosper and bloom like the rose."

In his concluding remarks, Howard deprecated any discussion of politics: "I have never had anything to do with politics." Instead, he urged his audience to "put down the pins and hold on to what we have, and be sure we have got it before we try to push ahead any further." When his audience responded with cries of "no," Howard pointed to events in the French Caribbean where, he maintained, disastrous consequences resulted when "people got divided up, pro and con by political agitations before labor was settled." Anarchy resulted "and everything went backwards. Some of these islands are now pointed at as showing that freedom is worse than slavery."[3]

Since July, the editorial staff of the *New Orleans Tribune*, the official organ of the Friends of Universal Suffrage as well as the nation's first black daily, had been forwarding copies of their radical, bilingual newspaper to Howard. In fact, Jean-Baptiste Roudanez, one of the Afro-Creole founders of the *Tribune*, sat on the stage with Howard as the commissioner delivered his address. Howard had paid little attention to the proffered newspaper, however, if he had expected to mollify the city's French-speaking black leaders with his references to the "French islands."[4]

The key architects of the Friends' coalition, the French-speaking Afro-Creoles of New Orleans, possessed close ties to the French

Antilles, and they viewed events in the Caribbean in an entirely different light. During the war, they had expressed solidarity with Haitian radicals and pointed to slavery's overthrow in France's 1848 revolution when the newly freed slaves won full citizenship rights. They had called attention to the subsequent Antillean elections when the former slaves elected black delegates to represent them in France's new Constituent Assembly. Determined to fulfill the democratic promise of the revolutionary age, black Creoles pressed for the unconditional assimilation of blacks into the national life. Their demands constituted an essential element in the nation's great tradition of black protest. For them, Howard's speech could hardly have been more disastrous.[5]

Initially, Afro-Creole radicals viewed the Freedmen's Bureau as an agency of social change and agrarian reform designed to assist the former slaves in their transition to citizenship. The Bureau's land distribution policy offered protection from northern speculators and held out the prospect of black autonomy in an economy of small, family-owned farms. The agency's mission reinforced the Afro-Creoles' aspirations for black voting rights and an economic equality grounded in land ownership. They anticipated a transformation of the region's political economy. By the fall of 1865, however, the compliant Howard had succumbed to presidential pressure. Under Johnson's influence, the Bureau in Louisiana was quickly transformed into an arm of Presidential Reconstruction designed to deliver black workers into the hands of Johnson's planter allies. In the end, the Freedmen's Bureau not only failed in its commitment to achieve meaningful economic and social reform, but it actually served to preclude black freedom. The ease with which Johnson sabotaged the Bureau's mission in Louisiana can be attributed to wartime developments when Federal army policies, which had been continued by the Bureau, foreshadowed presidential policy and provoked Afro-Creole resistance.[6]

With origins in the city's tripartite racial order and Latin-European religious culture, French-speaking people of color emerged as a cohesive and prosperous free black class during the eighteenth century. Inspired by the ideals of the American and French Revolutions, they nurtured their republican militancy in literary works and spiritualist séances. In the secession crisis of 1861, they offered their services to the Confederate army under threat of violence, expulsion, and confiscation. When Confederate forces withdrew from New Orleans in April 1862, free black leaders placed their troops at the disposal of the Union commander, General Benjamin F. Butler, and moved quickly to advance their political agenda.[7]

In September 1862, Afro-Creole leaders boldly announced their objectives in their newly created French-language newspaper, *L'Union*, the *Tribune*'s immediate predecessor. In the biweekly's premier issue, *L'Union*'s founders, Dr. Louis Charles Roudanez, his brother Jean-Baptiste Roudanez, and Paul Trévigne, condemned slavery and blasted the Confederacy. Rallying their readers to the Federal cause, they assured the free black community that the North's victory would usher in an era of reform and set the nation's democratic system on a solid foundation. With the commencement of the new "millennium" before the end of the century, the country would be able to promote republicanism around the world so that "our brothers in every country can profit from this divine gift."[8]

Afro-Creole leaders centered at *L'Union* viewed the Civil War as far more than a struggle to preserve the Union. They perceived the crisis within the context of an ongoing age of democratic revolution, and they proposed, as had the insurgents in the French Caribbean, to strike a blow for freedom and equal citizenship.

Enslaved Louisianians responded just as dramatically to the city's capture by Union forces. Seeking sanctuary from slavery, thousands fled to New Orleans. Through the spring and summer of 1862, they streamed toward military outposts as the Federal army advanced into the plantation parishes of south Louisiana. To their dismay, however, General Butler moved just as rapidly to maintain the region's plantation economy. After occupying the city in May, Butler, commander of the Department of the Gulf, acted to appease Unionist planters with the announcement that "all rights of property of whatever kind, will be held inviolate, subject only to the laws of the United States." Within the month, Butler directed the military to turn away fugitive slaves who could not be employed by Federal forces, "leaving them subject to the ordinary laws of the community." But runaways fought reenslavement, and violence erupted when they attempted to force their way into occupied New Orleans and Union outposts.[9]

During the early fall, the Preliminary Emancipation Proclamation and the advance of Union troops touched off renewed flight from

Confederate Louisiana. The surge of refugees and black resistance to slave labor forced Butler to devise a new strategy for sustaining the plantation system. General Orders, No. 91, issued in November, authorized the seizure of Confederate-owned plantations and introduced a slave-wage system. The program involved a contractual agreement whereby laborers worked for wages while planters secured a reliable and disciplined workforce. The contract required slaves to continue to work on the plantations of loyal masters or on confiscated plantations leased to northern investors in return for food, medical care, and a fixed minimal wage. Though prohibiting corporal punishment, the new labor code enforced strict controls denying rations to the unemployed and requiring written passes of workers who left plantations. It also sanctioned planter-dominated slave patrols with army provost marshals authorized to mediate disputes and discipline transgressors. This contract labor system—one that incorporated the recommendations of planters themselves—formed the basis for policies employed by the commanding officer, General Nathaniel P. Banks, who replaced Butler in mid-December 1862. Louisiana's halting transition to a free-labor system, first implemented in wartime Plaquemines, St. Bernard, and Lafourche Parishes, established the legal framework for the restructuring of the plantation regimen throughout much of the South.[10]

General Banks moved even more energetically than had Butler to accommodate planters. On January 30, 1863, on the heels of the Emancipation Proclamation, Banks issued modifications in his predecessor's labor system that lowered worker's wages, sanctioned increased autonomy for planter security forces, and virtually halted the seizure of plantations. Further, the regulations embodied in Banks's General Orders, No.12, threatened workers who left their place of employment with arrest on the charge of vagrancy. The new rules concluded with the stern warning that "all negroes not otherwise employed will be required to labor upon the public works, and no person capable of labor will be supported at the public expense." Finally, in the spring of 1863, the general designated an agency, the Bureau of Negro Labor (forerunner of the Louisiana division of the Freedmen's Bureau), to implement his policies. But as Banks moved to reconstitute the region's planter-dominated agricultural system and thereby win the loyalty of southern whites, he encountered intense criticism.[11]

Earlier in January, just as Banks was preparing to issue General Orders, No. 12, the Massachusetts Emancipation League, an association of some of the nation's leading abolitionists, had forwarded a petition to Congress that requested the creation of a federal bureau to assist and protect the freedmen. Anticipating slavery's destruction, abolitionists had begun urging the formation of a bureau of emancipation during the opening months of the war. Within weeks of the Emancipation Proclamation, the League presented its petition to the Senate. During the ensuing two-year debate over the creation of such an agency, congressional Radical Republicans argued that the newly liberated slaves would remain subject to the wills of their former masters without the economic security of land ownership. They insisted on the redistribution of confiscated lands to displaced black workers through the offices of the proposed government agency. The disposition of confiscated land proved to be one of the major obstacles to the establishment of an office of Federal assistance.[12]

In January, when the abolitionists accelerated their campaign to assist black southerners in their struggle for freedom and self-sufficiency, they pointed to Banks's Louisiana labor system as one of the major justifications for a federal bureau of emancipation. The general's contract-regulated policies, critics charged, left the planter-laborer relationship intact. They denounced Banks's General Orders, No. 12 as an "execrable proclamation" and labeled the general a "born slave-driver" who was intent upon "re-enslaving" the freedmen.

In February 1864, *New York Tribune* editorialist Sydney Gay compared Banks's system to serfdom: "The negro bound to the soil for a year, compelled to work for wages two-thirds less than he could command in open market, not permitted . . . to have a voice in the contract by which he becomes bound, exposed to the tyrannous caprices of lifelong slaveholders. . . . Such is the serfage which predominates on the soil of Louisiana." Gay's angry attack struck a resonant chord in Creole New Orleans.[13]

At first, Afro-Creole radicals had accepted the tight controls on plantation workers as a temporary necessity. In the spring of 1863 in *L'Union*, they even applauded Banks's "wise and equitable plan" as a means of restoring order and preparing the way for a free-labor system. Regarding vagrancy policy, they urged the avoidance of "cruel regulations" and looked forward to the day when freedmen would "become proprietors themselves." At the same time, *L'Union* radicals called for federal protection and assistance for the emancipated slaves. And, in agreement with abolitionist and congressional radicals in the North, they viewed land ownership as an essential prerequisite to freedom. They insisted on a government policy of land distribution. In February 1863, when reports of wartime atrocities accompanied news of land speculation, *L'Union* demanded action of the president and Congress.[14]

In January, Confederates had responded to the Emancipation Proclamation's authorization of black enlistments with threats that black soldiers would not be allowed to surrender. By the end of February, news reports of Confederate atrocities circulated in the press. One such dispatch related how fifteen black soldiers captured on board Federal transport vessels on the Cumberland River had been flogged, tied to trees, and starved to death.

Infuriated by the executions, one of *L'Union*'s editorial writers lashed out at the president in an essay titled "The Negroes and Their Liberators." "We predicted," he wrote, "that if Lincoln's proclamation was not accompanied by appropriate measures to assure the freed slaves of effective protection, it would have the most disastrous consequences." Lincoln was no less guilty of inhumanity to the former slaves than "les cannibales du Sud" for the commander in chief, "after having declared them free men, after having accepted their services, repays their good will by abandoning them, without saying a word, to their oppressors." The crisis required a presidential decree ordering the execution of two Confederates for every black Union soldier killed after capture.[15]

Partisans of "the rights of man," the writer continued, should consider it equally urgent to protect the freedmen from "enemies no less dangerous" than the Confederates. The editorial pointed to events in occupied South Carolina where Congress had authorized the auctioning of large parcels of land seized for nonpayment of taxes. In Beaufort, South Carolina, speculators stood ready, *L'Union*'s editorialist reported, to buy up large parcels of land, thereby creating "a new slaveholding aristocracy" because the freedmen who occupied the land were attached "body and soul to their native soil." The "one who becomes the proprietor of this soil holds them [the freedmen] in his power" unless, as abolitionists proposed, the government granted a plot of at least ten acres to each black family.

Because "blacks declared free by the January 1 proclamation all run more or less the same risk as those of Beaufort," Congress's most pressing duty, the editorialist concluded, must be "the fate of the millions of human beings who have been emancipated without being able to exercise their freedom and without having been assured of effective protection." In wartime Louisiana, security concerns, as well as increasing frustration over labor controls and land management, would elicit countless such appeals from the Afro-Creole press.[16]

Throughout 1863, black Creole radicals accepted General Banks's labor system as a military necessity. By the fall of 1864, however, the suppression of personal liberties, the exploitive nature of the labor regulations, and the realization that strict worker controls were not temporary convinced Afro-Creoles centered at *L'Union*'s successor, the *Tribune*, to reject the repressive system. With the lapse of the yearly contracts in December, the *Tribune* cautioned black workers against entering into new labor agreements. Banks's "bastard regime" paid freedmen "scarcely enough to put an extra pair of boots on their feet." Comparing the general's contract system with the labor regime on an antebellum plantation, the paper found that if "we except the lash . . . one is unable to perceive any material difference between the two sets of regulations." The editorial continued: "The free laborer, as well as the slave, has to retire into his cabin at a fixed hour in the evening; he cannot leave on Sunday, even to visit friends or simply to take a walk in the neighborhood, unless he be provided with a written authorization; he cannot listen to any preacher or hear divine service from any minister but those chosen by his master." Ministers who were unwilling "to proclaim slavery a blessing and a divine institution" were turned away. A white man, the paper concluded, "subjected to such restrictive and humiliating prohibitions, will certainly call himself a slave."[17]

As early as 1862, the Afro-Creole press had begun advocating the settlement of freedmen, white Unionist refugees, and Federal veterans on confiscated lands as a step toward "loyalizing" the South. Together with the division of plantations into self-sustaining freehold farms, the South's reconstruction required the freedmen's enfranchisement. Because federal military occupation ran contrary to the spirit of republican government, the South's rebel element, the *Tribune* insisted, must be counterbalanced by a loyal, landholding electorate protected by well-trained, well-armed Unionist militias. The "total failure" of Banks's labor policy and the general's sabotage in 1864 of an interracial Unionist coalition advocating black suffrage convinced French-speaking black leaders to move forward with their own plan of Reconstruction—a plan in which economic empowerment accompanied political equality.[18]

On February 27, 1865, the *Tribune* announced the formation of the New Orleans Freedmen's Aid Association. Determined to make emancipation a reality for black Louisianians, the members of the interracial benevolent organization proposed to buy land from the government and lease it to voluntary associations of farm workers. The former slaves, the *Tribune* insisted, "are entitled by a paramount right to the possession of the soil they have so long cultivated. . . . If the Government will not give them the land, let it be rented to them."[19]

In the association's cooperative economic model, the freedmen would generate the necessary capital by purchasing inexpensive shares in self-help banks that would, in turn, use the capital to make land, rations, and farming supplies available to workers. In the self-sustaining labor colonies, workers would enjoy freedom of movement, self-government, and wages, as well as a share of the crop. In the consequent reorganization of the plantation system, workers would take control of their own labor and thereby undermine planter domination.

European *associations d'ouvriers* funded by *banques du peuple* undoubtedly served as the model for the Louisiana experiment. The *Tribune* carried glowing reports of the spread of such communes throughout Europe, and two of the association's French-speaking white directors, New Orleanian Thomas Jefferson Durant and Belgian emigré Jean-Charles Houzeau, one of the *Tribune*'s editors, had belonged to Fourierist societies before the war. Indeed, French socialist Charles Fourier's communal ideal permeated the thinking and literary art of the city's interracial community of Francophone radicals.[20]

By August, the association had rented several plantations in a scaled-down version of its initial plan and launched a movement to apply the cooperative model to factory production in New Orleans.

From the beginning, however, a shortage of financial resources limited the organization's activities. After the war, moreover, the return of plantations to their former owners brought an effective end to the association's work.[21]

In the midst of its drive for economic democratization, the *Tribune* offered a cautious endorsement to a new federal agency designed, like the Freedmen's Aid Association, to assist the newly liberated slaves in the transition from slavery to freedom. Both Houses of Congress had finally passed the abolitionist-inspired bill calling for a federal aid agency. On March 3, 1865, President Lincoln signed the legislation creating the Bureau of Refugees, Freedmen, and Abandoned Lands. The new agency was to operate under the auspices of the War Department for one year following the end of hostilities.[22]

The act establishing the Bureau made newly appointed Commissioner Oliver Otis Howard responsible for the "supervision and management of all abandoned lands, and the control of all subjects relating to refugees and freedmen." More specifically, it directed the commissioner to distribute food, clothing, and other life-sustaining necessities and to assign every male freedman and white refugee a tract of confiscated land of up to forty acres. The former bondsmen and displaced whites could rent the tracts for three years on favorable terms with an option to purchase the land within the three-year period. Astonishingly, Congress appropriated no budget for the Bureau; hence, funds collected from land rents sustained the new federal agency. In essence, the freedmen's labor funded assistance to the destitute during the first year of Bureau operation.[23]

In May 1865, Howard designated Thomas W. Conway as his assistant commissioner of the Freedmen's Bureau in Louisiana. At the time of his appointment, Conway, an Irish immigrant and Protestant chaplain, headed the military's Louisiana Bureau of Free Labor. In 1864, under pressure from his abolitionist and Radical Republican detractors in the North, Banks had assigned Conway the task of reforming his troubled labor program. After taking control of the Bureau of Negro Labor in August 1864, Conway renamed the agency the Bureau of Free Labor, halted the arbitrary arrest of black Louisianians, collected back wages owed plantation workers, and assisted the destitute. Still, Conway remained a steadfast defender of Banks's policies and fitted his reforms within the framework of the general's compulsory labor system. Throughout the war, the maintenance of a stable workforce for Louisiana planters remained the military's top priority, and neither Conway nor Banks countenanced the leasing or sale of confiscated lands to aspiring black farmers.[24]

As part of his campaign to vindicate Banks's labor system and improve the general's image, Conway also had conspired against Banks's most persistent Louisiana critic, the Afro-Creole press. During the summer of 1864, Conway cut off the subsidy that *L'Union* received for printing the army's public notices and, after the demise of *L'Union*, conspired to have the military suppress the *Tribune*. In 1865, when his efforts to muzzle the Creole newspaper failed, Conway helped to found a pro-federal rival to the *Tribune*, the *Black Republican*, a short-lived weekly publication. The *Tribune* had good reason for skepticism when Howard named Conway to head the Freedmen's Bureau for Louisiana and transferred the Bureau of Free Labor to the new federal agency in June 1865.

At the outset, however, the new assistant commissioner's attempts to broaden the scope of his work offered some grounds for hope, and the newspaper offered a tentative endorsement: "For the moment, we content ourselves with giving our cordial approval to General Howard's policies. The manner in which Monsieur Conway applies them in Louisiana is energetic and bold. But the future will depend on the extent to which these measures are carried out, that is to say on the zeal and support of the military." Though perhaps encouraged by Conway's Bureau policies in the summer of 1865, Afro-Creole leaders could take little comfort from events in Washington.[25]

With Lincoln's assassination in April 1865, Johnson assumed the presidency with an entirely new set of political objectives. Determined to enhance his prospects for victory in the 1868 presidential election, the chief executive entered into secret negotiations with northern Democratic leaders and moved to reconstitute the southern wing of his old party by restoring the planter elite to political and economic dominance. In this scenario, the Freedmen's Bureau became an instrument of Johnson's electoral ambitions.

In his Amnesty Proclamation of May 29, 1865, the new president offered full pardons with restoration of confiscated lands to all former Confederates who would take an oath of allegiance to the national government. By the fall, Johnson had pardoned all but a handful of ex-Confederates. Confiscated lands slated for agrarian reform—lands used to fund the Freedmen's Bureau—were returned to their former owners. Finally, the president directed Bureau officials to help planters round up freedmen to work on their restored estates. Agents supportive of the freedmen's interests were replaced with conservatives who were willing to carry out presidential directives. Johnson's strategy produced an overwhelming Democratic victory in the fall elections throughout the South.[26]

As the head of Bureau affairs in Louisiana, Conway anticipated Johnson's accommodationist strategy by carrying forward the army's wartime policy of maintaining a stable labor force for white planters. But, early in 1865, Conway finessed his way into an alliance with New Orleans radicals after meeting with Chief Justice of the Supreme Court Salmon P. Chase, a proponent of black suffrage. As a former secretary of the treasury, Chase had used his extensive powers of patronage to build up a following in Louisiana. On a two-month tour of the South to fortify his political machine, Chase encouraged Conway's changeover to the radical cause in a June meeting at New Orleans. Soon after assuming the office of assistant commissioner, Conway joined forces with the Treasury agents who headed Chase's state coalition and accelerated his reformist approach to freedmen's affairs.

During the summer of 1865, Conway protested the city government's brutal crackdown on vagrancy and expanded his activities to include the most controversial aspect of the Bureau's mandate, the leasing of the state's abandoned and confiscated lands. At the same time, Conway joined with some of his severest critics, the members of the *Tribune* faction, in the formation of the new political coalition, the Friends of Universal Suffrage. The assistant commissioner's actions ran directly counter to presidential policy.

With the Confederate surrender on April 9, unrepentant returning Confederates and conservative Unionists had seized control of the state's provisional government. Johnson readily approved the destruction of Banks's regime and stripped the general of his military command. The reactionary backlash forced Banks and his allies to side with the radicals. Following Conway's lead, they converted to the cause of black suffrage and merged with the Friends organization.[27]

Johnson's new Louisiana allies, Governor J. Madison Wells and New Orleans Mayor Hugh Kennedy, an ex-Confederate, now targeted the only federal official capable of blocking a complete conservative takeover, the head of the Freedmen's Bureau. In July, they sent President Johnson regular reports attacking Conway's political activities and labor policies. In one such communication, Wells characterized Conway as a "radical negro suffrage man" who thinks "the black better than the white man and is an active political speaker and agitator for negro suffrage and equality." In another, the governor criticized Conway for "allowing the negroes to go where they please and to work for whom they please." The effect of such a policy, Wells continued, "will be to utterly demoralize the negroes."[28] Angered by such reports, Johnson called Commissioner Howard on the carpet and demanded that Bureau officials cooperate in the return of all abandoned and confiscated lands to pardoned Confederates. On September 13, an acquiescent Howard recommended the Louisiana assistant commissioner's dismissal with the president himself appointing Conway's successor. The new appointee, General Absalom Baird, could not fill the post immediately, and one of Johnson's allies on Howard's Washington staff, General Joseph S. Fullerton, was dispatched to Louisiana to reverse Conway's policies.[29]

In reporting the assistant commissioner's removal, the *Tribune* applauded Conway for having remedied "many injustices and proceeded against some of the most glaring crimes." As the head of the Freedmen's Bureau, he had shown himself to be "among the most advanced men of Louisiana's radical party." Had he applied himself with the same determination, the paper observed, "when, under General Banks, he had the opportunity to lay the groundwork for the future, he would be the greatest man in the South today. If he had exerted himself from that time in order to obtain universal suffrage of which he was frightened up to the end, blacks would vote, Louisiana would be admitted into the Union at the opening of the next session of Congress, and Monsieur Conway would have been its first senator." Both Banks and Conway had been victims of their own shortcomings. At the end of October, in an editorial titled "Adieux à Monsieur Conway," the *Tribune* noted that in the assistant commissioner's defeat, the "Freedmen's Bureau falls with him." The editorial continued: "We understand that we have been abandoned to our own resources and that from now on we must fight from a position of political inequality."[30]

General Fullerton, in his month-long role as Louisiana's acting assistant commissioner, inaugurated a massive restoration of abandoned and confiscated lands. By the end of the year, most of the 62,528 acres of land that had been leased to black farmers by either the Freedmen's Bureau or the Treasury Department had been returned to the former owners. In addition, some of the pardoned planters sued the black lessees for rent and damages to their property.

In his eagerness to return confiscated properties to white voters, Fullerton seized federally supported black schools and orphanages and effectively destroyed the black school system. He furnished information to white newspapers that described the procedure whereby readers could apply for the services of the displaced children who were to be bound out in an apprenticeship program. His authorization of a strictly enforced vagrancy law sanctioned the arrest of all black New Orleanians who lacked written evidence of employment. The police then leased the services of the black detainees to planters willing to pay their fines. Fullerton's actions opened the way for passage of Louisiana's black code.[31]

By the time Commissioner Howard appeared in the city's Orleans Theatre on November 5 to urge reconciliation between the freedmen and their former masters and to announce the destruction of the Bureau's forty-acres program, Johnson's drive to guarantee white dominance in the state's internal affairs was nearly complete. Howard's message of compliance, coming on the heels of the president's restoration policies, helped to produce the desired result. The day after the commissioner's speech, Johnson's slate of candidates triumphed in statewide elections.[32]

Far from operating as an agent of social and economic change, the Louisiana Freedmen's Bureau had helped to sustain the prevailing system of black economic subservience. One of the major reasons for the Bureau's failed mission can be traced to policies developed by the Federal army of occupation. Nearly three years of compulsory yearly labor contracts, fixed minimal wages, and a repressive pass system prepared the way for failure. Though Afro-Creole and abolitionist efforts in behalf of the former slaves had culminated in the creation of the Freedmen's Aid Association and the Freedmen's Bureau, Banks's contract-labor system helped to undermine the struggle for meaningful change. Under Conway, the Bureau carried over

Banks's compulsory labor program in its efforts to maintain a stable labor force. Conway's reforms notwithstanding, his continued prosecution of labor contract violations as criminal offenses confirmed the Afro-Creole perception of the federal agency as the lineal descendant of Banks's Bureau of Free Labor.

By the fall of 1865, the Bureau had been transformed from a carrier of black aspirations into an agency of the president's political ambitions. Landless black workers in rural Louisiana would move little beyond the wartime experience of annual labor contracts and sharecropping arrangements despite the temporary civil and political gains of the Reconstruction era. Even in the matter of protecting black Louisianians from major acts of violence, the Freedmen's Bureau failed its mission.[33]

On July 30, 1866, as a large procession of black workers converged on a designated meeting hall in New Orleans to press for voting rights, a mass of white policemen and former Confederates attacked the workers and killed more than forty of them during the assault. Even though Assistant Commissioner Baird, the senior military officer in New Orleans, who had assumed command of the Louisiana Bureau in November 1865 and served until early September 1866, possessed advance knowledge of the planned police action, he refrained from summoning army troops until the bloody attack was over. "Let the Freedmen's Bureau go down" the *Tribune* demanded in the aftermath of the riot. For black Louisianians, the agency had ceased to govern except in the capacity of accommodating the forces of reaction and violence.[34]

With the onset of congressional Reconstruction, the Afro-Creole intelligentsia pressed ahead with demands for voting rights, proportional representation in political officeholding, equal access to public accommodations, and land reform. Their activism and republican idealism ensured that delegates to Louisiana's constitutional convention of 1867 would draft one of the Reconstruction South's most advanced blueprints for change. Pointing the way to social revolution, the newly drafted 1868 charter required state officials to recognize, by oath, the civil and political equality of all men. It alone among Reconstruction constitutions explicitly required equal treatment in places of public accommodation. And it forbade segregation in public schools. The chances for meaningful change dimmed, however, with the ascendancy of Republican moderates.[35]

Through a series of well-calculated maneuvers, Conway, Henry Clay Warmoth, and other Republican moderates undercut their radical opponents and seized control of the Louisiana Republican Party in 1867. When Warmoth secured the 1868 gubernatorial nomination, the *Tribune*-led radicals bolted. Certain that a Warmoth victory would undermine the cause of black civil and political equality, they put forward an independent Republican ticket.

Conway, a nominee for superintendent of education on the Warmoth ticket, retaliated against the *Tribune* when Warmoth won the election. He convinced the Republican government to withdraw its patronage from his longtime critic. Stripped of its subsidy, the newspaper suspended publication within two weeks of the election. Conway had finally succeeded in silencing the *Tribune*.

Just as the *Tribune* had predicted, Governor Warmoth stymied civil-rights legislation, resisted desegregation of the public schools, opposed enforcement of the constitution's equal accommodations provision, appointed white Democrats to political office, and accumulated a personal fortune by exacting tribute from railroad companies. The "reign of knaves and adventurers," Afro-Creole writer Rodolphe Lucien Desdunes observed, "was of short duration." Besieged by charges of corruption, the regime's downfall began in mid-1870.[36]

Arguing for land distribution in the fall of 1864, the *Tribune* had envisioned "both banks of the Mississippi River peopled by . . . well-armed and well-drilled cultivators, from the Gulf of Mexico to Cairo [Illinois]; men of unquestioned and unquestionable loyalty to the 'old flag.' " The newspaper's Afro-Creole writers and supporters believed that black freedom hinged on political equality, physical security, and economic independence—an independence anchored in land ownership. Even after their purported allies in the Freedmen's Bureau and the Republican party derailed their efforts for meaningful change, they pressed ahead.[37]

In the 1872 governor's race, French-speaking black activists put forward the radical Afro-Creole philanthropist Aristide Mary as their gubernatorial candidate. When his bid for the Republican nomination failed, they joined the Louisiana Unification Movement, a bipartisan political coalition organized by the city's white business elite. In return for their support, Afro-Creole leaders exacted promises from the white Unifiers to guarantee black civil and political rights and to consider the breakup of large landholdings into small farms, so that "our colored citizens and white emigrants may become practical farmers and cultivators of the soil." The coalition crumbled in the face of a white supremacist resurgence in the state's rural districts.[38]

As Reconstruction's promise of freedom, opportunity, and equal citizenship descended into a nightmare of semiservitude, Jim Crow laws, and disfranchisement, Afro-Creole leaders refused to succumb. Insisting that "Revolutions never go backward," they linked the Civil War struggle to an ongoing age of democratic revolution and identified their egalitarian objectives with the highest ideals of the revolutionary age. Their tradition of protest offered a powerful vision for the future.[39]

NOTES

1. *New Orleans Times*, Nov. 7, 1865; *New Orleans Tribune*, Oct. 28, Nov. 6, 1865. In this study, the terms *free people of color*, *black Creole*, *Afro-Creole*, and *Creole of color* refer to native-born, French-speaking Louisianians of African descent.

2. *New Orleans Tribune*, Nov. 6, 1865; *Proceedings of the Convention of the Republican Party of Louisiana* (New Orleans: Office of the *New Orleans Tribune*, 1865), 1–18 (hereinafter cited as PCRPL); Caryn Cossé Bell, *Revolution, Romanticism, and the Afro-Creole Protest Tradition in Louisiana, 1718–1868* (Baton Rouge: Louisiana State University Press, 1997), 255–7.

3. William S. McFeely, *Yankee Stepfather: General O. O. Howard and the Freedmen* (New Haven: Yale University Press, 1968), 136–7, 180–1; Lawrence N. Powell, *New Masters: Northern Planters during the Civil War and Reconstruction* (New Haven: Yale University Press, 1980), 84–5; *New Orleans Times*, Nov. 11, 1865.

4. Charles J. Dalloz [pseudonym of Jean-Charles Houzeau] to O. O. Howard, July 24, 1865, Oliver Otis Howard Papers, Bowdoin College, Brunswick, Maine; PCRPL, iv; *New Orleans Tribune*, Nov. 6, 1865; Bell, *Revolution, Romanticism, and Afro-Creole Protest Tradition*, 252.

5. *L'Union*, Sept. 27, Oct. 18, 1862. In the great tradition of black protest, African Americans proclaimed their integral role in the national experience and insisted on equality with white citizens. See Vincent Harding, *There Is a River: The Black Struggle for Freedom in America* (New York: Harcourt Brace & Company, 1981), 117–9, 172–4, 255–7; Eric Foner, *Reconstruction:*

America's Unfinished Revolution, 1863–1877 (New York: Harper & Row 1988), 26–7.

6. McFeely, *Yankee Stepfather*, 1–8; Powell, *New Masters*, 84–5.

7. Relying on pro-Confederate newspaper reports, some historians have portrayed Afro-Creole men-at-arms as self-serving elitists who sided with the Confederates and switched their allegiance to the Union with the Federal occupation of the city. This view overlooks the origins of black Creole dissent and ignores a large body of firsthand testimony. For further discussion of this issue, see Bell, *Revolution, Romanticism, and Afro-Creole Protest Tradition*, 229–32.

8. In July 1864, the Roudanez brothers and their associates reorganized *L'Union* and renamed the paper the *Tribune*; *L'Union*, Sept. 27, Dec. 6, 1862. All translations are my own.

9. Approximately one-third of Louisiana fell to Federal forces with the occupation of New Orleans. The thousands of slaves who fled to the city constituted a fraction of a statewide population in 1860 of 331,726 slaves, 18,647 free blacks, and 357,629 whites. At the same time, the city of New Orleans contained 14,484 slaves, 10,939 free blacks, and 144,601 whites. The Department of the Gulf included Mississippi, Florida, and Alabama, as well as Louisiana. For a discussion of the Federal occupation's impact and population figures, see Howard A. White, *The Freedmen's Bureau in Louisiana* (Baton Rouge: Louisiana State University Press, 1970), 5–7. See also Bell, *Revolution, Romanticism, and Afro-Creole Protest Tradition*, 78; for quotations, see C. Peter Ripley, *Slaves and Freedmen in Civil War Louisiana* (Baton Rouge: Louisiana State University Press, 1976), 25, 27.

10. Ripley, *Slaves and Freedmen*, 36–46; Foner, *Reconstruction*, 54–5; Powell, *New Masters*, 84; W. E. B. Du Bois, *Black Reconstruction in America, 1860–1880* (1935; reprint, New York: Atheneum, 1975), 68–9.

11. Ripley, *Slaves and Freedmen*, 48–9; Peyton McCrary, *Abraham Lincoln and Reconstruction: The Louisiana Experiment* (Princeton: Princeton University Press, 1978), 108, 118–21, 135; White, *Freedmen's Bureau in Louisiana*, 103; for quotation, see McCrary, *Abraham Lincoln*, 118.

12. James M. McPherson, *The Struggle for Equality: Abolitionists and the Negro in the Civil War and Reconstruction*, 2nd ed. (Princeton: Princeton University Press, 1995), 75–6, 178–9; Claude F. Oubre, *Forty Acres and a Mule: The Freedmen's Bureau and Black Landownership* (Baton Rouge: Louisiana State University Press, 1978), 1–2, 20–1.

13. For quotations, see McPherson, *Struggle for Equality*, 290; George R. Bentley, *A History of the Freedmen's Bureau* (Philadelphia: University of Pennsylvania Press, 1955), 23–4 (quotation on 23).

14. *L'Union*, Jan. 6, Feb. 28, April 7, 1863; see also *New Orleans Tribune*, Aug. 31, 1865.

15. *L'Union*, Feb. 28, 1863. Lincoln refrained from taking retaliatory action until after May 1, 1863, when the Confederate Congress authorized the reenslavement or execution of captured black soldiers and their officers. Three months later, on July 30, 1863, Lincoln ordered that one Confederate soldier be executed for every Union captive killed in violation of the rules of war. Fear of setting off a spiraling cycle of vicious retaliation, however, prevented the Union government from acting on the president's recommendation. See James M. McPherson, *The Negro's Civil War: How American Negroes Felt and Acted during the War for the Union* (Urbana: University of Illinois Press, 1982), 174, 332 n. 7; and James M. McPherson, *Battle Cry of Freedom: The Civil War Era* (New York: Oxford University Press, 1988), 792–6.

16. *L'Union*, Feb. 28, 1863. Drawn by cotton cultivation's fabulous profitability, army officers, government officials, northern speculators, and cotton companies would ultimately snatch up over one-half of plantation land. Almost immediately, however, speculators would get hold of most of the land bought by military personnel (see Powell, *New Masters*, 4, 35; Foner, *Reconstruction*, 24–5).

17. Ripley, *Slaves and Freedmen*, 52–8, 73, 90–3; Louis S. Gerteis, *From Contraband to Freedman: Federal Policy toward Southern Blacks, 1861–1865* (Westport, Conn.: Greenwood Press, 1973), 102–3; quotations from *New Orleans Tribune*, Dec. 8, 1864, Aug. 13, 1865.

18. *New Orleans Tribune*, Aug. 13, Sept. 10, 24, 1864; Aug. 31, 1865; Bell, *Revolution, Romanticism, and Afro-Creole Protest Tradition*, 246–50; Joseph Logsdon and Caryn Cossé Bell, "The Americanization of Black New Orleans, 1850–1900," in Arnold R. Hirsch and Joseph Logsdon, eds., *Creole New Orleans: Race and Americanization* (Baton Rouge: Louisiana State University Press, 1992), 221–4.

19. *New Orleans Tribune*, Sept. 10, 1864.

20. Ibid., Feb. 24, Apr. 15, May 5, 1865; Bell, *Revolution, Romanticism and Afro-Creole Protest Tradition*, chaps. 4–6; for insight into Durant's radicalism, see Joseph G. Tregle, Jr., "Thomas J. Durant, Utopian Socialism, and the Failure of Presidential Reconstruction in Louisiana," *Journal of Southern History* 45 (Nov. 1979): 485–512; for Houzeau's association with Afro-Creole radicals, see Jean-Charles Houzeau, *My Passage at the New Orleans "Tribune": A Memoir of the Civil War Era*, ed. by David C. Rankin and trans. by Gerard F. Denault (Baton Rouge: Louisiana State University Press, 1984).

21. John W. Blassingame, *Black New Orleans, 1860–1880* (Chicago: University of Chicago Press, 1973), 57–9; Gilles Vandal, "Black Utopia in Early Reconstruction New Orleans: The People's Bakery as a Case-Study," *Louisiana History* 38 (fall 1997): 442–7; William F. Messner, *Freedmen and the Ideology of Free Labor: Louisiana, 1862–1865* (Lafayette: Center for Louisiana Studies, University of Southwestern Louisiana, 1978), 109–11.

22. McPherson, *Struggle for Equality*, chap. 8; White, *Freedmen's Bureau in Louisiana*, 8.

23. Bentley, *History of Freedmen's Bureau*, 49–52 (quotation on 49); Mc-Crary, *Abraham Lincoln*, 303; Oubre, *Forty Acres and a Mule*, xiii-xv; Foner, *Reconstruction*, 69.

24. Bentley, *History of Freedmen's Bureau*, 56–7; McFeely, *Yankee Stepfather*, 72; Messner, *Freedmen and Ideology of Free Labor*, 66–8.

25. Logsdon and Bell, "Americanization of Black New Orleans," 228–9; Ted Tunnell, *Crucible of Reconstruction: War, Radicalism and Race in Louisiana, 1862–1877* (Baton Rouge: Louisiana State University Press, 1984), 84–5; Messner, *Freedmen and Ideology of Free Labor*, 67 n. 43, 109 n. 104; White, *Freedmen's Bureau in Louisiana*, 19; *New Orleans Tribune*, July 20, 1865. To add to Afro-Creole concerns, in a letter published in the *Tribune*, Dec. 2, 1864, Conway angered the black community with the statement that there "is a great country beyond the sea, where Livingstone traveled, which must ultimately be reached by the children and grandchildren of those whose chains we are now breaking."

26. McCrary, *Abraham Lincoln*, 11–13, 308, 354–5; Powell, *New Masters*, 84–5; Bentley, *History of Freedmen's Bureau*, 70–1; Foner, *Reconstruction*, 47, 74, 178.

27. McCrary, *Abraham Lincoln*, 311–5, 320–2, 330–1; Bentley, *History of Freedmen's Bureau*, 56–8; McFeely, *Yankee Stepfather*, 170; Bell, *Revolution, Romanticism, and Afro-Creole Protest Tradition*, 255–8.

28. McCrary, *Abraham Lincoln*, 322. Quotations from Bentley, *History of Freedmen's Bureau*, 70, and McFeely, *Yankee Stepfather*, 172.

29. McCrary, *Abraham Lincoln*, 329–30; Bentley, *History of Freedmen's Bureau*, 70–1.

30. *New Orleans Tribune*, Oct. 5, 28, 1865.

31. Ripley, *Slaves and Freedmen*, 189–90; McFeely, *Yankee Stepfather*, 178–9; Messner, *Freedmen and Ideology of Free Labor*, 185 n. 7; Foner, *Reconstruction*, 157.

32. Foner, *Reconstruction*, 199; McCrary, *Abraham Lincoln*, 338.

33. Ripley, *Slaves and Freedmen*, 181, 187–98; Messner, *Freedmen and Ideology of Free Labor*, 184–5; McFeely, *Yankee Stepfather*, 273, 288.

34. Bell, *Revolution, Romanticism, and Afro-Creole Protest Tradition*, 261–2; McFeely, *Yankee Stepfather*, 283–5, 287 (quotation), 295. Despite its increasing obsolescence, the federal agency would survive until 1872, though most of its work would end on Dec. 31, 1868 (McFeely, *Yankee Stepfather*, 327–8).

35. Foner, *Reconstruction*, 319–22; Tunnell, *Crucible of Reconstruction*, chap. 6; Charles M. Vincent, "Black Constitution Makers: The Constitution of 1868," in Warren M. Billings and Edward F. Haas, eds., *In Search of Fundamental Law: Louisiana's Constitutions, 1812–1974* (Lafayette: The Center for Louisiana Studies, University of Southwestern Louisiana, 1993), 69–80.

36. Bell, *Revolution, Romanticism, and Afro-Creole Protest Tradition*, 270–7; for quotation, see Rodolphe Lucien Desdunes, *Our People and Our History*, trans. and ed. by Sister Dorothea Olga McCants (Baton Rouge: Louisiana State University Press, 1973), 135.

37. *New Orleans Tribune*, Sept. 10, 1864.

38. Bell, *Revolution, Romanticism, and Afro-Creole Protest Tradition*, 277–9 (quotation on 278).

39. Harding, *There Is a River*, 256–7; *New Orleans Tribune*, Sept. 10, 1864.

8

"Because They Are Women": Gender and the Virginia Freedmen's Bureau's "War on Dependency"

Mary J. Farmer

"THERE IS STILL a complaint that the freedmen exercise no control over their families," a somewhat perplexed Edwin Lyon, agent of the Freedmen's Bureau in Charlotte County, Virginia, reported to his superiors in May 1866. More than a year after the Civil War had ended, freedmen in his district were "allowing their children to follow their own inclinations" and, even more disappointing to him, some were "encouraging their wives to idleness." But perhaps what frustrated this agent more was that despite the growing inclination among most freedmen "to put their wives and grown daughters to work," freedwomen were "determined on resisting the authority of their liege lords."[1] This agent's frustrations underscore the importance that both the Freedmen's Bureau and its conceptions of gender played in defining the meaning of freedom for more than four million former slaves in the immediate aftermath of the Civil War. As part of their principal task, Bureau agents throughout the South were instructed to teach the freedpeople to be "a self-supporting class of free laborers" who understood the necessity of steady employment. Still, and as a component of this task, the Bureau also considered it crucial to teach freedmen to be responsible husbands and fathers who provided for their families and, similarly, freedwomen to be good wives and mothers.[2]

Despite the voluminous scholarship on the Freedmen's Bureau, remarkably little has been written about the role that gender played in the federal agency's efforts throughout the South; neglected as well in this scholarship has been the relationship between black women and the Bureau. Like other areas of historical inquiry, the history of the Freedmen's Bureau has taken on a gender-neutral undertone.[3] Consequently, scholars have often failed to see the historical significance of the Bureau in terms of its relationships with freedmen, freedwomen, and thus, to some extent, even the black community as a whole. Emancipation dramatically altered the legal and economic standing of blacks and transformed families and gender roles within the African-American community. Bureau policies impinged on these matters in a variety of important ways. Moreover, whatever the motives of the Bureau and its official policies, black women, as well as black men, responded to and used the Bureau to pursue their own objectives. As a result, and often despite the letter of the Bureau's own gender-neutral policies, Bureau agents were forced to apply and reshape their policies to freedmen and freedwomen accordingly. Scholars of the Freedmen's Bureau, then, must recognize, just as Bureau officials came to understand themselves, that the Freedmen's Bureau was a federal agency that dealt not only with freedpeople but with *freedmen* and *freedwomen*.

Perhaps nowhere was it more apparent that the Freedmen's Bureau was dealing with both freedmen and freedwomen than in the Bureau's "war on dependency." Getting freedpeople to work, irrespective of gender,[4] and often of age, so that they would not be dependent on the federal government for support was one of the Bureau's greatest concerns. Yet, in the Civil War's immediate aftermath, the devastation, dislocation, and destitution produced by the war made survival especially difficult. The signs of war blanketed the South: destroyed bridges, barns, and fences cluttered the landscape; crops no longer flourished in the fields; livestock was sparse; poverty was widespread; and blacks lined the roadsides in search of labor and lost family members. By spring 1865, many former slaves had left the plantations. They poured into Union-occupied areas, they collected in cities and camps near army posts, and an "unending stream" of freedpeople "without any visible means of support" seemed to flow throughout the countryside. Given this perceived state of upheaval, government officials believed that they had little choice but to make federal relief available to the former slaves. Basic humanity, as well as the devastation, dislocation, and destitution throughout the South, dictated that the federal government feed the hungry and care for the weak.[5]

Possessing the conviction that freedom required self-sufficiency, however, officials in both the Union Army and the Freedmen's Bureau did not want to create a permanent class of black indigents dependent on the government for survival. Thus, the army and the Bureau created policies aimed at preventing starvation among the former slaves while also inculcating the importance of labor, self-reliance, and independence, and at providing relief only to the "deserving" poor, while compelling others to enter the labor market. In developing and implementing such policies aimed at ending dependency and destitution in 1865 and 1866, the Freedmen's Bureau proved powerfully, if not consciously, influenced by gender. In its "war on dependency," the Bureau created policies that were, on their face, gender neutral: they denied relief to all "able-bodied" freedpersons and compelled those who could not find employment to move to areas where work was more plentiful. But, in practice, Bureau officials assumed that supporting black women was far more acceptable than supporting black men. Consequently, the letter of Bureau policy applied with few exceptions to able-bodied freedmen, who were compelled to find employment or face prosecution as vagrants. Invariably, however, the same did not hold true for similarly situated freedwomen. Bureau officials generally regarded able-bodied freedwomen who could not find labor as "dependents on the government," rather than vagrants, and provided them with government relief.[6]

This application of Bureau policy proved particularly true for freedpeople in Virginia, where the devastation, dislocation, and destitution caused by the war had combined with the state's historically large black population to create an especially large postwar population of needy, unemployed freedpeople dependent on the federal government for support. The destruction and loss of property in Virginia, where the principal fighting in the Civil War's eastern theater occurred, greatly surpassed that of other Confederate states. Moreover, this devastation was further intensified by the thousands of black refugees who fled into the state, both during and after the Civil War. "No other State, perhaps, was so unsettled by the war as the State of Virginia," Major General Oliver Otis Howard, commissioner of the Freedmen's Bureau, later reported to Congress. "The immediate theatre of active operations," he recounted, it "became in part a tract of deserted and broken up farms, and in part an asylum for the thousands of refugees that flocked within our lines from almost every section of the south."[7] In areas of the state occupied by Union troops, such as the James River peninsula, in particular, the already large black population more than doubled by war's end.[8] In these areas, the army placed many refugees in what became known as "contraband camps" or "government farms."[9] Although some of them would eventually return to their former homes, many refugees chose to make new homes in these communities. Unlike other southern states in the immediate aftermath of the Civil War, then, the condition in which the war left Virginia made the Bureau's task there particularly acute, as well as immediate. It also provides an excellent opportunity for a case study of the role gender played in shaping Bureau relief policy.[10]

The Virginia Freedmen's Bureau began operation in June 1865 with the appointment of Colonel Orlando Brown as assistant commissioner for the state. Having served as general superintendent of Negro affairs in the Union-occupied counties in and surrounding Norfolk since 1863, Brown brought invaluable experience to his position, particularly in dealing with refugees and with the destitute. As superintendent of Negro affairs, he had been expected to provide former slaves with food, shelter, and, perhaps more importantly, employment. But because military recruiters quickly claimed the healthy able-bodied black men as soldiers or laborers for the military, most of Brown's experience was the result of dealing more directly with the neediest of the ever-growing black refugee population: women, children, the elderly, and the infirm. By attempting to provide relief and employment to these former slaves, Brown began to assert the federal government's responsibility for the welfare of African Americans who were perceived as unable to care for themselves, whether only temporarily or perhaps more permanently.[11]

In his new role as assistant commissioner of the Freedmen's Bureau in Virginia, Brown set up headquarters in Richmond. For administrative purposes, he divided the state into ten districts and placed a superintendent in charge of each. These officers, in turn, directed the activities of local agents. Charged with the broad duty of "establishing peace and securing prosperity" by protecting "the negroes in their rights as free men," local agents were instructed to foster "friendly relations between the two races, to assist in organizing and maintaining schools, to discourage freedmen from wandering too widely, . . . to furnish rations, medicines, and doctors to destitute freedmen, and to adjudicate Negroes' cases or refer them to the proper military authorities." Brown also instructed these local agents in what he saw as perhaps the Bureau's most significant task: integrating blacks into the labor system as free laborers. "[I]n their present state of helplessness," he explained, see that the freedpeople "are not oppressed or injured by their former masters." In particular, Brown emphasized the need to help the former slaves find work and to urge them to enter and keep contracts, as well as to advise them on contracts and prevent them from being defrauded. Of utmost importance was explaining to blacks "the relations that exist between their labor and capital, and how each is dependent on the other." Blacks who were unwilling to labor, according to the letter of Bureau policy, were to be treated as vagrants who, "if after being admonished . . . do not provide themselves with honest labor," were to be turned "over to work under some military guard without payment until they are ready to work for themselves." Assistant Commissioner Brown understood the importance of employment. It was the foundation to all of the Bureau's tasks; if blacks possessed employment, at least in theory, they could become self-reliant, independent men and women who would support themselves and their families.[12]

Perhaps most pressing among its duties, at least during the early months of the Bureau's existence in Virginia, was providing relief rations of food and clothing, medicines, and medical care to the indigent and destitute freedpeople throughout the state. Although northern benevolent associations and freedmen's aid societies assisted the former slaves, federal law had placed the responsibility for destitution among the freedpeople throughout the South with the Freedmen's Bureau.[13] Bureau efforts to relieve such destitution were circumscribed from the start. Shaping its response to destitution were both the Bureau's lack of substantial financial resources[14] and collective fears that even the most temporary of charity could do more harm than good. Like contemporary benevolent organizations, the Bureau accepted antebellum notions of charity that cautioned against the "demoralization" and "pauperization" of the poor with assistance. "No greater harm," the Bureau insisted, "can be done the negro, than supporting those who can support themselves."[15] Moreover, Bureau officials understood that such philanthropic endeavors had been traditionally, and perhaps more appropriately, the duty of families, private charitable organizations, and state and local governments. Even Commissioner Howard considered such federal assistance "abnormal to our system of government" and thus had no intention of providing it to the freedpeople indefinitely.[16] Nonetheless, and at least for the time being, he understood the necessity of aiding the former slaves through the federal government. But in functioning as a federal relief agency, the Freedmen's Bureau acted as a temporary agency attempting to remedy an immediate exigency, rather than an enduring malady that would outlive even the Bureau's own existence.[17]

During the early months of the Bureau's existence, its efforts to provide relief were informal and attempted to grant some form of government relief to the most destitute of loyal southerners who requested it. In fact, during the late spring and early summer of 1865, the Bureau provided assistance to both destitute black and white southerners, even going so far as to supply white planters and farmers with rations to aid them "in the subsistence of their employees." But beginning in July and August 1865, Bureau headquarters in Washington, D.C., began to place limitations on the agency's relief policies by establishing eligibility requirements for federal assistance. By the end of summer in 1865, the Bureau had stopped government relief to white employers as well as destitute whites who were not refugees. "Only such white persons as have been forced to leave their homes, because of their loyalty," the commissioner of the Bureau directed agents, were to be "fed by the Gov[ernmen]t." And as the months progressed, so too did the restrictions on government relief. Bureau headquarters in Washington directed its agents in September to "carefully investigate the matter of issues of Rations to Refugees and Freedmen, and order their discontinuance, whenever in their judgement such issues can be dispensed with." As a result, by October 1866, restrictions within Bureau relief policies had essentially limited government aid to blacks who were orphans, elderly, disabled, ill, or members of black Union soldiers' families. In fact, the Bureau increasingly attempted to restrict the number of rations issued to freedwomen with small children, even though agents generally regarded them as "unproductives" who could not find work even if they wanted to work. By the end of 1866, the letter of Bureau relief policy had officially limited government assistance to black orphaned children and freedpeople in "regularly organized hospitals." Nonetheless, Commissioner Howard allowed his assistant commissioners the independence to use their own discretion in determining petitions for government assistance on a case-by-case basis. The message was clear: federal relief was only "to prevent extreme suffering."[18]

In furnishing support to the freedpeople throughout the South, then, Commissioner Howard instructed state assistant commissioners and thus local agents "not [to] issue rations to any person able to work, for whom employment can be found." Both white northerners and southerners were already concerned, albeit incorrectly, that African Americans would resort to idleness and refuse to contract out their labor without some force compelling them into the labor market. Providing blacks with aid from the federal government too easily, it was commonly believed, would contribute to black idleness and license. White northerners commissioned in the Freedmen's Bureau feared that the agency's relief policies might give credence to northern Democrats' and white southerners' frequent charges that it initiated and encouraged idleness among "able-bodied" freedpeople. Aware of critics who believed the Bureau would "feed niggers in idleness," Howard insisted on relief policies that were decidedly opposed to supporting "able-bodied" freedpeople, for providing them with aid from the government, if done too freely, could easily encourage such idleness.[19] The last thing the Bureau wanted was "to create a race of paupers or to encourage idleness." After all, the "principal function of this Bureau is not to supply a channel through which government aid or private charity shall be dispensed," Assistant Commissioner Brown later insisted. Rather, it was "to make the Freedmen a self-supporting class of free laborers, who shall understand the necessity of steady employment, and the responsibility of providing for themselves and [their] families."[20] Moreover, such fears that federal assistance could easily result in an unhealthy dependency on the government embodied antebellum northern concerns about poor relief, in general, and about how it undermined masculine responsibilities and independence, in particular. By accepting government relief or charity, one became not only dependent on others for support but also independent from the responsibilities of a family and employment. If carried too far, Bureau agents reasoned, government relief would encourage vagrancy. "A man who can work has no right to support by the government," one Bureau official insisted; after all, "[n]o really respectable person wishes to be supported by others."[21]

The Virginia Bureau went well beyond explaining its position on government relief simply to local agents. Assistant Commissioner Brown took the Bureau's policy a step further by issuing a circular directly to the freedpeople. Although "[t]he Government and charity will aid you," he told them, "this assistance will be of little advantage unless you help yourselves" by being "industrious and frugal." Brown also expressed his fears to the freedpeople that some might resort to idleness and refuse to work: "While it is believed that most of you will feel the responsibilities of your new condition, and will do all in your power to become independent of charity and of government aid . . . it is feared that some will act from the mistaken notion that Freedom means liberty to be idle." The Freedmen's Bureau in Virginia, Brown warned, would not tolerate those who lived in such idleness "known to the law as vagrants." Freedpeople who chose to live in idleness and refused to contract out their labor would be arrested, hired out, and forced to work without compensation.[22]

The aim of Bureau relief policy almost from its start, then, was to discontinue federal relief to the freedpeople as quickly as possible. Quite simply, the Bureau's policies were designed to end the need for such assistance by encouraging employment and returning the responsibility for destitution among blacks to state and local governments as soon as realistically possible.[23] The Bureau perceived its duty as temporarily providing for destitute freedpeople until state and local governments could properly "assume the responsibility for indigent blacks" as they did for white paupers. By mid-1866, the Virginia Bureau began turning over its relief efforts to county overseers of the poor whenever possible. Most counties resisted assuming sole responsibility for destitute and indigent blacks. Although limited financial resources and lack of space in poorhouses were the ostensible reasons for this resistance, hostility and hatred also played their roles. When asked whether his county would feed the poor freedpeople residing there should the Bureau cease issuing rations, William Armstrong, president of the overseers of the poor for Stafford County, replied, "[N]ot a *dam* bite will I give them, I would chose hell first." Nonetheless, by the fall of 1866, Commissioner Howard officially discontinued federal relief distributed by the Bureau, except for that in hospitals and orphan asylums. The harsh economic realities in Virginia, however, would severely undermine his orders.[24]

Bureau relief efforts in Virginia began almost immediately upon Assistant Commissioner Brown's appointment in June 1865 and continued even beyond Commissioner Howard's order for their discontinuance in late 1866. From its earliest days, the Virginia Bureau recognized a duty to help needy freedpeople by providing them food—"a ration[25] of pork, bacon, or fresh beef, flour or bread, with occasional issues of corn meal, beans, peas, or hominy, and coffee (or, for women, tea)"—as well as clothing and medical care. By August 1865, the Virginia Bureau was issuing 178,120 rations to 15,779 people; in September those numbers increased to 275,880 and 16,298, respectively. But instead of continuing to rise, by the end of September the numbers began declining, with the Bureau issuing only 235,786 rations to 11,622 people in October. Policy changes initiated by Bureau headquarters in Washington, D.C., had begun to have their desired effect in Virginia. By the spring of 1866, the Virginia Bureau had made drastic cuts in both the number of rations issued and the number of freedpeople receiving government assistance. As a result, the Virginia Bureau recorded a substantial decrease in the number of freedpeople who received rations in February, March, and April. By September 1866, the number of people fed by the Virginia Freedmen's Bureau had decreased to only 4,679 for the entire state.[26]

In their efforts to apply the letter of Bureau policy and prevent dependency among the freedpeople, Virginia Bureau officials increasingly took steps to limit distribution of government relief whenever possible. Without question, the Bureau's answer to dependency among the freedpeople was employment. In aiding the freedpeople in "their present state of helplessness," Bureau policies aimed at encouraging independence and responsibility among the former slaves by integrating them back into the labor system as free laborers. The Bureau's relief policies were closely tied to its labor policies. If blacks possessed employment, at least in theory, they could become self-reliant, independent men and women who would support themselves and their families. But what if employment was simply not available? Fostering a sense of independence and responsibility through employment would prove difficult in places where potential laborers were abundant but jobs scarce. Although agents regularly encouraged blacks to enter contracts to labor on nearby farms and plantations, this was not always possible in areas of the state where labor supply far outstripped demand in 1865 and 1866. Agents in western Virginia, for instance, reported a shortage of laborers as early as June 1865, but agents in the eastern and urban parts of the state simultaneously reported growing numbers of destitute blacks for whom employment could not be found. By November 1865, Assistant Commissioner Brown predicted that only with an exodus of some 50,000 blacks would the state's labor problem subside.[27]

Efforts by Bureau agents to reduce the freedpeople's dependency on government relief throughout the state varied greatly. In most parts of the state, agents were relatively unconcerned with providing government relief to the former slaves. Smaller black populations and a strong demand for labor in the Piedmont, in particular, ensured employment for the former slaves, and thus government assistance was limited in such areas. Containing predominantly agricultural counties, these areas depended on black laborers to cultivate and harvest crops. And, when jobs were available, at least in theory, blacks could support themselves and their families. Rather than concerning themselves with government relief policies, agents in these areas concentrated on Bureau labor policies (that is, ensuring that blacks contracted out their labor) and transportation policies (that is, transporting blacks into their districts to fulfill labor demands). In these areas of the state, federal assistance provided by the Bureau was truly limited to the old, infirm, and orphaned children.[28]

By and large, changes in Bureau relief policies proved challenging only to agents and blacks in areas of the state with large black refugee populations, such as the state's tidewater region, including the James River peninsula, and urban centers such as Richmond, Petersburg, and Norfolk. In fact, by spring 1866, the number of freedpeople receiving rations from the Freedmen's Bureau in these regions alone constituted almost 90 percent of the total number of freedpeople receiving rations in the entire state. By fishing and oystering, cultivating small plots of land on which they squatted or rented, and doing odd jobs around towns and army camps such as taking in laundry, chopping wood, or digging drainage ditches, blacks on the James River peninsula attempted to claim their freedom on their own terms. But because of the dense black populations, large number of refugees, and seasonal labor patterns, these areas had a surplus of labor and became the focus of the Bureau's relief efforts. As a result, when the Bureau took steps to reduce the amount of relief provided to blacks, freedpeople in these areas of the state felt the consequences.[29]

In an attempt to follow the letter of Bureau relief policy, Assistant Commissioner Brown directed local agents to deny government relief and assistance to all able-bodied freedpersons, to compel able-bodied freedpeople into the workforce, to transport able-bodied freedpeople who could not find employment to areas where work was more plentiful, and to discontinue government relief to any able-bodied freedperson who refused such transportation. By providing transportation to all "strong and healthy" freedpeople drawing rations, the Bureau hoped that they would "move to some locality where there is a reasonable prospect that they will become self supporting." Bureau agents informed blacks drawing rations for themselves or their children that they would be required to apply for transportation to any place where they believed they could find work or some means of support other than federal assistance or charity. At that point, each person would receive a ration ticket for two weeks, rather than a month, and be informed that it was his or her last ration ticket. Although "such a plan may seem hard," officials believed that "few would starve by reason of such a step" and "in the end [it would] be a blessing to those people." In the words of an agent in Hampton, it was time "to harden our hearts."[30]

Although agents in these regions of the state attempted to follow Bureau policy, they regularly voiced their concerns. Following the order to end government relief to those who refused transportation from the Bureau, agents in the cities, in particular, expressed apprehensions often resembling those of William P. Austin, an agent in Norfolk:

> The most needy are the aged, infirm and orphan children, most of whom formerly belonged to other parts of the state, or some other state. Efforts have been made to return them to their former homes,

with but little success, as they have been so long away that they have lost all attachment to and nearly all knowledge of their former homes. They utterly refuse to return unless by force. To such as have had transportation furnished them and have refused it the rations have stopped.

Although Austin enforced the Bureau's policy demanding that rations be stopped to those who refused transportation to other areas, he stressed that doing so would soon

cause suffering, especially with the children whom the parents retain. The prospects are that the small crops belonging to the colored people will be insufficient to subsist them through the winter, and they will be dependent more or less upon charity. Large numbers are scantily and poorly clad, and will also be dependent for clothing. . . . [R]ations are issued only to those entirely dependent, and those wholly unable to subsist themselves. If rations are stopped from these they must starve unless other provision is made for their support. These are very old men and women, cripples, idiots, and children who require the constant care of another to prepare their daily food after it is received.[31]

The situation seemed only to worsen in Virginia as the restrictions on government relief tightened. This was particularly true for freedwomen and children because, as many agents reported, there were always "more women than men and more children" who could not support themselves and thus required assistance from the government. Throughout the state, agents who recognized this problem, such as Stuart Barnes, assistant superintendent for the counties surrounding Petersburg, began modifying the Bureau's relief policy. Although he instructed agents not to issue rations to freedpeople who were able to work, Barnes made one exception: "[T]he only exception," he ordered, "will be in the cases of women, who have no husbands, living or present, to provide for them, who have large families of children, in which cases rations . . . may be issued."[32]

Clearly, the Freedmen's Bureau had created relief policies that were, on their face, gender neutral: they directed local agents to deny government relief and assistance to all able-bodied freedpeople; to compel able-bodied freedpeople to enter the workforce; to transport able-bodied freedpeople unable to find employment to areas where work was more plentiful; and to discontinue government relief to freedpeople who refused such transportation. In practice, however, these same policies proved anything but gender neutral. Bureau officials consistently excluded only able-bodied black men from government relief. The same did not hold true for able-bodied black women. In fact, agents often recorded that freedwomen receiving government assistance were able-bodied women who desired work but, for a variety of reasons, could not obtain it. As a result, exceptions were made, but they were made only for freedwomen. The precarious labor market in Virginia, in particular, made applying the letter of Bureau relief policy to both able-bodied freedmen and able-bodied freedwomen difficult. In providing government support or charity to black women, the Virginia Bureau found that it could not simply base its decision on whether or not women were physically able to work. Bureau officials consistently found themselves looking at other factors when it came to determining freedwomen's petitions for government assistance. Were these freedwomen married? Were they married to able-bodied freedmen? Had they been abandoned by their husbands? Did they have children? Were their children infants? All of these questions found their way into the Bureau officials' decision-making process regarding relief. Able-bodied freedwomen with small children and no husbands present found it especially difficult to find employment. Labeled the "unproductives" by both Bureau officials and white employers, these women were the last to be hired—if they were hired at all.[33] Their children were the crux of the problem. Agents often noted that "[e]mployment could be found for these parties were it not for their children who are so small that no one seems disposed to engage them."[34] Faced with such circumstances and following nineteenth-century assumptions about gender, Bureau officials proved more likely to view women as dependents, whether of fathers or husbands or, as in these cases, of the government. Consequently, despite their unease with providing relief to the able-bodied, Virginia Bureau agents refused to deny freedwomen relief. During the period in which the government was most active in supplying freedpeople with relief, that is, during the year and a half immediately following the war, 1865 and 1866, the Virginia Bureau treated unemployed and often destitute freedwomen, on the one hand, as "dependents on the government" to whom it provided relief while it encouraged them to find work. On the other hand, it defined unemployed freedmen as "vagrants" to whom it denied government support; it forced them to find employment or labor without compensation and arrested those men whom it deemed the most refractory.[35]

Although the Virginia Bureau was decidedly "opposed to feeding idle, indolent [black] men . . . who wont work," the same often was not true for black women. Agents found it much easier to deny government relief to freedmen than to deny it to freedwomen. This is evident with an examination of reports made by agents in each county during 1865 and 1866 that listed who received government relief.[36] The vast majority of recipients of relief in Virginia were freedwomen and children. Moreover, by looking more closely at the same reports, it is apparent that assumptions about gender informed the actions of agents. Their remarks as to why freedpeople received rations illustrate that, although not always the case for freedwomen, Bureau agents took extraordinary care to justify providing support to freedmen. For instance, the agent in York County reported some 248 destitute freedpeople provided for by the Bureau in 1866. Of that total, only 2 of the freedpeople were adult males and neither was "able-bodied." One, the agent noted, had no hands, and the other was blind. The remaining 246 blacks receiving rations from the Bureau in York County were recorded simply as women and children. Likewise, of the 195 destitute blacks receiving rations from the Freemen's Bureau in Mecklenburg County during the same period, only 16 were adult males, almost half of whom agents justified by noting that they were sixty-five years or older. The remaining 179 people were destitute women and children. Agents in other counties throughout the state also recorded few freedmen receiving relief from the government; when they did receive it, the agents were careful to note that these men were elderly, sick, or disabled. It appears, then, that the Virginia Freedmen's Bureau refused to provide government relief to adult black males whom it considered "able-bodied" and responsible for themselves.[37]

The assumptions of Bureau officials about masculinity and manhood clearly informed these practices. Men, they believed, should be independent, show initiative, and provide for the well-being of their families. Consequently, Bureau policy encouraged black men to take responsibility for themselves and their families, and agents were directed "to impressing upon the freedmen's minds their duties and responsibilities as free men and as husbands and fathers."

Agents regularly reminded black men of these duties. "Husbands must provide for their families," one agent told a group of freedpeople. "Your wives will not love you if you do not provide bread and clothes for them. They cannot be happy and greet you with a kiss, when you come home, if they are hungry, ragged, and cold. By industry and economy you can soon provide a real good home, and plenty of food and clothing for your family; and you should not rest until this is done." In the eyes of Bureau agents, providing able-bodied black men government assistance or charity would encourage them to live in idleness, and it would sap the very sense of manly independence and responsibility that the Bureau hoped to foster. Moreover, by accepting government relief, one became not only dependent on others for support but also independent from the responsibilities of family and employment. If carried too far, both white northerners in the Freedmen's Bureau and white southerners believed, Bureau relief policies could result in a large number of freedmen becoming vagrants who provided for neither themselves nor their families.[38]

Although Bureau officials were more willing to provide support for able-bodied women, they nonetheless had concerns about fostering a sense of dependence on the federal government among freedwomen and children. After all, the last thing the Bureau had wanted to do was "to create a race of paupers or to encourage idleness" among the former slaves, irrespective of their gender or age. But for black women and children, dependency took on a different meaning. Following nineteenth-century assumptions about gender, Bureau officials naturally viewed freedwomen as dependents; preferably, however, they and their children would be the dependents of fathers or husbands rather than the federal government. Freedwomen who lived in family units with adult male heads, whether fathers, husbands, uncles, or sons, caused little concern for Bureau officials, but black women and children who were dependent on the federal government for their survival made Bureau officials uneasy. Their greatest concerns were the many destitute freedwomen who "because they are women, helpless with infants either in their arms or unborn, with no place to go . . . totally destitute, utterly helpless who would be beggars anywhere [else]"[39] Fearful that "confirming one dependent population in their worst of habits or rather of crimes confirmed pauperism" and that it was now "compelled to feed them in idleness," a "condition that destroys self respect, demoralizes and ruins

any people," the Virginia Bureau took steps to end such "inappropri-
ate" dependency among freedwomen.[40]

One way the Bureau attempted to prevent dependency among
freedwomen was through its efforts to assist black women in holding
black men accountable for their responsibilities as husbands and
fathers. Bureau offices throughout the state were often besieged by
destitute freedwomen who had been abandoned by their husbands.[41]
Freedwomen, including Lucinda Molley and Ann Maria Brown, for
instance, found assistance from the Bureau in finding their husbands
in an effort either to bring them back or to compel them to provide
for their wives and children. Recognizing the numerous cases of
abandonment, the superintendent in Lynchburg, like others
throughout the state, directed agents in his district, whenever possible, to send home all able-bodied freedmen who had deserted their
families without "good" cause.[42] Lucinda Molley was fortunate in
that the Bureau found her husband, but, instead of sending him
home, the Bureau ordered him "to provide for his wife and family."
In the case of Ann Maria Brown, however, the Bureau endeavored to
reunite her with her husband, James. Ann Maria came to the Bureau
in 1866 to complain that her husband had deserted her, was living
in Maryland, and was doing well there, but he had neither sent for
her nor made any effort to support her. After hearing the case, Bureau officials in Charlottesville ordered James to send for his wife.[43]
In most cases of desertion, the Bureau took the opportunity to educate, or perhaps remind, freedmen of their marital responsibilities
and used its authority to compel them to support their families.[44]

Bureau agents also attempted to reduce the number of destitute
black women receiving government assistance in more coercive
ways. One approach sometimes advanced for dealing specifically
with those freedwomen "who have no husbands, but are blessed
with numerous children," who were "strong and healthy" women,
and who sought government relief was to issue rations only to some
of the children. The mother would then be required to provide for
herself and the children for whom rations were not issued.[45] Although this approach resulted in some assistance, it did not solve
the problem of unemployment for these freedwomen. In the eyes of
white Bureau agents and white employers, most unemployed freedwomen "encumbered" with children were jobless because of their
children. As a result, some agents urged freedwomen with many chil-

dren to have all or some of their children apprenticed to white employers who could provide "good homes" where the children could "be well fed, well clothed & receive a good education."[46] After apprenticing her children, the agents reasoned, a freedwoman would be able to find work. Although the Bureau officially advocated apprenticeship only for orphans or for children with the consent of their parents, Bureau officials, at times, took custody of children and apprenticed them in instances where parents were unable to provide for their families.

The policy of apprenticing these children often varied from district to district. In the district surrounding Lynchburg, for instance, agents were directed in "any case where the parents receive government support" to "bind out the child." In other areas, agents proved reluctant to go so far. Desiring parental consent, many officials in the Bureau chose to advise, counsel, or even urge destitute mothers receiving government support to apprentice their children voluntarily. Whatever the policy advocated, Bureau agents neither fully anticipated black women's responses nor their resistance. After advising several women to apprentice their children, one agent in Richmond reported back to his superiors that "in each case I was met with the reply that 'they could not part with them.' " Puzzled, this agent noted that "it seems they would rather see their children starve, than have them provided for" by being apprentices. But black women did resist Bureau efforts to take custody of their children. In fact, some of them did so even to the point of forsaking or rejecting government assistance altogether.[47]

Another, and perhaps more rudimentary, approach taken by the Bureau to reduce the number of destitute black women receiving government assistance was simply to encourage them to return to the workforce whenever possible. After all, the black woman's obligation to labor, at least in the white man's mind, had not ended with emancipation. Intent on ending blacks' dependency on government support and charity, one army official advocated gathering all the unemployed women in Richmond to "hire them out." Or, if that did not work, he recommended trying to find work for them, such as nursing in hospitals, making clothing or washing for prisoners and blacks, or detailing them out as laundresses to the military. Finally, if "every source of labor fails," he thought it wise to "gather these women and children into buildings and open a grand general washing establishment for the city, where clothing of any one will be washed gratis." But, unlike this army official, agents of the Bureau in Virginia proved unwilling to compel unemployed black women to work. Although many black women accepted employment when it was found for them and when it was agreeable to their terms, the Virginia Bureau neither treated those who refused as "vagrants" nor hired them out or forced them to work in such a grand washing establishment. Bureau officials believed that black women "were exempt from the middle class ideal of fulltime domesticity" and belonged in the workforce, but they were unwilling to use coercion to force them to labor.[48]

In areas of the state where jobs were scarce and finding employment for black men, let alone black women, was difficult, agents tried another approach: transporting the unemployed to areas where employment was more plentiful. Like other Bureau agents throughout the South, they regularly encouraged blacks to get "in tune with the rhythms of the labor market" and go "where the promise of economic betterment was greatest." Thus, Virginia Bureau officials attempted to provide workers for the labor-starved areas of their own state as well as for other states, such as Arkansas, Louisiana, Mississippi, and Texas. In the James River peninsula, where the black population was swollen and largely destitute, for instance, agents regularly complained of "hundreds of perfectly helpless yet strong and willing women who must be rationed or starved or resort to those crimes for which destitution is fertile soil." Agents advocated transporting these women to their former homes where family members could support them or to other areas where employment was more readily available. In doing so, the Bureau hoped that it would give freedwomen "a fair chance to find work elsewhere," relieve the government of their support, and reduce dependency among the black population.[49]

Many freedwomen seized the opportunity to return to their former homes. One of them was Charity Cox, then residing in Charlottesville, who went to the Bureau for help in returning to her home in Tennessee where she had last seen her children.[50] Other women took the opportunity to go North. With the assistance of the Bureau, as well as such private organizations as the American Freedmen's Friend Society, hundreds of women found work with families in New York, Brooklyn, Boston, and other northern cities as domestic servants, laundresses, and cooks.[51] Eventually, a large number of the freedpeople who had gathered on the James River peninsula relocated, but whether they did so as a result of the efforts of the Freedmen's Bureau is unclear. As historian William Cohen notes, by 1870, the black population in the four counties that made up the James River peninsula was at 13,654, only about 4,000 more than its 1860 level. If the peninsula's 1866 black population of 30,000, as recorded by Bureau officials in 1866, was accurate, more than half of the blacks had left. Whether they returned to their former homes or went where employment was more readily available is unclear. A considerable number, however, probably found homes in such nearby cities as Norfolk and Portsmouth, both of which experienced more than a doubling of their black populations between 1860 and 1870.[52]

Despite the combination of Bureau threats and incentives, many black women stood firm in the face of Bureau policy. In several instances where the Bureau offered black women transportation to their former homes or to areas where employment was abundant, they simply refused to go. In fact, many freedwomen refused to leave despite agents' threats that their government support would end if they failed to do so. Frustrated, agents reported that black women did "not desire regular work in the country" and were, in fact, "very unwilling to go any distance into the country and cling with pertinacity to" cities, towns, and government farms. Bureau agents were left perplexed. As one agent noted in disbelief, "women and children are here who could if removed to other places find employment and . . . comfortable homes but seem to live here in almost starvation." They seemed willing to risk starvation rather than move away from what had become their homes. Fearful of their former masters, these freedwomen refused to return to their old homes. Suspicious "of any effort to get them homes and employment elsewhere," freedwomen proved more resistant to moving north than freedmen; possessing "small lots of land under cultivation" or "having rented a small plot of land for the present year," freedwomen were determined to stay put in order to enjoy the fruits of their labor; and having been gone for so long, freedwomen also realized that family and friends may no longer be at their former homes.[53]

Bureau agents failed to understand why these freedwomen zealously resisted returning to their former homes or moving to areas where employment was more readily available, which, in both cases, usually meant returning to the countryside to work as field hands or domestic servants. As noted previously, the women who received rations from the Bureau and resisted so vehemently were principally those who had sole responsibility for young children whose fathers were dead, in the military, or, in some cases, had abandoned them. They were also the women whom both Bureau agents and white southerners often considered the "unproductives." Consequently, white planters and farmers, when willing to employ these women at all, paid them less than subsistence wages. Moving to the countryside also entailed considerable risk. Black women understood that accepting employment on farms and plantations often required them to leave secure communities in the cities or on the James River peninsula for areas where they would be subject to close supervision and abuse by whites in return for wages that would most likely not allow them to support their children. Moreover, particularly during 1865 and early 1866, local officials used the apprenticeship laws to take black children away from parents who were deemed incapable of supporting them and to apprentice them to labor-starved planters and farmers.[54]

In the end, many Afro-Virginian women quietly defied Bureau policies and chose personal autonomy and their children over the dictates of the market and of the Bureau. In some cases, black women's resistance forced Bureau agents to alter the letter of official policy. Although Bureau policy was to deny relief to all able-bodied freedpersons, to compel able-bodied freedpersons to enter the workforce, to transport able-bodied freedpeople who were unable to find work to areas where jobs were plentiful, and to discontinue relief to all who refused, agents consistently denied relief only to able-bodied men and made exceptions for unemployed, destitute, able-bodied women. Even though the Bureau significantly reduced support for black women during mid- and late 1866, several thousand black women remained on Bureau relief rolls at year's end. Moreover, even when the Bureau cut off relief, many black women refused to give up their children or to move to areas where employment was available. This combination of black women's assertiveness and the Bureau's grudging willingness to refrain from enforcing the letter of its policies afforded black women at least a modicum of protection against the vicissitudes of a labor market that both the Civil War and the Bureau's own policies had created.

The "problems" of unemployment, destitution, and dependency among freedwomen confounded Bureau agents in Virginia throughout the Bureau's existence. But despite official Bureau policies ordering the discontinuance of government support in the fall of 1866 to all freedpeople except orphans and those hospitalized, agents in Virginia continued to support destitute, able-bodied freedwomen and children. Because of the realities of the labor market, as well as agents' assumptions about women's natural dependence, the Virginia Bureau came to treat destitute, able-bodied black women who could not find work as "dependents on the government" and provided them with assistance. Bureau officials' gendered assumptions about dependency clearly informed these practices. Freedmen, they believed, should be independent, show initiative, and provide for the well-being of their families. Freedwomen, on the other hand, though clearly seen as having a responsibility to labor, were viewed by the Bureau as naturally dependent. No longer the dependents of a master, freedwomen became dependents of fathers, husbands, or, as in the case of these women with no men present in their lives, the federal government. The Virginia Freedmen's Bureau became the guardian and protector of these destitute freedwomen who "because they are women, helpless with infants either in their arms or unborn, with no place to go . . . [are] totally destitute, utterly helpless [and] who would be beggars anywhere [else]."[55]

NOTES

1. E. Lyon to O. Brown, May 31, 1866, reel 44, Records of the Assistant Commissioner for the State of Virginia, Bureau of Refugees, Freedmen, and Abandoned Lands, Record Group 105, National Archives Microfilm Publication M1048 (hereinafter cited as BRFAL-Va [M1048]). Some of my research in the Virginia Assistant Commissioner records was gathered prior to their microfilming; this material is cited as BRFAL-Va with descriptors indicated.

2. Circular (issued by O. Brown), Nov. 5, 1865, reel 41, BRFAL-Va (M1048); J. Gregg to O. O. Howard, July 16, 1865, reel 15, Registers and Letters Received by the Commissioner of the Bureau of Refugees, Freedmen, and Abandoned Lands, National Archives Microfilm Publication

M752 (hereinafter cited as BRFAL [M752]). For an excellent example of the Bureau attempting to teach blacks to be responsible laborers as well as husbands, fathers, wives, and mothers, see the series of pamphlets titled *Plain Counsels for the Freedmen* (Boston: American Tract Society, 1866) by Gen. Clinton B. Fisk, Assistant Commissioner of Tennessee. In "Be a Man," he instructed husbands to provide for their families: "By industry and economy you can soon provide a real good home, and plenty of food and clothing for your family; and you should not rest until this is done." To women, he emphasized the importance of knowing how to "knit and sew, to mend clothes and bake good bread, to keep a nice clean house and cultivate a garden, and to read and write." But perhaps just as important, Fisk maintained, was that a "wife must do her very best to help her husband make a living" for much of the family's success depended "on the good sense, economy, and industry of the wife." Excerpts of Fisk's lectures can be found in Dorothy Sterling, ed., *We Are Your Sisters: Black Women in the Nineteenth Century* (New York: W. W. Norton & Co., 1984), 319–20.

3. The best survey of writings on the Freedmen's Bureau can be found in LaWanda Cox's historiographical essay, "From Emancipation to Segregation: National Policy and Southern Blacks," in John B. Boles and Evelyn Thomas Nolan, eds., *Interpreting Southern History: Historiographical Essays in Honor of Sanford W. Higginbotham* (Baton Rouge: Louisiana State University Press, 1987), 224–8; although concerned with the Bureau in Texas, chapter one in Barry A. Crouch, *The Freedmen's Bureau and Black Texans* (Austin: University of Texas Press, 1992), and its footnotes provide a comprehensive analysis of literature on the Bureau as well. Although there seems to be no consensus in sight as to the success or failure of the Freedmen's Bureau, Donald G. Nieman, *To Set the Law in Motion: The Freedmen's Bureau and the Legal Rights of Blacks, 1865–1868* (Millwood, N.Y.: KTO Press, 1979), illustrates that a fair judgment of the Bureau must account for its actions as well as the environment in which it operated. More recently, two excellent state studies of the Freedmen's Bureau have appeared: Crouch, *Freedmen's Bureau and Black Texans;* and Paul A. Cimbala, *Under the Guardianship of the Nation: The Freedmen's Bureau and the Reconstruction of Georgia, 1865–1870* (Athens: University of Georgia Press, 1997). Other state studies include Randy Finley, *From Slavery to Uncertain Freedom: The Freedmen's Bureau in Arkansas, 1865–1869* (Fayetteville: University of Arkansas Press, 1996); Martin Abbott, *The Freedmen's Bureau in South Carolina, 1865–1872* (Chapel Hill: University of North Carolina Press, 1967); William L. Richter, *Overreached on All Sides: The Freedmen's Bureau Administrators in Texas, 1865–1868* (College Station: Texas A&M University Press, 1991); Laura Josephine Webster, *Operations of the Freedmen's Bureau in South Carolina* (Northampton, Mass.: Smith College, 1916); and Howard A. White, *The Freedmen's Bureau in Louisi-*

ana (Baton Rouge: Louisiana State University Press, 1970). Nonetheless, all of these studies deal primarily with "blacks" as black men and only peripherally with black women. As a result, they fail to depict the Bureau as a federal agency operating with a defined set of gendered assumptions that dramatically affected both its policies and practices. Exceptions are articles by Rebecca Scott, "The Battle over the Child: Child Apprenticeship and the Freedmen's Bureau in North Carolina," *Prologue* 10 (summer 1978): 101–13; and Sara Rapport, "The Freedmen's Bureau as a Legal Agent for Black Men and Women in Georgia: 1865–1868," *Georgia Historical Quarterly* 73 (spring 1989): 26–53, which have recognized freedwomen's relationship with the Bureau.

4. Both the black man's and woman's obligation to labor, at least in the white man's mind, had not ended with emancipation. Like white southerners, officials in the Freedmen's Bureau throughout the South expected both freedmen and freedwomen to work. As Jacqueline Jones notes, like "the Irish and French-Canadian immigrant women who labored in New England textile mills to help support their families, freedwomen were exempt from the middle-class ideal of full-time domesticity. . . . [B]y the end of the Civil War, it was clear that the victorious Yankees and the vanquished Confederates agreed on very little when it came to rebuilding the war-torn South; but one assumption they did share was that black wives and mothers should continue to engage in productive labor outside their homes." (*Labor of Love, Labor of Sorrow: Black Women, Work and the Family, from Reconstruction to the Present* [New York: Basic Books, 1985], 45; see also 58–9.)

5. Eric Foner, *Reconstruction: America's Unfinished Revolution, 1863–1877* (New York: Harper & Row, 1988), 152; George R. Bentley, *A History of the Freedmen's Bureau* (Philadelphia: University of Pennsylvania Press, 1955), 62, 76–9; William Cohen, *At Freedom's Edge: Black Mobility and the Southern Quest for Racial Control* (Baton Rouge: Louisiana State University Press, 1991), 58–9; and Eric Foner, *Politics and Ideology in the Age of the Civil War* (New York: Oxford University Press, 1980), 101–3.

6. *The War of the Rebellion: A Compilation of the Official Records of the Union and Confederate Armies*, 70 vols. in 128 (Washington, D.C.: Government Printing Office, 1880–1901) (hereinafter cited as *Official Records*), ser. 1, vol. 47, pt. 3, 607; *Official Records*, series 1, vol. 48, part ii, 295; *Official Records*, ser. 1, vol. 46, pt. 3, 1291; O. O. Howard, "Report of the Commissioner of the Freedmen's Bureau," Nov. 1, 1867, *House Executive Documents*, 40th Cong., 2nd sess., no. 1, 663; William T. Alderson, "The Influence of Military Rule and the Freedmen's Bureau on Reconstruction in Virginia" (Ph.D. diss., Vanderbilt University, 1952), 2–4, 7–9; and Mary J. Farmer, "Vagrancy and Gender: The Freedmen's Bureau and the Black Woman's Obligation to Labor," unpublished paper delivered at the American Society for Legal History Annual Meeting, 1996.

7. O. O. Howard, "Report of the Commissioner of the Freedmen's Bureau," Nov. 1, 1867, *House Executive Documents*, 40th Cong., 2nd sess., no.1, 663.

8. A. S. Flagg to O. Brown, July 13, 1865 , reel 13, BRFAL-Va (M1048); S. C. Armstrong to O. Brown, 30 June 1866, Letter Rec'd, BRFAL-Va; "Summary Report" (issued by O. Brown), 1865, reel 1, BRFAL-Va (M1048); Cohen, *At Freedom's Edge*, 51–2, 93–5; Nieman, *To Set the Law in Motion*, 37; Robert Francis Engs, *Freedom's First Generation: Black Hampton, Virginia, 1861–1890* (Philadelphia: University of Pennsylvania Press, 1979), 114–6; and Alderson, "Influence of Military Rule," 2–3, 7–9.

9. For a general discussion of wartime activities of the Union army in Virginia and contraband policies, see Part One of Louis S. Gerteis, *From Contraband to Freedman: Federal Policy toward Southern Blacks, 1861–1865* (Westport, Conn.: Greenwood Press, 1973). Gerteis, as well as J. Thomas May, "Continuity and Change in the Labor Program of the Union Army and the Freedmen's Bureau," *Civil War History* 17 (Sept. 1971): 245–54, emphasizes the continuity in army and Bureau policies that provided government assistance to blacks. See also Bentley, *History of Freedmen's Bureau*, chaps. 1, 2.

10. O. O. Howard, "Report of the Commissioner of the Freedmen's Bureau" Nov. 1, 1867, *House Executive Documents*, 40th Cong., 2nd sess., no. 1, 663; J. A. Bates to S. Barnes, Nov. 6, 1865, reel 11; A.S. Flagg to O. Brown, July 13, 1865, reel 13; S.C. Armstrong to O. Brown, June 30, 1866, reel 10; "Summary Report" (issued by O. Brown), 1865, reel 1, BRFAL-Va (M1048); *The Negro in Virginia*, compiled by Workers of the Writers' Program of the Work Projects Administration in the State of Virginia (New York: Hastings House, 1940), 239; Cohen, *At Freedom's Edge*, 51–2, 93–5; Nieman, *To Set the Law in Motion*, 37; and Alderson, "Influence of Military Rule," 2–3, 7–9, 44–5.

11. Ira Berlin et al., eds., *Freedom: A Documentary History of Emancipation, 1861–1867*, ser. 1, vol. 2: *The Wartime Genesis of Free Labor: The Lower South* (Cambridge, England: Cambridge University Press, 1993), 85, 95, 99, 101, 105; Ira Berlin et al., eds., *Freedom*, ser. 1, vol. 3: *The Wartime Genesis of Free Labor: The Lower South* (Cambridge, England: Cambridge University Press, 1990), 30; and Bentley, *History of Freedmen's Bureau*, 25, 56–57.

12. O. O. Howard, "Letter of Advice to Assistant Commissioners," June 14, 1865, reel 1, Records of the Commissioner of the Bureau of Refugees, Freedmen, and Abandoned Lands, Record Group 105, National Archives Microfilm Publication M742 (hereinafter cited as BRFAL [M742]); Circular Letter, June 15, 1865, reel 41; Introduction, reel 1; O. Brown to H. S. Merrell, June 15, 1865, reel 13; M. Woodhull to Col. O. Brown, Dec. 11, 1865 (with summary report enclosed), reel 20, BRFAL-Va (M1048); Robert

H. Bremner, *The Public Good: Philanthropy and Welfare in the Civil War Era* (New York: Alfred A. Knopf, 1980), 115, 117, 121–6; Bentley, *History of Freedmen's Bureau*, 25, 56–7, 136; and Hamilton James Eckenrode, *The History of Virginia during the Reconstruction* (Baltimore: Johns Hopkins University Press, 1904), 55–6.

13. *The Statutes at Large of the United States, 1789–1873*, 17 vols. (Washington, D.C.: Government Printing Office, 1850–1873), 13:508; for a more comprehensive analysis of nineteenth-century benevolence and philanthropy beyond the Freedmen's Bureau, as well as the ideological confines of such benevolent endeavors, see *Negro in Virginia*, 211–13; Bremner, *Public Good*; and Joe M. Richardson, *Christian Reconstruction: The American Missionary Association and Southern Blacks, 1861–1890* (Athens: University of Georgia Press, 1986).

14. Congress granted no official funds to the agency for assisting the former slaves in claiming their freedom. Using the Bureau's status as an agency of the War Department and his connections within the Army, Commissioner Howard managed to obtain food, clothing, and medical supplies for the freedpeople. By June 1865, the Commissary General of the Army, Amos B. Eaton, was providing food to the freedpeople; the food rations included enough cornmeal, flour, and sugar to last a person for approximately a week. In addition, Howard obtained clothing and medical supplies for the freedpeople. The Bureau issued poor blacks clothing that the Quartermaster of the Army had deemed unsuitable for the Union troops, as well as remaining medical supplies from the Army's Surgeon General. Oliver Otis Howard, *Autobiography of Oliver Otis Howard, Major General United States Army*, 2 vols. (New York: Baker & Taylor, 1907), 2:226, 256, 258; *American Annual Cyclopedia and Register of Important Events* (New York: D. Appleton and Co., 1862–1875), 1870:375; Bentley, *History of Freedmen's Bureau*, 76–7; Bremner, *Public Good*, 125; and Foner, *Reconstruction*, 152–3.

15. General Orders, No. 16 (issued by S. Barnes), Sept. 15, 1865, Circulars and Orders Issued, (Petersburg), Records of the Field Offices of the Bureau of Refugees, Freedmen, and Abandoned Lands, Record Group 105, National Archives, Washington, D.C. (hereinafter cited as BRFAL-Va [FO]); for similar assertions, see H. B. Scott to S. Barnes, Sept. 12, 1865, reel 1, BRFAL-Va (M1048); and Special Orders, No. 25 (issued by S. Barnes), Sept. 13, 1865, Circulars and Orders Issue, (Petersburg), BRFAL-Va (FO).

16. Howard, *Autobiography*, 2:226.

17. Cimbala, *Under Guardianship of the Nation*, 83–104. For further discussion of Bureau cooperation with northern benevolent associations, such as the American Missionary Association, National Freedmen's Relief Association, Society of Friends, and American Baptist Home Missionary, as well as

the inherent difficulties that the Bureau faced in providing this cooperation, see Bentley, *History of Freedmen's Bureau*, 62–88; *Negro in Virginia*,
211–3; Bremner, *Public Good*; and Victoria Marcus Olds, "The Freedmen's
Bureau as a Social Agency" (Ph.D. diss., Columbia University, 1966).

18. General Orders, No. 12 (issued by O. O. Howard), Aug. 19, 1865,
reel 41; O. Brown to I. A. Rosenkranz, July 14, 1865, reel 1; General Orders,
No. 20 (issued by O. Brown), Sept. 16, 1865, reel 41; Circular No. 28 (issued by J. M. Schofield), Sept. 22, 1865, reel 41; J. H. Keatley to O. Brown,
2 Aug. 1866, reel 3, BRFAL-Va (M1048). See also Herbert G. Gutman, *The
Black Family in Slavery and Freedom, 1750–1925* (New York: Vintage Books,
1976), 235; Bentley, *History of Freedmen's Bureau*, 76–7; Foner, *Reconstruction*,
152–53; Cimbala, *Under Guardianship of the Nation*, 87.

19. Howard, *Autobiography*, 2:214.

20. Circular (issued by O. Brown), Nov. 4, 1865, reel 41. See also O.
Brown to H. S. Merrell, June 15, 1865, reel 13; Circular (issued by O.
Brown), June 15, 1865. reel 41; M. Woodhull to O. Brown, Dec. 11, 1865
(and enclosed summary report), reel 20; O. Brown to O. O. Howard, 16
July 1865, reel 1, BRFAL-Va (M1048); Alderson, "Influence of Military
Rule," 32–3; Bremner, *Public Good*, 125; Foner, *Reconstruction*, 142, 152–3;
Cohen, *At Freedom's Edge*, 58–9, 76–7; Bentley, *History of Freedmen's Bureau*,
76–9; and John A. Carpenter, *Sword and the Olive Branch: Oliver Otis Howard*
(Pittsburgh: University of Pittsburgh Press, 1964), 104–5.

21. *House Executive Documents*, 40th Cong., 3rd sess., no. 1, 1058 and *House
Executive Documents*, 39th Cong., 2nd sess., no. 70, 155, as quoted in Foner,
Reconstruction, 152. For a more complete discussion of white northerners
assumptions regarding how government relief defied male gender roles and
could result in vagrancy, see James D. Schmidt, " 'Neither Slavery nor Involuntary Servitude': Free Labor and American Law, Ca. 1815–1880"
(Ph.D. diss., Rice University, 1992), 91–4.

22. "To the Freedmen of Virginia," O. Brown, July 1, 1865, reel 41,
BRFAL-Va (M1048). See also Howard, *Autobiography*, 2:214, 256; Circular
(issued by O. Brown), Nov. 4, 1865, reel 41; Circular (issued by S. Barnes),
Dec. 22, 1865, reel 11, BRFAL-Va (M1048); and Alderson, "Influence of
Military Rule," 33–4.

23. Throughout the nineteenth century, the administration of poor relief in Virginia was handled at the county level by an overseer of the poor
board, and the Freedmen's Bureau hoped to return its relief efforts to such
boards as soon as realistically possible. With an elected superintendent,
these boards determined who received "outside relief" (food and other
supplies) and who were placed into "workhouses." These workhouses employed the able-bodied poor while simultaneously, it was hoped, rehabili-
tating "the character of the dependent." Following emancipation, however,

these civil authorities often limited aid to white paupers and were especially reluctant to provide assistance to blacks who had not resided in the vicinity prior to the war and thus were not "their own poor Freedmen." W. P. Austin to O. Brown, June 30, 1866; S. C. Armstrong to O. Brown, June 30, 1866, reel 10, BRFAL-Va (M1048); and Crandall A. Shifflett, *Patronage and Poverty in the Tobacco South: Louisa County, Virginia, 1860–1900* (Knoxville: University of Tennessee Press, 1982), 70–5. For the history of poor relief and the development of a public welfare system in Virginia, see Arthur W. James, *The Disappearance of the County Almshouse in Virginia* (Richmond: State Department of Public Welfare, 1926); Robert H. Kirkwood, *Fit Surroundings: District Homes Replace County Almshouses in Virginia* (Richmond: Virginia Department of Public Welfare, 1948); and Frank William Hoffer, *Counties in Transition: A Study of County Public and Private Welfare Administration in Virginia* (Charlottesville: Institute of Research in Social Sciences, University of Virginia, 1929).

24. H. Sears to O. Brown, Feb. 28, 1866, reel 44, BRFAL-Va (M1048). For other responses of county overseers of the poor boards and their treatment of indigent blacks, see D. R. Bower to J. J. DeLamater, Jan. 22, 1866, reel 11; D. J. Saunders to unknown addressee, Nov. 30, 1865, reel 1; and W.P. Austin to O. Brown, 30 June 1866, reel 10, BRFAL-Va (M1048). See also *House Executive Documents*, 39th Cong., 2nd sess., no. 1, 713; and *House Executive Documents*, 40th Cong., 2nd sess., no. 1, 639–40, as cited in Foner, *Reconstruction*, 152.

25. Circular No. 8 issued by the Freedmen's Bureau headquarters in Washington, D.C. on June 20, 1865, defined a ration as "Pork or bacon, 10 ounces, in lieu of fresh beef; fresh beef, 16 ounces; flour and soft bread, 16 ounces, twice a week; hard bread, 12 ounces, in lieu of flour or soft bread; corn meal, 16 ounces, five times a week; beans, peas, or hominy, 10 pounds to 100 rations; sugar, 8 pounds to 100 rations; vinegar, 2 quarts to 100 rations; candles, adamantine or star, 8 ounces to 100 rations; soap, 2 pounds to 100 rations; salt, 2 pounds to 100 rations; pepper, 2 ounces to 100 rations. Women and children, in addition to the foregoing ration, are allowed roasted rye coffee at the rate of ten (10) pounds, or tea at the rate of fifteen (15) ounces to each one hundred (100) rations. Children under fourteen (14) years of age are allowed half rations." *House Executive Documents*, 39th Cong., 1st sess., no. 11, 47.

26. In general, see the records of destitution and rations for each county in Records Relating to Destitute Freedmen and Refugees, reel 57, BRFAL-Va (M1048). See also William N. Felt, "Statement of Freedmen and Refugees to whom Rations were Issued and number of Rations in Month of February 1866," March 16, 1866, "Report of number of Freedmen and Refugees to whom Rations were issued with number of Rations issued in

Month of March [1866]," [no date], and "Statement of Number of Freedmen and Refugees to whom Rations were issued in the State of Virginia, in
month of April 1866," [no date], reel 13, BRFAL-Va (M1048); Howard,
Autobiography, 2:214, 256; Bentley, *History of Freedmen's Bureau*, 76; "Report
of the Secretary of War," 40th Cong., 2nd sess., no. 1, 240; Eckenrode,
Political History of Virginia during Reconstruction, 56–7; and Bremner, *Public
Good*, 117.

27. O. Brown to H.S. Merrell, June 15, 1865, reel 13, BRFAL-Va
(M1048); "Report of Orlando Brown," Nov. 31, 1865, *Senate Executive Documents*, 39th Cong., 1st sess., no. 27, 146; S. Barnes to O. Brown, July 9, 1865,
reel 12; Circular (issued by O. Brown), June 15, 1865, reel 41; J. Post to O.
Brown, June 10, 1865, reel 18; W.S. How to O. Brown, Oct. 28, 1865, reel
19, BRFAL-Va (M1048); W. Moore to F. Crandon, Feb. 28, 1866; J. Wilson
to F. Crandon, Feb. 28, 1866, Report of Operations and Conditions; S. C.
Armstrong to A.A.A.G., Mar. 19, 1866, Letters Rec'd, BRFAL-Va; M. Woodhull to O. Brown, Oct. 6, 1865, and Dec. 11, 1865 (and enclosed summary
report), reel 20, BRFAL-Va (M1048); Nieman, *To Set the Law in Motion*, 37;
and Cohen, *At Freedom's Edge*, 51–2, 54–5, 93–4.

28. J. Post to O. Brown, June 10, 1865, reel 18; W. S. How to O. Brown,
Oct. 28, 1865, reel 19; S. Barnes to O. Brown, July 9, 1865, reel 12, BRFAL-
Va (M1048); W. Moore to F. Crandon, Feb. 28, 1866; J. Wilson to F. Cran-
don, Feb. 28, 1866, Report of Operations and Conditions, BRFAL-Va; M.
Woodhull to O. Brown, Oct. 6, 1865, reel 20, BRFAL-Va (M1048); T. P.
Jackson to A. G. Flagg, April 19, 1866, Letters Rec'd, BRFAL-Va; W. G.
Roberts to J. Johnson, February 28, 1866, reel 44, BRFAL-Va (M1048); S.
C. Armstrong to A.A.A.G., May 19, 1866, Letters Rec'd, BRFAL-Va; Bent-
ley, *History of Freedmen's Bureau*, 97; and Cohen, *At Freedom's Edge*, 44, 51–2,
54–5.

29. Percentage based on sources in "Statement of Freedmen and Refugees to whom Rations were Issued and number of Rations in Month of
February 1866," March 16, 1866, "Report of number of Freedmen and Refugees to whom Rations were issued with number of Rations issued in
Month of March [1866]," [no date], and "Statement of Number of Freedmen and Refugees to whom Rations were issued in the State of Virginia, in
month of April 1866," [no date], all by William N. Felt, reel 13, BRFAL-Va
(M1048). See also Nieman, *To Set the Law in Motion*, 37; and Cohen, *At
Freedom's Edge*, 51, 93–5.

30. General Orders, No. 12 (issued by O. Brown), Aug. 19, 1865; General
Orders, No. 14, Sept. 6, 1865; Circular (issued by O. Brown), Nov. 4, 1865,
reel 41, BRFAL-Va (M1048); "Report of Orlando Brown," Nov. 31, 1865,
Senate Executive Documents, 39th Cong., 1st sess., no. 27, 146; O. O. Howard
to O. Brown, 19 Dec. 1865, Letters Rec'd, BRFAL-Va; Circular No. 2 (is-

sued by O. O. Howard), April 10, 1866, reel 41; T. Jackson to A. S. Flagg, Dec. 26, 1865, reel 13; O. Brown to A. S. Flagg, Jan. 6, 1866, reel 1; Circular (issued by S. Barnes), Dec. 22, 1865, reel 11; C. B. Goodyear to S. C. Armstrong, March 28, 1866, reel 10, BRFAL-Va (M1048); Cohen, *At Freedom's Edge*, 44, 51–2, 54–5; Alderson, "Influence of Military Rule," 45; and Bentley, *History of Freedmen's Bureau*, 97.

31. W. P. Austin to J. W. Schofield, Sept. 3, 1866, reel 1, BRFAL-Va (M1048).

32. Ibid.; C. P. Goodyear to L. Bacon, April 1, 1866, Bacon Family Papers, Yale University, as quoted in William S. McFeely, *Yankee Stepfather: General O. O. Howard and the Freedmen* (New Haven: Yale University Press, 1968), 259; quotation is from General Orders, No. 16 (issued by S. Barnes), Sept. 15, 1865, Orders and Circulars, (Petersburg), BRFAL-Va (FO). See also, in general, Records relating to Destitute Freedmen and Refugees, which list by county, name, sex, and age of freedpeople receiving rations from the Freedmen's Bureau between March and June, 1866, reel 57, BRFAL-Va (M1048).

33. S. P. Ryland to O. Brown, Oct. 16, 1866, Letters Rec'd; G. Cook to W. S. How, May 3, 1866, Report of Operations and Conditions, BRFAL-Va; T. P. Jackson to A. S. Flagg, April 19, 1866, reel 13; S. C. Armstrong to O. Brown, May 4, 1866, reel 10, BRFAL-Va (M1048).

34. F. Crandon, "Report of Freedmen Able to Work and for whom Employment cannot be found in the 4th District," Jan. 31, 1866, BRFAL-Va (M1048).

35. M. Woodhull to O. Brown, Jan. 31, 1866; O. Brown to A. S. Flagg, Jan. 6, 1866, reel 1, BRFAL-Va (M1048); S. P. Ryland to O. Brown, Oct. 16, 1865, Letters Rec'd; T. Jackson to A. S. Flagg, April 19, 1866, Letters Rec'd; C. Johnson to S. P. Jackson, Oct. 24, 1865, Letters Rec'd, BRFAL-Va; S. C. Armstrong to O. Brown, March 28, 1866, and May 4, 1866, reel 10, BRFAL-Va (M1048).

36. Using an analysis of variance, a statistical test of the difference of the means for two or more groups known as ANOVA, I analyzed the differences among the Virginia Freedmen's Bureau districts in their distribution of government support to the freedpeople. After finding no sound statistical evidence of significant difference in the average distribution of rations to the freedpeople across time, I then turned to an analysis of the average distribution of rations to freedpeople in February, March, and April 1866 across district. In doing so, I analyzed the difference between the mean distribution of rations to freedpeople in each district as a whole, that is, the distribution of rations to all freedpeople, and then by group, that is, the distribution of rations to freed*men*, freed*women*, and freed*children*. All of the findings suggest that the gender or age of a freedperson contributed

significantly to whether the Virginia Freedmen's Bureau provided them with government support. The ANOVAs across districts for freed*people*, freed*men*, freed*women*, and freed*children* all resulted in strong findings that the distribution of rations across districts to blacks, in general, and to black women and children, in particular, did not occur as a result of chance. Interestingly, the finding for the ANOVA across districts for freed*men* proved the most robust. Its high F ratio of 142.23 and low P-value of 1.13606E-14 suggest that there is little likelihood that the distribution of rations to these black men, though few, was a result of random chance. When taken in conjunction with a comparison of the actual number of rations issued to black men versus black women and children, one is able to conclude that the Virginia Bureau's aversion to distributing rations to freedmen was not simply an aversion by one district but rather was statewide. Moreover, these analyses suggest that just as its aversion to issuing rations to freedmen was statewide, so too was the Virginia Bureau's general endorsement of issuing rations to freedwomen and freedchildren. ANOVAs are based on sources cited in n. 29.

37. M. Woodhull to O. Brown, Jan. 31, 1866, reel 1, BRFAL-Va (M1048). See also, in general, Records Relating to Destitute Freedmen and Refugees, reel 57; "Report of Destitute Freedmen in Mecklenburg County, Virginia, 2d Dist.," reel 57, BRFAL-Va (M1048); and Reports of Lieutenants Massey (York County) and Reed (Elizabeth City County), as cited in Engs, *Freedom's First Generation*, 118, 216, n56.

38. J. Gregg to O. O. Howard, July 16, 1865, reel 15, BRFAL (M752); *House Executive* Documents, 40th Cong., 3rd sess., no. 1, 1058. See also Clinton B. Fisk, "Be a Man," in *Plain Counsels for the Freedmen*, as quoted in Sterling, *We Are Your Sisters*, 319–20; Paul D. Phillips, "A History of the Freedmen's Bureau in Tennessee" (Ph.D. diss., Vanderbilt University, 1964), 125; and, for further discussion of assumptions regarding how government relief defied male gender roles and could result in vagrancy, see Schmidt, "Neither Slavery nor Involuntary Servitude," 91–4.

39. S. C. Armstrong to O. Brown, June 30, 1866, reel 10, BRFAL-Va (M1048).

40. S. C. Armstrong to O. Brown, March 28, 1866, reel 10, BRFAL-Va (M1048).

41. The number of abandoned women, particularly those with children, who came to the Bureau for assistance are numerous; for examples see, J. O. Hollis to S. Barnes, Dec. 15, 1865, reel 11, BRFAL-Va (M1048); J. A. Bates to C. B. Wilder, Nov. 23, 1866 and [F.I. Massey] to S. C. Armstrong, Jan. 28, 1867, vol. 500, Letters Sent, (Yorktown); W. A. McNulty to [Freedmen's Bureau agent at Leesburg], Aug. 16, 1866, vol. 85, Register of Letters Rec'd, (Alexandria); B. C. Cook to A. McDonnell, June 26, 1866, Unregis-

tered Letters Rec'd, (Richmond); Bunney v. Burden, May 22, 1865, Walhop v. Dennis, n.d., and Binney v. Binney, Aug. 20, [1866], Proceedings of the Freedmen's Court, (Drummondtown); and Brown v. Brown, June 13, [1866], Young v. Young, June 25, [1866], Richardson v. Richardson, July 4, [1866], Tarray v. Tarray, July 28, [1866], Johnson v. Johnson, Aug. 1, [1866], Hatten v. Hatten, Aug. 9, [1866], Whendleton v. Whendleton, Aug. 9, [1866], Storers v. Jones, Aug. 9, [1866], Brown v. Coles, Aug. 11, [1866], Commodore v. Commodore, Aug. 15, [1866], Spinner v. Spinner, Aug. 27, [1866], vol. 131, Register of Complaints (Charlotte Court House), BRFAL-Va (FO).

42. General Orders, No. 12, May 26, 1865, as published in *Daily Lynchburg Virginian*, June 1, 1865.

43. M. McKennel to J. Joyes, Mar. 9, 1866, reel 12, BRFAL-Va (M1048); and Ann Maria Brown v. James Brown, June 13–14, 1866, vol. 131, Register of Complaints (Charlotte Court House), BRFAL-Va (FO).

44. It is difficult to determine to what extent such orders were enforced if, in fact, they could be enforced at all. Judging from the registers of complaints kept by local Bureau agents and summaries of the Freedmen's Courts' proceedings in Virginia, orders and enforcement efforts varied widely and according to individual agents' personal views and interests, as well as the circumstances and policies they encountered. Moreover, ordering freedmen to return and/or support their abandoned wives and children usually proved easier than exacting compliance from them. More often, local agents and the courts found themselves relying on sermons instructing complainants and deserters in their marital obligations and urging them to "live together peaceably." For examples, see cases cited in note 41.

45. B. C. Cook to J. A. Bates, Nov. 27, 1866, reel 1, BRFAL-Va (M1048).

46. Endorsement of James A. Bates on B. C. Cook to James A. Bates, Nov. 27, 1866, reel 11, BRFAL-Va (M1048).

47. B. C. Cook to J. A. Bates, Nov. 27, 1866, reel 1, BRFAL-Va (M1048); J. F. Wilcox to R. S. Lacey, Dec.13, 1865, Letters Rec'd (Danville); and G. P. Sherwood to J. O. Oneill, July 27, 1866, vol. 2, Letters Sent (Wytheville), BRFAL-Va (FO).

48. "314B: Commander of Department of Virginia to the Commander of the District of Eastern Virginia," quoted in Ira Berlin, et al., eds., *Freedom: A Documentary History of Emancipation, 1861–1867*, ser. 2: *The Black Military Experience* (Cambridge, England: Cambridge University Press, 1982), 721; and Jones, *Labor of Love, Labor of Sorrow*, 45, 53.

49. Circular, Nov. 4, 1865, reel 41, BRFAL-Va (M1048); S. Barnes to O. Brown, July 9, 1865, reel 12, BRFAL-Va (M1048); Circular, June 15, 1865, *House Executive Documents*, 39th Cong., 1st sess., no. 70, 120; General Orders, No. 8, Aug. 7, 1865, reel 42; Circular (issued by S. Barnes), Dec. 22, 1865;

Circular No. 2 (issued by O. O. Howard), April 10, 1866, reel 41; S. C. Armstrong to O. Brown, March 28, 1866; C. B. Goodyear to S. C. Armstrong, March 28, 1866, reel 10, BRFAL-Va (M1048); Nieman, *To Set the Law in Motion*, 37; Alderson, "Influence of Military Rule," 45; Bentley, *History of Freedmen's Bureau*, 97; and Cohen, *At Freedom's Edge*, 44, 51–2, 54–5, 93–5.

50. M. McKennel to J. Joyes, March 9, 1866, reel 12, BRFAL-Va (M1048).

51. Rev. J. N. Glouchester to unknown, Jan. 2, 1866, reel 13, BRFAL-Va (M1048); "List of Colored Persons Going North," Misc. Records, (Fort Monroe); and Register of Freedmen Sent to New England, vol. 198 (Fort Monroe), BRFAL-Va (FO).

52. U.S. Census Office, *The Statistics of the Population of the United States* (Washington, D.C.: Government Printing Office, 1872), vol. 1 of the Eighth (1860) and Ninth Censuses (1870); Cohen, *At Freedom's Edge*, 93–5; and Engs, *Freedom's First Generation*, 118.

53. F. I. Massey to S. C. Armstrong, Oct. 7, 1866, Letters Rec'd, BRFAL-Va; T. Jackson to A. S. Flagg, Feb. 8, 1866; G. Cook to W. S. How, May 3, 1866, reel 44; S. C. Armstrong to O. Brown, April 3, 1866, reel 10, BRFAL-Va (M1048); W. S. How to O. Brown, Aug. 8, 1865, Letters Rec'd; E. B. Townsend to H. Merrell, Jan. 31, 1866, Letters Rec'd, box 8; J. Jones to O. Brown, May 31, 1866, Report of Operations and Conditions; C. P. Austin to O. Brown, Sept. 3, 1866, Letters Rec'd, BRFAL-Va; F. I. Massey to O. Brown, June 22, 1866, reel 44; S. C. Armstrong to O. Brown, June 30, 1866, reel 10, BRFAL-Va (M1048); F. I. Massey to S. C. Armstrong, Sept. 1, 1866, vol. 500, Letters Sent (Yorktown), BRFAL-Va (FO); and Alderson, "Influence of Military Rule," 282–4.

54. F. I. Massey to O. Brown, June 22, 1866, reel 10, BRFAL-Va (M1048); W. S. How to O. Brown, Aug. 8, 1865, Letters Rec'd; E. B. Townsend to H. S. Merrell, Jan. 31, 1866, Letters Rec'd, BRFAL-Va; and S. C. Armstrong to O. Brown, June 30, 1866, reel 10, BRFAL-Va (M1048).

55. S. C. Armstrong to O. Brown, June 30, 1866, reel 10, BRFAL-Va (M1048).

9

The Freedmen's Bureau and Wage Labor in the Louisiana Sugar Region

John C. Rodrigue

IN EARLY 1868, John H. Brough, the Freedmen's Bureau assistant subassistant commissioner at Donaldsonville, Louisiana, reported on the unsettled state of affairs in his district. "[T]he Freedmen are unwilling to go to work for such wages as the Planters can afford to give them," Brough noted, "but are insisting for very high wages, which as Planters have but barely cleared expenses and many are entirely broken up—cannot be given." Freedmen throughout the area were conducting meetings, he added, "addressed by persons who are advising the Laborers not to work unless they can get from $20 to $25 per month with rations included." Admitting that "it is the right of the freedmen to get the best wages possible," Brough nonetheless contended that "this holding aloof from work, because they cannot get high wages is ruinous to themselves and will eventually bring them to penury and want, and all the consequent results."[1]

Brough's report highlighted several key issues in the development of wage labor in the Louisiana sugar region—located in the southeastern part of the state—after the Civil War. Freedmen had mastered the internal workings of the labor market, and they had shrewdly discerned how, by acting collectively, they could make it work to their advantage, even going so far as to demand what Brough believed were unreasonably high wages. Although Brough acknowledged that the former slaves had the legal right to seek the highest possible compensation for their services, he also expressed the fear of many Bureau agents that the freedmen's "holding aloof from work" would prove to be self-destructive. Yet Brough's evident inaction signaled not the impotence of Freedmen's Bureau agents but rather their conviction that, so long as neither planters nor freedmen broke the law, the process of negotiation between them must be allowed to run its course.

Of equal importance, Brough also hinted at the central role of the Freedmen's Bureau in the advent of wage labor in the sugar region. Among the Bureau's many responsibilities were those of creating a free-labor system for the South and instructing freedmen and former slaveholders on its proper workings.[2] In southern Louisiana, the particular demands of sugar production gave freedmen considerable leverage in their struggle with employers to redefine life and labor on sugar plantations. In the contest over the contours of the new labor system, Freedmen's Bureau agents were neither passive spectators nor objective mediators. Instead, they played an active role in free labor's development by working to secure a legitimate free market in labor, seeing that freedmen enjoyed the rights of free workers, and intervening on freedmen's behalf when employers tried to cheat them or intimidate them with threats and violence. In their own minds, Bureau agents strove to maintain an ostensible neutrality between capital and labor, and they occasionally interceded on employers' behalf when they believed that freedmen acted in ways detrimental to their own interests. But by defending what they believed were the rights of the former slaves, Bureau agents enabled the logic of free labor to unfold with consequences that redounded to the freedmen's advantage.

The role of the Freedmen's Bureau in the development of wage labor must be understood as part of the larger transition to free labor in Louisiana's sugar region. In contrast to the various forms of sharecropping that replaced slavery in the cotton South, wage labor and centralized plantation routine supplanted slavery in the postbellum sugar region. Yet former slaveholders did not unilaterally impose wage labor on freedmen who opposed it. Instead, wage labor and centralized plantation routine came to dominate the postbellum sugar region only with the freedmen's acquiescence because planters could not have imposed the kind of labor organization that sugar production required on free workers who found it objectionable. Exploiting the distinctive environmental and geographical factors that imposed inescapable limitations on sugar production in Louisiana, freedmen achieved a significant degree of leverage in the contest with planters over the creation of a new labor system. Freedmen seized on the exigencies of sugar cultivation to gain advantageous terms on wages, the conditions of labor, and other matters. The willingness of former slaves to embrace wage labor was owed in part to the resolve of Bureau agents to secure its benefits for the freedmen.

But success in defining the particulars of free labor had profound repercussions, for it impelled freedmen to accept wage labor in principle. Freedmen thus participated, however unwittingly, in the process by which they ultimately became members of a permanent rural working class. If freedmen lost the larger struggle for economic independence by consenting to wage labor, however, that eventuality was not altogether clear during the immediate postbellum years when the former slaves could call upon the Freedmen's Bureau in defense of their interests.[3]

In creating a free-labor system for the sugar region, the Freedmen's Bureau built upon the unique attributes of sugar production in Louisiana, as well as upon wartime precedents. Sugar production spawned some of the South's wealthiest slaveholders, and it endowed sugar plantations with distinctive characteristics, including the concentration of land, labor, and capital. The labor demands of sugar cultivation, moreover, gave rise to large, complex slave communities. Sugar production involved a series of tasks that had to be performed in a timely manner lest the crop be jeopardized. They included planting and hoeing the cane, gathering and chopping wood, and maintaining the extensive network of plantation roads, ditches, and canals. Consequently, slaves on Louisiana's sugar plantations performed some of the most arduous labor in the antebellum South. In particular, the fall sugar harvest, known as the "rolling season," required a disciplined labor force to toil frantically, yet with clock-like precision. The uncompromising nature of sugar production, as well as the delicate equilibrium of plantation routine, caused contemporaries to liken sugar plantations to "factories in the field" and gave the plantations their hellish reputation among slaves of the antebellum South.[4]

The world of sugar was turned upside down forever in May 1862 with the Union army's capture of New Orleans. The federal presence prompted thousands of slaves to abscond from the nearby plantations and compelled military authorities to improvise a free-labor program. Free labor thus emerged not from a preconceived plan but from the Union army's pressing need to return fugitive slaves to productive labor and to revive the plantation economy. Hoping to gain the cooperation of southern Louisiana's influential slaveholders in his effort to create a loyal state government, President Abraham Lincoln exempted the area from the Emancipation Proclamation because southern Louisiana was under federal control in January 1863.[5] Free labor in southern Louisiana was shaped by the struggle among slaves, slaveholders, and military officials, by wartime politics, and by the demands of sugar production.

The contours of free labor in the sugar region reflected the circumstances of its birth. Adopted out of pure expediency, wartime free labor combined elements of northern free labor with certain customs of the slave regime; and it attempted to reconcile the slaves' desire to be free with the slaveholders' insistence that their slaves still belonged to them and owed them obedience and service. Planters and freedmen, for reasons of their own, pushed against the constraints of military labor policy. Union army officers, for their part, attempted to mediate affairs between slaves and slaveholders while simultaneously evading the question of slavery's fate. Yet their policies and actions gradually expanded and consolidated the rights of the former slaves.

Wartime free labor reached its apotheosis in General Orders, No. 23, issued by General Nathaniel P. Banks, commander of the Department of the Gulf, in February 1864. The order established monthly wage rates ($8 for first-class male workers and less for others), defined the hours of labor, and decreed that laborers and their dependents must receive "just treatment, healthy rations, comfortable clothing, quarters, fuel, medical attendance, and instruction for children." Laborers must contract with an employer, and once they had contracted they were to remain on the plantation. Corporal punishment was prohibited, but the army provided provost guards to ensure that laborers worked diligently. The order also directed the withholding of one half of laborers' monthly wages in reserve until the end of the year. This provision became a critical feature of free labor in the sugar region, for it constituted planters' only means of securing labor through the crop season. Just about everyone found something to criticize in Banks's order. But in terms of the laborers' rights, it marked a fundamental break with slavery. By the time Louisiana Unionists abolished slavery in September 1864, it had long since belonged to the past.[6]

Although free labor would continue to evolve in subsequent years, it had assumed its essential features. Wartime free labor also had provided former slaveholders, freedmen, and prospective Bureau agents with a wealth of experience on which to draw, and it had established important precedents that proved difficult to overturn. The architects of wartime free labor had attempted to assuage planters' concerns, while, at the same time, they tried to guarantee to former slaves the rights of free workers. But, in effect, wartime free labor had predisposed planters and freedmen toward distinctive attitudes about free labor. Indeed, as the postwar era dawned, it was clear that planters and freedmen harbored irreconcilable conceptions of free labor and, consequently, of free labor's prime emissary in the South—the Freedmen's Bureau.

Planters came out of the war convinced that free labor was a travesty. Maintaining that sugar was a "forced" crop in Louisiana and that black people would not submit to the discipline sugar production required, planters avowed that free labor, as understood in mid–nineteenth-century America, was incompatible with sugar production. The requirements of sugar cultivation must take precedence over the freedom of labor, they insisted, and the new labor system must afford them the control over labor to which they were accustomed and which they believed to be essential to sugar production. Sugar planters' critique of free labor derived in part from their pro-slavery vision, but it also stemmed from their genuine frustration over trying to operate the plantations during the war with laborers who were unwilling to work any longer as slaves. Refusing to concede control over labor, even after emancipation, planters castigated free labor and prophesied their doom under this concept.

The animosity of sugar planters toward free labor further intensified with the arrival of the Freedmen's Bureau. Owing to its avowed mission to implement free labor in the South and to protect the rights of the former slaves, the Bureau served, in the planters' minds, only to "demoralize" labor. Were it not for the Freedmen's Bureau, one planter complained, "we would get on as smoothly as we did during slavery. As it is now [the freedmen] have greatly the advantage over us. They are permitted to go when & where they please & if they choose be as impudent as they wish." Employers who at-

tempted to "chastise" their workers, he added, were "brought before the commissioner & either heavily fined or incarcerated for an
indefinite period."[7] Like former slaveholders throughout the South,
sugar planters relentlessly denounced the Freedmen's Bureau and
advocated its abolition during the entire period of its existence.
They proposed instead that the individual states regulate labor.

Freedmen offered a contrasting vision of free labor and of the
Freedmen's Bureau. Familiar with the dictates of sugar cultivation,
they admitted the need for centralized plantation routine but envisioned a free-labor system that ensured them a degree of autonomy
within the realm of sugar production. Freedmen willingly submitted
to the discipline that sugar production required as long as they were
paid for their labor, enjoyed access to the plantation's economic resources, and were not driven as slaves. Although freedmen had to
continue working in gangs under white overseers, they demanded a
voice in such matters as the conditions of labor and insisted that
overseers accord them the respect due free people. In reinterpreting
northern free-labor ideology to fit their own experiences and in
building on the communitarian ethos that had provided them psychological and spiritual sustenance under slavery, freedmen did not
see free labor and sugar production as incompatible. The two could,
and must, coexist. Nor did freedmen view wage labor as a repressive
form of social relations or as "wage slavery." Rather, they included
it within their larger definition of freedom. In trying to realize their
visions of free labor and of freedom itself, freedmen would continu-
ally look to the Freedmen's Bureau as an indispensable ally.

Thus, a sort of quasi–free-labor system had existed in southern
Louisiana for more than two years by the time the Civil War ended
in the spring of 1865. Nonetheless, the contrasting notions of free
labor espoused by planters and freedmen led to conflict that manifested itself at predictable times and in familiar ways during the
annual cycle of sugar production. Consequently, the Freedmen's Bureau played an essential role in mediating this conflict and in shaping
free labor's postwar evolution.

The Freedmen's Bureau provided the skeletal framework for free
labor through the orders and circulars issued by General O. O. Howard in Washington, D.C., and by the assistant commissioner for Louisiana. Among the most important of these directives were the labor
regulations that the assistant commissioner promulgated in Decem-

ber 1865. Retaining elements of Banks's wartime free-labor program, the Bureau regulations parted from it in important ways, for they neither explicitly compelled freedmen to contract nor prescribed wage rates. Instead, they declared it to be freedmen's "duty" to "obtain the best terms they can for their service." Freedmen were free to choose their employers, but the principle that they must sign yearly contracts remained understood. By retaining the practice of reserving half wages until year's end, the Bureau conceded to the planters' demand to have some means to control labor. A month's labor was defined as twenty-six days of ten hours each, except during the rolling season, when securing the sugar crop was a round-the-clock occupation. The regulations also continued wartime free labor by directing that freedmen receive, in addition to wages, such basic provisions as rations, clothing, housing, medical attention, and the use of half-acre garden plots per family. These regulations remained in effect throughout the Bureau's existence, and they marked a key moment in the consolidation of wage labor for the sugar region.[8]

In implementing free labor in the sugar region, the men of the Freedmen's Bureau did not regard wage labor as oppressive. To the contrary, by inducing freedmen to enter into annual contracts for monthly wages and by encouraging them to try to gain the best compensation for their services, Bureau agents endorsed the wage-labor system in the sugar region. The triumph of wage labor both coincided with and reflected the transformation of northern free-labor ideology—from a doctrine that championed the ownership of productive property as the bedrock of economic independence to one that celebrated the freedom of the laborer to sell his or her labor for the best possible terms on a free and open market.[9] "[T]he matter of wages must depend on the law of supply and demand," the assistant commissioner for Louisiana directed in early November 1865.[10] The particular variant of free labor that the Bureau sanctioned in the sugar region did not contradict prevailing notions of northern free-labor ideology. Instead, in the eyes of Bureau personnel, it was an attempt to reconcile free labor with the dictates of sugar production.

Important though Freedmen's Bureau policy directives were, responsibility for implementing this policy, and indeed for making free labor a reality, ultimately rested on the shoulders of local Bureau officials. As apostles of free labor, most Bureau agents saw their role as that of objective mediator between freedmen and planters. Yet, in arbitrating the labor disputes that arose on the plantations, Bureau agents inevitably became active participants in shaping free labor. Likewise, virtually all agents accepted as given the consensus of interests between labor and capital that underpinned free-labor ideology, and they believed free labor to be part of the natural order, the benefits of which both former slaveholders and freedmen would quickly come to see. But Bureau agents' faith that freedmen and planters could overcome slavery's bitter legacy and learn the workings of free labor was immediately put to the test. Conflict between planters and freedmen belied Bureau agents' optimism about the universal applicability of northern free-labor ideology, and it revealed that both former slaveholders and freedmen possessed a more realistic understanding of the challenges they faced: namely, that quickly surmounting slavery's legacy was a hopeless task and that little common interest existed between former slaves and former slaveholders.

Although Bureau agents overestimated the capacity of freedmen and former slaveholders to come to terms with the past, they had better success at mastering the distinctive world of sugar cultivation. Bureau agents did not customarily make explicit references in their reports to the particular demands of sugar production or to the unique problems that sugar planters faced after emancipation. But, in the course of mediating conflicts, they often developed a sophisticated understanding of the specific customs and traditions to which sugar cultivation in Louisiana gave rise, and they sometimes revealed remarkable sensitivity in trying to reconcile the demands of sugar production with the logic of free labor. Bureau agents' appreciation of sugar culture seems all the more noteworthy in light of the fact that, as outsiders, they had no previous knowledge of this highly technical and idiosyncratic agricultural endeavor. To be sure, Bureau agents' on-the-job training in the rudiments of sugar cultivation won them slight credibility among local planters, who had little use for the Bureau under any circumstances. But Bureau agents' understanding of sugar production was an important factor in free labor's development, if for no other reason than it enabled them to assess with some degree of competency the competing claims of employers and employees in labor disputes.

The predominance of wage labor in the sugar region was owing in part to wartime precedents and to Bureau policy, but it also resulted from the "failure" of land reform, as well as from developments within the sugar region during the immediate postwar period. During the war, former slaves had revealed a disposition to cultivate sugar on their own by working abandoned plantations.[11] After the war, the Freedmen's Bureau controlled several thousand acres of abandoned and confiscated land in southern Louisiana.[12] In late August 1865, Thomas W. Conway—the first assistant commissioner for Louisiana and one of the most radical of the original assistant commissioners—attempted to fulfill the Bureau's mandate to distribute this land to the former slaves. Conway invited freed families or "associations" of freedmen to apply to the Bureau for land, and hundreds of applications representing thousands of freedmen soon flooded Bureau headquarters.[13] But Conway's plans suffered a setback when President Andrew Johnson decided that abandoned property must be returned to its former owners. (Also, Conway's radicalism disturbed Johnson, who ordered his removal in October 1865.) By the fall of 1866, the Bureau had returned virtually all of the property in its possession to the former owners.[14]

If land reform made no progress in the sugar region, neither did alternatives to wage labor. To be sure, the historical development of sugar production in Louisiana militated against any search for alternatives to traditional methods and arrangements in making sugar. Nonetheless, the failure of some variant of sharecropping or tenancy to emerge on sugar plantations did not follow from the essential nature of sugar production or from "crop determinism." As other societies have shown, sugar production could succeed when organized around small landholdings and the disaggregation of field and mill operations.[15] Instead, the ascendance of monthly wage labor resulted from the complex interaction among planters, freedmen, and Freedmen's Bureau agents within the context of sugar culture.

Planters conceived of sugar production as an integrated process, one in which the growing of cane and the milling operations were inseparable. Sugar cultivation, they insisted, required a highly centralized plantation routine. Such claims were obviously self-serving; above all, planters wanted to reestablish control over labor and return their operations to antebellum production levels. Yet it is not entirely inconceivable that the freedmen themselves, being well versed in traditional methods of sugar production, shared the belief that sugar could not be made on any other basis. Unlike their counterparts in the cotton South during the years after emancipation, freedmen on sugar plantations did not repudiate the gang system or close supervision of labor. They believed that centralized plantation routine was necessary to sugar production, but they wanted to be compensated accordingly. The freedmen's acquiescence to wage labor is especially noteworthy because Freedmen's Bureau regulations allowed planters and freedmen to seek alternatives to monthly wage labor. Local Bureau agents, in overseeing labor agreements, did not closely supervise the terms of the contracts; they were interested in seeing that such contracts were voluntary and that freedmen received their proper compensation. Thus, it was a combination of the efforts of the Bureau agents to secure freedmen their due, the freedmen's ability to wrest advantageous terms from their employers, and the planters' desire to preserve the old organization of work that accounts for the triumph of wage labor and the "failure" of alternatives to emerge in the postbellum sugar region.

Freedmen's Bureau agents supervised negotiations between planters and freedmen over wage rates during the contracting period, usually from late December to mid-January, and they oversaw the settling of accounts from the previous year when the freedmen received the portions of their wages that employers had held in reserve. The overlapping processes of settling up for one year and negotiating terms for the next often provoked what one Bureau agent called "hard feelings."[16] Consequently, Bureau agents regularly mediated disputes between employers and freedmen, examined planters' books to ensure that the laborers' accounts were calculated fairly, and personally supervised the payment of freedmen's wages. "[F]or the past ten days I have been busily engaged in settling with the planters in behalf of the freedmen, for the past years work," John H. Brough, then Bureau agent for St. James and Ascension Parishes, had reported in early 1867, "Some of the planters are not disposed to settle upon fair terms."[17] Occasionally, Bureau agents had to go so far as to seize crops or to threaten planters with fines and even imprisonment if they did not settle fairly with their employees. But whether or not planters were inclined to deal justly with freedmen, Bureau agents customarily made sure that they did.

Although Bureau agents saw it as their responsibility to ensure that the former slaves entered into fair contracts, they nonetheless found it difficult to persuade freedmen to contract for the entire year. They were also at pains to compel freedmen to adhere to their contracts after they had agreed to them. Having once been bound to the plantation by other means, freedmen resented the principle of binding contracts, and they distrusted Bureau agents' admonitions that written contracts imposed obligations on the planters and thus offered freedmen a measure of protection. Not only did freedmen object to annual labor contracts in principle, but the lump sum payments they received at settlement made them especially reluctant to contract. "The Freedmen on the Plantations have not yet entered into any contract," the Bureau agent for Jefferson Parish reported in early 1868. "They do not seem very anxious to work in the Month of January, owing to the fact that they have received their final payment for the past year. And the most of them undoubtedly will not go to work until they spend the last cent they have."[18] The agent might have overstated the freedmen's frivolousness with their earnings, but he did not exaggerate their aversion to contracts or the Bureau agents' own frustration in convincing the freedmen to see the benefits of written agreements. Over time, Bureau agents achieved some success in getting freedmen to contract, but the matter of contracting remained a source of frustration, especially so because the freedmen's year-end earnings gave them negotiating leverage with their employers, who, anxious to commence spring planting, often had to meet freedmen's demands.

Bureau agents also found, much to their chagrin, that once planters and laborers came to terms, their arrangements did not preclude clashes over the regular payment of monthly wages. Disputes resulted when planters tried to defraud freedmen outright or, more commonly, when they made deductions for trifling reasons in order, as one agent put it, "to annoy the Freedmen in every way possible."[19] Unable to discharge an entire workforce in the middle of the crop season, employers tried to intimidate freedmen by firing certain of them for petty reasons and then denying back wages on the grounds that they had breached their contracts. Freedmen contested such practices by complaining to local Bureau agents and by refusing to work until the agents assured them that they would be paid as promised. When the Bureau agent at Donaldsonville inspected one plantation in April 1867, he found that the freedmen "had become demoralized" for fear of not being paid. "I organized the force anew gave them assurance of their prompt pay and set them to work again," he reported, "they being well pleased that they would be the recipients of all that had been assured them in their contract."[20] Bureau agents' ability to mediate this and similar disagreements relatively amicably might have reinforced their faith in free labor's prospects, but only if they overlooked the very source of conflict between planters and freedmen.

Not only did Freedmen's Bureau agents intercede on the former slaves' behalf in order to secure them their wages, they also recoiled from compelling freedmen to remain with planters who were in financial straits and could not pay them. In such cases, Bureau agents directed that freedmen whose employers were delinquent in paying wages were, as the agent for St. Mary's Parish noted, "at liberty to work some where else until the gathering of the crop."[21] Having familiarized themselves with the essentials of sugar cultivation, Bureau agents were well aware that, by adopting such a stance, they were passing a death sentence on certain planters. Because a few days' neglect of the cane could devastate a sugar crop, a planter whose employees left him, even if only temporarily, in mid-season would most likely not be around at the end of the year to pay them what they had accumulated in back wages. Most Bureau agents, not to mention most planters, did not let matters reach this point if they could help it. But, as the advocates of free labor, Bureau agents were not about to compel freedmen to remain with an employer who could not meet his payroll, especially in cases when neighboring planters were willing to hire them.

On the other hand, Freedmen's Bureau agents, in attending to their self-imposed role as objective mediators, also protected employers' interests when they deemed it necessary. Planters' routine condemnations of the Freedmen's Bureau did not preclude them from regularly petitioning local Bureau agents to mediate labor disputes or to force former slaves to adhere to their contracts. On those occasions when Bureau agents investigated disputes on plantations and found freedmen at fault, they usually tried to persuade them that they were mistaken; however, they did not hesitate to threaten the freedmen with dismissal from their jobs, fines, or even imprisonment, but they rarely, if ever, carried out these threats. In resorting to such tactics, Bureau agents, in their own minds, were not doing the planters' bidding. Rather, they were ensuring that both parties fulfilled the obligations of their contracts because, for Bureau agents, voluntary contracts constituted the foundation of the free-labor system. The freedmen were no more at liberty to violate the contracts than were the planters.

Events on one plantation in Plaquemines Parish in early 1867 offer a case in point. During the spring planting season, a group of freedmen on the place, as the local Bureau agent later recounted, "stopped work and demanded higher wages." Having already agreed to work for $15 per month, the freedmen now wanted $18. The employer reported the incident to the Bureau agent, who visited the plantation in order to mediate the dispute. When the agent arrived, however, the freedmen at first refused to discuss the matter. Instead, they announced that "they were born and raised on the plantation and would fight before they would leave." Deeming their demands unreasonable—inasmuch as they had already agreed to work for $15 per month—and their stance intemperate, the agent informed the freedmen that they must return to work or leave the place. After discussing the matter among themselves, the freedmen eventually decided to accept the lower figure and, as the Bureau agent noted, "quietly" returned to work. The trouble arose, the agent surmised, because this particular group of freedmen had "always been indulged in their every wish, and they thought if they stopped work and demanded more wages their demand would be complied with at once."[22] Just where the Bureau agent drew the line between, on the one hand, the freedmen using the logic of free labor and the exigencies of sugar production to their best advantage, and, on the other hand, their making extravagant demands that must not be "indulged," he did not say. Presumably, however, such a line existed, and Bureau agents held them to account when they believed that the freedmen had crossed it.

Nonetheless, it was far more often the case that freedmen solicited the aid of the Freedmen's Bureau in disputes with employers. Just as former slaves looked to the Bureau to secure their wages, they also enlisted its aid to guarantee proper treatment from employers and overseers who directed their labor. Familiar with sugar cultivation, the freedmen did not shrink from the discipline and physical exertions that it required. Instead, they protested vociferously to Bureau agents whenever employers and overseers dealt with them harshly or tried to drive them as they had under slavery.[23] Bureau agents put a halt to employers' and overseers' efforts to threaten, intimidate, and harass freedmen, usually by calling them before Bureau courts and fining them or even threatening them with imprisonment. Although Bureau agents took care not to give the appearance of indulging freedmen or favoring them in disputes, planters often accused them of doing just that. Still, if fines and the threat of incarceration were not motivation enough, planters and overseers slowly came to realize that smooth plantation operations hinged upon their treating freedmen fairly and decently. Former slaveholders, contended the Bureau agent for St. Mary's Parish in 1867, "seem to become more and more convinced that kind treatment and courteous language toward the Freedmen is necessary in order to receive a good days work."[24]

Employers might have come to see the importance of "kind treatment and courteous language" in dealing with freedmen, but they also insisted on retaining control over daily plantation operations and over the freedmen's working lives. Because centralized plantation routine predominated in the sugar region, decisionmaking authority in the quotidian world of work became a critically important issue and tested the diplomatic skills of the Bureau agents. They often resolved the more trivial disputes between planters and freedmen by persuading both parties to shake hands and make up. But serious disagreements were less easily resolved, arising as they did from the contrasting visions of free labor espoused by former slaveholders and freedmen. Even former slaveholders who reconciled themselves to free labor argued that close control of labor was necessary, whereas freedmen refused to submit to work routines that too closely resembled those of the slave regime. Believing that they could enjoy independence within the parameters of traditional sugar cultivation, freedmen objected in particular to white supervisors who tried to make unilateral decisions about their work. Thus, confrontation over ostensibly mundane aspects of daily plantation labor elucidated the larger issue of power and authority. It fell to Bureau agents to sort out the resulting controversy.

A seemingly innocuous matter, such as rainy weather, could provoke bitter recrimination and necessitate the intervention of Bureau agents. In June 1867, for instance, the freedman Winfield Branch complained to the local Bureau office that his employer, Babylon LeBranch, had not only dismissed him but had refused to pay his back wages. As it began to rain, Branch left work and was later con-

fronted by LeBranch, who demanded to know why he was not at
work, the rain having since stopped. Branch responded that it was
raining when he had left the fields, but LeBranch announced "that
he would not honor such work." When the freedman countered that
he would not work in the rain, LeBranch interpreted his response as
insubordination. "[I]f you don't want to work the way I want you to
work I want you to leave," he declared, and he discharged Branch.
Intervening in the matter, the Bureau agent arranged a settlement
in which Branch agreed to leave the place but only after receiving
his full back wages, which his employer had originally denied him.[25]
The Bureau agent's attempt to steer a middle course probably
wound up leaving both parties somewhat dissatisfied. Yet, if the
agent's decision upheld the employer's authority to control matters
on his plantation and to discharge workers whom he regarded as
recalcitrant, it also sustained the freedman in his refusal to work in
the rain, to submit to a harshly dictated order, and to allow his employer to deny him the fruits of his labor.

The difficulties that Bureau agents experienced in implementing
free labor in the sugar region were complicated by planters' insistence on retaining certain elements of slavery. These difficulties
were further magnified by freedmen's determination to preserve
those customs and practices of the slave regime that they found
beneficial even as they demanded the rights of free people. In the
struggle with planters to recast plantation routine on a free-labor
basis, former slaves endeavored to incorporate what historians have
come to call the "slaves' economy" into the new labor system.[26]
Under the slaves' economy, slaves had undertaken a host of activities
on their own time—tending to garden plots; raising animals; repair-
ing roads, levees, and ditches; cutting and hauling wood; and gathering Spanish moss, among other tasks—for which they customarily
had received sums of money or credit on the plantation books. They
also had enjoyed access to the plantation's economic resources—
land, work animals, and farm implements—with which to conduct
these activities. Building upon the traditions of the slaves' economy,
freedmen demanded access to these economic resources as an essential supplement to their monthly wages, which prompted protests
from their employers. "[I]n many instances the Planter complains
of having to pay [freedmen] wages, give them land, and then have

to keep their hogs and horses," explained one Bureau agent in 1868, "but still they allow it."[27]

Bureau agents tried to convince the former slaves that they must now assume responsibility for the upkeep of their animals and that they could no longer lay claim to the use of their employers' property, but these were difficult lessons to teach. Freedmen saw no inconsistency in receiving wages for their labor while retaining the traditional privileges they had enjoyed as slaves. Indeed, the preservation of such privileges made wage labor tolerable. Employers, for their part, rankled at the notion that they must continue to recognize the freedmen's traditional rights in addition to paying them wages.

Nonetheless, Bureau agents customarily enforced the provisions of Bureau regulations directing that freedmen receive garden plots, and they defended the freedmen's right to grow the crops of their choice on them. Moreover, when freedmen were shrewd enough to have the use of their employers' draft animals and farm implements written into their contracts, Bureau agents protected that privilege as well. One plantation mistress, who refused her employees the use of animals and plows and who tried to dictate to them the crops to grow on their provision grounds, was soon informed by the local Bureau agent that "it was no matter of hers what the freedmen chose to plant," and that, by her contract, she must allow them the use of teams and plows.[28] Most employers might have seen such a decision as further evidence of the partiality of the Freedmen's Bureau, but, to the Bureau agents, it was a way for them to reconcile free labor with sugar production. Owing to planters' need for labor, of which freedmen were well aware, and to the freedmen's knowledge and skill in making sugar, any effort to apply the principles of free labor to sugar production ultimately worked to the freedmen's advantage in the construction of a new labor system to replace slavery.

In the annual routine of a nineteenth-century Louisiana sugar plantation, nothing matched the rolling season. The culmination of the year's efforts, the rolling season demanded extraordinary exertion from everyone on the plantation. From mid-October through the end of the year, day in and day out, the tasks of cutting the sugarcane, transporting it to the sugar mill, and converting the cane juice to sugar went on relentlessly. The rolling season was a time of arduous labor that had tested the limits of the slaves'—and later the freedmen's—physical endurance.

Even after emancipation, freedmen voluntarily put forward the extraordinary labor demanded by the sugar harvest. They knew what their employers expected of them, and they did not shirk their responsibilities. In return, freedmen made their own demands clearly known: they wanted good wages, respectful treatment, and a voice in the conditions of labor. "I am well satisfied that the Freedmen . . . will do the fair thing," observed the Bureau agent for St. Mary's Parish during the 1867 harvest, "if they are only used in a decent, and respectable manner, and are satisfied about their pay."[29] But if freedmen were willing to "do the fair thing," they also protested to Bureau officials when they thought their employers did not deal with them in a "decent and respectful manner." Consequently, Bureau agents, in mediating disputes during the rolling season, often had to draw a fine distinction between, on the one hand, the normal frantic and hectic pace of the rolling season, and, on the other, modes of behavior by employers toward freedmen that bordered on abuse.[30]

In disputes concerning the hours and conditions of labor, Bureau agents tended to be more solicitous of the freedmen. One particular aspect of harvest work that freedmen rejected and on which Bureau agents did not try to persuade them differently was Sunday work. Employers ignored freedmen's aversion to working on Sunday at their peril, and many of them rearranged the harvest work schedule in such a way as to conform to the freedmen's wish to enjoy Sunday to themselves. Not only did Bureau agents forgo any attempt to persuade freedmen to work against their will on Sunday, but they noted that planters who tried to impose Sunday work courted their employees' disaffection. "[O]n plantations where they have commenced grinding there was considerable trouble to induce the Freedmen to work on Sunday," a Bureau agent near New Orleans observed in 1867. "In several cases [freedmen] worked on without saying anything until Saturday evening and then all stopped and said they would not work on Sunday." Some planters responded by threatening to dismiss freedmen who did not return to work because Sunday work was stipulated in their contracts. But even then, the agent added, freedmen did not go back to work "cheerfully as the planters would like." Fearing the prospects of "demoralization," he concluded, most of the planters "will avoid running on Sunday when it can be possible for them to do so without loss."[31]

Planters who were determined to prove a point might try to impose Sunday work, but, in doing so, they risked alienating their employees. As every sugar planter knew, a disgruntled, dispirited labor force would not work with the élan necessary to meet the demands of the rolling season. Consequently, most employers concluded that it was better to give their employees the time off rather than risk losing their cooperation.[32] In the emergence of this modus vivendi, Bureau agents were not simply disinterested bystanders. By refusing to intervene on planters' behalf in order to induce freedmen to work on Sundays, Bureau agents were, in effect, permitting the burgeoning labor market in the sugar country to run its course. Freedmen, in turn, parlayed planters' dependence on their labor and cooperation into bargaining power to shape the particulars of free labor on sugar plantations.

Bureau agents helped to ensure that freedmen were not driven as slaves during the rolling season, but they also intervened on planters' behalf when they believed freedmen made unreasonable demands. In particular, Bureau agents usually took the employer's side on those occasions when freedmen violated the terms of their contracts by striking for higher wages during the harvest. Despite the depressed condition of the sugar industry after the Civil War, planters displayed an insatiable need for labor during the rolling season, when freedmen knew their labor was at a premium. "The rolling season is now coming on," remarked the Bureau agent for Assumption Parish in October 1867, "and many more laborers are needed in this Parish who could get very high wages."[33] Experience told employers that the best way to secure sufficient labor and to ensure high morale throughout the harvest was to increase wages or even double them. Some planters hoped to preempt trouble by agreeing during the contracting period in January to increase wages for the rolling season.[34] Yet even the most prudent employers found that stipulating wage rates for the rolling season in advance could not prevent labor difficulties. As the rolling season approached, freedmen attempted to capitalize on the bidding war for their services to gain better wages. Because freedmen "can get higher wages for the next 3 months," observed the Bureau agent at Thibodaux on the eve of the 1868 sugar harvest, "they have not hesitated to break their contracts."[35]

Planters whose employees struck for higher wages during the rolling season usually assumed an uncompromising position and refused to raise rates. But the outcome of these small-scale, spontaneous strikes depended as much on the intervention of the local Bureau agent as it did on an individual employer's perseverance. In mediating strikes, Bureau agents customarily resorted to the familiar tactics of threatening strikers with dismissal and loss of back wages, or, if that did not work, with arrest and imprisonment. Milder forms of suasion usually sufficed. When freedmen who earned $15 per month on a Terrebonne Parish plantation struck for $45 at the commencement of the 1867 harvest, the Bureau agent intervened and persuaded several of the strikers to return to work. The others, "who are the ringleaders and still demand the higher wages," as the agent put it, evidently left.[36] Bureau agents not only condoned but encouraged freedmen to bargain for the best possible terms during the contracting period, but for freedmen to break their contracts at the critical point in the crop season in order to capitalize on the labor market was carrying things too far. Having undertaken to instruct freedmen and planters in the principles of free labor, Bureau agents now found themselves in the awkward position of having to rein in former slaves who seemed to have mastered at least some of those principles all too well.

In building upon the wartime origins of free labor, in attempting to reconcile the contrasting notions of free labor advanced by planters and former slaves, and in undertaking to harmonize the logic of free labor with the exigencies of sugar production, the Freedmen's Bureau played a central role in the development of the free-labor system that came to prevail in the Louisiana sugar region. After slavery, freedmen translated their employers' need for labor and their own knowledge of the art of making sugar into powerful bargaining leverage during the contest over the new labor system. Although Bureau agents might have seen themselves as impartial middlemen between capital and labor, they actively fashioned many of the particulars of free labor to the freedmen's advantage as they mediated the disputes that inevitably arose between planters and former slaves. Yet an irony lies embedded within the many successes that the freedmen achieved with the aid of the Bureau. By seeing that the freedmen and their employers entered into voluntary labor contracts as putative equals, by protecting freedmen from their employers' attempts to control their working lives, and by ensuring that the freedmen received the fruits of their labor, Bureau agents facilitated the process by which freedmen in the sugar region eventually became reconciled to monthly wage labor during the years after emancipation.

To be sure, theory often did not correspond to reality. One of slavery's legacies was that freedmen and employers did not always engage one another as equals within a free and open market. Former slaveholders did everything within their power to block free labor's development and to crush the freedmen's aspirations. Nor were Bureau agents immune from either the unconscious racism or the outright animosity toward black people that impelled them to favor employers in labor disputes. Yet it is also true that the burgeoning free-labor market that the Freedmen's Bureau helped to create enabled freedmen to wrest concessions from employers on wages, the conditions of labor, and the general reconstitution of plantation routine. Wage labor might not have been the freedmen's first choice, but they did not necessarily view it as oppressive. Indeed, wage labor held certain advantages for freedmen—so long as other forms of compensation supplemented their wages and planters were prevented from imposing their own definitions of free labor.

Thus, wage labor did not negate freedom in the sugar region. Rather, such autonomy as freedmen there enjoyed under wage labor derived from the larger political context within which free labor developed. In other words, the freedmen's ability to gain a measure of control over their working lives was a reflection of the balance of power on the plantations. Also, during the relatively short period of its existence, the Freedmen's Bureau guaranteed some semblance of a balance of power between freedmen and former slaveholders. Likewise, despite Bureau agents' testimonials, there was nothing "natural" about free labor. Instead, the variant of free labor in southern Louisiana evolved out of the conflict between planters and freedmen—a conflict forged by the demands of sugar cultivation and mediated by the Freedmen's Bureau. The Bureau's success in inaugurating free labor in the sugar region might be measured by the fact that freedmen continued for many years after the Bureau's demise to withstand employers' efforts to control their labor. The decades after emancipation found employers bemoaning the "labor problem" and lamenting their inability to achieve the control over labor that they believed essential to sugar production in Louisiana.

NOTES

1. J. H. Brough to J. M. Lee, Jan. 11, 1868, vol. 263, Letters Sent, Donaldsonville Agent (Agt) and Assistant Subassistant Commmissioner (Asst. SAC), Records of the Subordinate Field Offices for the State of Louisiana, Bureau of Refugees, Freedmen, and Abandoned Lands, Record Group 105, National Archives, Washington, D.C. (hereinafter cited as BRFAL-La). I wish to express my appreciation to Charles J. Shindo for helpful comments and suggestions on earlier drafts of this article. I also thank Leslie S. Rowland, Steven F. Miller, and Susan E. O'Donovan, my former colleagues on the Freedmen and Southern Society Project at the University of Maryland, for their assistance in the formulation of many of the ideas contained herein. The writing of this article was supported by a summer stipend from Louisiana State University's Council on Research in the Office of Research and Economic Development.

2. No attempt is made here to cite general works on the Freedmen's Bureau. On the Freedmen's Bureau in Louisiana, see Howard A. White, *The Freedmen's Bureau in Louisiana* (Baton Rouge: Louisiana State University Press, 1970); and John C. Engelsman, "The Freedmen's Bureau in Louisiana," *Louisiana Historical Quarterly* 32 (Jan. 1949): 145–224.

3. For a fuller discussion of the themes presented in this and the preceding paragraph, see John C. Rodrigue, "Raising Cane: From Slavery to Free Labor in Louisiana's Sugar Parishes, 1862–1880" (Ph.D. dissertation, Emory University, 1993). Other works that examine, from various perspectives, the beginnings of free labor in the Louisiana sugar region include Ira Berlin et al., eds, *Freedom: A Documentary History of Emancipation, 1861–1867*, ser. 1, vol. 1: *The Destruction of Slavery* (Cambridge, England: Cambridge University Press, 1985), chap. 4; Ira Berlin et al., eds., *Freedom: A Documentary History of Emancipation, 1861–1867*, ser. 1, vol. 3: *The Wartime Genesis of Free Labor: The Lower South* (Cambridge, England: Cambridge University Press, 1990), chap. 2; John Alfred Heitmann, *The Modernization of the Louisiana Sugar Industry, 1830–1910* (Baton Rouge: Louisiana State University Press, 1987); William F. Messner, *Freedmen and the Ideology of Free Labor: Louisiana, 1862–1865* (Lafayette: Center for Louisiana Studies, University of Southwestern Louisiana, 1978); Joseph P. Reidy, "Sugar and Freedom: Emancipation in Louisiana's Sugar Parishes," unpublished paper presented at the annual meeting of the American Historical Association, 1980; Charles P. Roland, *Louisiana Sugar Plantations during the American Civil War* (Leiden,

The Netherlands: E. J. Brill, 1957); Mark Schmitz, "The Transformation of the Southern Cane Sugar Sector, 1860–1930," *Agricultural History* 53 (Jan. 1979): 270–85; Rebecca J. Scott, "Defining the Boundaries of Freedom in the World of Cane: Cuba, Brazil, and Louisiana after Emancipation," *American Historical Review* 99 (Feb. 1994): 70–102; Ralph Shlomowitz, " 'Bound' or 'Free'? Black Labor in Cotton and Sugarcane Farming, 1865–1880," *Journal of Southern History* 50 (Nov. 1984): 569–96; J. Carlyle Sitterson, *Sugar Country: The Cane Sugar Industry in the South, 1753–1950* (Lexington: University of Kentucky Press, 1953), 205–51.

4. On the distinctiveness of the Louisiana sugar region within the antebellum South, see Rodrigue, "Raising Cane," chap. 1.

5. James D. Richardson, comp., *A Compilation of the Messages and Papers of the Presidents of the United States,* 20 vols. (New York: Bureau of National Literature, 1897–1917), 8:3358–60. Historians have devoted considerable attention to Lincoln's reconstruction policy in Louisiana. The most important works include LaWanda Cox, *Lincoln and Black Freedom: A Study in Presidential Leadership* (Columbia: University of South Carolina Press, 1981); William C. Harris, *With Charity for All: Lincoln and the Restoration of the Union* (Lexington: University of Kentucky Press, 1997), chaps. 4, 8; Peyton McCrary, *Abraham Lincoln and Reconstruction: The Louisiana Experiment* (Princeton, N.J.: Princeton University Press, 1978); Joe Gray Taylor, *Louisiana Reconstructed, 1863–1877* (Baton Rouge: Louisiana State University Press, 1974), chaps. 2, 3; Ted Tunnell, *Crucible of Reconstruction: War, Radicalism and Race in Louisiana, 1862–1877* (Baton Rouge: Louisiana State University Press, 1984), chaps. 1–4.

6. For Banks's order, see General Orders, No. 23, Headquarters, Department of the Gulf, Feb. 3, 1864, in Berlin et al., *Freedom,* ser. 1, vol. 3: *Wartime Genesis,* 512–7.

7. R. C. Martin, Jr., to R. C. Martin, Aug. 3, 1866, Martin-Pugh Collection, Allen J. Ellender Archives, Nicholls State University, Thibodaux, La. (hereinafter cited as NSU). For other complaints by sugar planters about the Freedmen's Bureau, see Report of S. R. Oren, Sept. 8, 1865, vol. 90, Inspection Reports, Plantation Dept.; W. Dougherty to D. G. Fenno, Nov. 7, 1865, reel 8, Records of the Assistant Commissioner for the State of Louisiana, Bureau of Refugees, Freedmen and Abandoned Lands, National Archives Microfilm M1027 (hereinafter cited as BRFAL-La [M1027]). On this point generally, see Rodrigue, "Raising Cane," *passim.*

8. Circular No. 29, Headquarters Bureau of Refugees, Freedmen, and Abandoned Lands, State of Louisiana, Dec. 4, 1865, in "Letter from the Secretary of War, in answer to a resolution of the House of March 8, transmitting a report, by the Commissioner of the Freedmen's Bureau, of all orders issued by him or any assistant commissioner," *House Executive Docu-*

ment, 39th Cong., 1st sess., no. 70, 30–3 (hereinafter cited as "Freedmen's Bureau Orders.") For the reasoning of the Freedmen's Bureau assistant commissioner in issuing the regulations, see Brevet Major General A. Baird to Major General O. O. Howard, December 20, 1865, Letters Rec'd, Washington Headquarters, Bureau of Refugees, Freedmen, and Abandoned lands (hereinafter cited as BRFAL) [A-8746]. (The bracketed alpha-numeric designation refers to the filing system of the Freedmen and Southern Society Project at the University of Maryland, College Park, where these documents were examined.)

9. On free labor ideology in the North before the Civil War, see Eric Foner, *Free Soil, Free Labor, Free Men: The Ideology of the Republican Party before the Civil War*, 2nd ed., with a New Introductory Essay (New York: Oxford University Press, 1995); and Jonathan A. Glickstein, *Concepts of Free Labor in Antebellum America* (New Haven: Yale University Press, 1991). On the transformation of northern free-labor thought during the Civil War and Reconstruction, see Eric Foner, *Reconstruction: America's Unfinished Revolution, 1863–1877* (New York: Harper & Row, 1988).

10. Circular No. 26, Headquarters Bureau of Refugees, Freedmen, and Abandoned Lands, State of Louisiana, Nov. 7, 1865, "Freedmen's Bureau Orders," 29.

11. See, for instance, Charles Harris et al. to Honorable Captain Stiles, Jan. 8, 1865, in Berlin et al., *Freedom*, ser. 1, vol. 3: *Wartime Genesis*, 572–3; G. P. Davis to Capt. H. Stiles, Jan. 21, 1865, and C. L. Dunbar to Capt. H. Stiles, Apr. 26, 1865, in Berlin et al., *Freedom*, ser. 1, vol. 3: *Wartime Genesis*, 573n.; and C. L. Dunbar, "Report of Inspection of Govt. Plantations being worked in the Parishes of 'Terrebone and Lafourche, for the year 1865 (by Freedmen)," [mid-June? 1865], in Berlin et al., *Freedom*, ser. 1, vol. 3: *Wartime Genesis*, 617. There were relatively few abandoned plantations in southern Louisiana during the war. Most sugar planters remained on their estates and swore allegiance to the Union rather than "refugee" to the Confederate interior. Nor did Lincoln enforce the Direct Tax Act in Louisiana, concerned as he was with winning planter support for his loyal state government. On the Direct Tax Act, see Berlin et al., *Freedom*, ser. 1, vol. 3: *Wartime Genesis*, 36, 222n.

12. "Report of the Commissioner of the Bureau of Refugees, Freedmen and Abandoned Lands" [Nov. 14, 1866], in *Annual Report of the Secretary of War*, *House Executive Document*, 39th Cong., 2nd sess., no. 1, 708 (hereinafter cited as "Report of the Commissioner, 1866").

13. Circular No. 10, Headquarters, Bureau of Refugees, Freedmen, and Abandoned Lands, State of Louisiana, Aug. 28, 1865, "Freedmen's Bureau Orders," 19.

14. On Conway's removal as assistant commissioner for Louisiana, see

William S. McFeely, *Yankee Stepfather: General O. O. Howard and the Freedmen* (New Haven: Yale University Press, 1968), chap. 9. On the return of abandoned and confiscated property in Louisiana, see "Letter of the Secretary of War, communicating, in compliance with a resolution of the Senate of December 17, 1866, reports of the assistant commissioners of freedmen, and a synopsis of laws respecting persons of color in the late slave States," *Senate Executive Document*, 39th Cong., 1st sess., no. 6, 69; "Report of the Commissioner, 1866," 708.

15. On sharecropping on Cuban sugar plantations after emancipation, for example, see Rebecca J. Scott, *Slave Emancipation in Cuba: The Transition to Free Labor, 1860–1899* (Princeton: Princeton University Press, 1985),104–5. On the importance of sugarcane farmers in Brazil, even under slavery, see Stuart B. Schwartz, *Sugar Plantations in the Formation of Brazilian Society: Bahia, 1550–1835* (Cambridge, England: Cambridge University Press, 1985).

16. J. W. Keller to J. M. Lee, Jan. 10, 1868, vol. 384, Trimonthly Reports, New Iberia Asst. SAC, BRFAL-La.

17. J. H. Brough to W. H. Sterling, Jan. 12, 1867, vol. 262, Letters Sent, Donaldsonville Agt and Asst. SAC, BRFAL-La. In two instances, Brough seized sugar crops in order to secure the payment of laborers' wages from unscrupulous planters. J. H. Brough to Sterling, Feb. 8, 21, 1867, vol. 262, Letters Sent, Donaldsonville Agt and Asst. SAC, BRFAL-La. See also G. A. Ludlow to W. H. Sterling, March 10, 1867, Narrative Trimonthly Reports of Operations and Conditions from Subordinate Officers, reel 27, BRFAL-La (M1027).

18. Tri-Monthly Report of G. Bruning, Jan. 31, 1868, Letters and Telegrams Received, reel 22, BRFAL-La (M1027). For other examples of the freedmen's aversion to written contracts, see R. Daigre to E. J. Gay, Dec. 3, 1866, Edward J. Gay Papers, Louisiana and Lower Mississippi Valley Collections, Louisiana State University, Baton Rouge (hereinafter LSU); Jan. 4, 1867, Plantation Diary, Palfrey Family Papers, in Kenneth M. Stampp, ed., *Records of Antebellum Southern Plantations* (microfilm), ser. 1 (LSU), pt. 1 (4:748); Consolidated Quarterly Report of Provost Capt. R. Folles, Mar. 31, 1867, Reports of Assistant Inspector of Freedmen, Algiers Agent and SAC, BRFAL-La; W. A. Webster to J. M. Lee, Sept. 30, 1867, vol. 218, Letters Sent, Baton Rouge Asst. SAC, BRFAL-La; W. Woods to J. M. Lee, Dec. 31, 1867, reel 21, BRFAL-La: (M1027); J. W. Keller to J. M. Lee, Jan. 10, 1868, vol. 384, Trimonthly Reports, New Iberia Asst. SAC; C. E. Merrill to L. H. Warren, Jan. 31, 1868, vol. 427, Letters Sent, Plaquemine Agt and Asst. SAC; J. H. Brough to T. L. Morris, Feb. 10, 1868; and J. H. Brough to L. H. Warren, March 16, 1868, vol. 263, Letters Sent, Donaldsonville Agt and Asst. SAC, BRFAL-La.

19. W. A. Webster to J. M. Lee, Sept. 30, 1867, vol. 218, Letters Sent, Baton Rouge Asst. SAC, BRFAL-La. See also A. F. Hayden to J. H. Brough, Aug. 15, 1866, vol. 262, Letters Sent, Donaldsonville Agt and Asst. SAC; G. A. Ludlow to L. C. Parker, Aug. 31, 1867; and W. Woods to J. M. Lee, Dec. 20, 1867, vol. 294, Letters Sent, Houma Agt and Asst. SAC, BRFAL-La.

20. J. H. Brough to W. Sterling, Apr. 1, 1867, vol. 262, Letters Sent, Donaldsonville Agt and Asst. SAC, BRFAL-La.

21. J. W. Keller to W. H. Sterling, Aug. 31, 1867, vol. 275, Letters Sent, Franklin Agt and Asst. SAC, BRFAL-La.

22. I. D. McClany to W. H. Sterling, March 10, 1867, Reports of Operations and Conditions, Louisiana Asst. Comr., reel 27, BRFAL-La.

23. See, for example, Report of J. F. Harrison, Sept. 15, 1865, vol. 90, Inspection Reports, Plantation Dept., Louisiana Asst. Comr.; C. E. Merrill to A. F. Hayden, April 30, 1866, Narrative Trimonthly Reports of Business Transacted, Franklin Agt and Asst. SAC; R. Folles, Monthly Report, May 31, 1866, Reports of Asst. Inspector of Freedmen, Algiers Agt and Asst. SAC; R. Folles to A. F. Hayden, Sept. [?] 1866, vol. 187, Letters Sent, Algiers Agt and Asst. SAC; and J. White to L. H. Warren, Feb. 29, 1868, vol. 384, Trimonthly Reports, New Iberia Asst. SAC, BRFAL-La.

24. J. W. Keller to W. H. Sterling, Aug. 31, 1867, vol. 275, Letters Sent, Franklin Agt and Asst. BRFAL-La. Another Bureau agent similarly noted: "[I]f Planters treat freedmen kindly and with respect they return the compliment and work well, but if they find their employers scorn them and talk harsh to them freedmen are apt to do as little work as they possibly can. . . . My experience among freedmen is that if employers adopt a system of treating Freedmen with kindness and give them to understand that they mean to deal honorably and fairly with them everything will work well." Monthly Report of R. Folles, Jan. 31, 1868, Reports of Assistant Inspector of Freedmen, Algiers Agt and Asst. SAC, BRFAL-La.

25. R. Folles to W. W. Tyler, June 28, 1867, vol. 187, Letters Sent, Algiers Agt and Asst. SAC, BRFAL-La. For similar episodes, see I. D. McClany to W. W. Tyler, June 10, 1867, vol. 535, Letters Sent, St. Bernard and Plaquemines Parishes, New Orleans Asst. SAC; and J. H. Brough to W. W. Tyler, July 5, 1867, vol. 263, Letters Sent, Donaldsonville Agt and Asst. SAC, BRFAL-La.

26. On the slaves' economy in the Louisiana sugar region, see Roderick A. McDonald, *The Economy and Material Culture of Slaves: Goods and Chattels on the Sugar Plantations of Jamaica and Louisiana* (Baton Rouge: Louisiana State University Press, 1993), especially chap. 2.

27. R. W. Mullen to L. H. Warren, July 20, 1868, vol. 286, Trimonthly Reports, Franklin Agt and Asst. SAC, BRFAL-La. See also R. C. Martin, Jr., to R. C. Martin, Sept. 17, 1865, Martin-Pugh Collection, NSU.

28. J. White to L. H. Warren, Feb. 29, 1868, vol. 384, Trimonthly Reports, New Iberia Asst. SAC, BRFAL-La. For a similar episode, see S. W. Purchase to J. M. Lee, Nov. 20, 1867, vol. 384, Trimonthly Reports, New Iberia Asst. SAC, BRFAL-La.

29. S. W. Purchase to J. M. Lee, Nov. 30, 1867, vol. 284, Monthly Reports, Franklin SAC (3rd Subdistrict), BRFAL-La. See also J. H. Brough to A. F. Hayden, Nov. 13, 1866, vol. 262, and J. H. Brough to J. M. Lee, Nov. 21, 1867, vol. 263, Letters Sent, Donaldsonville Agt and Asst. SAC, BRFAL-La.

30. The records of local Freedmen's Bureau agents are so replete with labor disputes during the rolling season that it would be impractical to cite particular instances. For a general discussion of the problem, see Rodrigue, "Raising Cane," 225–6, 296–9, 349–53.

31. I. D. McClany to J. H. Hastings, Nov. 20, 1867, vol. 535, Letters Sent, St. Bernard and Plaquemines Parishes, New Orleans, Asst. SAC, BRFAL-La.

32. Well into the postbellum period, sugar planters acquiesced to freedmen's resistance to Sunday work during the rolling season. See Oct.–Dec. 1876, Plantation Journal 7, William A. Shaffer Papers, Southern Historical Collection, University of North Carolina at Chapel Hill (hereinafter SHC); Letter from Henry Studniczka in *Louisiana Sugar-Bowl*, Feb. 14, 1878; Nov.–Dec. 1880, Magnolia Plantation Journal, vol. 12, Henry Clay Warmoth Papers, SHC; and T. C. Porteous to Mr. Salvisberg, Nov. 5, 1880, Porteous Letterbook, LSU.

33. O. H. Hempstead to J. M. Lee, Oct. 10, 1867, Letters and Telegrams Received, reel 16, BRFAL-La. See also J. W. Keller to J. M. Lee, Nov. 10, 1867, vol. 275, Letters Sent, Franklin Agt and Asst. SAC, BRFAL-La.

34. Employers who were not as sagacious paid the price. "Sugar planters who had neglected to stipulate the amount of wages during Sugar making, when making agreement last spring," the Bureau agent for St. Mary's Parish noted in 1867, "have had some trouble with the Freedmen before they agreed to work extra hours." J. W. Keller to J. M. Lee, Nov. 20, 1867, vol. 275, Letters Sent, Franklin Agt and Asst. SAC, BRFAL-La.

35. J. H. Van Antwerp to B. J. Hutchins, Oct. 10, 1868, vol. 472, Letters Sent, Thibodaux Agt and Asst. SAC, BRFAL-La. See also J. W. Keller to J. M. Lee, Oct. 31, 1867, vol. 275, Letters Sent, Franklin Agent and Asst. SAC, BRFAL-La.

36. M. W. Morris to B. J. Hutchins, Nov. 10, 1868, vol. 295, Letters Sent, Houma Agt and Asst. SAC, BRFAL-La. See also *Thibodaux Sentinel*, Oct. 19, 1867; and A. L. Boeuf to H. S. Peire, Dec. 1, 1867, Consolidated Association of Planters of Louisiana Papers, LSU.

10

"A Full-Fledged Government of Men": Freedmen's Bureau Labor Policy in South Carolina, 1865–1868

James D. Schmidt

WHEN BREVET MAJOR GENERAL ROBERT KINGSTON SCOTT assessed his previous year's work as assistant commissioner of the Freedmen's Bureau in South Carolina in early 1867, he used the standard of northern free labor. "That free labor is a success," Scott declared, "there can be no doubt in every instance where it has been tested by practical and fair minded men, who were willing to treat the black men as laborers are treated at the north and in other parts of the country." By invoking the benchmark of northern free labor, the assistant commissioner acted in accord with many other northerners, both in and out of the Bureau of Freedmen, Refugees and Abandoned Lands. As the work of Eric Foner and other historians has made clear, the Bureau operated primarily as an agent of free-labor ideology, trying to balance out the needs of planters and freedpeople with the assumptions of bourgeois society in the North. By the time of the Civil War, however, those assumptions had come to mean many things for many different groups of people. For some, free labor implied the ownership of productive property, either in the form of land or in the form of a small shop or other petty proprietorship. For others, it meant simple self-ownership, which implied freedom from the will of another and the ability to sell one's labor power freely in the marketplace. For still others, as historians of labor law have uncovered in recent years, free labor implied a set of legal relationships that regulated both the marketplace and the shop floor.[1]

This contrast between the ideological and legal constructions of free labor has been frequently noted by historians of Reconstruction. Yet many northerners, at the time of the Civil War, would not have seen the apparent paradox. In fact, most nineteenth-century northerners did not see legal control of the employment relation or the labor market as contradictory with the free-labor ethic. In the five decades between 1815 and 1865, northern courts and legislatures had fashioned rules that specified the legal terms of free labor. Of these legal developments, the most important for what would take place in the postbellum South were labor-contract rules and vagrancy laws. Contracts crystallized the relationship of workers to individual employers, whereas vagrancy statutes defined the meaning of work in the community at large. Before the Civil War, northern courts, in adapting labor-contract rules to specific modes of production, had constructed stringent rules about marketplace movement for agricultural workers but less restrictive ones for industrial labor. In addition, jurists and law writers formulated two opposing conceptions of labor-contract law. One of these, the rule of entire contracts, sought to bind workers to their agreements through the threat of wage forfeiture; the other, the rule of apportioning contracts, looked to recompense workers for work performed regardless of the nature of the contract. Although no clear consensus had been reached by 1865, many northerners envisioned legal regulation of labor, especially for agricultural workers.[2]

For northerners who sought to construct free labor in the postbellum South, therefore, law was central. If read properly and used creatively, law could be a positive force to aid freed African Americans. For example, the common-law entirety rule required employers to pay workers their full wages if they were fired without cause. But implementing free labor in this manner rested on the presence of a Freedmen's Bureau assistant commissioner and staff who possessed a knowledge of labor law or, at least, a commitment to using what they knew about it to secure the rights of laborers. Even then, field agents could undermine directives from headquarters. In other words, the influence of Freedmen's Bureau field agents in setting the terms of freedom through labor regulations was crucial. Perhaps nowhere was this more clear than in South Carolina. There, neither Scott nor his predecessor, General Rufus Saxton, took as coordinated an approach to labor law as had been done in some other states.

Saxton was certainly committed to the cause of the freedpeople, but, like other officers with abolitionist connections, he was removed by late 1865. Although Scott relied on free-labor discourse, as did most other assistant commissioners, he manifested neither an unwavering commitment to black rights nor the legal training necessary for formalist remedies.[3]

As a result, labor law in Reconstruction South Carolina depended to a large extent on local Bureau agents. Studying such local emissaries of the Bureau has been a noticeable trend in recent scholarship on the Bureau. These studies have done much to advance historical knowledge about its daily workings and have demonstrated that the actions of local agents were far from uniform. Freedmen's Bureau scholars, however, continue to make relatively uncomplicated judgments about the Bureau's effectiveness with regard to its mission to assist freedpeople. Most of their studies have not closely considered the ideological commitments of local agents, yet the ways in which abstract principles of free-labor ideology and free-labor law were translated into daily reality depended heavily on the world views of the average northerners and southerners who occupied local outposts of the Bureau. Because they represented the power of the national state to shape labor law and hence the legal boundaries of the employment relation, local agents opened some options and closed others.[4]

Understanding this process requires analyzing army and Bureau officials, whether at the top of the hierarchy or in the field, as people with a complex intellectual history. The ideology they carried into the South drew on common antecedents and contained an embedded common consciousness, but it was not monolithic. If viewed from the perspectives of both free-labor ideology and free-labor law, at least three positions emerged. A sizable group of "conservatives" often supported coercive labor law with few restrictions and with little commitment to elements of free-labor ideology that promoted social mobility. Additionally, this group more consistently supported state action on the part of employers rather than workers. A small minority of "liberals," clinging to some version of the free-labor ethic, usually desired a labor system ultimately disciplined by market forces instead of the state. Often antagonistic to or unaware of free labor's legal system, these men more often supported state action on the part of workers than of employers. The "moderate" majority tried to combine the two and saw state control of the labor market as one of the best ways to achieve the ultimate result of social mobility. Many of these agents, as well as their superior, General Scott, displayed little hesitation to wield the Bureau's coercive power over both planters and freedmen.[5]

Historians who have studied the policies created by this diverse group of men often have seen their efforts as experimental. For such scholars, Union Army officials during the war and Bureau agents afterward created labor policy in the field as they reacted to the confused social relations of production generated by the sudden end of slavery. Bureau records certainly support the view that agents' daily policy decisions varied; however, the variance in Bureau labor regulations from state to state, as well as within states, did not necessarily reflect a purely experimental approach. Rather, agents in all three of the political categories mentioned above drew both on a developing bourgeois vision of work and, more important, on an antebellum legal system already in the process of embedding this language of class in law.[6]

Northerners who worked in the South as Bureau agents carried with them a vision of labor that was sometimes at odds in its particulars but generally consistent in its overall structure. By 1865, the central hallmarks of the developing capitalist work culture of the North—time discipline, the commodification of labor power, the cash nexus, and the inviolability of contracts—already had begun to take on the cemented quality of lived reality. Moreover, reform writers and courts had been working hard to establish the notion that free labor did not mean control of workers, which would give employers dominion over power relations in the workplace. At the same time, self-reliance bought through waged labor had become a cultural shibboleth. Imagined in part through fiction, prescriptive writing, sermons, and other forms of bourgeois discourse, self-reliance also had been lodged in the legal concept of vagrancy, a notion that moved to the forefront of the bourgeois imagination during Reconstruction.[7]

By the time slaves and their allies destroyed the peculiar institution, this vision of labor had not become irreparably fixed. Nonetheless, it had penetrated the consciousness of many northerners. To say that such people were "bourgeois" does not necessarily mean that they constituted a socially cohesive class. Rather, it means that they shared an increasingly stable language of class, one that exerted a considerable influence on how they imagined people freed from bondage. Although racial ideologies and gender conventions prevalent in northern culture formed part of northern perceptions, at least for Bureau agents, class provided the primary lens. Bureau policymakers envisioned freedpeople first as workers. Doing so connected freedpeople not only to a particular set of imaginative constructs but, more important, to a particular set of legal ones.[8]

Prevailing labor law became especially important in Bureau policy because the agency represented one of the first manifestations of the modern, bureaucratic state in U.S. history. If state power, as Stephen Skowronek points out, previously lay embedded in courts and parties, the Bureau now became a much more obvious incarnation of a monopoly on the legitimate means of coercion. The Bureau not only had jurisdiction over both millions of people and a myriad of social relations, including labor and beyond, but it also came with the guns (quite literally) to make its decisions stick. Even though much of the Union army had been mustered out, Bureau officers could nonetheless call on provost marshals for small detachments of troops, or even a single officer, to enforce directives in extreme cases. This power meant that Bureau decisions became more than mere directives, for they sought to alter the social relations of production, at least temporarily. Whereas bourgeois reformers back home had to work slowly and persuasively within at least nominally democratic processes, the Bureau represented something closer to a modern, administrative bureaucracy with direct power. That it ultimately failed testifies to the powerful resistance that the planters and freedpeople raised.[9]

In implementing labor policies, the Bureau acted like a modern state in another manner, for it evinced the use of previous policy, even if in the most informal of ways. Agents in South Carolina, as elsewhere, drew on previously existing principles of labor law that had been created by state legislatures and courts during the antebellum period. Most consistently, agents implemented the vagrancy laws of the antebellum North. Less invariably, they invoked the principles contained in northern contract law. That Bureau policy regarding labor contracts varied from place to place reflected the inchoate state of law at home. Although some northern courts had begun to move toward an unrestricted market in labor power, many jurists still clung to older notions of contract that were closer to bound labor than free labor. Because northern courts had not completed the task of anchoring bourgeois notions of labor securely in the rule of law, Bureau agents drew on many strains of popular legal discourse when they tried to construct a capitalist South. The internal tensions in that discourse, as well as resistance by its black and white recipients, eventually unhinged the Bureau's mission.[10]

This dynamic of class language filtered through a modern state and, drawing on legal notions, appeared clearly in the daily operations of the South Carolina Bureau. In making policy decisions, its officials carried into practice a capitalist conception of labor ill fitted to the preindustrial work culture of the state. For four years, Bureau agents preached the gospel of commodities, cash, and contracts to suspicious planters and freedpeople. They sought to establish both worker rights and employer power, a balance some envisioned as the proper "management" of free labor. Above all, they sought to ensconce the idea of participation in the labor market as the true path to self-reliance. To carry out this vision, agents used the power of the state in ways unprecedented in antebellum labor relations and almost without parallel in the twentieth century.[11]

Whereas field agents in South Carolina were the ultimate conduits for free labor, their actions and ideas must be seen in the context of policies that originated at the top of the Bureau hierarchy. Although reconstituting northern law became a central goal of the Bureau in South Carolina by 1866, Assistant Commissioner Saxton did not initiate this focus. Like many other top Bureau officers, Saxton brought to the job a set of life experiences common to the professional classes at the center of the northern bourgeoisie. Raised in the family of a Massachusetts lawyer, Saxton had become a career military officer. Having headed the Port Royal experiment during the war, he already had considerable experience with the establishment of free labor. Nevertheless, Saxton continued in 1865 to see the Bureau as an experiment whose first step involved the simple enforcement of legal emancipation. Freedpeople needed to understand their new "status" and must be protected in maintaining their newly formed rights, whereas former owners must be convinced that the federal government would no longer sanction slavery. Self-ownership, however, represented only a first step in freedom. Like other early assistant commissioners, Saxton believed strongly in land distribution not only as the surest guarantee of freedom but also the conduit to full citizenship.[12]

Saxton's goal of independent proprietorship for freedpeople directed the way he structured early labor policy in the state. The assistant commissioner became an early proponent of sharecropping, presumably as a quick way to secure some access to productive property. In the summer of 1865, he advised agents to form "fair and liberal" contracts on fifty-fifty shares and enjoined his men to remember the oft-quoted biblical injunction that "the laborer is worthy of his hire." By fall, Saxton's hopes for black landowning waned as President Andrew Johnson pardoned former Confederates and restored their lands. Still, Saxton continued to advocate a contract system that was simpler and more open than the systems that many of his contemporaries adopted. Hoping to secure "equitable contracts" for freedpeople, Saxton issued a brief contract form that required payment of monthly wages plus provision of housing, rations, fuel, medical attention, and other necessaries. Although Saxton did not intend rigorous intervention in the labor market, he did believe in the sanctity of contract. "Where fair and equitable contracts are made," Saxton counseled South Carolinians, "they must be kept by both parties." Still, he preferred the free-market capitalism supported by most liberals in the Bureau. Although he did suggest $10 per month as a possible minimum wage, he refused to use the Bureau's power to fix local wage rates and preferred to "leave it to seek its own value in the market." A free market in wages went hand in hand with the unfettered exchange of commodities. As reports came into his office of "river traders" who coasted the low country's waterways to barter cheap goods in exchange for freedpeople's crops, Saxton refused to interdict the practice. Freedpeople, he maintained, must learn how to act in the marketplace. "In many cases the freedmen would probably be imposed upon by dishonest and unscrupulous men," he admitted, "but as freedmen they must be taught self-reliance."Even in the inculcation of self-reliance, Saxton preferred to give freedpeople more freedom than many contemporaries. In late 1865, for example, Colonel J. J. Upham, an agent in Lawtonville, notified Saxton that he intended to arrest as vagrants all freedpeople not under contract by January 1. When Saxton wrote back, he advised Upham to delay enforcement of the order.[13]

In creating these policies, Saxton had followed a line not unlike that taken by abolitionists during the war. Liberals, such as prominent abolitionist Wendell Phillips or James McKaye, a member of the American Freedmen's Inquiry Commission that had established the basis for the Bureau, argued consistently for a laissez-faire market in labor. Phillips believed that what he called the "Idea of Massachusetts Liberty" consisted of an unfettered wage bargain, the right to quit, and the availability of legal redress. He rejected explicitly the binding nature of contracts and the fixing of wage rates. McKaye followed a similar course in commenting on the wartime labor system in Louisiana. Wages and work conditions must remain unregulated, he declared, so that ex-slaves could attain self-mastery and a sense of personal responsibility.[14]

The faith in the free market maintained by such liberals as Phillips, McKaye, and Saxton usually drew on a particular racial vision of freedpeople. Unlike moderates, who tended to see freedpeople primarily in class terms as workers, liberals invoked racial constructs that imagined freedpeople as long-suffering supplicants for white goodwill. Responding to the prevalent insurrection scares of 1865, Saxton informed Bureau Commissioner O. O. Howard that no danger existed among freedpeople, for "at the slightest show of kindness they seem to forget all their past grievances. . . . If but simple justice is done to them, a more orderly, peaceful people could not be found than this same 'barbaric race.' " Even when Johnson's pardons foreclosed access to land, Saxton predicted that ex-slaves would "submit with the same patient resignation that they do to their other disappointments." Although in some ways a paternalist language of uplift, Saxton's racial ideology nonetheless supported a liberal approach to policy and simultaneously placed him on a collision course with the president and with Howard. As early as August 1865, Saxton had begun to worry about the safety of his job, and, by January 1866, he had been replaced by Scott.[15]

During the waning days of Saxton's tenure, Bureau labor policy in South Carolina came to conform more closely to the program being established elsewhere by the Bureau when District Commander Major General Daniel E. Sickles issued a new set of regulations. Even more than Saxton's, Sickles's prewar experiences had been those of the emergent bourgeoisie. Born and raised in the nation's new commercial and industrial center, New York City, Sickles had graduated from City University. After college, he studied law with

Attorney General B. F. Battle and gained admission to the bar in 1846. By the 1850s, Sickles began to build an impressive political career that culminated with his 1857 election to Congress. The political connections that he made there served him well in South Carolina. As a friend of James Orr, South Carolina's governor under Presidential Reconstruction, Sickles influenced the making of the state's black codes. Corresponding with Orr in December 1865, Sickles helped to form an agreement that replaced the racial legislation of the immediate postwar era with color-blind laws. Although he would later become a Radical Republican, Sickles's insistence on simple equality of law suggests that in 1865 and 1866 he remained a moderate.[16]

His position as commander of the Department of South Carolina gave Sickles the authority to direct labor policy, and, in late 1865, he began to do so. In December, he notified freedpeople that no government land distribution would occur and that the army would not issue rations to people able to work. Having thus created, by state action, the need for a labor market, Sickles instructed his officers in the legal means of its inauguration. Union officials needed to help freedpeople make "fair contracts to labor," but they must also teach those unaccustomed to free labor the consequences of not making contracts. Both planters and freedpeople must be admonished to undertake cultivation to "avoid the losses, privations, and sufferings, which must follow idleness on the one hand, and harsh and unreasonable exactions on the other." Apparently unsure of the willingness of Saxton's officers to follow his directives, Sickles declared that officers who prevented or discouraged ex-slaves from employment faced arrest and punishment. Having thus begun the transition to a much greater role for the state in creating a labor market, Sickles continued his efforts on January 1, 1866, by issuing a much more comprehensive set of labor laws. The general ordered what amounted to a sweeping program of intervention in the emergent labor market as an effort both to secure "civil rights and immunities" and to define "the rights and duties of the employer and the free laborer." These military orders would return the land to its former owners and secure its cultivation. Compared with Saxton's labor policy, Sickles's actions seemed to place the power of the Union army on the side of the planters, yet he did not necessarily intend to be their willing accomplice. Rather, the general cast his actions in the language of the northern poor laws. His order, he averred, would ensure "that persons able and willing to work may find employment, that idleness and vagrancy may be discountenanced and encouragement given to industry and thrift; and that humane provision may be made for the aged, infirm and destitute."[17]

Sickles's employment of this language of poverty was not simply a veneer to cover direct assistance to the planters. Indeed, he aimed to realize ambitions that Saxton and other Liberals certainly respected. But for Sickles, as both a military man and a lawyer, the state rather than the market itself was the best guarantor of success. As a result, Sickles melded a number of existing northern legal principles into a new code for free labor in South Carolina. Fulfilling his promise to establish civil rights, Sickles required equal protection of the law and endorsed the right of blacks to testify in court. With regard to the labor market, the order ensured that all occupations would remain open to all races and that no combinations to suppress wages would be formed. The order also began to shift the burden of social welfare from personal paternalism to that of the state by authorizing provision for the old and infirm and by allowing planters to evict ex-slaves who refused to work or who were "rightfully dismissed or expelled for misbehavior." Having thus ensured that planters could push unwanted laborers into local markets, Sickles made certain that unemployed people would seek work. Officers should discountenance idleness when handing out rations. Drawing directly on the northern poor laws, Sickles empowered officers to employ those arrested as vagrants on public works and to use the proceeds of their labor to assist orphaned children. Sickles thus employed the bourgeois notion that state power should be used to construct a labor market and force participation in it instead of compelling work for any particular individual. His comments on the existing vagrancy codes in South Carolina make this clear. Ex-slaves were bound to obey existing vagrancy statutes "applicable to free white persons," but the army would not enforce these statutes against "persons who are without employment, if they can prove that they have been unable to obtain employment after diligent efforts to do so." In other words, as long as freedpeople looked for work, they broke no law.[18]

These rules laid the initial groundwork for the new Bureau policy instituted by Scott when he took over the assistant commissioner's office. Although not trained as a lawyer, as was Sickles, Scott also came to the position as a member of the northern bourgeoisie. A Pennsylvanian by birth and upbringing, Scott had attended college in Ohio and eventually had studied medicine. A checkered career before the war had found him in real estate, medicine, and merchandising. Later a Republican governor of South Carolina, Scott in 1866 was a political moderate. Although charged with carrying out the results of the sudden destruction of slavery during the war, he professed support for gradual abolition and believed that it "would have educated and prepared both classes for the new regime and enabled the civil authorities to have anticipated the requirement of the new condition by appropriate and timely legislation." Scott's gradualism, however, did not grow primarily out of racial sentiments. By 1867, for example, he favored integration and praised the president of the Charleston Rail Road Company for opening its cars to blacks. Rather than race, Scott viewed the problem of Reconstruction primarily through the lens of class. The war, he believed, had "suddenly disarranged" social, industrial, civil, and financial interests, and had "induce[d] antagonism of feeling between the two classes" in the South. Lacking both Saxton's previous experience with labor policy and Sickles's training as a lawyer, Scott dealt with this class conflict, in part, by gathering information from state constitutions but mostly by employing popular conceptions of northern labor law combined with a nebulous concern for "equity."[19]

Drawing on these roots, Scott worked throughout 1866 to structure a new Bureau labor policy. Eschewing Saxton's willingness to rely on the market, the new assistant commissioner issued a lengthy sample contract. The new agreement called for families or larger groups of laborers to undertake yearly obligations paid by a one-third share in the crop and organized by tasks or a ten-hour day. It established clearly the right to receive at least some cash wages when dismissed, but it also allowed planters to fine workers for such offenses as injury to farm animals. The contract enjoined workers to take care of tools, to keep their homes and gardens "neat and orderly," to refrain from entertaining visitors during working hours, and to provide a nurse and stockminder. Scott proposed to deal with workplace conflicts by allowing planters or overseers to select a foreman from among the hands. Reminiscent of a slave driver, this foreman would inform the owner of "all abuses, refusals to work, and disorderly conduct of the employees" and then read the list to the hands. Although these provisions, if carried out, might have opened an opportunity for a modicum of workplace control, Scott made sure that neither local labor markets nor plantation discipline would be disrupted. In April, he reissued an order from Howard that limited charity to extreme instances. When the height of the cultivation cycle arrived in June, Scott advised field officers to discountenance freedpeople from bringing small conflicts into Bureau offices for litigation and to "enjoin upon them the necessity of steadiness of purpose."[20]

After reviewing this program at the end of 1866, Scott altered the system considerably for 1867. Gone were the minute controls over workers' lives, as well as the system of direct fines, which Scott had concluded was "productive of more evil than good and . . . not adapted to free labor." Gone, too, were the foremen selected by the planter. With regard to compensation, Scott's 1867 contract offered separate sections for shares and cash wages. Share contracts continued the practice of giving one-third of the gross proceeds to the laborer, whereas wage contracts stipulated monthly payments with the amount open. Scott clearly preferred the latter option. Although he admitted that a shortage of capital might require share wages, he had urged South Carolinians in late 1866 "to follow as nearly as practicable the labor system of the agricultural districts of the North and West paying each laborer fair compensation for his services by the day, week, or month as may be agreed upon." Hoping to implement this capitalist model, Scott also continued to curtail charity, uphold workplace discipline, and secure wages. A January circular letter warned freedpeople who refused to contract that they would face military eviction from their homes and would find no government relief. In March, he ordered officers to make sure that contracts provided enough compensation so that workers would not apply for relief after their agreements expired. When voter registration meetings began in June 1867, the assistant commissioner advised officers not to allow such proceedings to interfere with farm work. While thus attempting to keep freedpeople at work, Scott also sought to ensure that wages would be paid. In September, he warned employers that all freedpeople entitled to a share must be paid and that charges would be brought against anyone who attempted to "defraud them of their just dues."[21]

By the time Scott became South Carolina's governor in summer 1868, he had shifted Bureau labor policy considerably in the direction of an open market tempered by equity. As early as January 1867, his office had advised an agent in Rockville that when freedpeople became "inharmonious . . . unsettled and Stubborn," he could simply leave contracts open and neither approve nor disapprove them. In 1868, Scott refrained from issuing a contract form as in previous years but instead recommended contracts of "briefness and simplicity" that paid cash wages, although he acknowledged that share wages would probably prevail. Increasingly aware of the exactions of unscrupulous planters, he advised freedpeople to avoid contracting with employers who had "persistently wronged and defrauded them." This partial retreat from the contract system had come from Scott's ongoing reliance on the concept of equity as the surest resolution to class conflict. Labor agreements should not "work in any manner but that of Equity between the parties." As a result, he reported, his office frequently annulled contracts that were "inconsistent with justice and the principles of free labor." Such arrangements were "made by the planter with a sole view to *their* interests, and without reference to those of the freedmen." Yet, he assured Governor Orr, his agents did not go to plantations "for the purpose of annuling equitable contracts or creating disaffection among the laborers but for the purpose of securing strict justice in the settlement of *all* contracts."[22]

The unintended outcome of Scott's adherence to equity was a Bureau labor policy not unlike what Saxton and other liberals desired—one with a limited role for the state in policing labor arrangements. In part, this consequence originated in Scott's reading of the conflict between planters and freedpeople primarily as a class conflict. In late 1866, for example, Scott blamed failures in the system on "mutual distrust between the planter and the laborer" that led both sides to ignore "the principle that the interests of capital and labor are identical." In 1866, and to a lesser extent in 1867, Scott had tried to use the Bureau's power to resolve this conflict. But, in the end, Scott remained a moderate. He refused to abandon entirely the Bureau's power to intervene in wage disputes and continued to believe that his office had the power to stop organized efforts by both parties to control local wage rates. Still, Scott had discovered, as would his agents, that using state power to construct free labor was not an easy task.[23]

As the assistant commissioner in South Carolina during the key years of 1866 and 1867, Scott did much to establish a system of free labor in the state. Stressing a balance of interests between capital and labor, he followed a moderate line. How these policy directives worked out in practice, however, depended on the administrations of Bureau field agents. Hence, the daily operations of the Bureau depended heavily on what local agents thought about free labor and the law's role in bringing it into existence. The men who made Bureau policy a reality for thousands of freedpeople and their former masters followed a variety of paths. Some agents, acting more in line with Saxton's liberal stance, took up the cause of freedpeople and tempered the potentially oppressive effects of northern labor law. Others followed a course more rigid than Scott's and aligned themselves with Bureau conservatives in other states who turned local field offices into labor police available to planters. Most agents, however, operated similarly to Scott and other moderate assistant commissioners. These men struggled to combine both the free labor ethic and the legal system that had brought it into being. Like their commanding officer, they, too, sometimes came to find northern ideology and law inadequate to deal with the social conflicts created by emancipation.

Few agents in South Carolina occupied a consistent liberal position, but one of the most unfailing advocates of the freedpeople was Major Martin R. Delany. Northern born and educated and one of the nation's premier black nationalists before the war, Delany had been one of the first commissioned officers in the United States Colored Troops. In July 1865, the War Department assigned Delany as a special agent to ex-slaves at Hilton Head, and he eventually became a regular officer in the Bureau. Delany spent his early days in the Sea Islands, where he worked on behalf of black workers to ensure that they would not immediately slip back into forced labor. An army official in the area reported in late July that Delany was "endeavoring to persuade the col. people on the adjacent Islands not to work for Whites." In a July 23 speech on St. Helena, Delany urged freedmen to gain land, insist on a one-third share in the crops, and refuse to work for wages so low that they would equate with slavery.

"I tell you slavery is over, and shall never return again," the major declared.[24]

As Delany's career as a Bureau agent continued, his local policies moved from a liberal position based on free-labor ideology to one that invoked greater state intervention on the part of the freedpeople. During the fall of 1865, Delany announced in a series of letters to the *New South*, a Hilton Head newspaper, his "Triple Alliance." "Capital, land, and labor require a copartnership," Delany wrote, sounding like a good northern Republican. Land needed to be made available to ex-slaves to buy or rent. Consequently, he invited northern capitalists, southern landholders, and black workers to join together, with each equally sharing the profits of their efforts. The motives behind Delany's plan would have fit well with such liberals as Phillips and McKaye. Freedpeople, he believed, were "unaccustomed to self-reliance by the barbarism of the system under which they had lived." A proper system of free labor, however, would solve this problem. If blacks could gain small tracts of land, as well as civil and political rights, they would become productive members of society. Such a system would benefit all, for it would call forth "a great market, . . . a new source of consumption of every commodity in demand in free civilized communities." Freedpeople would be "great consumers" who would purchase farm implements and new houses. Better food would replace black-eyed peas, hominy, and salt pork; "osnaburgs and rags would give place to genteel apparel becoming a free and industrious people." In practice, Delany sought to write this vision into freedpersons' contracts. When a Colonel C. J. Colcock contacted Delany about help in securing a contract, Delany's response characterized Colcock's letter as asking whether workers could be "obtained on the basis of copartnership of capital, land, and labor, or what I term the domestic triple alliance." Generally approving of the colonel's arrangements, Delany amended the contract's "injunction to frugality and economy"; he believed it best that such admonitions come from the freedpeople's "own representative."[25]

As Delany endeavored to establish his plan, he increasingly drew on the Bureau's power. In early 1866, he supervised the making of contracts in the islands with enough zeal that some freedpeople started to complain. By the end of January, the *New South* could report that Delany acted as a "medium between employers and employees." A month later, the editors praised Delany for telling the freedpeople to "go to work at once; that labor surely brings its own reward." Indeed, Delany's contract form included much that could make planters happy. It allowed share forfeiture for "negligence of duty in cultivation," required proper treatment of animals and good care of tools, and prohibited liquor. Yet, the major also prevented planters from requiring handwork for what could be done with machines or animals, allowed the adjudication of disputes by mutually selected third parties, and advised workers to keep account books to make sure "that no advantage be taken by incorrect charges." Apparently, Delany tried to make this contract uniform throughout his district; in March, Scott's office sent a letter noting that it was "entirely impracticable to attempt to establish a uniform form of contract" and warning him not to interfere with "fair and equitable contracts."[26]

Although much of Delany's program would have met with the approbation of northern liberals, he eventually came to favor greater market intervention than most agents would have accepted. In the fall of 1866, Delany set up what he called "a freedman's cotton agency," where freedpeople on the islands could have their cotton sorted, ginned, and bagged. He wanted more than simply a cotton warehouse. Delany intended the depot as an effort in black mutualism. He found a suitable building, gathered all the freedmen with foot gins to work there, and paid them out of the proceeds of the ginning. His efforts brought a stern letter from Scott, who told him that Delaney could allow freedmen to obtain a fair weight from his depot but that he must not act as a cotton factor. "The people must be free to sell when they think proper," Scott instructed.[27]

Although Delany's eventual use of market intervention was a more extreme step than those taken by many agents, he was not the only South Carolina agent who acted on behalf of the freedmen. Benjamin P. Runkle, who worked at several local offices in the state, also followed a liberal line. Runkle understood the depths of white resistance to emancipation and worked to counter it. In late 1866, he voiced his concerns about planters' willingness to "take advantage of the ignorance of the freedman and cheat and defraud him out of his hard earned share of the crop." When he reported on theft by freedpeople, he blamed it on their having been "thrust out and unjustly deprived of their earnings." Whites, on the other hand, often exhibited "a spirit of utter lawlessness," hated the Bureau, and tried to "wreak their vengeance upon the freedman for no other reason than the fate of the war has made them free."[28]

More than just sentiment, Runkle carried his advocacy of the freedpeople into practice. Witnessing the repeated violation of contracts by planters, he frequently used military force to secure workers' rights. In September 1866, for example, he warned an employer that he must pay his employees for the time they had worked or Runkle's office would send a guard to confiscate property to cover the debts. That same month, he decided that freedpeople were bound to perform only the work stipulated in their contracts. Workers should be compelled to perform their agreements, he admitted, but it would be "unlawful and unjust to compel them to perform labor not contemplated by them." In addition to adjudicating contracts in favor of freedmen, Runkle, unlike many of his colleagues, also refused to apply a strict construction of northern poor laws to freed slaves. Although he reported that many "vagrant freedmen" in his district displayed "a general disposition to avoid work and violate contracts," he also denounced "vagrant whites" who committed "outrages" upon freedpeople. Moreover, he advocated swift action for infant and elderly freedpeople. "Surely if we desert them cast out as they are in their old age and helplessness by their former heartless taskmasters for them they wasted their strength and vigor," he wrote, "to these poor people is liberty indeed a curse."[29]

On one level, Runkle's concern for the very young and very old drew on the common northern construction of poverty that legitimated relief to the "worthy poor." Certainly, both his and Delany's views of ex-slaves did not stray much beyond received middle-class wisdom. Still, the more liberal nature of their positions becomes clear when their actions appear next to those of their more conservative colleagues. These men operated from open or thinly veiled racial predilections, and they showed little restraint on their use of the military's power to ensure plantation labor and uphold plantation discipline.

One of the most conservative of all the agents in the state was E. R. Chase. Viewing the same rash of violence that Runkle had witnessed, Chase placed the onus on the victims. The Aiken District, he reported in August 1866, had seen several assaults and one murder. Yet he found the freedmen "to a certain extent blameable in many cases, they being insolent and neglecting to fulfill their contracts &c." Moreover, Chase seemed quick to believe charges of theft against ex-slaves. His reports complained of "petit thefts" on their part, and when a freedman named Davy appeared in Chase's office to complain of nonpayment of wages, Chase dismissed the case after Davy's employer appeared to charge him with theft. In general, Chase's complaint register recorded many of the racial appellations commonly applied to blacks. Whereas other agents usually referred to ex-slaves simply as "freedmen" or "blacks" or "Negroes" in their records, Chase faithfully recorded the accusations of a planter who claimed his hogs had been "killed by Mr. Duncan's niggers." Moreover, Chase usually recorded blacks' cases only with their first names, and he consistently accepted planters' descriptions of blacks as "insolent," "saucy," and "unruly."[30]

In practice, Chase's racial ideology turned the Bureau into something approximating the slave patrols. In April 1866, he sent soldiers to arrest workers on William Davis's place and hold them until they promised to work better. When Grace, a worker for J. S. Stanley, complained of sickness, Chase sent out a doctor to examine her and a guard to compel her to work. He detained Jim Duncan as a vagrant and held him in the guardhouse at Aiken for more than two weeks until "promising to do better [when he] was released." In early June 1866, Chase removed a freedwoman's children, returned them to a Mrs. Crowley, *"a very fine lady,"* who claimed to have raised them and to have written permission to keep them. Chase thus used the Bureau to carry out the wishes of nearly every planter who presented himself or herself. On the other side, he was much less active. When a freedwoman named Carolina reported that her employer had beaten and driven her off, Chase simply sent out a letter to the planter.[31]

Chase was probably the most conservative agent in the state, but his colleague, A. J. Willard, also took a hard line with regard to labor law. In November 1866, Willard issued a lengthy set of instructions for officers who visited plantations in his Georgetown district. Such visits, he stated plainly, should aim to "preserve order," enforce contract provisions, and "induce the Freed people to contract for another year." For officers to achieve this end, Willard approved wide powers. A list of "Rules as to Plantations" prohibited outsiders from coming on the place, required all present to work, prevented hunting or trading without permission, and severely restricted the ownership of firearms. A separate set of rules for work made it clear that employers or overseers could force freedpeople to work at their discretion. If workers failed to perform, they could be fired, evicted, and made to "pay out of their crops, stock, poultry, and other property, any loss sustained by the Planter in consequence of their not performing their contract."[32]

Georgetown-area planters must have been overjoyed by the power that Willard endowed, but he saw these rules as stemming from military law, not from personal authority. Displaying an incredibly blunt view of the Bureau's role, Willard ordered his officers to "instruct the people that the government has the right to decide what work they are bound to do under the contract, and that the decision of the Military Authorities is binding and they are bound to obey it." Willard must have realized that this decree might not meet with unqualified approval, for he cautioned officers "not to have too many people, at one time, removed from a plantation for disobedience of orders." These orders also appear to have regularized a policy that Willard had been following for some time. A year earlier, he had written to the assistant commissioner that in cases of general "misconduct" he had rounded up "the leading spirits" and dealt with them accordingly, "trusting the force of such an example to secure obediance to lawful authority on the part of the rest of the people on the plantation."[33]

For Willard, labor law represented a tool to restore plantation discipline and to set freedpeople to work. Although appearing not to possess Chase's overt racism, Willard nonetheless enforced the Bureau's labor policy almost entirely in favor of planters. By their actions, such conservative agents as Willard and Chase created one end of a spectrum, whereas the actions of such liberal officers as Runkle and Delany formed the opposite extreme. Most South Carolina agents fell somewhere in between. These moderates usually pursued policies based on a middle-class version of the free-labor ethic, and they tried to apply existing concepts of labor law relatively equally to both ex-slaves and ex-masters.

German-born agent Frederick W. Liedtke, who spent most of his tenure stationed at Moncks Corner, provides a particularly clear example of the mixture of ideas followed by the moderates. Liedtke clearly had imbibed the tenet of free-labor ideology before the war—

when he sought to explain freedom to ex-slaves, he invoked the image of wage labor creating social mobility so common in republican discourse. He reported that, during the winter of 1866, he had gone to the plantations and "explained to the freedpeople their position as free men, and . . . endeavored to impress upon their minds that by honest, industrious and peaceable labor they would gradually be able to buy homes for themselves and become good citizens." Liedtke put these rhetorical flourishes into practice by sponsoring the causes of freedpeople, such as Cuffy Glover, who claimed more than $100 in wages from his employer. Unable to leave work to sue in the local courts, Glover turned to Liedtke for help. The agent took up Glover's case with Scott's office, which eventually authorized Liedtke to seize property to satisfy Glover's claim.[34]

Believing in the value of wage labor, Liedtke also trusted the power of labor law to ensure its performance and followed closely the poor laws of his adopted homeland. In July 1866, he decried the presence of "a very low class of white people, male and female, who have intermixed with Negroes and Indians and who themselves as well as their offspring are so unwilling to work that charity expended to them would be the very inducement to make them lazy." These people, Liedtke recommended, should be cut off from Bureau relief. In the same report, he blamed the destitution of freedpeople on their having "squandered" their earnings in transactions with the river traders. Earlier in the month, Liedtke had revealed an unusual part of his relief policy. For freedpeople too old or infirm to work in the fields, he urged them to do handiwork, such as making baskets, axe handles, and horse collars, for self-support. If "those too lazy to do anything at all" refused to become petty capitalists, Liedtke informed them that they "need not look to the Government for support."[35]

Liedtke's application of vagrancy concepts across racial lines paralleled his application of contract laws. Clearly, he saw law as necessary for establishing free labor. Commenting on Glover's case, Liedtke deplored the unwillingness of local magistrates to act and insisted that the Bureau officers needed more "power to act." In working out the contract system, Liedtke sought to use the power he did possess, and he did so for both planters and freedpeople. With regard to freedpeople, for example, he sentenced a freedman named Evans to three hours of "hard labor" for "striking [the] foreman," and a woman named Jenny received the same punishment for "insolence." He also arrested freedpeople directly for "breach of contract" and allowed planters to dismiss freedpeople from their plantations. If these actions are viewed by themselves, Liedtke would appear little different from conservatives, such as Chase. The difference lies in the fact that he also used his authority against the planters. When Joseph Davis reported to Liedtke that his employer, Robert Jackson, had driven him off with a gun, Liedtke ordered Jackson arrested, confined, and dispossessed of his gun. He had a planter arrested for "refusing to make [a] contract" and another for "breach of contract." In the latter case, Liedtke recorded the offender as a "mean fellow" and directed that half the crop be given to the freedpeople. During the fall of 1867, Liedtke adjudicated many such cases and ordered crop divisions when planters refused to settle.[36]

Bureau agent George Pingree also sought equal application of the law. As did many other agents, Pingree had to decide numerous cases relating to the dismissal of freedpeople. He reinstated workers who had been fired for such after-work activities as voter registration and church attendance, yet he upheld the case of a group of workers who apparently left work to attend a Union League meeting. In resolving discharge cases, Pingree reported that he never allowed a dismissal after six months "unless it has been proved by black witnesses that the laborer is insolent and unworthy." In such cases, he apportioned contracts at $6 per month. Pingree's test of a worker having been "insolent" or "unworthy" imported tropes from both racial and class discourse, but his strong reliance on black testimony put him out of step with many of his colleagues. Beyond dismissal cases, Pingree enforced labor law against planters in ways similar to Liedtke. He arrested planters in order to make them pay wages and to register contracts, and he issued numerous orders to settle crop divisions. Occasionally, in a mirror image of Chase's general policy, Pingree merely sent letters to freedpeople whose employers had complained about their refusal to work.[37]

Underneath this application of law lay policy aims similar to those of other moderates. Pingree, like Liedtke, purveyed the idea of material gain through hard work. "You must remember," he wrote to a freedman named Ford Parker, "that the harder you work, the larger crop you will make and the more money you will have at the end of the year." This belief in advancement through hard work connected to the sanctity of contracts. Commenting on the workers who had left for a Union League meeting, Pingree called on Scott to "announce whether Laborers have a right to leave the Plantations of their Employers whenever they see fit, without regard to whether their services are indispensable on the Plantation." Clearly, Pingree thought they did not. "Too many of the Freedmen are getting the idea that they have charge of the plantations, and are not bound to obey the orders of the owners thereof," he opined in his monthly report for the period that included the Parker case.[38]

Pingree's desire for uninterrupted labor drew on northern poor laws, but, in the end, he found them inadequate to deal with the poverty of Reconstruction South Carolina. As did many moderate agents, Pingree applied these concepts to both blacks and whites. When planters complained of theft and blamed it on freedpeople, Pingree instead implicated "ignorant 'Poor Whites' [who] are lying about with no intention of working and no visible means of support." In view of this situation, he recommended a law for "the arrest of these vagrants both black and white." Here, Pingree drew directly on the formal language of northern vagrancy laws, and, in dispensing relief to poverty-stricken South Carolinians, he also tried to use northern standards. When issuing rations to both black and white recipients, he tried to "discriminate justly" and give assistance "to those only who are really destitute and worthy." Although Pingree tried to apply this rule, the destitution in his district, which he called "absolutely appalling," pushed him beyond received wisdom. In an August 1867 report to Scott, he admitted that he had "fed many who are able bodied, but only because they had neither money or credit, their crops would have been abandoned without help, and I believed it better to assist them in making a crop that they might not be objects of Charity next year." Appearing frustrated with the situation, he acknowledged that he had probably been "swindled" and concluded that the people in his district had "no pride in the matter" and would "beg rather than work."[39]

As Pingree struggled with received notions about free labor and law, he wrestled with the dilemmas of Reconstruction similar to other moderate agents. Concomitantly, these officers' lack of certainty made them different from both liberals and conservatives, who relied on considerably different understandings of labor, law, and race. Consequently, the labor policies promulgated by Bureau officers were often inconsistent. Some officers acted practically as agents of the planters; others advocated the causes of freedpeople; others sought a balance. At the level of policy, then, Bureau actions in the state appear to be little more than a collection of reactions to specific problems in postemancipation labor relations. To conclude that local agents displayed absolutely no coherence, however, would be to misconstrue both the nature of the Bureau's program and the reasons for its ultimate failure. Beneath a diverse set of labor regulations lay a relatively consistent set of imaginative constructs, a language within which agents of all stripes envisioned their mission.

That language was a capitalist language of class. Although Bureau officers in the state diverged over how to balance free-labor law and the free-labor ethic, most agreed on certain notions of capitalist work culture. For them, work and time were commodities to be traded under a contract for cash in a market. Waged labor thus purchased self-reliance and personal independence as the precondition of full political and civil rights. Agents saw themselves as involved in creating a market society and a society with industrial class relations, even if production remained agricultural. Conflicts between planters and freedmen, consequently, were class conflicts. Liberal agents thought these conflicts best solved by the market itself, but most of the rest accepted the need for a coercive state to establish a capitalist labor market and the labor relations of a market society.

As the starting point for all else, the agents in the state had to teach the notion of commodified labor power to people unused to buying and selling it and time discipline to people used to living by seasonal rhythms. In a state where the task system had been more common than elsewhere, this goal proved particularly difficult to achieve. Garret Nagle complained from Summerville in November 1866 that freedmen did not understand the nature of contracts. "They were under the impression," he reported, "that when their usual tasks were finished they were at liberty to do as they pleased, regarding their contract as meaning so much work per day in the field and when the crop is harvested to have their share." Similarly, Bureau agent Chase found freedmen in Barnwell disposed to enter local labor markets after the crops were laid by. Other agents bemoaned the lack of steady work on the plantation. B. F. Smith alleged that freedpeople in the vicinity of Georgetown finished their allotted work by noon and refused to work for the rest of the day.

"They seem to understand that the more they labor the larger their share of the crop will be," a confused Smith confessed, "but they prefer to idle away the rest of the day." For Smith, labor meant steady work for the entire day, a concept ill-fitted to people with a preindustrial understanding of work. This conceptual gap appeared even more clearly in a story recounted by Bureau agent Willard, also stationed in Georgetown. A sawmill owner who had contracted for $25 per month plus rations came to Willard to resolve a dispute. The two workers in question, "very intelligent and good laborers" in Willard's opinion, claimed an hour off between 8 and 9 A.M. for breakfast and another between 12 and 1 P.M. for lunch. Trying to resolve the situation, Willard explained to them that "laborers at the North got less wages and worked from sunrise to sunset, this season of the year, only having an hour at noon. Their [the workers'] answer was, 'we want to work just as we have always worked.' "[40]

To remedy this perceived deficiency in bourgeois values, the Bureau sanctioned wage deductions for time lost. Scott's February 1866 contract form allowed deductions of fifty cents for every day's labor lost. When agents carried this policy into practice, however, they found that it proved quite useful to planters who wanted to maintain plantation discipline or to avoid paying wages altogether. After two years of using time deductions, Scott felt moved in January 1868 to remind planters that fines for disobeying petty plantation regulations or deductions for such infractions as "impertinence" were "inconsistent with the laborers status as a freeman and accountable person." Fines, Scott averred, aimed to keep laborers at work. "If a laborer absents himself from his allotted task he should be charged for the time so lost, at the rate which he would have received if he had worked," the assistant commission explained, "all addition of extra fines for lost time is improper where the free-labor system is expected to succeed."[41]

If time deductions were pointed at freedpeople who worked too little in the eyes of the Bureau, another question about time dealt with those who worked too much. The binding contracts implanted by the Bureau gave planters the opportunity, in the words of Aiken officer Orlando H. Moore, to bring freedmen "as near to the condition of slavery as possible and exact from them unremunerative labor which was never contemplated by the freedmen when making the contract." Planters, it seemed, also failed to understand the sale of tightly commodified labor. This conflicting view of labor appeared in an exchange between Bureau agent Liedtke and a planter named Dr. Dwight. When Dwight appeared at Liedtke's office in Moncks Corner to complain about a freedman who refused to perform work not stipulated in a contract, Liedtke informed him that he must pay more for extra labor. When the planter tried to convince the officer that "plantation" meant land and all work connected to it, Liedtke informed him that "plantation" merely signified land under cultivation and that no amount of land could make one man wiser than another. Dwight grew agitated at these remarks, and Liedtke threw him out of the office. A similar conflict led Nagle to suggest a novel, but telling, solution to Henry Hood, a freedman employed by Joel Witsell. Witsell had put Hood to work at hauling trash, a task to which Hood objected. After hearing Hood's case, Nagle wrote to Witsell that he had "directed Hood to keep a strict account of the time that they are employed at work not legitimately connected with the crop, the same may be charged against you."[42]

Nagle's remedy for Hood's problem reflected a central goal of Bureau policy, the inculcation of time discipline and commodified labor. Keeping accounts represented the division of toil into discrete parcels that could be bought and sold in the marketplace. Clearly, as the freedmen involved in Willard's visit to the sawmill and the planter in Liedtke's office indicate, not all southerners were prepared for this northern construction of a labor market. For the northerners in the Bureau, participation in that labor market also implied a promise to pay. Consequently, a near obsession with the cash nexus became central to Bureau policy. John R. Chance, one of a string of agents in Georgetown, put the case flatly: "Money is the basis of labor," he declared. Charleston agent George A. Williams agreed that contracts need to be for wages, not shares or tasks. Agent C. S. Allen reported that freedmen in Abbeville were being "victimized out of their just due." Scott reiterated this principle in a letter to Governor James Orr in late 1866. Contracts that allowed even a "moderate compensation" to freedmen would be upheld by the Bureau, Scott assured him, but those "intended to defraud the freedman out of compensation" would be considered "null and void." Moreover, proper contracts, Scott and his officers believed, should be made for cash wages paid in a timely fashion, preferably by the month.[43]

Implementing capitalist modes of exchange appeared in Bureau policy regarding wage forfeitures. In Scott's 1866 contract form, he allowed planters to dismiss any hand missing from the plantation for three days, and the worker was to forfeit his or her share of the crop. Such a principle invoked an established legal practice in northern agricultural labor contracts—withholding wages until the end of the crop season. Strict adherence to prevailing northern law could have meant that such workers forfeited their entire year's earnings. As a result, Scott also employed the rising doctrine of contract apportionment. Workers who forfeited their shares were to be paid $5 per month for the time they had already worked. When put into practice, however, this commonplace northern practice worked to the advantage of planters who could withhold all compensation for the slightest of infractions. As a result, Scott's office worked to instill the true meaning of wage forfeiture into employers. When Garrett Hayward fired Green Hawood without wages in September 1867, Scott's office wrote back that "it would be unjust in any case to deprive him of his whole seasons labor for some light misdemeanor and contracts made in contradiction to this principle are not in accordance with the laws of justice and equity."[44]

Hawood's case points toward the most common dispute that Bureau officials were asked to resolve, those involving freedmen dismissed without wages. In such conflicts, local Bureau agents put into practice the mixture of northern legal principles that Scott had suggested. Occasionally, Bureau agents allowed dismissed workers to claim their whole wages or shares, but more often they apportioned the contract and required planters to pay wages to the date of dismissal. Generally, the outcome depended on whether an agent believed that a planter had a just cause in dismissing a worker. Agents William F. DeKnight in Abbeville and William H. Holton in Columbia both employed this policy. At other times, agents simply apportioned contracts, such as Nagle did in the case of Samuel Smith. "You will show this office good cause for discharging him," Nagle wrote to Benjamin Durant, Smith's employer, "and [you] will pay him at once for what is due him for his labor." Whether freedpeople received wages in such cases, however, depended on agents' conceptions of what constituted an unjust discharge and what did not. Whereas agents might void discharges for such actions as church attendance or voting, they generally upheld those directly related to work performance.[45]

Agents' adjudication of planter dismissals represented one side of another central concept of the bourgeois vision that they had brought south. The inviolability of contracts and its larger social accompaniment, the importance of promise keeping, have constituted a core value in capitalist cultures, and even a cursory look at Freedmen's Bureau records anywhere reveals that agents spent a great deal of time trying to spread this ideal to southerners, both white and black. Because the Bureau chose to organize freed labor with contracts, it necessarily summoned both judicial precedents and cultural constructs associated with binding agreements. As Bureau agents found out, however, social relations in the South did not match those of the bourgeois North.[46]

As elsewhere, South Carolina agents worked to promote contract inviolability among freedpeople. The assistant commissioner's office issued the usual perorations about binding obligations, and local agents tried to carry these precepts into practice, sometimes with a considerable amount of zeal. Benjamin F. Stone, for instance, issued a circular in early 1868 that authorized "a forfeiture of all rights" for "absolute abandonment without cause" under a written contract. Agent Holton in Orangeburg frequently called freedmen into his office for a "reprimand" about performing their contracts. After one such visit with a freedman named Toney, he recorded that "Toney's conduct is now very satisfactory." Such actions should not be taken as evidence that the Bureau acted unilaterally on the side of planters. Generally, agents enforced contracts with equal ardor against planters, as the dismissal cases reveal. In other instances, agents declared a planter in violation for not upholding part of his or her end of a bargain, as did J. W. De Forest when he told Jacob Beck that his workers would be free to leave if he had not provided them with rations as the contract required. These decisions represent more than a simple settling of affairs in favor of one party or the other. Agents in South Carolina and across the South repeatedly saw contracts as central to work in a capitalist culture. As agent Ralph Ely intoned in early 1866, "Freedpersons now see the folly of not making contracts—by this alone can they expect their just rights." George Gile made the connection even more pointedly when he directed one of his assistants to "admonish" a group of freedpeople working under a contract as to "the imperative necessity of a strict compliance with its provisions if they wish to retain the protection of the officers of the Government."[47]

This belief in the sanctity of contracts led agents to employ northern labor contract law in ways both commonplace and novel. Although agents usually apportioned contracts, they also enforced, at times, the northern rule of entirety—contracts had to be performed in full. In at least some cases, agent DeKnight in Abbeville ordered planters to give fired workers a whole year's pay. George McDougall in Aiken was even more direct. In July 1866, he threatened to send out a guard if a planter did not either take back his employee or pay the man his whole year's wages. Using entirety in this manner to compel performance on the part of an employer called on a common practice in northern law, but an agent's use of the common law tort of enticement did not. Northern courts had heard a few cases for enticing away workers during the antebellum period, but the heyday of this old action's revival came after the war. Bureau officials, however, occasionally used this action or at least the concept contained within it. C. R. Becker in Abbeville proposed in March 1866 that planters be fined for "enticing" freedmen away from their written contracts. In the same month, Scott advised agents to prohibit interference by outside parties in contracts and to use military authority to return workers "to the plantation where they first contracted." By May 1866, agents, such as Chase in Barnwell, had carried the order into practice. In November 1867, agent William Stone disposed of a case with even more direct use of the legal language of enticement. Stone advised Henry Hammond that he could tell his employees they were bound to stay until their contract was up. If they failed to do so, Hammond could forbid them from working for anyone else and sue both the hands and other employers for damages.[48]

The ways in which agents used entirety and enticement originated in a central contradiction in the Bureau's contract system. The Bureau expected freedmen to work for planters as good and faithful labor, but it also expected planters to perform their ends of a bargain, especially with regard to sustenance. When planters refused to provide food for contracted workers, the workers often left to seek subsistence wages in day labor. Planters then called on the Bureau to return the workers, or they used the absences as excuses to deny wages. Given the Bureau agents' beliefs in the strict inviolability of contracts, these actions left them in somewhat of a quandary. Although some agents arrested and returned freedpeople with glee, others seemed to sense the contradictions inherent in the contract system. William Harkisheimer reported from Columbia in the summer of 1866 that he had arrested freedpeople who had left under such circumstances and returned them to their "legitimate work." Yet, he also noted that it was "almost beyond the power of these Hdquarters to keep these people at work while they are in such a destitute condition really suffering from the want of food."[49]

The idea of contract inviolability also created tensions with regard to workplace discipline. If planters inserted clauses about proper respect for employers, many agents felt themselves duty bound to uphold them. Whether or not such language appeared in contracts, the bourgeois notions of the agents dictated a certain amount of respect for one's boss. Scott voiced this assumption in a December 1866 circular letter. "It is your duty to treat your employer with courtesy and respect and obey his lawful orders," Scott informed the freedpeople, "and it will be for your interest to so conduct yourselves as to deserve his respect and regard." These sentiments led a good number of Bureau agents to uphold discharges for "insolence" or "insubordination," although almost unfailingly with wages. The belief in respect also led some of the more conservative agents to enforce plantation discipline with almost sadistic enthusiasm. For example, Chase called freedpeople into his headquarters for shaming punishments, such as standing on a barrel or having their heads shaved. He also sent a guard to arrest a freedwoman, held her long enough so as to browbeat her into performance of her contract, and used her as an example to other hands to "be faithfull and perform *their contracts*."[50]

Such harsh actions, however, existed in tension with the desire to inculcate the proper "management" of free labor. The provost marshal in Moncks Corner wrote a stinging letter about the use of black drivers. "The days of 'nigger drivers' have passed and the colored people have equal rights with one another and they must be protected in them," he declared. "No man white or black has any right to abuse another." Absenteeism also caught the attention of some agents. "Where the plantations are carefully attended to by the owners or agents, all incidental matters looked to, and the necessities of the employees supplied, as is necessary for the success of free labor everywhere," D. T. Corbin noted, "there is little or no cause of complaint." Scott put the case in the most sentimental of terms. If employers would simply display "consideration and respect" for workers' rights and undertake "acts of kindness," they would find "a more faithful performance of labor than can be obtained by acts of coercion."[51]

If Scott and his fellow agents believed that kindness worked better than coercion in workplace management, they did not present this belief to the labor market at large. Like most of their fellow northerners, they believed that all people had a duty to participate in the labor market and that the state could force them to do so. As elsewhere, agents in South Carolina did not hesitate to use vagrancy law to compel participation in the labor market. Throughout the Bureau's tenure, agents followed the general directives contained in Sickles's 1866 vagrancy order; they encouraged freedpeople not under contract to seek employment and punished those who did not by forcing them to work on the public roads.[52]

Vagrancy orders of this type represented a near copy of northern legislation, and agents' explanations of the offense went even further toward revealing the sentiments behind such regulations. Like contracts, vagrancy codes aimed to teach freedpeople market values and relations. The more conservative agents frequently railed about freedpeople not understanding their proper places in the labor market. Williams complained that "quiet" had been disturbed by black preachers who told freedpeople not to contract, and Willard declared that freedmen possessed an inflated notion of the wages they deserved. J. E. Cornelius reported that freedpeople entertained the notion that "*all* the produce of the soil should be theirs." This ostensible deficiency in market values, he averred, made them poor workers. "They have been preached to about '*their rights*' until they are persuaded that nobody else has any rights, and until they learn better no dependence can be placed on them as laborers," Cornelius concluded. Even agents not so disposed to conservative views proclaimed the benefits of market relations. In late December 1867, Harkisheimer noted that he had to instruct disgruntled freedmen about "the fluctuations in the value of cotton," but, he continued, "it is very hard to make a man almost upon the verge of starvation understand such matters."[53]

Harkisheimer's difficulties suggest the extent to which bourgeois notions of the market penetrated agents' thinking. As a result, some agents came to see subsistence itself as akin to vagrancy and hence illegal. By 1866, freedpeople had begun to use the kinds of subsistence strategies that historian Jacqueline Jones has noted in sharecropping households during the latter part of the nineteenth century. Agent B. F. Smith reported in 1866 that freedpeople around Georgetown spent a great deal of time fishing in the low country's rivers and bays as well, as appropriating local rice stores and livestock. Several agents reported on groups of freedmen who squatted on abandoned plantations, where they hunted and fished, gathered roots, berries, and other edibles in the woods and streams, and planted subsistence crops. The important point here, however, is how agents imagined these activities. Agent Williams referred to such people as "a large vagrant class," and agent J. M. Johnston pointed toward large numbers of "vagrant freed families" who exerted "a most baneful influence" on "contract freedmen." Bureau officer Edward F. O'Brien found freedpeople in Christ Church Parish who lived on green corn, alligator meat, and pond lily beans, but he nonetheless described many as "idle, vicious vagrants whose sole idea consists in loafing about without working." O'Brien and other white observers usually tied such "vagrancy" to theft, but it appears that they were mostly witnessing simple subsistence. O'Brien admitted as much in another communication. "Always accustomed to look upon freedom as immunity from labor," he wrote in October 1866, the majority of freedmen "prefer to wander about hunting and fishing neglecting everything that they ought to attend to and becoming idle worthless vagrants." Even Scott, usually moderate in all matters, felt compelled to nip in the bud any freedmen's ideas about life outside the market. When he learned that Sea Island freedpeople were planting watermelons among the cotton, he ordered the vines destroyed. Beyond such direct measures to prevent mere subsistence, Scott and his subordinates declared that no freedmen not under contract could receive relief rations from the Bureau.[54]

Scott's restriction of subsistence and rations suggests the powerful role that the Bureau played as an agency of the bourgeois state. As educator and author W. E. B. Du Bois noted many years ago, the Bureau was "a full-fledged government of men" for "it made laws, executed them, and interpreted them." As Du Bois saw quite clearly, the Bureau's actions represented an unprecedented intervention into social relations, in general, and the labor market, in particular. In trying to carry out their visions of class, Bureau agents used the state in ways usually not witnessed until the twentieth century, but, in doing so, they employed legal precedents of the antebellum period or conjured up others long since moribund in Anglo-American law. The most obvious examples of the latter were the arrests made by Bureau agents for breach of contract. American legal historians remain divided about whether early American courts had ever sanctioned the direct use of arrest to compel performance, but whether or not colonial courts employed specific performance, the practice had certainly died out before the Civil War. When Bureau agents revived this practice, they aimed it both at planters and at freedpeople. Not only did they arrest freedpeople who had abandoned their contracts and compel them to return to work, but, more often, they took the unparalleled action of forcing employers to take back workers whom they had fired. On balance, the bourgeois state ironically acted out workers' demands. In addition to compelling planters to retain freedmen, agents sent military guards to force the payment of wages or division of shares; instituted, in some cases, a laborer's first lien on the year's crop; and threatened the seizure of crops or other property to compel compensation.[55]

These actions certainly helped freedpeople involved in the daily struggle for a decent life. Yet, in the larger sense, they also aimed to incorporate into social relations the bourgeois vision of class relations that the Bureau had brought south. The importance of class appeared repeatedly in agents' talk about poverty and especially vagrancy. Agents and officers who held varying views on other policies consistently used vagrancy as a standard to judge the success of free labor as a system. E. A. Kozlay plainly used this benchmark in a February 1866 report on the freedpeople of his district. "It is gratifying to know, that they are doing well," he divulged. "So far, there is not a vagrant within my district; or one able bodied man or woman, to whom I would be compelled to issue government rations. They are so far self-supporting." These flattering comments on freedmen take on more significance when placed in contrast to similar comments about white South Carolinians. Johnston claimed that white applicants for relief were often Irish women who told "most thrilling tales of suffering" but if given clothing "for 'poor ragged and father-less children you can see it floating along the streets on the back of a robust drayman or other laborer." Other agents cast comments about poor whites directly in class language. Liedtke complained about a "low class of whites," and Runkle blamed a local "insurrec-tion" scare on a group of "vagabond whites." John W. De Forest, a northern novelist employed as an agent in Greenville, compared freedmen favorably to "the idleness, shiftlessness, and begging hab-its of a large part of the 'low down whites.'" Nonetheless, De Forest conceded, the war had caused much "honest and worth[y] suffer-ing" among them.[56]

The tension evident in De Forest's consciousness reinforces the extent to which Bureau agents relied on class. In fact, this broader vision of class and class conflict sometimes came quite close to the surface. Scott and others often complained about how neither side understood the proper relation of capital to labor. When planters refused to institute northern forms of free labor, Scott believed, "a conflict arose between the landowner and the laborer, the former struggling to retain absolute control, and the latter determined to maintain his newly acquired freedom to its fullest extent." Willard understood this dynamic as well and realized the depths of the divi-sion. When reflecting on his narrative about the freedmen employed at the sawmill, he imagined employer and employees "so widely sep-arated in their ideas on this subject as to offer little encouragement of an early solution."[57]

Scott and Willard were right. Emancipation involved planters and freedmen in a class struggle that the northern, bourgeois state could influence only so far. As historian Julie Saville has noted, freedpeople in South Carolina plainly rejected the vision of labor proffered by the Bureau. Agent Gile found these attitudes and the planter re-sponse much in evidence in his Darlington district. In the middle of June 1866, Gile heard the case of a group of freedmen against their employer, Reuben Beasly. When the men found that they were in debt to Beasly instead of him to them, "some very threatening lan-guage was used," Gile reported. "You have stolen from us and we may steal from you," the freedmen told Beasly. "What you have taken from us will never do you any good." Having relayed their feelings to their employer, the men turned to Gile and used "disre-spectful language concerning the 'Justice' which they were receiving as black men at the hands of the Bureau." Gile settled the dispute in proper bourgeois fashion by drawing up an account for each worker. Unfortunately for Gile, his week of trials was not over. Three days later, he recorded a reply from Wiley Bell, who had been ordered to appear regarding a dispute with his employee, Peter. Bell returned Gile's letter unopened and told Peter he would "not report here for no damn Yankee . . . that he would shoot the first man that offered him another damn Yankee letter . . . [and] that he had four guns in the house loaded for that purpose."[58]

Like his colleagues, Gile was caught in the midst of an intense class struggle that complaints about the disharmony between capital and labor scarcely captured. Bureau agents, such as Gile, sought to embed bourgeois notions of class in a society where the social relations of production hardly matched those of the wage labor North. Although their efforts to supply southerners with time discipline, commodified labor power, inviolable contracts, and waged self-reliance ultimately failed, they did not fail because the agents lacked guiding principles. In South Carolina, as elsewhere, Bureau agents sought to create a free-labor society by using the state. That they did so was not anomalous to antebellum experience. Rather, their efforts grew out of the project undertaken by northern legislatures and courts after the turn of the nineteenth century. Although the diversity of policy created by the Bureau reflected, in part, the divergent social conditions of the South, it also reflected the effects of an only partially developed labor market and state in the bourgeois North.[59]

NOTES

1. R. K. Scott to O. O. Howard, November 1, 1867, reel 1, Records of the Assistant Commissioner for the State of South Carolina, Bureau of Refugees, Freedmen, and Abandoned Lands, National Archives Microfilm Publication M869 (hereinafter cited as BRFAL-SC [M869]). The starting point for understanding the influence of free-labor ideology in the mid-nineteenth century is in three works by Eric Foner: *Free Soil, Free Labor, Free Men: The Ideology of the Republican Party before the Civil War* (New York: Oxford University Press, 1970), 1–39 and *passim*; *Politics and Ideology in the Age of Civil War* (New York: Oxford University Press, 1980), 34–76, 97–127; and *Reconstruction: America's Unfinished Revolution, 1863–1877* (New York:

Harper and Row, 1989), esp. 54–60. For a good summary of what free-labor ideology meant in the Civil War era and how it constrained the alternatives available during Reconstruction, see Ira Berlin et al., eds. *Freedom: A Documentary History of Emancipation, 1861–1867*, ser. 1, vol. 3, *The Wartime Genesis of Free Labor: The Lower South* (Cambridge, England: Cambridge University Press, 1990), 2–6; and Ira Berlin et al., "The Terrain of Freedom: The Struggle Over the Meaning of Free Labor in the U.S. South," *History Workshop* 22 (autumn 1986): 109. The most comprehensive treatment is Jonathan A. Glickstein, *Concepts of Free Labor in Antebellum America* (New Haven: Yale University Press, 1991). On these abstract formulations of free labor, see also David Montgomery, *Beyond Equality: Labor and the Radical Republicans, 1862–1872* (New York: Alfred A. Knopf, 1967), 30–2; David Montgomery, *Citizen Worker: The Experience of Workers in the United States with Democracy and the Free Market During the Nineteenth Century*, (Cambridge, England: Cambridge University Press, 1993); David Brion Davis, *The Problem of Slavery in the Age of Revolution, 1770–1823* (Ithaca, N.Y.: Cornell University Press, 1975), esp. 469–524; and Jonathan A. Glickstein, " 'Poverty Is Not Slavery': American Abolitionists and the Competitive Labor Market," in Lewis Perry and Michael Fellman, eds., *Antislavery Reconsidered: New Perspectives on the Abolitionists* (Baton Rouge: Louisiana State University Press, 1979), 195–218. Berlin et al., *Freedom*, ser. 1, vol. 3: *Wartime Genesis*, 2–8, 15–6, 29–30, and passim, is especially good at noting the influence of northern social welfare concepts on Union policy, though they do not mean vagrancy in particular.

Many older works see the Bureau primarily as an agent of the planters. See, for example, William S. McFeely, *Yankee Stepfather: General O. O. Howard and the Freedmen* (New Haven: Yale University Press, 1968), 7–8, 149–65; Leon F. Litwack, *Been in the Storm So Long: The Aftermath of Slavery* (New York: Alfred A. Knopf, 1979), esp. 364–86; Louis S. Gerteis, *From Contraband to Freedmen: Federal Policy toward Blacks, 1861–1865* (Westport, Conn.: Greenwood Press, 1973), 183–92; and Daniel A. Novak, *The Wheel of Servitude: Black Forced Labor After Slavery* (Lexington: University Press of Kentucky, 1978), 9. McFeely, *Yankee Stepfather*, 1–7, is a valuable overview of earlier works.

Paul A. Cimbala's insightful and sophisticated study of the Bureau in Georgia represents the best work so far on the agency in one state. Unlike many previous historians, Cimbala explores fruitfully the role of northern ideology in Bureau policy making and argues forcefully the Bureau's actions as central to the failure of Reconstruction. See Paul A. Cimbala, *Under the Guardianship of the Nation: The Freedmen's Bureau and Reconstruction of Georgia, 1865–1870* (Athens: University of Georgia Press, 1997). Cimbala expressed some of the points of this work in earlier articles; see, for example, "The

'Talisman Power': Davis Tillson, the Freedmen's Bureau, and Free Labor in Reconstruction Georgia, 1865–1866," *Civil War History* 28 (June 1982): 153–71.

For other examples of generally sympathetic treatments, see Foner, *Politics and Ideology in the Age of the Civil War* 101; Dan T. Carter, *When the War Was Over: The Failure of Self-Reconstruction in the South, 1865–1867* (Baton Rouge: Louisiana State University Press, 1985), 178, 204, 214; and Barry A. Crouch, *The Freedmen's Bureau and Black Texans* (Austin: University of Texas Press, 1992), ix–x and passim.

2. For a more detailed exploration of these ideas, see James D. Schmidt, *Free to Work: Labor Law, Emancipation, and Reconstruction, 1815–1880* (Athens: University of Georgia Press, 1998).

3. For an example of a state where legal remedies were used creatively and effectively, see ibid., chap. 4.

4. For representative studies of local agents, see James Smallwood, "Charles E. Culver, A Reconstruction Agent in Texas: The Work of Local Freedmen's Bureau Agents and the Black Community," *Civil War History* 27 (Dec. 1981): 350–61; William L. Richter, " 'This Blood-Thirsty Hole': The Freedmen's Bureau Agency at Clarksville, Texas, 1867–1868," *Civil War History* 38 (Mar. 1992): 51–77; William L. Richter, " 'A Dear Little Job': Second Lieutenant Hiram F. Willis, Freedmen's Bureau Agent in Southwestern Arkansas, 1866–1868," *Arkansas Historical Quarterly* 50 (summer 1991): 158–200; William L. Richter, " 'The Revolver Rules the Day!': Colonel DeWitt C. Brown and the Freedmen's Bureau in Paris, Texas, 1867–1868," *Southwestern Historical Quarterly* 93 (Jan. 1990): 303–2; Paul A. Cimbala, "On the Front Line of Freedom: Freedmen's Bureau Officers and Agents in Reconstruction Georgia, 1865–1868," *Georgia Historical Quarterly* 76 (fall 1992): 577–611; and Paul D. Escott, "Clinton A. Cilley, Yankee War Hero in the Postwar South: A Study in the Compatibility of Regional Values," *North Carolina Historical Review* 68 (Oct. 1991): 404–26.

As noted above, the works of Cimbala and Crouch pay much more attention to ideology. For another notable exception to this inattention to ideology in local studies, see Sara Rapport, "The Freedmen's Bureau as a Legal Agent for Black Men and Women in Georgia: 1865–1868," *Georgia Historical Quarterly* 73 (spring 1989): 26–53, esp. 29–39. Rapport notes the Bureau's goal of teaching freedpeople "the main tenets of free-labor thinking, among which contractualism was perhaps the most important." Ibid., 32. On the formative power of the state in labor relations generally, see esp. Christopher L. Tomlins, *Law, Labor, and Ideology in the Early Republic* (Cambridge, England: Cambridge University Press, 1993); and Karen Orren, *Labor, the Law, and Liberal Development in the United States* (Cambridge, England: Cambridge University Press, 1991).

5. Michael Les Benedict has divided politicians during Reconstruction into these three groups, though not on this basis. See his *A Compromise of Principle: Congressional Republicans and Reconstruction, 1863–1869* (New York: W. W. Norton, 1974), 27–33. For a study of South Carolina that argues Bureau agents and army officers in provost courts consistently discriminated against African Americans on the basis of color, see Thomas D. Morris, "Equality, 'Extraordinary Law,' and Criminal Justice: The South Carolina Experience, 1865–1866," *South Carolina Historical Magazine* 83 (Jan. 1982): 15–33.

6. For an example of viewing the Bureau's work as experimental, see Foner, *Reconstruction*, chap. 4.

7. The works by Foner, Glickstein, and Berlin cited above make this point. The classic formulation is, of course, Max Weber, *The Protestant Ethic and the Spirit of Capitalism*, trans. by Talcott Parsons (New York: Charles Scribner's Sons, 1958), esp. chap. 5. Another near classic is E. P. Thompson, "Time, Work-Discipline, and Industrial Capitalism," *Past and Present* 38 (Dec. 1967): 56–97. Also useful is Richard Stott, "British Immigrants and the American 'Work Ethic' in the Mid-Nineteenth Century," *Labor History* 25 (winter 1984): 86–102. Stott suggests that U.S. workers in the early nineteenth century had internalized industrial work time far more than labor historians acknowledge.

8. My thinking about class has been informed mostly by historians who use the concept in practice, not theorists who set up ideal types. For some discussions of class formation and class consciousness for the period under consideration here, see Sean Wilentz, *Chants Democratic: New York City and the Rise of the American Working Class, 1788–1850* (New York: Oxford University Press, 1984), 3–19 and passim; Stuart M. Blumin, *The Emergence of a Middle Class: Social Experience in the American City, 1760–1900* (Cambridge, England: Cambridge University Press, 1989), 1–16; and Allan Kulikoff, *The Agrarian Origins of American Capitalism* (Charlottesville: University Press of Virginia, 1992), 1–9.

9. Stephen Skowronek, *Building the New American State: The Expansion of National Administrative Capacities, 1877–1920* (Cambridge, England: Cambridge University Press, 1982), 3–35. Theda Skocpol, *Protecting Soldiers and Mothers: The Political Origins of Social Policy in the United States* (Cambridge, Mass.: Belknap Press of the Harvard University Press, 1992), 43.

10. On autonomous power of preexisting structures, see Skocpol, *Protecting Soldiers and Mothers*, 57–61. For a critical discussion of the literature on antebellum labor law, see Schmidt, *Free to Work*, chap. 1.

11. The best single treatment of labor in Reconstruction South Carolina is Julie Saville, *The Work of Reconstruction: From Slave to Wage Labor in South Carolina, 1860–1870* (New York: Cambridge University Press, 1994). Saville

also sees the importance of class in Reconstruction South Carolina, though she focuses primarily on the class consciousness of freedpeople. For other treatments of emancipation in the state, see Martin Abbott, *The Freedmen's Bureau in South Carolina, 1865–1872* (Chapel Hill: University of North Carolina Press, 1967); and Joel Williamson, *After Slavery: The Negro in South Carolina during Reconstruction, 1861–1877* (Chapel Hill: University of North Carolina Press, 1965).

12. R. Saxton to N. C. Dennet, Aug. 15, 1865; R. Saxton to Col. J. C. Beecher, Aug. 17, 1865; R. Saxton to E. A. Wild, no date (probably early July 1865); and R. Saxton to E. A. Wild, Aug. 11, 1865, reel 1, BRFAL-SC (M869). For biographical information on Saxton, see *National Cyclopedia of American Biography*, 49 vols. (New York: James T. White, 1907), 4:219–20 (cited hereinafter as *NCAB*). On Port Royal, see Willie Lee Rose, *Rehearsal for Reconstruction: The Port Royal Experiment* (Indianapolis: Bobbs-Merrill, 1964); and Berlin et al., *Freedom*, ser. 1, vol. 3: *Wartime Genesis*, 87–113.

13. General Orders, No. 11, Aug. 28, 1865, and Circular No. 5, Oct. 19, 1865, reel 37; R. Saxton to O. O. Howard, Dec. 25, 1865; R. Saxton to J. J. Upham, Dec. 27, 1865; and R. Saxton to Bvt. Maj. Gen. C. Devens, Dec. 13, 1865, reel 1; and J. J. Upham to R. Saxton, Dec. 20, 1865, reel 8, BRFAL-SC (M869).

14. For Phillips's remarks, see his speech before the Massachusetts Anti-Slavery Society, Jan. 26, 1865, printed in the *Liberator*, Feb. 10, 1865. For McKaye, see James McKaye, *The Mastership and Its Fruits: The Emancipated Slave Face to Face with His Old Master* (New York: William C. Bryant, 1864), esp. 26–7.

15. R. Saxton to O. O. Howard, Oct. 13, 1865, reel 1; and O. O. Howard, Special Field Orders, No. 1 and No. 2, Oct. 19, 1865, reel 37, BRFAL-SC (M869). Saxton was aware of his precarious position almost from the start. See R. Saxton to Maj. Gen. James B. Steedman, August 19, 1865, reel 1; and Circular No. 1, Jan. 20, 1866, reel 36, BRFAL-SC (M869).

16. Williamson, *After Slavery*, 77–8.

17. Ibid.; General Orders, No. 75, Dept. of South Carolina, Dec. 15, 1865, reel 37, BRFAL-SC (M869); *The Free American* (San Francisco), Mar. 27, 1866.

18. *The Free American* (San Francisco), Mar. 27, 1866.

19. General Orders, No. 5, Feb. 6, 1866, reel 36; and R. Scott to J. Cordossa, Feb. 11, 1867, and R. Scott to J. L. Riggs, May 4, 1867, reel 1, BRFAL-SC (M869). In 1867, Scott requested copies of state constitutions from Pennsylvania, Massachusetts, and Iowa. See R. Scott to Gov. John Geary of Pennsylvania, Apr. 21, 1867, and accompanying note that similar letters were sent to the governors of the other two states, reel 1, BRFAL-SC (M869). For biographical information on Scott, see *NCAB*, 12:175–6.

Even though he played a key role in South Carolina's Reconstruction politics, Scott maintained that he did so only reluctantly. See R. Scott to the editor of the *Great Republic*, May 20, 1867, reel 1, BRFAL-SC (M869).

20. Circular No. 5, Feb. 5, 1866; General Orders, No. 14, Apr. 14, 1866; and R. Scott, Circular Letter, June 22, 1866, reel 36, BRFAL-SC (M869).

21. R. Scott, Circular Letter, Dec. 26, 1866; Circular No. 1, Jan. 1, 1867; Circular No. 2, Jan. 9, 1867; General Orders, No. 5, March 4, 1867; Circular Letter, June 19, 1867; and Circular Letter, Sept. 13, 1867, reel 36, BRFAL-SC (M869).

22. R. Scott, Circular Letter, Jan. 1, 1868, reel 36; Edward L. Deane to Corbin, Jan. 27, 1867; R. Scott to O. O. Howard, Nov. 1, 1866; and R. Scott to Gov. J. L. Orr, Dec. 13, 1866, [emphasis in original] reel 1, BRFAL-SC (M869). The influence of equitable concepts on the Bureau's program has been noted by Charles Hoffer, *The Law's Conscience: Equitable Constitutionalism in America* (Chapel Hill: University of North Carolina Press, 1990), 128–9.

23. R. Scott, Circular Letter, Dec. 26, 1866, and R. Scott, Circular Letter, Jan. 1, 1868, reel 36, BRFAL-SC (M869).

24. Acting Adjutant General to C. H. Howard, July 22, 1865, reel 1, BRFAL-SC (M869); Cyril E. Griffith, *The African Dream: Martin R. Delany and the Emergence of Pan-African Thought* (University Park: Pennsylvania State University Press, 1975), 87–9; Frank A. Rollin, *Life and Public Services of Martin R. Delany* (New York: Kraus Reprint Co., 1969 [1868]), 227–8.

25. Rollin, *Life and Public Services of Delany*, 222–3, 229, 239, 244.

26. Ibid., 251, 263, 261; H. W. Smith to M. R. Delany, March 5, 1866, reel 1, BRFAL-SC (M869).

27. Rollin, *Life and Public Services of Delany*, 273–4; R. Scott to M. R. Delany, Oct. 16, 1866, reel 1, BRFAL-SC (M869).

28. Excerpt in R. Scott to O. O. Howard, Oct. 22, 1866, and Excerpt in R. Scott to O. O. Howard, Nov. 1, 1866, reel 1, BRFAL-SC (M869).

29. B. P. Runkle to William Kemble, Sept. 10, 1866; B. P. Runkle to H. W. Smith, Sept. 13, 1866; and B. P. Runkle to H. W. Smith, Oct. 3, 1866, Letters Sent, Aiken Subdistrict; B. P. Runkle to H. M. Smith, Aug. 3, 1866, Letters Sent, Columbia Subdistrict, Records of the Subordinate Field Offices for the State of South Carolina, Record Group 105, National Archives, Washington, D.C. (hereinafter cited as BRFAL-SC).

30. Report of E. R. Chase, July 17, 1866, and Report of E. R. Chase, July 27, 1866, reel 34, BRFAL-SC (M869); Davy v. Wm. Davis, July 6, 1866, Register of Complaints, Barnwell Subdistrict, BRFAL-SC. Chase's use of racial language appears repeatedly in Register of Complaints, Barnwell Subdistrict, BRFAL-SC.

31. Register of Complaints, Barnwell Subdistrict, BRFAL-SC, 3, 9, 23, 13, 15.

32. Circular No. 1, Nov. 10, 1866, Georgetown Subdistrict, reel 37, BRFAL-SC (M869).

33. Ibid.; A. J. Willard to H. M. Smith, Dec. 6, 1865, reel 34, BRFAL-SC (M869).

34. Annual Report of F. W. Liedtke, Nov. 1, 1866, reel 34; and Excerpt in R. Scott to O. O. Howard, Jan. 23, 1867, and Edward L. Deane to F. W. Liedtke, Mar. 31, 1867, reel 1, BRFAL-SC (M869).

35. Report of F. W. Liedtke, July 31, 1866, reel 34; Excerpt in R. Scott to O. O. Howard, June 20, 1866, reel 1, BRFAL-SC (M869).

36. Excerpt in R. Scott to O. O. Howard, Jan. 23, 1867, reel 1, BRFAL-SC (M869); Registers of Complaints, Moncks Corner Subdistrict, BRFAL-SC, vol. 1: 4, 162–3, 164–5, 176–7, and vol. 2: 4–5. These complaint books record many more cases similar to those cited.

37. These conclusions draw on numerous cases that Pingree heard. In order to preserve space, I have not cited exact case names or letter dates. These records can be found in Excerpt in R. Scott to O. O. Howard, July 20, 1867, reel 1, BRFAL-SC (M869); Letters Sent, vol. 2: 144, 153; Journal of Complaints, 44–5, 73–4, 78–9, 83–4, 93–9; Register of Complaints, 1–15, Darlington Subdistrict, BRFAL-SC.

38. F. W. Liedtke to Ford Parker, May 1, 1867, Letters Sent, Darlington Subdistrict, BRFAL-SC; Excerpt in R. Scott to O. O. Howard, Oct. 26, 1867, reel 1, BRFAL-SC (M869).

39. G. Pingree to E. L. Deane, Oct. 31, 1867, Letters Sent, Darlington Subdistrict, BRFAL-SC; Excerpt in R. Scott to O. O. Howard, May 23, 1867; and Excerpt in R. Scott to O. O. Howard, Aug. 24, 1867, reel 1, BRFAL-SC (M869).

40. Annual Report of Bvt. Lt. Col. Garret Nagle, Nov.1, 1866; Report of Capt. E. R. Chase, July 27, 1866; Report of Bvt. Lt. Col. B. F. Smith, April 26, 1866; and Report of A. J. Willard, Nov. 13, 1865, reel 34, BRFAL-SC (M869). On the issue of controlling conditions of labor generally, see Berlin et al., *Freedom*, ser. 1, vol. 3: *Wartime Genesis*, 45–51. For a more detailed discussion of later African-American labor actions in Reconstruction South Carolina, see Eric Foner, *Nothing But Freedom: Emancipation and Its Legacy* (Baton Rouge: Louisiana State University Press, 1983), 74–110. For an excellent treatment of freedpeople's ideology about work, see Saville, *Work of Reconstruction*, esp. chap. 4.

41. Circular No. 5, Feb. 5, 1866, and R. Scott, Circular Letter, Jan. 1, 1868, reel 36, BRFAL-SC (M869).

42. Report of Bvt. Lt. Col. Orlando H. Moore, July 31, 1866, and Report of Capt. F. W. Liedtke, Aug. 31, 1866, reel 34, BRFAL-SC (M869); G. Nagle to Joel M. Witsell, Sept. 7, 1867, vol. 1, Letters Sent; Register of Complaints, Summerville Subdistrict, BRFAL-SC.

43. Report of Lt. John R. Chance quoted in R. Scott to O. O. Howard, Nov. 1, 1866, reel 1, and Annual Report of Bvt. Lt. Col. G. A. Williams, Oct. 24, 1866, reel 34, BRFAL-SC (M869); C. S. Allen to L. Walker, Oct. 31, 1867 in Misc. Documents, Abbeville District, BRFAL-SC; R. Scott to Gov. J. L. Orr, Dec. 13, 1866, reel 1, BRFAL-SC (M869).

44. Circular No. 5, Feb. 5, 1866, reel 35, and E. W. Everson to Garrett Hayward, Sept. 27, 1866, reel 1, BRFAL-SC (M869).

45. W. F. DeKnight to D. Dowden, June 11, 1868, Letters Sent, Abbeville Subdistrict; Geo. O'Neal et al. v. Robert Curry, July 16, 1866, Register of Complaints, Columbia Subdistrict; Nagle to Benjamin Durant, Aug. 21, 1867, Letters Sent, Summerville Subdistrict, BRFAL-SC. For discharge cases, see passim in Letters Sent, 3 vols., Columbia Subdistrict and Journal of Complaints, Darlington Subdistrict, BRFAL-SC.

46. On the importance of contracts to the Bureau, see Donald G. Nieman, *To Set the Law in Motion: The Freedmen's Bureau and the Legal Rights of Blacks, 1865–1868* (Millwood, N.Y.: KTO Press, 1979), vxii, 56, and passim.

47. Circular No. 1, Jan. 22, 1868, Letters Sent, Aiken Subdistrict; Register of Complaints, 9, 17, Orangeburg Subdistrict; and J. W. De Forest to J. Beck, Sept. 19, 1866, Letters Sent, Darlington Subdistrict, BRFAL-SC; Report of Bvt. Brig. Gen. R. Ely, Jan. 9, 1866, reel 34, BRFAL-SC(M869); G. Gile to J. J. Wright, May 30, 1867, Letters Sent, Beaufort Subdistrict, BRFAL-SC.

48. Chete [?] Alexander v. M.C. Miller, June 4, 1868, and P. Harrison v. C. T. Harrison, n.d., Register of Complaints, Abbeville Subdistrict, BRFAL-SC; H. M. Smith to D. T. Corbin, Mar. 5, 1866, reel 1, BRFAL-SC (M869); C.R. Becker to Bvt. Lt. Col. J. Devereaux, Mar. 20, 1866, Miscellaneous Documents, Abbeville Subdistrict, BRFAL-SC; Register of Complaints, vol. 1: 7, Barnwell Subdistrict; and B. F. Stone to H. Hammond, Nov. 3, 1867, Letters Sent, Aiken Subdistrict, BRFAL-SC.

49. Johnston quoted in R. Scott to O. O. Howard, June 22, 1867, reel 1; Report of W. Harkisheimer, July 12, 1866, reel 34, BRFAL-SC (M869).

50. R. Scott, Circular Letter, Dec. 26, 1866, reel 36, BRFAL-SC (M869); Register of Complaints, vol. 1:29, 47, 17 [emphasis in original], Barnwell Subdistrict, BRFAL-SC.

51. Prov. Marshal to W. J. Ball, July 24, 1866, Register of Complaints, Moncks Corner Subdistrict, BRFAL-SC; Report of Corbin, May 31, 1866; R. Scott, Circular Letter, Dec. 26, 1866, reel 34, BRFAL-SC (M869).

52. General Order 5, Feb. 6, 1866, reel 1, BRFAL-SC (M869). For examples of enforcement, see G. P. McDougall to Freedman Stuart and others, June 8, 1866, Letters Sent, Aiken Subdistrict, BRFAL-SC; Report of E. A. Kozlay, Jan. 29, 1866, reel 34, BRFAL-SC (M869).

53. Williams quoted in R. Scott to O. O. Howard, Mar. 20, 1867, reel 1;

Report of A. J. Willard, Nov. 13, 1865; and Report of J. E. Cornelius, Nov. 30, 1866, reel 34, BRFAL-SC (M869); W. Harkisheimer to T. S. Guenther, Dec. 31, 1867, Letters Sent, Columbia Subdistrict, BRFAL-SC.

54. Report of B. F. Smith, July 1866, reel 34; Report of G. A. Williams, Oct. 24, 1866; Report of Bvt. Maj. E. F. O'Brien, Sept. 5, 1866; and Annual Report of Lt. J. M. Johnston, Oct. 24, 1866, reel 34; and E. L. Deane to J. E. Cornelius, June 6, 1866, reel 1, BRFAL-SC (M869).

55. The South Carolina records contain hundreds of such cases. For examples, see the following documents in BRFAL-SC: Register of Complaints, Barnwell Subdistrict; Letters Sent, Marion Subdistrict; Letters Sent, Aiken Subdistrict; Misc. Reports, Aiken Subdistrict; Letters Sent, Columbia Subdistrict; Register of Complaints, Columbia Subdistrict; Journal of Complaints, Darlington Subdistrict, Register of Complaints, Darlington Subdistrict; and Register of Complaints, Summerville Subdistrict. For Du Bois's comment, see *The Souls of Black Folk: Essays and Sketches* (Nashville: Fisk University Press, 1979), 27. On the legal history of specific performance, see Robert J. Steinfeld, *The Invention of Free Labor: The Employment Relation in English and American Law and Culture, 1350–1870* (Chapel Hill: University of North Carolina Press, 1991); and Tomlins, *Law, Labor, and Ideology*.

56. Report of E. A. Kozlay, Feb. 28, 1866, and Report of Johnston, Dec. 8, 1866, reel 34; and Liedtke quoted in R. Scott to O. O. Howard, June 20, 1866, reel 1, BRFAL-SC (M869); B. P. Runkle to H. W. Smith, Oct. 4, 1866, Letters Sent, Aiken Subdistrict, BRFAL-SC; Bvt. Maj. J. W. De Forest quoted in R. Scott to O. O. Howard, May 23, 1867, reel 1, BRFAL-SC (M869).

57. R. Scott to O. O. Howard, Nov. 1, 1866, reel 1; and Report of A. J. Willard, Nov. 13, 1865, reel 34, BRFAL-SC (M869).

58. R. Beasly v. Freedmen, June 15, 1866; and Peter v. W. Bell, June 18, 1866, Journal of Complaints, Darlington Subdistrict, BRFAL-SC. For Saville's assessment, see *The Work of Reconstruction*.

59. My analysis here intends to suggest that emancipation must be seen as a part of the transition to a capitalist labor market in the United States. For other works along this line, see Barbara J. Fields, *Slavery and Freedom on the Middle Ground: Maryland during the Nineteenth Century* (New Haven: Yale University Press, 1985), esp. chap. 6; Saville, *Work of Reconstruction*; Joseph P. Reidy, *From Slavery to Agrarian Capitalism in the Cotton Plantation South, Central Georgia, 1800–1880* (Chapel Hill: University of North Carolina Press, 1992), esp. chap. 6; and, in a broader sense, John Ashworth, *Slavery, Capitalism, and Politics in the Antebellum Republic*, vol. 1: *Commerce and Compromise, 1820–1850* (Cambridge, England: Cambridge University Press, 1995).

11

"To Enslave the Rising Generation": The Freedmen's Bureau and the Texas Black Code

Barry A. Crouch

IN LATE 1866, the Eleventh Texas Legislature enacted labor, vagrancy, and apprenticeship legislation (a black code) to control work arrangements, behavior, and family life of the former slaves. Samuel C. Sloan, the Freedmen's Bureau agent in Millican, Texas, wrote that a "practical application" of the laws would render "an intolerable system of oppression and revive African Slavery under another name and with increased horrors." From Sumpter, agent H. S. Johnson described the statutes as of an "execrable character" and the "most detestable thing on earth." The Liberty, Texas, agent, A. H. Mayer, said the apprenticeship law aimed to "enslave the rising generation" of freedpeople in a "worse condition of slavery than they have ever been."[1]

Sloan, Johnson, and Mayer, as agents of the Freedmen's Bureau, served as advisers to the emancipated slaves in their transition to freedom. Agents of the Freedmen's Bureau arrived in Texas in September 1865, just three months after the Union Army had occupied the state, to assert national sovereignty and confirm the abolition of slavery. The military character of the army's mission, which was to restore and maintain order, defined its response to black freedom. The men in blue sought to enforce state law but left the resolution of social and economic issues related to emancipation to the Bureau.[2]

Although it has been contended that the 1866 Texas code was "an honest attempt by the legislature, blinded as it was by racial prejudice" to deal with the freedpeople, the onus for the severe character of the laws has been placed upon the action of the army and the Bureau. Allegedly, the Bureau favored such restrictive legislation, had originated similar ideas, and encouraged state initiative in the labor, apprenticeship, and vagrancy arenas. Naturally, the legislators detested the Bureau's presence and hastened the organization's removal by merely codifying army orders and Bureau promulgations. Thus, it is concluded, two national agencies entrenched an iniquitous labor and social system on the Texas African-American community.[3]

The reaction of the field agents (subassistant commissioners, to use the proper terminology of the Texas Bureau) belies this belief. Further, the Bureau did not follow army guidelines, as that particular organization had not established any clear-cut policy by the time Bureau officials arrived in Texas. Neither the Bureau nor its agents conspired with legislators to enact such restrictive legislation. The actions of the Texas Freedmen's Bureau assistant commissioners, and specifically the field agents, suggest that a majority of the Bureau personnel perceived the code as oppressive and took active steps to negate its pernicious influence. Two areas, apprenticeship and vagrancy, suggest how the Bureau approached these terrible laws.

As Texas reorganized politically, the Bureau, with limited personnel, used contractual order to avoid economic chaos. In mid-November 1865, Provisional Governor Andrew J. Hamilton had proclaimed that an election would be held in January 1866 to select delegates to a constitutional convention. In framing a new constitution (and refusing to ratify the Thirteenth Amendment), the members severely restricted rights for black Texans. The document was ratified by white voters (black men could not vote until 1867), and those elected to office under the new government focused on the protection of white settlers on the Indian frontier rather than on the murder of blacks in the interior. Also, the legislature sought to remove the Freedmen's Bureau from the state.[4]

In 1865 and early 1866, months before the Eleventh Legislature decided to subjugate black Texans with a new legal code, five southern states (South Carolina, Mississippi, Alabama, Louisiana, and Florida) had attempted this ploy and sought to frustrate Congress in its drive to provide legal equality for blacks. In response, the Republicans enacted the 1866 Civil Rights Act, which generally negated the various black codes that had been previously established. It became increasingly clear by mid-1866, at least to Radical Republicans, that Johnson's plan of Reconstruction was much too lenient, did not promote the concept that blacks should be equally protected under the law, and allowed the former slaves to suffer numerous injustices.[5]

The southern black codes can be defined as those series of laws passed by the states comprising the defeated Confederacy that applied directly or indirectly to African Americans. Enacted between the close of the Civil War and the imposition of Congressional Reconstruction in early 1867, the statutes dealt with labor and contracts, apprenticeship, vagrancy, enticement, domestic relations, property ownership, court testimony, litigation procedures, criminal penalties, a revised penal code, convict leasing, and various other aspects of regulating the freedpeople. Although some of the statutes might have appeared nondiscriminatory, they provided for penalizing, fining, and imprisoning blacks for the slightest legal transgressions.[6]

In September 1866, an Austin correspondent, who was familiar with the intention of the majority of the members of the Eleventh Legislature, informed Assistant Commissioner Joseph B. Kiddoo of the Freedmen's Bureau that the legislators were "intensely rebel in sentiment." All the laws that they were considering in relation to the freedpeople, he wrote, were "very unfriendly to their interests." Even before the lawmakers finalized the black code, Kiddoo had reason to suspect that they were about to enact several bills that one writer believed would require the "increased vigilance" of the Bureau field officers in order to prevent social and economic injustice upon the freedmen. In a quandary about how to deflect these potential statutes, Kiddoo at first vacillated and then disregarded them.[7]

Members of the Texas Eleventh Legislature disagreed with Congress and the Bureau over the protection and rights that should be granted to the former slaves. In late October, they resoundingly defeated the Fourteenth Amendment, which ensured citizenship to all African Americans. Governor James W. Throckmorton disingenuously asked President Johnson if there was anything he could recommend to the assembly to "facilitate restoration." Johnson urged the legislature to "make all Laws, involving Civil rights, as Complete as possible, so as to extend equal and exact justice to all persons without regard to color." The Texas legislature's response was crafty and underhanded.[8]

With the conflict between Congress and the president looming over their deliberations, the Texas legislators began to debate a different type of code. Although their collective thinking cannot be determined, the final result suggests that they had observed what occurred on the national scene and believed they had found a way to circumvent the new Civil Rights Act. They avoided any reference to race but copied the harshest of codes from those that had been previously legislated by the five southern states. All of these laws emphasized three major features: labor, apprenticeship, and vagrancy. Except for labor (antebellum laws were largely unnecessary because of slavery), the South, including Texas, as did the North, had existing statutes relating to apprenticeship and vagrancy.[9]

On the surface, the 1866 Texas black code appeared to ignore race, but it was designed to apply only to the freedpeople. The legislators followed the lead of Thomas Affleck, a representative of the Texas Land, Labor, and Immigration Company, who "drew up the preliminary drafts for the bills passed." Affleck had personally clashed several times with the local Bureau agent over his treatment and payment of the black workers who labored on his plantation. Moreover, like Affleck, other assemblymen had had similar experiences with Bureau agents. A majority of the legislators desired two related goals: (1) to make certain that whites controlled blacks, and (2) to eliminate the operation of the Freedmen's Bureau in the state.[10]

When Austin Bureau agent Byron Porter, an alleged conspirator in the enactment of the 1866 black code, learned of what the legislature planned to enact, he informed state headquarters of what many Texans already understood. "Of course it is a matter of common notoriety," he wrote, "that these laws were intended to be enforced against negroes only and can never be and will never be enforced against whites." A member of the lower house of the state legislature had informed Porter that those members who had recommended the passage of the code "did not scruple" to declare that they planned to use the series of statutes only against the freedmen. The laws maintained a nondiscriminatory façade that fooled no one.[11]

The 1866 Texas code deviated little from previous southern efforts. Laborers received minimal legal protection, and efforts to redress grievances were difficult and costly. Heavy fines, strict obedience, and movement restriction were matched in character by the apprentice statute, which allowed whites to indenture black children for a long period of time (as a cheap source of labor). Whites had to meet only minimal obligations. To make it even easier for whites to bind black children, the legislature did not sanction black marriages. Finally, the vagrancy law (and a vagrant was very loosely defined) was used to round up what authorities termed "unemployed" blacks and force them into either private or public service.[12]

Commenting on the legislature's completed code, William H. Sinclair, a Texas Bureau inspector, wrote that these laws gave blacks "about the same protection a wolf does a lamb." He believed that planters could not "control labor under the famous state laws passed to regulate this matter" because of the power that the blacks possessed in their "strong black arms[,] their willing hands and honest hearts." If not for these attributes, their condition would be "sad indeed." Sinclair concluded, "[T]here is no such thing as civil law justly and fairly administered in this state." The "feelings of the people in whose hands the administration of law and justice is placed are such that it is *morally impossible* for the freedpeople to receive it."[13]

After William Alexander, the state attorney general under Provisional Governor Andrew J. Hamilton, heard about the 1866 (Eleventh Legislature's) passage of the black code, he eventually resigned. Alexander simultaneously observed that "had the rebels been victorious in the field, what could they have won beyond the establishment of their laws? When they have lost," he clearly understood, "must the result be the same?" Alexander realized that the legislators desired to set aside the results of the war and legally strangle the freedpeople in every way possible. It is clear that the members of the legislature felt such laws were necessary, but the Bureau should not be held responsible for their implementation.[14]

The first Texas Bureau assistant commissioner, Edgar M. Gregory, had not condoned the wholesale apprenticing of black children nor had he sanctioned the roundup of vagrants. Kiddoo, his successor, nullified the 1866 code that the legislature had enacted, although local jurisdictions attempted to enforce the statutes. In early 1867, Kiddoo was replaced by Charles Griffin, who told Bureau Commis sioner Oliver Otis Howard that it was his belief that the laws violated the 1866 Civil Rights Act and were "oppressive and tyrannical." In a legal quandary, Griffin surmised that the laws particularly referred to and were "only enforced against the freedmen." They made no "literal distinction on account of color or race," so he did not feel at "liberty to disregard them."[15]

The black code aside, Griffin believed that the majority of wrongs perpetrated on the freedmen violated existing law. Public opinion encouraged the idea that offenders would go unpunished. He did not have sufficient troops to spread over the state and, "by overawing the people, compel the enforcement of the laws."[16] No matter what an assistant commissioner promulgated about how agents should negotiate contracts or protect freedmen's legal rights, the personnel in the field would have the most intimate connection with the black code trinity of labor, apprenticeship, and vagrancy. The performance of the Bureau field agents is worth considering because the Texas black code was not repealed by the state legislature until the Republicans assumed power in 1870.

Simultaneously with the enactment of the black code, the Texas Freedmen's Bureau standardized the monthly reporting procedure for its agents. They were required to answer a host of questions about their duties, responsibilities, and actions, and one section of the form requested each agent to comment on the three laws that comprised the heart of the Texas black code. Headquarters desired that a field officer "include in [his] Report the operations of the State laws as applied to freed people, with special reference to the Apprentice Law, Vagrant Law, and Law regulating labor."[17] Attitudes varied among the agents about the effectiveness of this legislation, but a majority was horrified by what they deemed to be the legislation's callous intent.

Nevertheless, even before these forms were instituted, the few Bureau agents in the vast Texas landscape attempted to rectify particularly grievous situations involving black children. Although headquarters promulgated certain mandates, field personnel often had to make immediate decisions concerning the affairs of the freedpeople. They might have been middle-class white male northerners, but they clearly evinced an understanding of the deleterious effects of slavery and a better perception of black family patterns that emerged from slavery than most writers have been willing to grant.

It is too easy to assume that these individuals would "necessarily" or "automatically" respond in a certain way and thus support the former masters and ruling class. Such was not the case.[18]

From the emancipation of the slaves in Maryland in November 1864 until the final freeing of the remainder of the bondspeople throughout the South in 1865, black children became the center of a social, economic, and legal controversy. As soon as blacks became free, whites moved with dispatch to apprentice black children. Through legal arrangements, in which white people became guardians and surrogate parents, they hoped to secure the labor of these black youngsters for a period of years. This system, also known as binding out or indenturing, created considerable alarm in every southern black community and became one of the three major cornerstones of the oppressive black codes enacted by many of the former Confederate states.[19]

Indenturing did not come about because of the Civil War. It had been long practiced in both the North and the South. Black and white orphans were apprenticed for a variety of circumstances. In the South, free black children were bound out if the parents did not exhibit the trait of industry. The law was so skewed that it practically assured white success before the local courts. These types of laws and practices were transferred to the postbellum era with only a change in the wording to describe the status of the child. It is impossible to ascertain how many black children fell into the apprentice category, but the number was sufficiently large for the authorities to take legal steps to avoid any problems in determining who had authority over the children.[20]

Thus, children did not become burdens on the public charge, much to the relief of local and county officials. And, in certain particulars, apprenticeship actually might be said to resemble a form of adoption. Nevertheless, during the early years of Reconstruction, it became common enough for whites to attempt to bind black children, which prompted many adults to show some concern about how the youngsters were quickly apprenticed without the black community being consulted. Real or fictive kin knew that local authorities probably would not assist them, so when a Bureau agent appeared in a town, they immediately apprised him of the circumstances. Seeking to break the indenture or to modify its terms, black Texans found a sympathetic ear at the Bureau.[21]

It must be made clear at the outset that binding out children was not the same as hiring them out. Indenturing involved a lengthy term of service, and the individual making the agreement had enormous control, similar to that of a parent, over a child. Hiring out involved a much shorter tenure, generally from a few months to a maximum of one year. Black parents seem to have had much more influence in making certain their children were treated fairly under hiring-out arrangements than they did with apprenticeship agreements. But regardless of the type of arrangement, Texas blacks endeavored to take care of their own and bring orphaned or so-called "parentless" children into the confines of the black community.[22]

During the three or four years immediately following the Civil War, apprenticing created quite a stir among southern blacks. During this period, they often turned to the agents of the Freedmen's Bureau for assistance in annulling apprenticeship agreements and regaining control of black children. The former slaves also used the Bureau and the military to reclaim members of their families who were being detained by force. Children in this situation were in a separate category, however, because they never had been part of a legal arrangement; rather, they were forced to remain with an individual through the threat of violence. The nonlegal nature of this type of detention allowed the military to compel a white to give up black children who had been forcibly held.

In Texas, blacks did not actually become free until June 19, 1865, and the assistant commissioner of the Freedmen's Bureau did not arrive until that September. During this hiatus, white Texans took advantage of the confusion surrounding emancipation, the legal limbo in which blacks found themselves, and sympathetic local officials who were willing to bind black children for long periods. Until the Freedmen's Bureau became more widely established, local blacks had few options. The usual consensus of the courts, generally manned by former Confederates, was that orphaned black children were better off if they were bound to white families. They quickly shunted aside black objections to this practice and indentured the children to serve for a decade or more.

A major problem that confronted Bureau agents, as it has historians, is the term *orphan*. It can be persuasively argued that a small percentage (perhaps 30 percent) of black children in Texas were actually orphans, that is, a girl or boy without mother or father. Slavery was responsible for the aberrant definition in the postwar era. With parents being sold away to other states and communication nonexistent or sporadic, the whereabouts of parents was often lost to memory. Certainly, a massive hunt for separated children began in the aftermath of war, but black parents had little information to guide them. If they did locate their offspring, they usually learned that they had been bound out because they had been legally classified as orphans.[23]

When an individual, white or black, signed an indenture, he or she generally posted a sum of money (a surety) and was required to have two other signers who vouched for the bond. In return, the child was bound to the individual until the youngster became twenty-one. Although this pattern varied somewhat for girls (they could be released if they married anytime after age eighteen), it ensured a long period of service for the apprentice. The person who assumed the guardianship, in turn, had to agree to perform specific duties and responsibilities that included providing the child with some education (which probably meant to read and write), teaching the apprentice a skill or trade, and rewarding him or her with some form of compensation at the termination of the apprenticeship.

Bureau Assistant Commissioner Gregory condemned the indenture system and later, as Bureau chief in Maryland, reiterated his stand. Gregory was quite cautious in allowing whites to retain black children, but his options were limited and he did allow his agents to grant retention rights to some whites. Bureau agents were ordered to make the "best disposition" of black children as they could under the circumstances, but it "would be only temporary until some settled policy could be adopted." In turn, when agents confronted planters over this issue, the latter had to agree to "retain minor orphans" under Bureau supervision until "further orders." All previous laws were to be considered obsolete.[24]

In Columbus, Texas Bureau agent John T. Raper was soon confronted with all of the questions and problems relating to black children. The status of black offspring who were either orphans or whose parents resided in another state or in some other section of Texas stymied Raper. He had no guidelines on which to depend and had to inquire of headquarters "in what light" he should hold minor children whose parents resided in another state. Was he authorized to make provision for them until they attained their majority if they were not claimed by the parents in the meantime? Raper also observed that, since emancipation, a number of parents had abandoned their children and moved to other parts of the state, and he inquired about what arrangements he should make for these children.[25]

Raper had learned that by the ruling of the courts of Texas, a "*fatherless* child" was considered an orphan. For minors, Raper informed headquarters, he acted as a chief justice and was binding out children or indenturing them to "good responsible men" until the boys became twenty-one and until the girls were married. The agreement covered "all possible points" that he thought might arise. First, he stipulated that the children were free and the individual assuming "control" of the youngster would furnish "good wholesome food, clothing, and medical attendance." In addition, they would receive "kind" and "humane treatment," and he reserved for the Bureau the privilege of "interfering to prevent anything unjust."[26]

Slavery left a strange legacy. From Washington County (the largest black enclave in the state) in 1865, Chief Justice O. H. P. Garrett wrote Provisional Governor Hamilton of "quite a number of orphan colored children" in his section. Because of its pitiful financial condition, the county could assume no responsibility. Garrett's alternative to government stewardship was to apprentice the children to "good comfortable homes" that would do "justice to these children" and where they would "receive some education." Garrett admitted that blacks were "anxious to take these children and carry them over the country where they have nothing to support and maintain" them and they would "certainly be much worse off." County personnel believed that they had acted properly under Texas law.[27]

Garrett contradicted himself in his letter when he suggested that the children were not orphans at all. Planters desired to gain legal control of these black children; by using the charge that blacks could not maintain the children, they discovered a rather large social and legal loophole for whites to maneuver to their advantage. Two Bureau agents suggested a plan because, as they complained, there were too many women with too many children and no husbands present, so why not allow the agent to "give [the children] to some one who could be trusted." Opposing this action were other Bureau personnel and the freedpeople, who desired the return of their children. If they were competent to support their offspring, they thought that they should be allowed to do so.[28]

In turn, when agents confronted planters over the binding-out issue, the latter had to agree to "retain minor orphans" under the supervision of the Bureau until "further orders." One agent in Sterling encountered a youngster, previously apprenticed by the county court, who had obviously received very "harsh treatment." This fact, in itself, was enough to invalidate the agreement. The Bureau agent believed that the young man (no age was given) was old enough to work for more than provisions and clothes and should be compensated for his labor. The agent refused to release the boy to the planter until a contract was signed, with the agent as guardian, which entitled the minor to his earnings.[29]

During the immediate postwar years, before the legislature enacted an apprenticing statute, the Texas Bureau, as a consequence of black persistence, adopted a four-point policy regarding indentures. First, the agents were to be the guardians of "orphan freedmen" if no members of the black community could be found to care for them. Second, courts were forbidden to bind out black children. Third, agents were to make every attempt to find "good homes" for these children, and the party would retain them until otherwise ordered. Fourth, the individuals were "required" to provide "proper treatment," among other requirements. In the final analysis, when the agent had to make a decision in such cases, he was to "look to the best interests of the child."[30]

Agents were constantly "importuned by planters to recognize their right to appeal to the civil authorities to bind orphan children." Whites in Madison, Brazoria, and Walker Counties, as a typical sample, first applied to the Bureau agent to have children bound or retained. The latter was essentially the same as apprenticing; in each case, all signed a similar contract or gave written assent through the mail. W. S. Rogers of Chappel Hill was given permission to keep Levi Rogers, a "colored orphan minor." Rogers was required to pay Levi $10 specie a month, plus board; to provide the "rudiments of an English education"; and to "treat" him kindly, thereby promoting the boy's mental, moral, and physical welfare.[31]

The Bureau agents did assess the ability of the parents to care for their children, and they also consulted the desires of those directly involved. Headquarters directed that, above all, the "character of the parents and the wishes of the children" should be the guiding principle in determining whether a youngster should be apprenticed. Standard Bureau policy dictated that the mother had "first claim to her child and interference with this right" would not be tolerated, unless specific exceptions were indicated. Parents, moreover, were allowed control of their daughters until they were eighteen years of age and of their sons until they were twenty-one years of age. Wherever possible, the two factors of character and wishes were intertwined.[32]

Before the Eleventh Legislature enacted an apprenticeship law, the Texas Freedmen's Bureau and its relatively few field agents had attempted to establish a fair-minded policy where indentures were involved. Indeed, some agents readily bound black children with little consideration for the wishes or desires of the black community. But, more often than not, they had an abiding concern for black youngsters, and, although they agreed to bind them out, they attempted to provide as much legal protection for the children as was humanly possible. Once the legislators entered the equation and the Bureau expanded its field personnel, clashes over the status of black children were destined to occur.

In its black code, the Texas legislature declared that any minors (under fourteen years old), including indigent, vagrant, or those whose parent or parents could not support them, could be bound until they were twenty-one years of age. If older than age fourteen, a minor could agree to the indenture if unopposed by his or her parents. When a minor's age could not be ascertained (most black children had no birth-date evidence), the judge affixed it. Applications required ten days' public notice, and minors could be apprenticed only at the regular term of the court. Enticing, concealing, or harboring an apprentice was punishable by a fine plus liability for damages. Judicial authorities retained considerable power under the code and used it accordingly.[33]

A bond required that the apprentice be furnished sufficient food and clothing, treated humanely, taught a "specified trade or occupation," and provided medical attendance. Moreover, the guardian was required to comply faithfully with the terms "stipulated in the indentures." Power was granted to the master or mistress to "inflict such moderate corporeal chastisement as may be necessary and proper." If the apprentices ran away, refused to return, or left without "good and sufficient cause," they would be jailed, allowed to post bond for an appearance at the county court, or punished. The apprentice could not reside outside the county in which the agreement had been made without written permission from the county judge.[34]

One Bureau agent neatly summarized how the apprentice law was intended to work against the freedmen. This enactment is "a very unjust one," Gregory Barrett wrote from Tyler, "as it only requires a notification in the papers of the intention to indenture, and as very few of the freedpeople can read, those interested immediately have no knowledge of the apprenticeship until after its consummation by the Court." He planned to revoke all such indentures unless otherwise ordered by headquarters. A Corpus Christi government official, John Dix, declared that "I never apprentice colored children to white people, for the reason, that colored children would be generally treated as slaves."[35]

Writing from Sherman, Albert Evans contended that the attempted application of the apprentice law was unfavorable to the freedmen. Every "orphan boy and girl (of the colored persuasion) is snatched up (those who can do full work) and put under an indenture till they are twenty one; the court fixing their ages as young as conscience will allow." He had released sixteen- and seventeen-year old juveniles who had been bound out. The court established their ages at twelve and thirteen. Small orphan children were not disturbed because they needed close attention. A similar set of circumstances prevailed in Clarksville, where adolescents between the ages of sixteen and eighteen had been apprenticed without any notice.[36]

From Paris, Texas, the much harassed and threatened agent De-Witt C. Brown emphasized that the binding-out law had been "much abused from the fact that many children have been bound out as orphans when they had parents." The freedchildren had been snatched from their mothers and fathers and "held, under color of the law, when the provisions of the law have not been complied with." In Livingston, M. H. Goddin observed the same phenomenon. The "slave worshiping power" dictated the apprentices' rights under the articles of apprenticeship, Goddin alerted headquarters, and this made it almost impossible to negotiate equitable indentures. But, in general, he believed the condition of the indentured could never benefit while the apprentice code was on the law books.[37]

Agents performed the dual roles of both revoking apprenticeship agreements and simultaneously consenting to the binding out of children. But when they allowed a black youngster to be apprenticed, the terms were much different than those stipulated by the legislature, which were largely ignored. A planter requested that P. F. Duggan, the Columbia Bureau agent, allow him to apprentice a black boy whom he had raised. The man proposed to give the lad forty acres of land, a yoke of oxen, a horse, saddle, bridle, and sufficient clothes for a year, plus the necessary seed to begin a farm at the expiration of the agreement. The boy's mother, reportedly unable and unwilling to care for him, consented to the indenture.[38]

In Victoria, agent Edward Miller said the apprentice code had been in force in his area, but he informed the chief justice that the Bureau would not recognize the law. Now, Miller had a great many orphan children, along with those of sick and indigent parents, and but two persons were willing to care for small children and raise them unless they were indentured. He had no power to bind them because of Bureau directives. Unless something was done to find homes for orphan children and secure their services until they came of age, he could not imagine what would happen to those in his and adjoining counties. Many mothers had no husbands, and, Miller opined, it would be a great advantage if some of their children were indentured under a system that would protect their rights and be given to families who could properly provide for them.[39]

As Miller's situation indicates, not all Bureau officials thought that the binding out of black children was in every case deleterious to the youngsters or to black society. Some believed that this was the only method by which certain children could be cared for and supported. Texas Bureau agents indentured youngsters, but their requirements varied considerably from those outlined by the state legal system. In general, they perceived the law, as written, to be detrimental to all concerned and an attempt by whites to provide themselves with a source of long-term labor. The apprentice and vagrancy statutes presented the agents with controversies and tested their legal acumen, but, by employing common sense, the Bureau agents learned to be fair.

In state, county, and city attempts to control the black population, vagrancy also came within the Bureau's purview. A vagrant was defined as "an idle person, living without any means of support" who made "no exertions to obtain a livelihood." The law encompassed prostitutes, gamblers, pimps, beggars, fortune-tellers, and those who exhibited "tricks or cheats in public." These types of people mingled "about the streets," were homeless, and exhibited "no honest business or employment." If convicted, a fine of not more than $10 could be levied, but the defendant could not be released until the fine and costs were paid. If they were not remitted within a reasonable time, the individual could be forced to labor for the town or county.[40]

Texas lawmakers attempted to cover every situation with their vagrancy law. They directed that sheriffs, justices of the peace, and county civil officers report to the judges of the county court "all indigent or vagrant minors" and also those minors whose parent or parents did not have the means or who refused to support their youngsters. The county judge then initiated the process to apprentice these youngsters to some "suitable or competent person" under direction of the court, "having particular care to the interest of said minor." The legislature obviously did not intend to provide extensive protection for the rights of children or vagrants who would be apprenticed.[41]

Youthful and juvenile vagrants would be sent before the police court to be bound out under the apprenticing act. The fines and penalties prescribed in the vagrancy statute conformed to the criminal code. County courts, justices of the peace, mayors, and recorders of incorporated towns and cities could order the arrest of vagrants "of their own motion" or on written complaint by some "credible person." After a magistrate issued a warrant, a peace officer would arrest the offender. If a law official were unavailable, the authority to arrest could be directed to any "private person." The accused could demand a trial by jury, but, if convicted, the "vagrant" had to pay a fine of up to $10, as well as court costs, before being released.[42]

The vagrancy law was designed to prevent the freedpeople from congregating in cities or towns. In Houston, agent W. B. Pease informed headquarters that "we are now trying what effect the enforcement of the *State* and *City* vagrant *laws* will have in driving the crowd of lazy freedpeople who have congregated in the city to work, and thus far with good success." The local authorities found the

"*City Laws*" more effective than the state enactment. In Liberty, although he said nothing about the state statute, Bureau agent A. H. Mayer asserted that a town ordinance of this nature was "right and proper" and calculated to "benefit white and black." At all times, Mayer attempted to carry it into effect equally for both races.[43]

Edward Collins, the Brenham official, had little faith in how town officials would use the statute. "The operation of the vagrant law will depend much on the justice of the local tribunals," he wrote. Collins observed that it would "most likely be abused to the oppression of the freedmen for whom it was evidently intended." Bureau agents generally believed the vagrancy law to be unfair but occasionally used it as a warning to force black men to rejoin their families. In Columbia, Duggan said that the law itself had not been applied, but he was "compelled to threaten" two black men, who had abandoned their families, with its enforcement. Duggan explained the law to them and, since that time, they had been "industrious."[44]

Depending on the location of an agent, the vagrancy law did engender some ambiguity. Anthony M. Bryant of Sherman stated that, in his region, there was "no attention whatever paid to the vagrant law." Many other subassistant commissioners either expressed the same outlook or reported that there were no vagrants in their subdistricts. In an urban environment or in the larger towns of the state, agents did have a somewhat different perspective. Because local and county officials complained that they had no funds to care for true black vagrants (those who had become so because of some specific action or catastrophe), or even the homeless, agents believed they had no recourse but to force these individuals to labor either for private employers or for the public good.[45]

The vagrancy part of the 1866 black code was used sparingly against black Texans; more often, local laws were implemented. So-called vagrants seem to have become a concern after the crops had been gathered and before the next seasonal cycle began. Vagrancy was not perceived as a major problem in the Lone Star State, however, and the majority of Bureau agents simply ignored the legislation. Actually, after a brief flurry of activity in regard to the law in early 1867 (just after its enactment), Bureau field officers mostly dismissed the statute and refused to allow its enforcement by local officials. In sum, the Texas agents occasionally threatened to classify some blacks as vagrants, but doing so was rare.[46]

The Bureau's policy toward the black code, as enunciated through the assistant commissioners, was neither as discriminatory nor as detailed as the 1866 laws of the legislature. Bureau announcements were race-specific because that was the job of the agency. The key to the differences between Bureau policy and the dictates of the legislators, however, was that Bureau regulations provided black Texans more negotiating latitude, safeguards, and a relatively convenient arena for the hearing of their complaints, along with an entering wedge into the legal system. It is far off the mark to blame the Texas Bureau for the introduction of sharecropping, indenturing or apprenticing of black children, or the enforcement of harsh vagrancy laws.[47]

Not only did the Texas assistant commissioners find the black code abhorrent, so did most of their subalterns. They might have equivocated somewhat, but their attitudes toward the black code were a far cry from the blueprint that the Bureau allegedly gave the legislature. Both assistant commissioners and subassistant commissioners had difficult positions to fill. The men who headed the state agency had to negotiate a treacherous political road as they frequently became embroiled in clashes between the president and Congress or between the president and the Bureau's national commissioner. Contrary to previous historical assumptions, the field agents were usually effective in blocking the implementation of the black code.

The majority of the subassistant commissioners believed that the apprenticeship and vagrancy sections of the code were repugnant and designed to repress black Texans. By allowing the legal stealing of children, the laws also intended to limit the mobility of blacks, destroy their families, develop a cheap labor pool, and discourage individual entrepreneurship. The agents were neither so naive nor, as some have argued, so bigoted that they failed to realize what the legislation portended.[48] Although a few agents participated in the system and acquiesced in the coercion of black labor, apprenticing black children, and rounding up vagrants to work on local projects, most refused to allow these actions and tried to rectify injustices.

The Bureau and its agents did issue circulars and orders relating to apprenticing and vagrancy. Such promulgations had their roots in antebellum northern and southern laws. To be sure, some of these pronouncements were restrictive, but they were never as harsh, demeaning, or degrading as the policies sanctioned by the black code. Bureau agents, driven by a host of motives, often angered the local white community with their decisions. They annulled apprentice-ship agreements and forced jailers to free "black vagrants." What-ever else may be said about the Bureau and its personnel (and they have often been viewed negatively), the organization did not abet, encourage, or implement the 1866 Texas black code.[49]

William Alexander, first appointed attorney general by Provisional Governor Hamilton, also served briefly under Governor Throckmor-ton but resigned because of the black code. He was later selected for the same position by the Radical Republican governor, E. J. Davis. Alexander believed that the 1866 Texas Constitution and the laws of the Eleventh Legislature were "incompatible with and hostile to the supreme law of the land." Specifically, Alexander found twenty-four of the General Laws of 1866 inimical to black Texans; in his view, the black code was the most nefarious. The individuals who framed the state constitution and their successors in the legislature who enacted the code, Alexander said, desired the "restoration of African slavery, in the modified form of peonage." The code, which he labeled "a very ingenious thrust at the freedmen," denied Texas freedpeople basic civil rights guaranteed by the national law of 1866.[50]

In Texas, it was not the Freedmen's Bureau and its local agents who had an unenlightened outlook. To condemn the agency for the origins and establishment of the 1866 black code is to deny what the sources reveal and to ignore the Bureau's reaction to the code. The treatment of the freedpeople by the local authorities and the lack of respect for black rights alarmed Bureau officials. The Texas Bureau, in general, and the field agents, in particular, responded in a fashion that clearly suggests they did not acquiesce in the code. A majority of the Bureau agents found this series of laws to be abominable and an attempt by the state authorities to impose a form of legal slavery. In effect, the agents served as ombudsmen for the freedpeople.

NOTES

1. Samuel C. Sloan to Assistant Commissioner, Texas, Jan. 1, 1867; and H. S. Johnson to J. T. Kirkman, Apr. 11, 1867, Operations Reports, Records

of the Assistant Commissioner for the State of Texas, Bureau of Refugees, Freedmen, and Abandoned Lands, Record Group 105, National Archives, Washington, D.C. (hereinafter cited as Assistant Commissioner, BRFAL-Tx); A. H. Mayer to Henry A. Ellis, Nov. 24, 1866, vol. 120, Letters Sent, Liberty Subdistrict, Records of the Subordinate Field Offices for the State of Texas, Bureau of Refugees, Freedmen, and Abandoned Lands, Texas, Record Group 105, National Archives, Washington, D.C. (hereinafter cited as BRFAL-Tx preceded by the appropriate subdistrict name).

2. Nancy Cohen-Lack, "A Struggle for Sovereignty: National Consolidation, Emancipation, and Free Labor in Texas, 1865," *Journal of Southern History* 58 (Feb. 1992): 57–98. Historians continue to posit the idea that the Bureau followed the army in numerous policy decisions; William S. McFeely, *Yankee Stepfather: General O. O. Howard and the Freedmen* (New Haven: Yale University Press, 1968); J. Thomas May, "Continuity and Change in the Labor Program of the Union Army and the Freedmen's Bureau," *Civil War History* 17 (Sept. 1971): 245–54; Louis S. Gerteis, *From Contraband to Freedman: Federal Policy toward Southern Blacks, 1861–1865* (Westport, Conn.: Greenwood Press, 1973).

3. William L. Richter, *The Army in Texas during Reconstruction, 1865–1870* (College Station: Texas A&M University Press, 1987), 49–50, 59–61, 72, 97, 219–20; William L. Richter, *Overreached on All Sides: The Freedmen's Bureau Administrators in Texas, 1865–1868* (College Station: Texas A&M University Press, 1991), 94–100, 290. A convenient summary is William L. Richter, "The Army and the Negro during Texas Reconstruction, 1865–1870," *East Texas Historical Journal* 10 (spring 1972): 7–19. A different interpretation can be found in Barry A. Crouch, *The Freedmen's Bureau and Black Texans* (Austin: University of Texas Press, 1992); James Marten, " 'What Is to Become of the Negro?': White Reaction to Emancipation in Texas," *Mid-America* 73 (April-July 1991): 115–33; Billy Don Ledbetter, "White Texans' Attitudes toward the Political Equality of Negroes, 1865–1870," *Phylon* 40 (Sept. 1979): 253–63; James M. Smallwood, *Time of Hope, Time of Despair: Black Texans during Reconstruction* (Port Washington, N.Y.: Kennikat Press, 1981), 54, 56, 58. The agents, Smallwood correctly perceived, "tended to be fair with blacks," condemned the code as oppressive and unjust, even though whites continued to "misrepresent" their true intention. Except for Richter, historians of the Lone Star State experience have not concluded that the Bureau's presence led to the baneful laws of 1866.

4. There is no full, modern history of Reconstruction Texas, but for background to these events see Randolph B. Campbell, *Grass-Roots Reconstruction in Texas, 1865–1880* (Baton Rouge: Louisiana State University Press, 1997); John Conger McGraw, "The Texas Constitution of 1866" (Ph. D. dissertation, Texas Technological College, 1959), 197–255; Nora Estelle

Owens, "Presidential Reconstruction in Texas: A Case Study" (Ph. D. dissertation, Auburn University, 1983), 87–155; Allan C. Ashcraft, "Texas in Defeat: The Early Phase of A. J. Hamilton's Provisional Governorship of Texas, June 17, 1865 to February 7, 1866," *Texas Military History* 8 (1970): 199–219; Allan C. Ashcraft, "Texas: 1860–1866, The Lone Star State in the Civil War" (Ph. D. dissertation, Columbia University, 1960), 238–305; John Pressley Carrier, "A Political History of Texas During the Reconstruction, 1865–1874" (Ph. D. dissertation, Vanderbilt University, 1971), 1–105. Before Congress enacted the Civil Rights Act in 1866, Mississippi Bureau officers had been stymied in their efforts to nullify the dictates of the legislature when they enacted a code to continue the former slaves in a subservient status. The push to protect the rights of southern blacks engaged the national legislature that placed the burden for implementing the idea of legal equality squarely upon the shoulders of the Bureau. But even with congressional enactments, which provided the southern freedpeople with basic civil rights and nullified the efforts of several southern states to place blacks in an inferior position, Texas continued to challenge the course of national events and the concept of equal rights under the law for the freedpeople. See Donald G. Nieman, "The Freedmen's Bureau and the Mississippi Black Code," *Journal of Mississippi History* 40 (May 1978): 91–118; Donald G. Nieman, "Andrew Johnson, the Freedmen's Bureau and the Problem of Equal Rights, 1865–1866," *Journal of Southern History* 44 (Aug. 1978): 399–420; Donald G. Nieman, *To Set the Law in Motion: The Freedmen's Bureau and the Legal Rights of Blacks, 1865–1868* (Millwood, N.Y.: KTO Press, 1979).

5. Barry A. Crouch, " 'All the Vile Passions': The Texas Black Code of 1866," *Southwestern Historical Quarterly* 97 (July 1993): 20; Eric Foner, *Reconstruction: America's Unfinished Revolution, 1863–1877* (New York: Harper & Row, 1988), 199–216, 243–51.

6. Older views are expressed in J. G. de Roulhac Hamilton, "Southern Legislation in Respect to Freedmen, 1865–1866," in *Studies in Southern History and Politics* (New York: Columbia University Press, 1914), 137–58; George A. Wood, "The Black Code of Alabama," *South Atlantic Quarterly* 13 (Oct. 1914): 350–60; John M. Mecklin, "The Black Codes," *South Atlantic Quarterly* 16 (July 1917): 248–59; Theodore Brantner Wilson, *The Black Codes of the South* (University: University of Alabama Press, 1965). Newer ideas are set forth in Joe M. Richardson, "Florida Black Codes," *Florida Historical Quarterly* 47 (Apr. 1969): 365–79; Nieman, "Freedmen's Bureau and Mississippi Black Code," 91–118; Nieman, *To Set the Law in Motion*, 72–102; Wayne K. Durrill, "The South Carolina Black Code," in William Graebner, ed., *True Stories From the American Past* (New York: McGraw-Hill, 1993), 1–15. With Wilson's book now more than three decades old and with

the changed status of Reconstruction historiography, a new examination of the southern black codes that relates them to previous state legislation and their attempted application to the freedpeople would seem to be worth an inquiry.

7. O. E. Pratt to J. B. Kiddoo, Sept. 27, 866, vol. 46, Letters Sent, Austin Subdistrict, BRFAL-Tx.

8. James W. Throckmorton to Andrew Johnson, Oct. 29, 1866 (telegram), Andrew Johnson Papers, Library of Congress, Washington, D.C.; Johnson to Throckmorton, Oct. 30, 1866, in LeRoy P. Graf et al., eds., *The Papers of Andrew Johnson*, 15 vols. to date (Knoxville: University of Tennessee Press, 1967–), 11:408; McGraw, "Texas Constitution of 1866," 197–270. Johnson's racial attitudes are chronicled in David Warren Bowen, *Andrew Johnson and the Negro* (Knoxville: University of Tennessee Press, 1989). On Throckmorton, see the old but unreliable Claude Elliott, *Leathercoat: The Life History of a Texas Patriot* (San Antonio: Standard Printing Co., 1938). A more balanced assessment of Throckmorton is Owens, "Presidential Reconstruction in Texas," 156–91. The Twelfth Legislature eventually ratified the Fourteenth Amendment in 1870.

9. Several writers, including Richter, seem to believe that the heart of the southern black codes was copied from antebellum northern laws. Although there may be a grain of truth in this assertion, in actuality southerners had to look no further than their own law books. After all, the South had long harshly regulated free blacks, so why not apply a similar concept to a larger population? That the North had stringent laws in these areas cannot be denied, but the South had matched them stride for stride. It is useless to debate whose laws were harsher; this leads nowhere. Suffice it to say that, during the early stages of Reconstruction, the South had not yet learned that old customs could not be simply grafted upon new conditions. The rules had changed. Beginning with the laws and decrees of the state of Coahuila and Texas and continuing through the antebellum era, enactments concerning vagrancy and guardians (apprentices) graced the statute books; see: H. P. N. Gammel, comp., *The Laws of Texas, 1822–1897*, 10 vols. (Austin: The Gammel Book Company, 1898), 1:124, 140; 2:39–40; 3:285–6; 4:32.

10. Richter, *The Army in Texas*, 61, 59; Richter, *Overreached on All Sides*, 24, 27, 69–70, 153–4. On Affleck, see Fred C. Cole, "The Texas Career of Thomas Affleck" (Ph.D. dissertation, Louisiana State University, 1942); Robert W. Williams and Ralph A. Wooster, eds., "Life in Civil War Central Texas: Letters from Mr. and Mrs. Thomas Affleck to Private Isaac Dunbar Affleck," *Texana* 7 (summer 1969): 146–62; and the Affleck Papers at Louisiana State University, Baton Rouge. Richter, *Army in Texas*, 97, claims that the Republicans "believed that the Black Codes had given the black vote

to the rebels through economic intimidation." For a different perspective, see Crouch, " 'All the Vile Passions,' " 13–34. The only other work on the code is the older and sympathetic Winnell Albrecht, "The Black Codes of Texas" (M.A. thesis, Southwest Texas State University, 1969). The debates (or lack thereof) suggest that the code was not meant to apply to whites.

11. Byron Porter to Ellis, Dec. 3, 1866; Byron Porter to W. H. Sinclair, Dec. 24, 1866, vol. 48, Letters Sent, Austin Subdistrict, BRFAL-Tx; see also Richter, *Overreached on All Sides*, 95. One of the problems with Richter's book is that he did not investigate the local volumes kept by the Texas Bureau agents that are in the National Archives but not on microfilm.

12. An analysis of the nature and legal intention of the Texas black code is in Crouch, " 'All the Vile Passions',," 13–34. The code, along with all the other laws that involved the freedpeople, are in Gammel, *The Laws of Texas*, vol. 5. On the lawmakers' failure to recognize black marriages, see Barry A. Crouch, "The 'Chords of Love': Legalizing Black Marital and Family Rights in Post War Texas," *Journal of Negro History* 79 (fall 1994): 334–51. See also Harold D. Woodman, *New South—New Law: The Legal Foundations of Credit and Labor Relations in the Postbellum Agricultural South* (Baton Rouge: Louisiana State University Press, 1995).

13. W. H. Sinclair to Kirkman, Feb. 26, 1867, Letters Rec'd, Assistant Commissioner, BRFAL-Tx (italics mine). See also William L. Richter, "Who Was the Real Head of the Texas Freedmen's Bureau?: The Role of Brevet Colonel William H. Sinclair as Acting Assistant Inspector General," *Military History of the Southwest* 20 (fall 1990): 121–56. Richter's view of the army and the Bureau is riddled with inconsistencies.

14. William Alexander to Bvt. Maj. Gen. J. J. Reynolds, Oct. 28, 1867, in *Journal of the Reconstruction Convention, Which Met at Austin, Texas, June 1, 1868* (Austin: Tracy, Siemering & Co., 1870), App., 956.

15. Charles Griffin to O. O. Howard, Feb. 12, 1867, vol. 4, Letters Sent, Assistant Commissioner, BRFAL-Tx. On Griffin, see William L. Richter, "Tyrant and Reformer: General Griffin Reconstructs Texas, 1866–1867," *Prologue* 10 (winter 1978): 225–41; Richter, *Overreached on All Sides*, 149–214; Crouch, *Freedmen's Bureau and Black Texans*, 27–32. Griffin was the first individual to assume simultaneously the positions of district commander and head of the Bureau. He died during the 1867 yellow fever epidemic.

16. Griffin to Howard, Feb. 12, 1867, vol. 4, Letters Sent, Assistant Commissioner, BRFAL-Tx.

17. See any of the Reports of Operations and Conditions from December 1866 to December 1868 in the Texas Bureau records for examples. Although opinions of historians have been divided about the status and intent of the 1866 Texas black code, the most recent and thorough publica-

tion suggests that it was nasty, brutish, and vindictive. Clearly, it did not mention race or color, but even though nondiscriminatory, everyone understood that it was meant to ostracize the former slaves. To maintain, as Richter does, that the Bureau was responsible for the enactment of these laws or, on the other hand, that the Bureau established some precedents for this legislation is quite another type of argument.

18. In the most recent effort to blame the Freedmen's Bureau for all the ills of the black community, especially where family was concerned, in what has become a favorite pastime of uninformed scholars, see Donna L. Franklin, *Ensuring Inequality: The Structural Transformation of the African-American Family* (New York: Oxford University Press, 1997), 27–49.

19. Herbert G. Gutman, *The Black Family in Slavery and Freedom, 1750–1925* (New York: Pantheon Books, 1976), 402–12; W. A. Low, "The Freedmen's Bureau and Civil Rights in Maryland," *Journal of Negro History* 37 (July 1952): 221–46; Low, "The Freedmen's Bureau in the Border States," in Richard O. Curry, ed., *Radicalism, Racism, and Party Realignment: The Border States during Reconstruction* (Baltimore: Johns Hopkins University Press, 1969), 246–50; Victoria Marcus Olds, "The Freedmen's Bureau as a Social Agency" (Ph.D. diss., Columbia University, 1966), 185–7; Clayton M. Fuller, "Governmental Action to Aid Freedmen in Maryland, 1864–1869" (M.A. thesis, Howard University, 1965), 93–5. For a succinct and well-grounded perspective on apprenticeship, see Michael Grossberg, *Governing the Hearth: Law and Family in Nineteenth-Century America* (Chapel Hill: University of North Carolina Press, 1985), 259–68.

20. Ira Berlin, *Slaves Without Masters: The Free Negro in the Antebellum South* (New York: Pantheon Books, 1974), 226–7. For slave conditions, see Wilma King, *Stolen Childhood: Slave Youth in Nineteenth-Century America* (Bloomington: Indiana University Press, 1995).

21. In general, see Barry A. Crouch, "To Bind Them Out: Apprenticeship of Texas Black Children during Reconstruction," unpublished ms.; Barry A. Crouch, "The Freedmen's Bureau in Colorado County, Texas, 1865–1868," *Nesbitt Memorial Library Journal* 5 (May 1995): pt. 1, 84–9; Barry A. Crouch, "Guardian of the Freedpeople: Texas Freedmen's Bureau Agents and the Black Community," *Southern Studies*, new series, 3 (fall 1992): 185–201.

22. One of the real problems with past historiography about this nomenclature is that historians, by using only the administrative records of the Bureau, failed to realize the difference between hiring and indenturing. A classic example is Rebecca Scott, "The Battle Over the Child: Child Apprenticeship and the Freedmen's Bureau in North Carolina," *Prologue* 10 (summer 1978): 101–13. Scott also misrepresents the intentions and actions of the local agents in the Tarheel State. See Barry A. Crouch, "Black

Dreams and White Justice," *Prologue* 6 (winter 1974): 260–3; Barry A. Crouch and Larry Madaras, "Reconstructing Black Families: Perspectives from the Texas Freedmen's Bureau Records," *Prologue* 18 (summer 1986): 109–22. Blacks did understand the significance of controlling the labor of their children, a subject that is examined in Richard Paul Fuke, "Planters, Apprenticeship, and Forced Labor: The Black Family under Pressure in Post-Emancipation Maryland," *Agricultural History* 62 (fall 1988): 57–74. In Georgia, the state supreme court had to admonish local officials to be extremely cautious about apprenticing children; see Edmund L. Drago, *Black Politicians and Reconstruction in Georgia: A Splendid Failure* (Baton Rouge: Louisiana State University Press, 1982), 112. To compare how the Bureau responded in other states, see Elaine Cutler Everly, "The Freedmen's Bureau in the National Capital" (Ph.D. diss., George Washington University, 1971); Paul A. Cimbala, *Under the Guardianship of the Nation: The Freedmen's Bureau and the Reconstruction of Georgia, 1865–1870* (Athens: University of Georgia Press, 1997); Randy Finley, *From Slavery to Uncertain Freedom: The Freedmen's Bureau in Arkansas, 1865–1869* (Fayetteville: University of Arkansas Press, 1996).

23. Crouch and Madaras, "Reconstructing Black Families" 109–22.

24. Gregory to Howard, Dec. 9, 1865; Morse to George C. Abbott, Dec. 22, 1865; Morse to O. H. Swingley, Dec. 22, 1865, vol. 4, Letters Sent, Assistant Commissioner, BRFAL-Tx. See also Peter W. Bardaglio, "Challenging Parental Custody Rights: The Legal Reconstruction of Parenthood in the Nineteenth-Century American South," *Continuity and Change* 4 (Aug. 1989): 259–92; Peter W. Bardaglio, *Reconstructing the Household: Families, Sex, and the Law in the Nineteenth-Century South* (Chapel Hill: University of North Carolina Press, 1995), xv, 14, 99, 102–11, 157, 161–3.

25. John T. Raper to Gregory, Nov. 29, 1865, Unlisted Letters 1865–1866, Assistant Commissioner, BRFAL-Tx. On Raper, see Crouch, "Freedmen's Bureau in Colorado County," 82–4.

26. Raper to Gregory, Nov. 29, 1865, Unlisted Letters 1865–1866, Assistant Commissioner, BRFAL-Tx.

27. O. H. P. Garrett to A. J. Hamilton, Dec. 11, 1865, Governor's Papers [Hamilton], Texas State Library, Austin; Crouch and Madaras, "Reconstructing Black Families," 114.

28. Sinclair to Philip Howard, Apr. 17, 1866, vol. 4, Letters Sent; Edward Miller to J. P. Kiddoo, Jan. 11, 1867, Operations Reports, Assistant Commissioner, BRFAL-Tx.

29. Gregory to Howard, Dec. 9, 1865; Morse to George C. Abbott, Dec. 22, 1865; Morse to O. H. Swingley, Dec. 22, 1865, vol. 4, Letters Sent, Assistant Commissioner; George Gladwin to O. A. Normand, Dec. 27, 1865, vol. 100, Letters Sent, Houston Subdistrict; Champ Carter to Kiddoo, June

11, 1866, Letters Rec'd, Assistant Commissioner; Sinclair, June 11, 1866, box 43, Endorsements, Assistant Commissioner, BRFAL-Tx.

30. Morse to Eugene Smith, March 2, 1866; Sinclair to Ira C. Pedigo, April 17, 1866, vol. 4, Letters Sent, Assistant Commissioner; David S. Beath to Vernou, Sept. 18, 1868, vol. 86, Letters Sent, Cotton Gin Subdistrict, BRFAL-Tx.

31. James C. Devine to Ellis, Nov. 23, 1866, Letters Rec'd; Ellis, Nov. 27, 1866, Endorsements, Assistant Commissioner; Porter to John Hill, Mar. 30, 1866; Porter to W. S. Rogers, Mar. 27, 1866, vol. 110, Letters Sent, Houston Subdistrict, BRFAL-Tx.

32. Richardson to S. C. Plummer, May 29, 1867, vol. 49, Letters Rec'd, Prairie Lea Subdistrict; Morse to F. D. Inge, Feb. 22, 1866, vol. 4, Letters Sent, Assistant Commissioner, BRFAL-Tx..

33. Gammel, *The Laws of Texas*, 5:979, 981; "Laws in Relation to Freedmen," *Senate Executive Document*, 39th Cong., 2nd sess., No. 6 (Serial 1276), 224–7 (hereinafter cited as "Freedmen Laws"). Additionally, the legislature passed a separate punishment law to prevent individuals from persuading, tampering with, enticing away, harboring, secreting, and feeding a laborer or apprentice. Liable for damages, upon conviction the violator would be punished by a fine not to exceed five hundred or less than ten dollars, imprisonment in the county jail for six months, or both. Any individual who employed a laborer or apprentice under contract, thus depriving the contractor of that individual's services, would be guilty of a misdemeanor. If convicted, a fine of not less than $10 nor more than $500 "for each and every offence," or imprisonment not exceeding thirty days in the county jail, or both, and liability for damages could be imposed; Gammel, *Laws of Texas*, 5:998; "Freedmen Laws," 221–2.

34. Gammel, *Laws of Texas*, 5:979–81; "Freedmen Laws," 225–6. The legislature surely realized that the freedpeople would not have money to initiate suits for an individual's failure to abide by apprenticeship agreements. In most cases, neither apprentices nor their families or kin would have had the necessary cash to post bail.

35. Gregory Barrett to Vernou, June 30, 1868, vol. 162, Letters Sent, Tyler Subdistrict; John Dix to Richardson, May 31, 1868, Operations Reports, Assistant Commissioner, BRFAL-Tx. On Barrett, see Barry A. Crouch, "The Freedmen's Bureau and the 30th Sub-District in Texas: Smith County and Its Environs During Reconstruction," *Chronicles of Smith County, Texas* 11 (spring 1972): 15–30; Barry A. Crouch, "View from Within: Letters of Gregory Barrett, Freedmen's Bureau Agent," *Chronicles of Smith County, Texas* 12 (winter 1973): 13–26. On Dix, see Randolph B. Campbell, "Reconstruction in Nueces County, 1865–1876," *Houston Review* 16 (1994): 3–26. For apprenticeships in Smith County, see John Pressley Carrier,

"The Era of Reconstruction, 1865–1875," in Robert W. Glover, ed., *Tyler & Smith County, Texas: An Historical Survey* (Tyler, Tx.: Walsworth, 1976), 65–6; and the "Book of Indentures to Bonds of Apprenticing, 1867–1870," 2 vols., Smith County Records, James Gilliam Gee Library, East Texas State University, Commerce.

36. Albert Evans to Sinclair, Jan. 18, 1867; Albert H. Latimer to Kirkman, June 1, 1867, Operations Reports, Assistant Commissioner, BRFAL-Tx.

37. DeWitt C. Brown to Richardson, Dec. 31, 1867; Jan. 31, 1868; M. H. Goddin to J. A. Potter, Aug. 31, 1867; Duggan to Acting Ass't Adj't Gen., Aug. 1, 1867; Bryant to Kirkman, June 30, 1867, Operations Reports, Assistant Commissioner, BRFAL-Tx. On Brown's performance see William L. Richter, " 'The Revolver Rules the Day!': Colonel DeWitt C. Brown and the Freedmen's Bureau in Paris, Texas, 1867–1868," *Southwestern Historical Quarterly* 93 (Jan. 1990): 303–32.

38. Duggan to Acting Ass't Adj't Gen., Aug. 1, 1867; Bryant to Kirkman, June 30, 1867; E. C. Hentig to Vernou, July 1, 1868; Howard to Richardson, Jan. 31, 1868; J. H. Archer to Richardson, Nov. 1, 1867; A. G. Malloy to Garretson, Sept. 30, 1867; Malloy to Richardson, Jan. 1, 1868; Charles F. Rand to Garretson, Oct. 1, 1867; C. E. Culver to Kirkman, September 1, 1867; A. A. Metzner to Kirkman, July 31, 1867; George H. Smith to Kirkman, Feb. 4, 1867, Operations Reports, Assistant Commissioner, BRFAL-Tx. On Rand, see William L. Richter, " 'This Blood-Thirsty Hole': The Freedmen's Bureau Agency at Clarksville, Texas, 1867–1868," *Civil War History* 38 (Mar. 1992): 51–77. On Culver, who was shot down in the street in Cotton Gin, see James M. Smallwood, "Charles E. Culver, a Reconstruction Agent in Texas: The Work of Local Freedmen's Bureau Agents and the Black Community," *Civil War History* 27 (Dec. 1981): 350–61. On Archer, see Barry A. Crouch, "The Freedmen's Bureau in Beaumont," *Texas Gulf Historical and Biographical Record* 28 (1992): pt. 1, 8–27; 29 (1993), pt. 2, 8–29.

39. Edward Miller to Kiddoo, Jan. 11, 1867; Howard to Kirkman, Aug. 31, 1867; Howard to Garretson, Oct. 31, 1867, Operations Reports, Assistant Commissioner, BRFAL-Tx.

40. Gammel, *Laws of Texas*, 5:1020–2; "Freedmen Laws," 226–7. To ensure that local jurisdictions would receive some benefit from vagrants, days spent in incarceration would not be computed "in estimating the time for satisfying the fine and costs." Youthful and juvenile vagrants would be sent before the police court to be bound out under the apprenticing act. The fines and penalties prescribed in the vagrancy statute "shall conform to the provisions of the Criminal Code in relation to the same offences."

41. Gammel, *Laws of Texas*, 5:979, 1020–1; "Freedmen Laws," 224, 226.

42. Gammel, *Laws of Texas*, 5:979, 1020–2; "Freedmen Laws," 226–7. Richter, *Overreached on All Sides*, 95, views the vagrancy law as part of the Bureau's "legislative desire."

43. W. B. Pease to Kirkman, Jan. [31], 1867; Pease to Kirkman, Mar. 6, 1867; A. H. Mayer to Kiddoo, Jan. 9, 1867; Devine to Sinclair, Jan. 12, 1867; Dix to Kirkman, Aug. 31, 1867, Operations Reports, Assistant Commissioner, BRFAL-Tx. Amy Dru Stanley, "Beggars Can't Be Choosers: Compulsion and Contract in Postbellum America," *Journal of American History* 78 (March 1992): 1285, suggests that the Bureau was responsible for the harsh southern vagrancy laws.

44. Collins to Richardson, Dec. 31, 1867; Duggan to Acting Ass't Adj't Gen., Aug. 1, 1867, Operations Reports, Assistant Commissioner, BRFAL-Tx.

45. Bryant to Kirkman, June 30, 1867, Operations Reports, Assistant Commissioners, BRFAL-Tx. For similar attitudes, see Collins to Richardson, Dec. 31, 1867; Pease to Kirkman, Jan. 31. 1867; Howard to Kirkman, Aug. 31, 1867; Howard to Garretson, Sept. 30, Oct. 31, 1867; Howard to Richardson, Dec. 31, 1867; Metzner to Kirkman, July 31, 1867; Miller to Kiddoo, Jan. 11, 1867; Evans to Sinclair, Jan 18, 1867, Operations Reports, Assistant Commissioner, BRFAL-Tx.

46. Frequently, the operations reports of the agents, from early 1867 until the Bureau's demise in December 1868, had a line drawn through the section about the black code and they often commented that the laws were simply ignored.

47. For the view that the "general principle guiding the sponsors of Reconstruction legislation was that of equality in fundamental rights, based on the principle that 'all men are created equal,' " see Paul Moreno, "Racial Classifications and Reconstruction Legislation," *Journal of Southern History* 61 (May 1995): 303.

48. Diane Neal and Thomas W. Kremm, " 'What Shall We Do with the Negro': The Freedmen's Bureau in Texas," *East Texas Historical Journal* 27 (fall 1989): 23–34, which is marred by superficial research and wrong conclusions about the abilities of the local agents.

49. Smallwood, *Time of Hope, Time of Despair*, 54, 56, 58; Alwyn Barr, *Black Texans: A History of Negroes in Texas, 1528–1971* (Austin: Jenkins Publishing Company, 1973), 56–7; Randolph Campbell, *A Southern Community in Crisis: Harrison County, Texas, 1850–1880* (Austin: Texas State Historical Association, 1983), 265–6.

50. William Alexander, "Pretended Laws of 1866 Against the Freedmen," in *Journal of the Reconstruction Convention, Which Met at Austin, Texas, June 1, 1868* (Austin: Tracy, Siemering & Co., 1870), App. 953–5.

12

Land, Lumber, and Learning: The Freedmen's Bureau, Education, and the Black Community in Post-Emancipation Maryland

Richard Paul Fuke

IN RECENT YEARS, historians have examined several aspects of black education in the post-emancipation South. Of critical interest has been the role played by the government of the United States—and its chief agent, the Bureau of Refugees, Freedmen and Abandoned Lands—in the process of building schools, providing teachers, and shaping southern educational objectives. To the extent that such study has recognized the contribution of blacks themselves, it has usually focused on their obvious enthusiasm at the prospect of acquiring an education, their determination to send as many children to school as possible, and their commitment to the same sort of liberal reform ideology that motivated the U.S. government and its educational program.[1]

The educational efforts of blacks in post-emancipation Maryland certainly reflected this combination of factors, but, at the same time, they represented something else: their need and desire to make their schools their own. As much as education was a part of a wider liberal venture in educational reform, it was also a part of the free black community's effort to create for itself as much local autonomy as possible amid trying circumstances. Such effort depended heavily on the support of the Freedmen's Bureau and northern freedmen's aid societies, but it drew equally from the hard work of the black community itself.

In November 1864, immediately after the state emancipation proclamation, a group of several prominent white Baltimoreans—Quakers, businessmen, lawyers, and clergymen—met to commit themselves to black education.[2] The new state constitution of 1864 had, for the first time, provided a public education system in Maryland, but it did nothing to compel local school boards to establish institutions for blacks.[3] Most of these prominent white men had been in the thick of the fight for emancipation, and they all belonged to or sympathized with the Radical Republican minority of the Union Party. To a man, they wanted more for blacks than a simple declaration of their freedom. Consequently, they organized the Baltimore Association for the Moral and Educational Improvement of Colored People to further their broader goals. On December 12, 1864, the Baltimore Association defined its mission and petitioned the Baltimore City Council for financial support:

> The New Constitution [of Maryland] has added to the eighty thousand free colored people of our state, eighty-seven thousand others, recently slaves. For the most part they are ignorant. . . . Thrown upon their own resources, they cannot be expected to know the necessity of industry, or how to seek permanent occupation and employment. We think it is the duty of every citizen of Maryland . . . to make this population most useful to the state . . . [and to] instruct them in their industry . . . that they may rise in the scale of being, and be better fitted for the varied duties they are called upon to perform.[4]

On May 31, 1865, the Baltimore City Council allocated $10,000 to the association's school program within the city.[5] The association received an additional $7,000 from northern and European philanthropists during its first year and further contributions in 1866 and 1867.[6] In addition, northern societies provided Maryland with teachers. Their sponsors—the New England Freedmen's Aid Society, the National Freedmen's Relief Association, the Pennsylvania Freedmen's Relief Association, and the American Missionary Association—paid their transportation and a part of their salaries.[7] By the end of 1865, the Baltimore Association had opened seven schools in Baltimore and eighteen in the rural counties of southern Maryland and the Eastern Shore.[8] A year later, in November 1866, it reported double that number of schools and an enrollment of more than 6,000 students.[9]

Much of this expansion came about as a consequence of the Baltimore Association's new partnership with the Freedmen's Bureau. In the summer of 1865, the Bureau extended its operations to the southern Maryland counties close to Washington and, in 1866, incorporated the rest of the state into its new District of Maryland.[10] On July 11, 1866, the Bureau sought a formal cooperative venture with the Baltimore Association, which responded quickly with the request for "any aid you can afford us" and stressed especially the need for money and material to build new schoolhouses.[11] Expansion into Maryland's tidewater counties had exhausted most of the association's money and all of the available space for schools in black churches and private dwellings. Despite its considerable backing, the Baltimore Association had to allocate practically all of its funds to teachers' salaries and other operating expenses. Successful beyond even its most optimistic projections in attracting black interest in schools, the association had outstripped its resources.[12] In fact, it had been facing a building crisis since the end of 1865, when it was no longer able to construct new buildings.

The Freedmen's Bureau moved into this breach. Within a short time, it was actively engaged in providing lumber for schoolhouses. By the summer of 1866, it had commandeered empty buildings at Fort Marshall, Maryland, and Hicks United States Army General Hospital in Baltimore to be stripped for their lumber.[13] Together, these buildings provided the essential construction material for more than sixty schoolhouses.[14] The Bureau also assumed the greater part of transportation costs and sent the lumber to its destinations at no charge to either local blacks or the Baltimore Association.[15] The contribution of the Freedmen's Bureau in dollars and lumber constituted a significant measure of support for both the Baltimore Association and Maryland's black schools. After only six months of active participation, it had spent over $5,000 on lumber for county schools and had agreed to underwrite the rent of schools already established in Baltimore.[16] Moreover, the Bureau's aid extended well beyond building materials and money. Throughout the tidewater counties, its agents worked closely with the Baltimore Association and local blacks in starting new school boards, canvassing for funds, buying land, and constructing the buildings.[17]

Clearly, black education in post-emancipation Maryland was a joint venture combining the common efforts and philosophy of the

Bureau, the Baltimore Association, and the blacks themselves. Equally clear, however, was the fact that each school was a part of the community in which it was built and, as such, was also shaped by factors beyond the control of either the Freedmen's Bureau or the Baltimore Association. Nowhere in the state did either the Bureau or the Association possess sufficient resources to purchase the land for black schools, to build and maintain them, to conduct the education provided in them once they had been erected, or to protect them and their occupants from white abuse. In the final analysis, black schools were community schools that reflected both the accomplishments and the failures of a recently freed people in their efforts to establish as much independence as possible in a society almost entirely dominated by their white ex-masters.[18] Just as blacks sought to control the disposition of their families' labor and to acquire small pieces of land to blunt the control of their ex-masters, they also built schools.

"Being in almost daily receipt of requests from the colored people for schools," explained the Baltimore Association in its *First Annual Report* in November 1865, "[w]e have engaged to open schools at Cambridge, Dorchester County; Clearspring, Washington Co.; Centreville, Queen Anne's Co.; Denton and Preston, Caroline Co.; Uniontown, Carroll Co., and Long Green, Baltimore Co. We have also from 14 Counties, 38 applications for schools, which we anticipate having in operation before the first of January next."[19] In fact, the Baltimore Association and the Bureau were hard pressed to meet the educational demands of the black population. Between 1865 and 1867, both agencies were flooded by applications for lumber to build schools and for teachers to teach in them. "[T]he colored people in every neighborhood [are] anxious for schools," explained the Baltimore Association in June 1865.[20] "They require school houses very much at present" reported the Bureau the following May, and, in June, "The want of proper accommodation is severely felt. . . . Many applications are made from various localities for assistance in establishing schools."[21] By January 1, 1867, in response to such requests, the Baltimore Association and Bureau had assisted blacks in establishing more than sixty schools with a total enrollment of more than 5,000 students.[22]

Behind such statistics lay the expressed enthusiasm of the black community. "You must build up your schools and educate your children," insisted Frederick Douglass in December 1864. "Hitherto you were wont to pride yourself on your muscles. . . . But you need something else now. You must have minds."[23] The Colored State Convention meeting in Baltimore a year later agreed: "We advise you to educate your children, give them trades and thereby qualify them for any position in life. For if ever we are raised to that elevated summit in life for which we are striving, it must be done by our individual exertion; no one can do it for us."[24] Indeed, "[t]he colored people of this State have settled down with the calm and firm resolution," explained Bureau officer Charles McDougall, "to make this work the one great and earnest effort of their life, thus demonstrating their manhood in the face of opposition and accumulated wrongs of many years."[25] As one freedwoman put it, "I was a poor slave only a little time ago, and now when I tinks I can send my child to school it makes me so tankful that 'pears I mus do all I can for de school; we poor colored folk never seed anything like dis afore."[26] Nor was it just for the children. "I am determined to make the effort to learn to read my Bible before I die," explained an eighty-year-old woman, "and if I fail I will die on the way."[27]

Across the state, such enthusiasm translated into action as communities sought the assistance of the Bureau and association. In August 1866, a Bureau officer from Charles County reported that "[t]he freedmen manifest a strong desire to be educated and to educate their children."[28] "The colored people . . . are deeply interested in this building," explained a white observer in Potter's Landing, Caroline County, in May 1867, "and will do all they can toward putting it up."[29] By September of the same year in Davidsonville, Anne Arundel County, school attendance had increased so rapidly "as to entirely fill the building now used and many have been turned away."[30] The message seemed clear. "The colored people," explained Bureau Superintendent of Education J. W. Alvord, "are alive to the importance of the work, and feel that it is a vital point in their future welfare. They are doing all they can to help along *plans* for their education."[31]

Such grassroots involvement in educational planning by the black community was of vital importance. William Perkins, a black merchant and a Bureau field agent in Chestertown, Kent County, provided eloquent testimony of this fact as he traveled the county to visit rural churches and talk to their congregations. "*Sir*: I went to

Centreville yesterday according to your request. I met . . . a small congregation [at Spanish Neck Church], and found them anxious for a school. . . . I left Spanish Neck Church at 2 o'clock and went to Centreville, found a small congregation there still *more* anxious for a school and had been ready for the last six weeks. . . . I left Centreville at 5:30 P.M., arriving at Salem at 8 P.M., met a pretty large congregation there, [and] found them very anxious for a school."[32]

From the start, the schools supported by the Baltimore Association and the Freedmen's Bureau occupied black churches or were constructed on black-owned land. Between 1866 and 1868 in the counties of southern Maryland alone, blacks purchased more than fifty pieces of such property—most of them costing between $100 and $300. The acquisition of this land represented a tremendous commitment of time, energy, and resources on the part of a rural community with little at its disposal. Alone, or with the assistance of Bureau officers or temporary field agents—some of them black—the freedmen met, organized committees, and raised the money for such property.

The results of their determination were impressive. In one of a series of reports on the work of John H. Butler, a black field agent hired by the Bureau to assist freedmen in Calvert and Anne Arundel Counties, Bureau agent William VanDerlip informed headquarters in February 1868 that "I am informed by Mr. Butler that the lot at Swamp Dist is deeded to Colored Trustees exclusively for a school. I will endeavor to ascertain if it is recorded. . . . Land has been purchased at Mt. Zion but is not quite all paid for yet. Land has also been purchased at a point between Owensville and Birdsville about a mile north of Owensville. You can see the point on the map as there is a mill very near it. This with the Swamp school will serve better than the land at Chews Chapel. The money is ready to be paid. . . . We also expect very soon to have land at Tracey's Landing. Money is raised."[33]

The acquisition of land for schools was very much a cooperative affair that was rooted in the activities of rural community life. Few individual blacks possessed or could afford to buy sufficient land on which to erect a school. With the assistance of the Freedmen's Bureau, blacks organized boards of school trustees among leaders in the community for the purpose of negotiating the purchase of small (one- or two-acre) plots of land. "It is suggested," read a Bureau directive in July 1867, "that the colored people form themselves into a school society and elect five of their best men as a board of managers, one of whom shall be President and one Secretary and treasurer of the board. The ground should be procured and an estimate made of the amount of money necessary to haul the lumber and put up the house."[34]

Blacks vigorously responded to this plan of action. "Sire I seand you this," wrote David Williams, a black school trustee in My Lady's Manor, Baltimore County, "informing you that the trustees for the school in whitch we are about to organiz . . . [are] appinted. [T]he following nams is appinted trustees of this school. David Williams, John Govans, Joshua Staritt, J. Huston, Joshua Johnson."[35] Reporting from Montgomery County in October 1867, Bureau officer R. G. Rutherford described similar participation:

> At Norbeck . . . the colored people have some money subscribed to put up the school house and I recommend that the material be furnished them. . . . Samuel Lytton, Cato Johnson, and Clem Johnson are the leading colored men. . . . At Damascus, the colored people are in treaty for an acre of land. . . . Samuel Mason is the leading colored man there. . . . Some two or three months since, Mr. Kimball handed me a paper dated at Barnesville and signed by a number of colored men stating that the ground was ready for a school house. . . . Lem Awkward is the principal colored man. . . . At Poolsville it is represented that the colored people want a school, and that they are endeavoring to buy ground upon which to build a church and school house. John Adams is one of the leading colored men there. . . . I am informed that the colored people have bought ground about six miles above Rockville on the Damestown Road and that they are anxious to have a school. Benj. Richardson, Chas Bearly, and Geo. Johnson are some of the leading colored men of the neighborhood.[36]

To purchase land for schools, blacks had to raise money among themselves. It was a simple and direct process of asking a hardworking and poverty-stricken community to donate what little it could. "The colored people have collectors out soliciting aid," explained a white observer in Caroline County. "[They] . . . are none of them men of means. Living as they do by such work as they can find . . . from day to day in a farming community it is hard for them to 'make ends meet.' . . . Still, they are deeply interested in this building and will do all they can toward putting it up. They will furnish all the money they can, anywhere from $50 to $150."[37] To buy such land for their schools, blacks somehow dug into their own pockets to provide the necessary funds. And when private solicitation wasn't enough, the entire community pitched in. "I was over last Wednesday at Galesville," reported Bureau agent John H. Butler from Calvert County in June 1868. "They have done well. . . . We want to have a big time there on July 16. . . . We intend to lay the cornerstone and hold a fair that day."[38] On another occasion, Butler described the situation in Island Creek, Calvert County, succinctly but effectively. "The people have had many disadvantages to labor under. They have paid $150 for the ground."[39]

The relationship between school land and the rural black community was apparent also in the close connection between newly purchased property and church property already owned by the free blacks. Throughout southern Maryland and the Eastern Shore, black churches—already important religious and social centers—assumed even greater significance during the post-emancipation period because the freedpeople could now openly associate with them. The churches served as focal points of rural black aspirations and expression. As the only totally black-owned institutions in their communities, they provided a vital source of group strength and mutual support; they were places where blacks could meet relatively free from white interference.

Church buildings themselves served as the location for the first post-emancipation black schools. "These schools are generally held in the churches of the colored people," explained the Baltimore Association in November 1865.[40] "The want of proper accommodation is severely felt," reported a Bureau officer in June 1866, "Churches and private dwellings being used in almost every instance."[41] In time, buildings on land purchased by blacks for school purposes replaced churches, but the schools often adjoined the churches. In some instances, blacks bought school land from whites whose property lay alongside black churches; in others, they bought it from themselves. Near Union Town in Carroll County, in December 1866, Singleton Hughes and William Mathews, black school trustees, explained: "The lot of ground . . . contains between ½ and ¾ of an acre of ground. It is Church property conveyed to the colored population of the Methodist Episcopal Church."[42] In September 1867, William VanDerlip reported from Mount Hope, Calvert

County, that "[t]he house is to be built on land adjoining the colored church." And from Davidsonville, "[t]he freedpeople . . . completed the purchase of the lot by the payment of the last instalment of money. Mr. Davidson was to give a deed to the Colored M. E. Church."[43]

For rural blacks, the church-school combination served as a highly visible center of community aspirations on land that they owned themselves. As such, its real and symbolic importance struck the white community with immediate force. As early as December 1864, arsonists in Newtown, Somerset County, burned a church in which blacks were trying to start a school.[44] During the next few months, flames destroyed similar efforts in Cecil and Queen Anne's Counties.[45] In October and November of 1865, during a three-week period, whites destroyed black church schools in Millington and Edesville, Kent County. In each case, only a month had passed since the school opened its doors for the first time. Such attacks were aimed directly at the capacity of the black community to buy land and to organize schools. As Addie T. Howard, the teacher at Millington, reported to the Baltimore Association:

> I write in great haste to inform you of the calamity which befell us last night. Some malicious person or persons set fire to the church in which we have been holding our school. . . . The fire was set on the north side of the Church and was not discovered until it had made considerable headway. Of course, nothing could be done to save the building. It is a great loss to the people here, as they are very poor, and will not be able to build another, perhaps for years. . . . The people here now think it will be useless to hold a school here for some time, and perhaps for the rest of the year. They were trying to make preparations to put up a school house soon, but it would meet with the same ill luck.[46]

Some time elapsed before the burning of churches and school houses had run its course. On November 11, 1865, whites burned a building in Baltimore County, and, on March 11, 1866, the school in Spanish Neck, Queen Anne's County, went up in flames.[47] Several more were to follow. It was not until late that year or early in the next year that the danger began to dissipate. By that time, the determination of blacks in rural Maryland and of the Baltimore Association and Freedmen's Bureau to build schools and to replace them, when necessary, was evident for all to see. Even the state government was compelled to recognize the legitmacy of such effort and to extend it some protection. After the Kent County fires, Governor Augustus W. Bradford offered a $500 reward for information leading to the arrest of the incendiaries.[48]

Opposition to or ambivalence toward the acquisition of land for school purposes was part of a generally negative white attitude toward black land ownership of any sort. Although a handful of blacks managed to acquire substantial private holdings during the immediate post-emancipation period, the vast majority did not. Most land acquisitions were small, and many of them were made by families who long had been free and who had owned property for years. Essentially, whites would sell only small plots of land to freed slaves—never more than an acre or two and never enough to break their new owners' dependence on wage labor or sharecropping.

Small plots of land—whether purchased individually or by groups—did, however, contribute something to the autonomy of black families who owned them and to those who shared in the process of cultivating them or raising churches or schools on them. Through the purchase of these small plots, blacks could redirect a portion of their labor to personal, family, and community use. Alongside their struggle for fair contracts and the release of their children from enforced apprenticeship, access to even scattered pieces of land on which blacks might live, grow food, and build schools helped to blunt the effect of the otherwise tight control by whites over their daily lives and labor.[49]

After buying the land, black Marylanders built their own schools. Again, with the assistance of the Baltimore Association and the Freedmen's Bureau and with the use of U. S. government–donated lumber from dismantled army barracks and hospitals, blacks erected several dozen buildings, each of them approximately thirty by forty feet and capable of accommodating forty to fifty students.[50] The Bureau shipped the lumber from Baltimore and Washington to points up and down the Potomac River and Chesapeake Bay where freedmen unloaded it, hauled it, and combined it with local materials to construct school buildings. From time to time, the Bureau hired local carpenters, but most of the work was done by black field hands.

The process required detailed planning and coordination. "The work of building more school houses will be pushed forward as soon as the weather is of a character to justify operations," explained the *Baltimore American* on February 4, 1867. "During the bad weather which has prevailed for some time past the only thing that could be done was to transport lumber for school houses to such points as could be reached by railroad. The lumber now on hand, it is estimated, is sufficient to put up forty-five school houses of the size required."[51] By March 1, lumber from Baltimore had been sent to twenty-two locations from which blacks hauled it to the school sites.[52] "To get this lumber conveninent [*sic*]," explained Butler in August 1867, "it should be shipped to this place on board of the Plum Point Packet as she has conveniences to land it. . . . The people are very anxious to get a house here and say they will have [it] ready for use in four weeks after the Materials are landed. I have great confidence in these people doing what they say."[53]

Once the lumber was on the spot, rural blacks devoted whatever spare time and energy they could muster to the construction of the actual buildings. "[W]e wish you to send the lumber as soon as you can make it convenant," wrote My Lady's Manor school trustee Williams in June 1867. "[P]lease send me a letter in answar to this when you can seand the Lumber to Monkton Stasion we want to be thear to unlode it and make ore Reagements to have teams thear to take it away at the same time."[54] "I am here at this school house," agent Butler reported from Nottingham, Prince George's County, in January 1868, "and the frame set up [is] a very substantial one. . . . I made an agreement with them [the workers] to go in the woods and get out the sleepers and perhaps the rafters and shingle the house and I would write to you for windows and sash and flooring and plank for the house. If we had . . . [these] I think the House could be finished in a few weeks."[55]

In Davidsonville, Anne Arundel County, local blacks committed their energy to a project even bigger than that originally called for. "They think a house less than 24 by 40 too small," reported Thomas Davidson, in September 1867. "[T]hey have now over 90 children enrolled and think that the number will be greatly increased next summer. They are willing to pledge themselves to furnish the sills, posts, braces, and plates for such a building, and commence at once. And if they should not be able to finish it this fall they will do so next spring."[56] "The . . . estimate [below] comprises the materials for the School house," explained Davidson:

Lumber

2 Side Sills	8 × 10	40 ft. long	
1 Girder	8 × 10	40 " "	
2 End Sills	8 × 10	30 " "	
11 Posts	6 × 4	11 " "	
44 Rafters	3 × 4	15 " "	
20 Scantlin	3 × 4	12 " "	
20 Scantlin	3 × 4	24 " "	Collar beams
10 Scantling	3 × 4	15 " "	
38 Sleepers	3 × 11	16 " "	

1300 feet flooring
5000″ weather boarding & Sheathing
Shingles fir 10 Square
5 window frames & Sash
12 lights 10 × 12
1 Door frame & folding door
Brick for underpinning & chimney
Laths, Lime & hair, Nails, Hinges & Lock[57]

By necessity, such effort had to take into account the priorities of a working community. "The harvest which is commencing," explained a white observer in Prince George's County in July 1867, "will prevent their doing anything before that time."[58] "They are willing to do all they can to build the house," Butler wrote from Calvert County a month later, "[and] will work as they can spare time."[59] In November, from Plum Point, Calvert County, Butler explained, "The people are getting their corn in now . . . and [will] complete as much of the work as possible by Christmas."[60] "I have been to look after the lumber," he said, "It has been landed and put neatly in a barn shed and will be hauled next week but those who will haul it have not yet finished sowing their corn and killing their hogs, but say next week all will be hauled up and house commenced if the weather is favorable."[61]

By early 1868, rural blacks had accomplished a remarkable feat. In less than two years, they had constructed sixty such schoolhouses at a pace that outstripped the Baltimore Association's capacity to supply them with teachers. "[O]ur Colored People have very willingly and very liberally helped on this cause in Maryland," reported the association. "[T]hey have, from the lumber obtained by us . . . built at *their own unaided* expense *Sixty School Houses*, all of them good structures, and most of them very far surpassing the county school houses for whites."[62]

Once the freedpeople built their schools, they sustained them. The Baltimore Association provided teachers and paid their salaries, but, beyond that, the blacks were on their own. The extent of the freedpeople's efforts was considerable. Blacks boarded their teachers, maintained their buildings, effected necessary repairs, provided light and fuel, and paid cash for supplies that they themselves could not provide. Moreover, such support required organization. The boards of trustees, which had purchased the land and facilitated construction of the buildings, also had to organize the community to maintain the schools once they were in operation.

In November 1865, after one year of operation, the Baltimore Association reckoned that rural blacks had contributed $2,000 to its school program, or 11 percent of its total expenditures.[63] "The colored people . . . have uniformly paid the board of teachers, besides the incidental expenses of the schools; thus contributing . . . some $6,000 or $7,000," reported the Freedmen's Bureau in July 1866, a figure that, by November, had grown to $9,000, or 26 percent of the association's budget.[64] A year later, in November 1867, these figures had grown to $21,000 and 36 percent.[65] Clearly, as one observer noted in October 1867, "The effort in Maryland . . . to make the schools partially self-sustaining has been a great success."[66] William J. Albert, president of the Baltimore Association, agreed. "It is a heavy tax upon them . . . but it shows that at no distant date their schools can be made almost self-supporting."[67]

To raise this money, the entire black community chipped in. "I am striving to get sufficient means," reported a teacher in Harford County. "During the holidays we had a fair in the church and raised one hundred and forty dollars."[68] "I am just now closing up a fair," Butler wrote from Asbury, Calvert County. "I am glad to inform you that after working hard two days and nights in the rain we succeeded in raising one hundred and forty dollars. . . . I also intend to hold another fair Friday and Saturday next at Parkers Creek."[69] On another occasion, in yet another Calvert County village, Butler explained, "It is very hard to raise money here for anything; the colored people are cheated so badly they have not the money, but I have gathered the females together and we are about to hold fairs at different places and by doing so we expect to raise money enough."[70]

To sustain such effort, blacks formed societies to raise money and to organize its expenditure. "The colored people are forming school societies," explained Joseph Hall from Calvert County, in September 1866. "In regard toward paying the board and washing of the teacher in my neighborhood the subscribers to the society number something over one hundred which pays something over twenty-five dollars."[71] "We the undersigned hereby pledge ourselves for the support of a school at Rockville," wrote a number of black men in Montgomery County in February 1867, "and agree to hold ourselves responsible for such sum as may be necessary to pay the board and washing of the teacher and to provide fuel and lights for the Schoolhouse":

Feb 14/67	–William Kelley	signed
	–Louis Proctor	mark
	Reuben Hill	"
Feb 15/67	–Samuel Martin	"
	Solomon Williams	"
	Adam Baker	"
	Hilliary Powell	"
Feb 20/67	–William Baker	"
Feb 21/67	–Barney Lilles	"
Feb 22/67	–Henry Tyler	signed
Feb 27/67	–Henson Morris	"
	Alfred Rose	mark
Feb 28/67	–Hezekiah Williams	signed
	Richard Williams	mark
	Mason Martin	signed
Mar 2/67	–Henry Dove	mark
	Levi Hopkins	"
Mar 7/67	–Israel Butler	"
Mar 13/67	–George Blair	"
Mar 14/67	–Tilghman Graham	" [72]

However important were the money and organizational structure, the bedrock of black community support for its schools came from the students—both children and adults—and the families who sustained them. Educational aspirations occupied a central place in the post-emancipation agenda of the rural black community, and, despite the many obstacles in their path, mothers, fathers, and children strove mightily to make their schools a success.

Teachers regularly reported on their students' eagerness and diligence. "My work in the school room is light," wrote M. S. Osbourne from Church Creek, Dorchester County, in October 1865. "I hardly realize that I have any governing to do. My pupils seem so eager to learn."[73] Later that month, teacher Harrison T. Fletcher added, "I never saw scholars take so much pains to obey their teacher, and endeavor to learn. . . . I am confident they will make very rapid progress."[74] And from teacher Matilda Anderson in Edesville, Kent County, "[their] artlessness of manner, the eagerness with which they seize upon their instruction, and their . . . affectionate manners are all subjects of deepest admiration."[75]

Tied to such enthusiasm was the blacks' obvious delight in attending their *own* schools. According to Osbourne, her children "have an unbounded love for and pride in their school. I never say 'this is your school' without bringing, if possible, a blacker hue to their eyes, and a happy color to their cheeks. I can't describe the emotions on their faces. . . . They show plainly they appreciate their school."[76] Phineas Waterhouse, a teacher at Muirkirk, Prince Georges County, commented that "[the] colored pupils manifest a good degree of interest in the school and all feel proud of the beautiful new school house."[77]

To send their children to school called for significant sacrifice from black parents. They had their work to think of first and usually required the help of their children simply to make a living. A child at class could not contribute as much to the support of his family as could one who worked all day. This was particularly the case with older children. "Parents are taking their grown children away and hiring them out," explained a teacher in Burkettsville, in April 1866, "while they continue to send the younger [to school]."[78]

Indeed, in spite of all of their educational aspirations, the black community could ill afford to send more than a few of its children to school. In a typical election district of Anne Arundel County, for example, fewer than 10 percent of the children listed in the 1870 U.S. census had attended school during the previous year. A similar situation applied in the Chestertown area in Kent County. The first annual report of the Baltimore Association in 1866 recorded 82 students in the Chestertown school. The 1870 census listed 100 black children as having attended school in 1869, a number that represented 10 percent of the children in the area.[79] The fact was that most black children had to work to support their families. "I have four children," explained Henna Howard of Worcester County in April 1865, "one son nineteen and one daughter fourteen which I have hired out. . . . I have one girl eleven and one son nine at home with me. [M]y husban workes with his old master at ten dollars a month . . . and I do all the worke that I can and my husban and mee can support our children and them that is hired out can support themselves and help me."[80]

Such sacrifice did nothing, however, to diminish the dedication of the black community to its schools or to its determination to educate as many people as possible. In a letter published in the *American Missionary* in February 1868, a teacher in Darlington, Harford County, described the level of such involvement and the profound impression it had upon her:

> There is an increasing interest among the people for education. We have more names on our register this term than ever before. A number of adults attend the day school, whose distance of residence forbids them from attending the night school. Several of them come four miles every day, and they learn with a rapidity which is truly astonishing. While the progress of the little ones acts as a stimulus for the older portion, the correct deportment of the latter has an influence for good on the former. So with all it is more of a benefit than a disadvantage for young and old to meet on a level, although it presents an odd appearance.
>
> It is interesting to look into our school; every nook and cranny is occupied, with all sizes and all ages. I think we have a fair representation of the four stages in life, for they rank from five years to sixty. Here and there a listless scholar, but mostly eager, anxious faces to greet you. As the school is Primary and Intermediate, seventy scholars keep me busily employed from nine o'clock in the morning until five in the afternoon, and at half past seven o'clock at night the school opens.[81]

Although many blacks could not afford to attend school or to send their children, others somehow managed. Every rural school had its night classes for adults who attended after working a full day in the fields. Although weary, they struggled to absorb what they could. "It is truly encouraging," wrote Waterhouse, "to see these men and women, after working all day, come in and study so attentively. It is true their tired bodies . . . often say, silently if not in words, 'I am unfit for study'; and not infrequently the nodding head falls involuntarily on the desk before it . . . [but] I have not the heart to chide for such sleeping in school time . . . [for] those who attend do not spend their hours altogether in vain."[82]

Such dedication and determination expressed itself in a more public and dramatic fashion in a series of public educational meetings held throughout the state in 1867. Sponsored by the Baltimore Association and the Freedmen's Bureau as a means to stir up both political and educational enthusiasm, these occasions turned out to be far bigger than expected and accomplished much more than the two groups had originally intended. Where modest or moderate crowds were anticipated, hundreds and even thousands showed up in eloquent public testimony to the strength of black educational aspirations. At one such meeting in Dorchester County in June, "a vast throng of people" gathered to hear speeches by General Edgar M. Gregory, Bureau assistant commissioner for Maryland, and prominent Republican Hugh Lennox Bond, judge of the Baltimore Criminal Court. "As the steamboat approached the wharf," reported the *Baltimore American*, "their greetings were loud and enthusiastic. At 3 o'clock P.M., after music from Smith's cornet band, of Cambridge, the meeting was organized. . . . There must have been three thousand people in front of the Court House."[83]

In late July, an estimated 2,000–3,000 blacks showed up at a similar meeting in Havre de Grace, Harford County, and, a week later, another 1,100–1,200 blacks met near Prince Frederick, Calvert County, and 1,000–1,500 appeared at Centreville, Queen Anne's County.[84] At the latter meeting, "The General, the Judge . . . and a few other gentlemen of this city took the morning boat and arrived at Queentown in good time," reported the *Centreville Citizen*, "and taking the conveyances provided, [they] started for Centreville . . . (six miles distant), and were met on the road about a mile from the latter place by a procession of about four or five hundred colored men, a hundred or more of whom had served in the Union army during the war. The greatest enthusiasm prevailed at the reception, and ranks were opened for the carriages to pass through and then closed up in the rear of the vehicles, making a procession somewhat imposing in its length and enthusiasm."[85] Similarly excited responses met the speakers at meetings in early September at Port Tobacco, Charles County, and at Leonardtown, St. Mary's County, where more than 1,000 rural blacks turned out on each occasion."[86]

Black participation in the establishment, organization, and support of post-emancipation rural schools constituted, in essence, a community grassroots educational movement of considerable force that, by 1868, was responding to an annual enrollment of some several thousand students.[87] None of this would have been possible without the encouragement and assistance of the Freedmen's Bureau and the Baltimore Association. The government supplied lumber. Bureau officers and agents helped to find land, instructed rural blacks in the fine arts of constituting committees, and provided public speakers. The Bureau also offered whatever physical protection its scattered agents could manage, and the association hired teachers and paid their salaries.

Both the Freedmen's Bureau and the Baltimore Association acted, at best, as facilitators of an educational movement shaped by the practical realities and priorities of the black community. In large part, rural black schools were what they were because they had no choice. In the absence of sufficient money, manpower, and sympathy from the whites surrounding them, they became institutions built and maintained by blacks on land purchased by the community. By necessity, these were local, cooperative enterprises and, as such, were similar to other activities that blacks felt compelled to undertake for and by themselves.

Nothing demonstrated such necessity better than the general opposition by rural whites to the presence of black schools in their midst. The burning of a dozen buildings during the period 1865–1866 provided the most dramatic evidence of such opposition. "[T]he school houses have all been rebuilt by the colored people themselves," reported the Baltimore Association in February 1867, "no assistance has been given by the white people in the neighborhood who sympathize in the outrages committed."[88] "In their present condition they have no encouragement," explained a white observer in Calvert County in June 1867.[89] "The owners of land are so much opposed to schools down in these counties," Bureau agent Butler noted, also from Calvert County, in October 1867.[90]

Teachers and students also felt the brunt of such opposition. On October 18, 1865, teacher Osbourne reported—with some sarcasm—from Church Creek:

> Last week there was considerable agitation about my work, and a meeting was held in which it was decided that I should leave the town. A committee of five was appointed to wait on me, and a letter written to inform me of the good feeling of the people of Church Creek in regard to me. The committee thus far has failed to do their duty, and I very much fear that I shall not have an opportunity of seeing what "Southern chivalry" is. Excuse me if I haven't much respect for this peculiar characteristic of Southern rebels. I cannot refrain from comparing 1860 with 1865; *then* one Southern boy could whip five Yankee men; *now* five Southern men, if they dared, would visit one Yankee girl to force her to leave a legal pursuit. "How the mighty have fallen!"[91]

Later that month, Martha Hoy, a teacher in Trappe, Talbot County, reported: "On arriving at my school house last Wednesday morning, I found that one of the window shutters had been forced open and all the lower panes of glass broken in. . . . The school house is located in such a lonely place, and it seems to me that the whites are so wicked here that they would, if they got the opportunity, injure us badly."[92] Nor did it get any better. On November 25, she described the nature of white opposition to her school in detail:

> Men, apparently intoxicated, would come and rush to my schoolhouse door and frighten the children in such a manner that the parents of my scholars would not send them to school. . . . When my scholars would be returning from school, the whites would take their slates away from them and rub out the copies that I had set for them, and return the slates when they felt disposed to do so; at other times they would have a rope laid to trip them and beat them with, or else they would chase them. In the morning when I would be going to school; they would lay hoops and other impediments in my way to trip me; in the afternoons or on returning home, they would push me off the walk, throw dirt on me, and stone me; they have threatened my life, and they said they would kill me any way, if I attempted to teach at night. They also threatened to burn the school.[93]

And it could get worse. From Spanish Neck in Queen Anne's County, J. W. Cromwell, a male teacher, reported in March 1866:

The crisis of affairs has at last arrived. Last night returning from school I met on the road five men posted four on one side in the opening to a bypath and one on the other side, "*at a charge bayonet.*" It was so very dark that I was in their grasp before I beheld them. . . . One advanced, placing his muzzle near my breast and said, Halt! Halt! You d—b—k s— of b—s halt! I clung to one who accompanied me, then, turned and ran across the road, they all immediately fired, balls went whining all around me but the crooked road, dark night, and dense woods alone protected me and rendered their firing uncertain, so I barely escaped with my life.[94]

With so few agents at their disposal, there was little either the Freedmen's Bureau or the Baltimore Association could do to protect schools, teachers, and students, other than to rely on good fortune and the assistance of the few rural whites who supported blacks and their education. Such support, however, did not normally amount to much. According to Martha Hoy, a magistrate who was supposedly sympathetic toward the black community told her "that he could not advise me what to do in such a case . . . and that they did not allow colored people to have any say against a white person in their State."[95]

Under the circumstances, blacks were compelled to fend for themselves much of the time. "The colored people ought to learn to make the best of present opportunities," counseled prominent black Marylander Henry Highland Garnet, "and use the hands made free . . . [to] show that they can and will do for themselves."[96] It was good advice because, essentially, the blacks had no choice. Generally speaking, rural blacks confronted emancipation utterly bereft of the economic support necessary to escape the restraints of subsistence wage labor, tenancy, or sharecropping. Regardless of the original good intentions of the U.S. government, freed Marylanders received neither forty acres nor a mule. To make matters worse, nearly 3,000 black children had awakened to emancipation in November 1864, only to find themselves dragged off to court to be apprenticed to ex-masters who were under no obligation to provide for their education.[97]

Amid such circumstances, blacks resorted to the strength of their own community to wrest whatever autonomy they could from their reluctant employers. In doing so, they sought at least partial control over the disposition of their families' labor and access to at least small plots of land, through sharecropping, tenancy, renting, or even purchasing, on which they might grow food and build churches and schools.

Such behavior constituted a part of what scholars have recently identified as blacks' search for autonomy within a generally coercive system. "At least in a limited way," comment Roger Ransom and Richard Sutch, freed blacks "possessed the power . . . to shape their own destinies."[98] "Autonomy was the lens," explains Eric Foner, "through which . . . [blacks] viewed labor conditions during Reconstruction. Those who could rent or purchase land did so; those who could not sought modes of labor that secured the highest degree of personal independence."[99] Barbara Fields argues that freedmen and women sought to dispose of their labor as they saw fit by "cultivating their own gardens, working for wages just long enough to earn a family subsistence, and refusing to establish themselves on a permanent basis with a single employer." Together, these historians define the tactics of what Fields calls a "subsistence-oriented" community, as blacks sought to establish as much control as possible over their daily lives.[100]

To place black schools entirely in this context would do a disservice to the efforts of the Freedmen's Bureau and the Baltimore Association, and to the fact that rural black Marylanders shared with the officers of both organizations an enduring faith in the essentially liberating potential of the northern educational ideology. It was not, after all, that blacks *wanted* their schools to occupy a place within the defensive strategies of an oppressed community. There is, however, no escaping the fact that, although both the U.S. government and black Marylanders aspired to an educational system and curriculum similar to those offered whites, the mechanics of the situation compelled them to operate within drastically different and reduced circumstances.

NOTES

1. Ronald E. Butchart, *Northern Schools, Southern Blacks, and Reconstruction: Freedmen's Education, 1862–1875* (Westport, Conn: Greenwood Press, 1980), 97–168; Robert C. Morris, *Reading, 'Riting, and Reconstruction: The Education of Freedmen in the South, 1861–1870* (Chicago: University of Chicago

Press, 1981), 149–212; Jacqueline Jones, *Soldiers of Light and Love: Northern Teachers and Georgia Blacks, 1865–1873* (Chapel Hill: University of North Carolina Press, 1980); James D. Anderson, *The Education of Blacks in the South, 1860–1935* (Chapel Hill: University of North Carolina Press, 1988), 4–32. See also Roberta Sue Alexander, "Hostility and Hope: Black Education in North Carolina during Reconstruction, 1865–1867," *North Carolina Historical Review* 53 (Jan. 1976): 113–32; James Smallwood, "Black Education in Reconstruction Texas: The Contributions of the Freedmen's Bureau and Benevolent Societies," *East Texas Historical Journal* 19 (spring 1981): 17–40; Kenneth B. White, "The Alabama Freedmen's Bureau and Black Education: The Myth of Opportunity," *Alabama Review* 34 (Apr. 1981): 107–24; Paul A. Cimbala, "Making Good Yankees: The Freedmen's Bureau and Education in Reconstruction Georgia, 1865–1870," *Atlanta Historical Journal* 29 (fall 1985): 5–18.

2. Baltimore Normal School Account Book, MS. 94, Maryland Historical Society, Baltimore, Md.; Baltimore Yearly Meeting, Religious Society of Friends, Orthodox, "Meeting of Sufferings, 1828–1877," Quaker Records, Maryland State Archives, Annapolis, Md.

3. Francis N. Thorpe, comp., *The Federal and State Constitutions, Colonial Charters, and Other Organic Laws of the States, Territories, and Colonies,* 7 vols. (Washington, D.C.: Government Printing Office, 1909), 3:1772–3; *Laws of the State of Maryland . . . 1865* (Annapolis: Richard P. Bayly, 1865), 269.

4. Baltimore Normal School Account Book; Bond-McCulloch Family Papers MS. 1159, Maryland Historical Society, Baltimore, Md.; *Baltimore American,* Dec. 12, 1864.

5. City Council, Reports and Resolutions, Record Group 16 S1, WPA 65: 605, Baltimore City Archives, Baltimore, Md. *Journal of Proceedings of the First Branch City Council of Baltimore at the Sessions of 1864 and 1865* (Baltimore: James Young, 1865), 572; *The Ordinances of the Mayor and City Council of Baltimore, Passed at the Sessions of 1864 and 1865* (Baltimore: James Young, 1865), 100.

6. *First Annual Report of the Baltimore Association of the Moral and Educational Improvement of the Colored People* (Baltimore: J. B. Rose and Company, 1866), 8; *Second Annual Report of the Baltimore Association for the Moral and Educational Improvement of the Colored People* (Baltimore: J. B. Rose and Company, 1866), 7; *Third Annual Report of the Baltimore Association for the Moral and Educational Improvement of the Colored People* (Baltimore: J. B. Rose and Company, 1868), 8.

7. *First Annual Report of the Baltimore Association,* 8: *Freedmen's Record* 1 (July 1865): 119 and (Nov. 1865): 119; *National Freedman* 1 (Oct. 15, 1865): 310–1; *American Missionary* 9 (Oct. 1865): 217.

8. *First Annual Report of the Baltimore Association,* 4, 7.

9. *Second Annual Report of the Baltimore Association*, 14–16.

10. *The Statutes at Large of the United States of America, 1789–1873*, 17 vols. (Washington, D.C.: Government Printing Office, 1859–1873), 13:507–508; 14:174; J. W. Alvord, *Third Semi-Annual Report on Schools for Freedmen, January 1, 1867* (Washington, D.C.: Government Printing Office, 1868), 5, 7.

11. Fielder Israel to John Kimball, July 11, 1866, Letters Rec'd, Bladensburg Agent, Records of the Subordinate Field Offices for the State of Maryland, Records of the Bureau of Refugees, Freedmen, and Abandoned Lands, Record Group 105, National Archives, Washington, D.C. (hereinafter cited as BRFAL-Md).

12. Ibid.

13. G. W. Bradley to E. M. Gregory, June 27, 1866, vol. 1, Register of Letters Rec'd; Robert Chandler to [–] Ketchum, July 14, 1866, vol. 3, Letters Sent; R. M. Janney to E. M. Gregory, Aug. 31, 1866, Letters Rec'd, Records of the Assistant Commissioner for the State of Maryland, Bureau of Refugees, Freedmen, and Abandoned Lands, Record Group 105, National Archives, Washington, D.C. (hereinafter cited as Assistant Commissioner, BRFAL-Md); *Baltimore American*, Oct. 15, 1866.

14. *Third Annual Report of the Baltimore Association*, 6; *Baltimore American*, Oct. 15, 1866.

15. E. M. Gregory to O. O. Howard, Nov. 3, 1866, vol. 3, Letters Sent, Assistant Commissioner; Frederick Von Shirach to A. C. Knower, Mar. 31, 1867, Letters Rec'd, Annapolis Agent, BRFAL-Md.

16. E. M. Gregory to O. O. Howard, Oct.13, 1866, vol. 3, Letters Rec'd, Assistant Commissioner, BRFAL-Md; J. W. Alvord, *Fourth Semi-Annual Report on Schools for Freedmen, July 1, 1867* (Washington, D.C.: Government Printing Office, 1868), 4; Frederick Von Shirach to A. C. Knower, Mar. 31, 1867, Letters Rec'd, Annapolis Agent, BRFAL-Md.

17. C. H. Howard to John Kimball, May 31, 1866, vol. 26, Special Orders and Circulars, Records of the Assistant Commissioner for the District of Columbia, Bureau of Refugees, Freedmen, and Abandoned Lands, Record Group 105, National Archives, Washington, D.C. (hereinafter cited as BRFAL-DC); G. E. Henry to W. H. Rogers, June 4, 1866, vol. 50, Letters Sent, Bladensburg Agent, BRFAL-Md.

18. My research in the areas of black labor and land acquisition in tidewater Maryland suggests that the purchase of property for schools, the construction of the buildings themselves, and their ongoing maintenance and organization constituted a part of a broader emphasis based as much on community survival as on individual self-help. In a *collective* response, as well as in *individual* responses, to difficult postemancipation circumstances, blacks sought to control the disposition of their families' labor, gain access to small plots of land on which they could live and supplement the returns

of daily wages, and—as this paper suggests—build schools, which reflected the necessity of community strategies. See Richard Paul Fuke, "Planters, Apprenticeship, and Forced Labor: The Black Family Under Pressure in Post-Emancipation Maryland," *Agricultural History* 62 (fall 1988): 57–74; and Fuke, "Peasant Priorities?: Tidewater Blacks and the Land in Post-Emancipation Maryland," *Locus* 3 (fall 1990): 21–45.

19. *First Annual Report of the Baltimore Association*, 9, 18.

20. *Freedmen's Record* 1 (July 1865): 116.

21. A. W. Bolenius to Freedmen's Bureau, May 26, 1866, Letters Rec'd; George W. Stannard to O. O. Howard, June 5, 1866, vol. 3, Letters Sent, Assistant Commissioner, BRFAL-Md.

22. Alvord, *Third Semi-Annual Report*, 6–7.

23. *Baltimore American*, Dec. 5, 1864.

24. *Baltimore Sun*, Jan. 1, 1866.

25. *Third Semi-Annual Report*, 6.

26. M. S. Osbourne to John T. Graham, Oct. 31, 1865, contained in *First Annual Report of the Baltimore Association*, 23.

27. Alvord, *Third Semi-Annual Report*, 6.

28. J. C. Brubaker to W. W. Rogers, Aug. 26, 1866, vol. 1, Register of Letters Rec'd. Assistant Commissioner, BRFAL-Md.

29. Rev. C. B. Boynton to E. M. Gregory, May 23, 1867, Letters Rec'd, Assistant Commissioner, BRFAL-Md.

30. William L. VanDerlip to W. W. Rogers, Sept. 28, 1867, Letters Rec'd, Annapolis, BRFAL-Md.

31. J. W. Alvord, *Second Semi-Annual Report on Schools and Finances of Freedmen, July 1, 1866* (Washington, D.C.: Government Printing Office, 1868), 11.

32. W. Perkins to John T. Graham, Nov. 1, 1865, contained in *First Annual Report of the Baltimore Association*, 28–29.

33. William L. VanDerlip to John Kimball, Feb. 18, 1868, vol. 48, Letters Sent, Annapolis Agent, BRFAL-Md.

34. R. G. Rutherford to Freedmen's Bureau, July 23, 1867, vol. 53, Letters Sent, Rockville Agent, BRFAL-Md.

35. David Williams to Edgar M. Gregory, June 12, 1867, Reports & Schools Misc., BRFAL-Md.

36. R. G. Rutherford to W. W. Rogers, Oct. 2, 1867, vol. 53, Letters Sent, Rockville Agent, BRFAL-Md.

37. Rev. C. B. Boynton to Edgar M. Gregory, May 23, 1867, vol. 1, Register of Letters Rec'd, Assistant Commissioner, BRFAL-Md.

38. John H. Butler to William L. VanDerlip, June 22, 1868, Letters Rec'd, Annapolis, BRFAL-Md.

39. John H. Butler to William L. VanDerlip, Aug. 22, 1867, vol. 47, Register of Letters Rec'd, Annapolis, BRFAL-Md.

40. *First Annual Report of the Baltimore Association*, 5.

41. George J. Stannard to O. O. Howard, June 5, 1866, vol. 3, Letters Sent, Assistant Commissioner, BRFAL-Md.

42. Singleton Hughes to Edgar M. Gregory, Dec. 24, 1866, vol. 1, Register of Letters Rec'd, Assistant Commissioner, BRFAL-Md.

43. William L. VanDerlip to W. W. Rogers, Sept. 23, 1867 (two letters), vol. 48, Letters Sent, Annapolis Agent, BRFAL-Md.

44. *Baltimore Clipper*, Dec. 9, 1864.

45. *First Annual Report of the Baltimore Association*, 29.

46. Testimony in Investigation of the Government of Maryland, 1867, Committee on the Judiciary, Records of the House of Representatives, Record Group 233, National Archives, Washington, D.C.

47. Charles A. Watkins to O. O. Howard, March 13, 1866, Letters Rec'd, Assistant Commissioner, BRFAL-DC.

48. "Proceedings of the Governor of the State of Maryland [1861–1869]," State Papers, Maryland State Archives, Annapolis, Md.

49. Fuke, "Peasant Priorities," 21–45.

50. R. M. Janney to Freedmen's Bureau, Aug. 31, 1866; Fielder J. Israel to E. M. Stanton, Sept. 28, 1866, Letters Rec'd, Assistant Commissioner, BRFAL-Md; *Baltimore American*, Oct. 15, 1866.

51. *Baltimore American*, Feb. 4, 1867.

52. R. M. Janney to Freedmen's Bureau, March 1, 1867, Letters Rec'd, Assistant Commissioner, BRFAL-Md.

53. John H. Butler to William L. VanDerlip, Aug. 28, 1867, vol. 47, Register of Letters Rec'd, Annapolis Agent, BRFAL-Md.

54. David Williams to Edgar M. Gregory, June 12, 1867, Reports, School Misc., BRFAL-Md.

55. John H. Butler to William L. VanDerlip, Jan. 4, 1868, vol. 47, Register of Letters Rec'd, Annapolis Agent, BRFAL-Md.

56. Thomas Davidson to John Kimball, Sept. 13, 1867, Letters Rec'd, Annapolis Agent, BRFAL-Md.

57. Thomas Davidson to William L. VanDerlip, Aug. 18, 1867, vol. 47, Register of Letters Rec'd, Annapolis Agent, BRFAL-Md.

58. S. J. Alsop to George E. Henry, July 2, 1867, Letters Rec'd, Bladensburg Agent, BRFAL-Md.

59. John H. Butler to William L. VanDerlip, Aug. 22, 1867, vol. 47, Register of Letters Rec'd, Annapolis Agent, BRFAL-Md.

60. John H. Butler to William L. VanDerlip, Nov. 18, 1867, Letters Rec'd, Annapolis Agent, BRFAL-Md.

61. John H. Butler to William L. VanDerlip, Nov. 10, 1867, Letter Rec'd, Annapolis, BRFAL-Md.

62. *Third Annual Report of the Baltimore Association*, 6.

63. *First Annual Report of the Baltimore Association*, 8.

64. *Second Annual Report of the Baltimore Association*, 7.

65. *Third Annual Report of the Baltimore Association*, 6.

66. Baltimore Yearly Meeting, Religious Society of Friends, Orthodox, Records Deposited at Homewood Meeting House, Minutes, Meetings for Sufferings, 1829–1877, M781, p. 311, Maryland State Archives, Annapolis, Md.

67. William J. Albert to American Freedmen's Union Commission, Mar. 21, 1868, Baltimore Normal School Minute Books, MS95, Maryland Historical Society, Baltimore, Md.

68. *American Missionary* 12 (May 1868): 101.

69. John H. Butler to William L. VanDerlip, Nov. 29, 1867, Letters Rec'd, Annapolis Agent, BRFAL-Md.

70. John H. Butler to William L. VanDerlip, Nov. 18, 1867, Letters Rec'd, Annapolis Agent, BRFAL-Md.

71. Joseph Hall to William L. VanDerlip, Sept. 4, 1866, Letters Rec'd, Annapolis Agent, BRFAL-Md.

72. Subscription list, Feb. 1867, Letters Rec'd, Rockville Agent, BRFAL-Md.

73. *Freedmen's Record* 1 (Dec. 1865): 194.

74. *First Annual Report of the Baltimore Association*, 19.

75. Ibid., 22.

76. Ibid., 24.

77. *Freedmen's Record* 3 (Apr. 1867): 62–63.

78. *National Freedman* 2 (May 1866): 148–49.

79. Ninth Census of the United States, 1870, Schedule 1: Inhabitants, National Archives, Washington, D. C; *First Annual Report of the Baltimore Association*, 7.

80. Henna Howard to Andrew Johnson, Apr. 25, 1865, State Papers, Maryland State Archives, Annapolis, Md.

81. *American Missionary* 12 (May 1868): 101.

82. *Freedmen's Record* 3 (April 1867): 62–63.

83. *Baltimore American*, July 1, 1867.

84. Ibid., July 30, Aug. 3, 12, 1867.

85. *Centreville Citizen*, n.d., as quoted in *Baltimore American*, Aug. 5, 1867.

86. *Baltimore American*, Sept. 5, 1867.

87. *Third Annual Report of the Baltimore Association*, 4.

88. Testimony in Investigation of the Government of Maryland, 1867, Committee on the Judiciary, Records of the House of Representatives, Record Group 233.

89. Joseph Hall to William L. VanDerlip, June 18, 1867, Letters Rec'd Annapolis Agent, BRFAL-Md.

90. John H. Butler to William L. VanDerlip, Oct. 31, 1867, Letters Rec'd., Annapolis Agent, BRFAL-Md.

91. *Freedmen's Record* 1 (Dec. 1865): 194.

92. *First Annual Report of the Baltimore Association*, 20.

93. *Baltimore American*, Dec. 4, 1865.

94. Testimony in Investigation of the Government of Maryland, 1867, Committee on the Judiciary, Records of the House of Representatives, Record Group 233.

95. *Baltimore American*, Dec. 4, 1865.

96. *Liberator* 34 (Nov. 25, 1864): 190.

97. Fuke, "Peasant Priorities," 21–22; Fuke, "Planters, Apprenticeship, and Forced Labor," 58.

98. Roger L. Ransom and Richard Sutch, *One Kind of Freedom: The Economic Consequences of Emancipation* (Cambridge, England: Cambridge University Press, 1977), 1.

99. Eric Foner, *Nothing But Freedom: Emancipation and Its Legacy* (Baton Rouge: Louisiana State University Press, 1983), 86.

100. Barbara J. Fields, *Slavery and Freedom on the Middle Ground: Maryland During the Nineteenth Century* (New Haven: Yale University Press, 1985), 165.

13

Reconstruction's Allies: The Relationship of the Freedmen's Bureau and the Georgia Freedmen

Paul A. Cimbala

YEARS AFTER THE PASSING of the Freedmen's Bureau, one Georgia freedwoman succinctly described what she had expected from the agency: "to get things to going smooth after the war."[1] If pressed, she probably would have admitted that the Bureau had fallen short of accomplishing that goal, and, to some degree, many of Reconstruction Georgia's approximately half-million African Americans would have confirmed her disappointment.[2] By the time of the Georgia Bureau's demise in 1870, freedpeople throughout the state still knew racism, fraud, and violence as common and constant hurdles placed in the way of their pursuit of the rights of free individuals by their unsympathetic white neighbors. It was a legacy that the Freedmen's Bureau had not intended to leave behind.[3]

The men of the Freedmen's Bureau were motivated by an ideology that had its roots, for most of them, in antebellum free-labor thought and, for a few of them, in antebellum reform. Their attitudes about the Union and freedom were nurtured by wartime developments that included a growing commitment to black civil rights; their commitment to Reconstruction was energized by a desire to secure the fruits of Union victory. Because of this ideological heritage, they did not find it difficult to pursue goals that—more often than not—intersected with the freedpeople's own goals. Working within fairly consistent intellectual parameters, they supported honest labor relations; assisted in establishing schools; offered temporary relief to the hungry; fought for equal justice for the freedpeople; and, when the time came, attempted to make sure that the freedpeople could express their political preferences without fear of white retribution.[4]

Hindered by inadequate resources and confronted by significant obstacles, Bureau men continued to fight the Civil War—if not the one that started on April 12, 1861, then certainly the one that began on January 1, 1863—against an enemy unwilling to retreat from its commitment to maintaining Georgia as a white man's country.[5] Abandoned by the nation and discouraged by their own impotence, they eventually suffered defeat at the hands of the unreconstructable white Georgians, this time the superior forces on the field. Along the way, however, they forged alliances with ex-slaves who witnessed the commitment of their northern friends to the mutual goals that would give substance to their freedom.

To understand the complex relationship that grew between the Freedmen's Bureau and the freedpeople, one must understand that despite these views, or perhaps as a consequence of them, the Bureau was not inclined to act solely as an ombudsman for the ex-slaves of Georgia. Because the Bureau was committed to creating a just free-labor society in which black and white Georgians recognized their mutual rights and obligations, because the agency was willing to give the complaints of planters a fair hearing, because the agency assumed that white Georgians had to be convinced that Reconstruction would be just and beneficial to all, and because the agency was not necessarily willing to support the freedpeople in all of their desires, the relationship between the Bureau and the freedpeople of Georgia was sometimes strained and ofttimes ambiguous. The attitudes of the Bureau agents toward the freedpeople provide a starting point for understanding this relationship.

During 1867, Lieutenant Douglas G. Risley, a Bureau assistant commissioner stationed at Brunswick, Georgia, was particularly interested in establishing schools for the freedpeople to move them out of the wake of slavery. Nevertheless, it was a concern that did not stop him from threatening to close those schools if the freedpeople did not make an effort to support them. Risley brought a patriotism to his Bureau service that was not uncommon to other Bureau men who had served in the Union army. Paternalistic and pugnacious, he often quarrelled with the northern schoolteachers working in his district who failed to accept his authority. But his views about Reconstruction were heavily influenced by his abolitionism, which he did not hide during the war, and by his wartime experiences, which included severe wounds received in 1864 while leading black troops in Virginia.[6]

Risley believed that by joining the Bureau he had become a missionary, as well as a soldier, in the nation's war against the white South and for the freedmen. "By proper exertions, and an unobstructed course, we might be ready to begin the work of Enlightening those heathen, and helping them cast off the yoke of bondage, still imposed with impunity upon them in a thousand ways by their self-styled 'best-friends'—their former masters—with the opening of the New Year," Risley explained to an American Missionary Association official. "Profoundly ignorant as Africa is upon all other subjects, she is not so deeply sunken in her 'Slough of Despond' as ever to believe that the Southerners are her 'true friends' as they claim. Instinct, reason or inspiration saves them from the Evils that a belief in this delusion and snare would entail upon them. They look towards the North, for their advisers, their helpers and their friends. Haveing set their faces that way during the years of bondage, it is difficult for them to 'face about'—And I call it an hopeful, encouraging sign."[7]

Risley clearly believed that the freedpeople were not yet ready to become masters of their own affairs, but he did not expect their situation to be static. He was committed to helping the freedpeople stand on their own two feet. In June 1867, he expressed his belief that Union Leagues, organizations that supported Republican Party goals, would prevent the freedpeople from suffering from white intimidation and "that their self protection is better insured by conferring upon them the elective franchise and their self-respect greatly increased thereby."[8] These are not the thoughts of a man who wished to keep the freedpeople in a subservient position.

For many Bureau men, such as Risley, slavery, not necessarily race, had diminished the capacity of Georgia's freedpeople to understand the full implications of their new status. That legacy was not a permanent one, but it demanded the attention of the Bureau until things changed. Lieutenant Colonel Homer B. Sprague, who had been a subassistant commissioner for a short time in late 1865 and early 1866, was unambiguous on this point.

Sprague's northern origins and military background were common to all of the forty men who served as subassistant commissioners—middle managers in the state hierarchy who were positioned between the state assistant commissioner and local agents—throughout the Georgia Bureau's existence.[9] Before the war, Sprague had been a principal of the Worcester, Massachusetts, High School. During the war, he had commanded a Connecticut regiment and had led a charge at Port Hudson. Also, participating in army recruiting efforts, he had once urged residents of his old hometown to come "down upon traitors like an Alpine avalanche" and to "march on for humanity, and strike for all the world."[10]

During the first autumn of Reconstruction, Sprague volunteered to work in the Bureau because he not only hoped to convince the freedpeople to be productive laborers but also to make sure that they received justice in a reconstructed Georgia.[11] For Sprague and other Bureau men like him, freedom placed a significant responsibility on the shoulders of the ex-slaves, one that required them to prove themselves capable of earning their way in a free-labor economy. The freedpeople, however, could count on their northern mentors to show them the right path to a sound future.

During his time in Georgia, Sprague became disturbed by accounts in the newspapers of harsh treatment of the ex-slaves and by expressed views concerning the freedpeople that many of his Bureau colleagues shared. "Now the negroes are bad enough, Heaven knows, without exaggerating—idle enough, vicious enough—just as slavery had left them," he once complained to Brigadier General Davis Tillson, the Georgia Bureau's second assistant commissioner. But the freedpeople "need to be trained with a firm and vigorous yet a kind hand. They need to be encouraged, to have their manhood appealed to. They need to have praise judiciously mixed with blame." Most important, the freedpeople need "to be protected in their rights as well as punished for their misdeeds, to be instructed in their duties and treated as men with immortal souls rather than as beasts of burden or machines for pulling cotton. They need a guardian rather than a jailor or a hangman."[12]

Bureau men, such as Risley and Sprague, might have had mixed opinions of the freedpeople, but they also had high expectations of what their agency could do for the ex-slaves and, in turn, what the ex-slaves could do for themselves. As subassistant commissioners, their influence was geographically limited, but their views were not out of line with those of most other Bureau officials and especially the four men who served as the Georgia Bureau's assistant commissioners, men who had the authority to set the tone of the agency during each of their administrations.

Brigadier General Rufus Saxton, who served as the Georgia Bureau's assistant commissioner from May 20, 1865, until September 22, 1865, was the only Georgia assistant commissioner who emphasized the importance of land distribution for the ex-slaves. Because of his emphasis on what land grants could do to uplift the freedpeople, he was arguably the most radical Georgia Bureau assistant commissioner. Yet his views were complex, and his policies encompassed more than just pushing this one issue. He assumed that the freedpeople required his paternalistic advice about work, marriage, morality, frugality, and patience. He urged the freedpeople to prove that they were worthy of their freedom, but he also promised them that hard work within the context of a system of labor contracts could improve their lives, that slavery no longer limited their future prospects, and that they now had a chance to shape their own destiny.[13] Tillson, Saxton's successor, also acknowledged that work was the most important of the northerners' ideals that they brought south, for through hard work protected by Bureau-supervised contracts, all things were possible, including the acquisition of property.[14] Colonel Caleb C. Sibley, who suceeded Tillson on January 14, 1867, agreed with Tillson's views on the importance of work and fair contracts, but probably because of the influence of his subordinate, Major John Randolph Lewis, he placed a greater emphasis on the role of formal education to create independent individuals. For Major Lewis, who succeeded Sibley and served as the last Georgia Bureau assistant commissioner from October 16, 1868, until the middle of 1870, labor was important, but educated freedpeople were "the seed sown in this land of oppression that shall spring up soldiers strong and mighty to resist the oppressor and strive for their rights."[15]

Regardless of the emphasis, all Georgia Bureau assistant commissioners, as well as most of their Union subordinates, expected to secure justice for the ex-slaves and leave them in circumstances that would allow them to advance their own cause when Congress inevitably shut down the Bureau.[16] They assumed that they knew what was best for the freedpeople, but they had no intention of abandoning them to the mercy of their employers or white judges and juries. Tillson, for example, made it clear that the freedpeople were "under the guardianship of the Nation."[17] That idea alone was sufficient justification for Tillson to interpose the power of the Bureau between the freedmen and aggressive, racist white Georgians in their civic and economic dealings, especially after he concluded that the freedpeople were more attuned to his plans for labor than were their ex-masters.[18] In the end, the northern Bureau men, who had started out placing so much faith in moral suasion and the reasonableness of white Georgians, concluded that only continued military pressure applied to such erstwhile rebels would save the day and secure the fruits of the Union's hard-fought victory.[19]

To be sure, some freedpeople wondered about an agency that placed ex-masters in positions of authority as local agents in what they thought was "their Bureau," which happened in Georgia during 1865 and 1866. And ex-slaves certainly considered of dubious worth a government policy that deprived them of the economic base for their freedom when the Bureau made it clear to them that they would have to earn the land that they so much desired—land that they considered to be their Civil War inheritance. If freedpeople did not understand why the Bureau did these things, there were reasons for such policies that did not diminish the Bureau's commitment to securing justice for black Georgians. These two factors—the use of native white Georgians to staff local Bureau agencies and the inability to comply with the freedpeople's desire for land—provide examples of how actions that appeared to be contrary to the freedpeople's greater good were not implemented by the Georgia Bureau with the intention of harming the progress of its black charges.

The freedpeople's first contact with Freedmen's Bureau officials during the spring and summer of 1865 was almost exclusively confined to the Georgia coast and, almost without exception, cordial. Along the Savannah River, in the Ogeechee district of Chatham County, and on the barrier islands along the coast, ministers-turned-government agents—first under the authority of General William T. Sherman, who set aside the area for the sole use of black Georgians in January 1865, and then under the authority of the Freedmen's Bureau, assisted the freedpeople in running their own affairs. In this black reservation, the Reverends Tunis G. Campbell (Saxton's one black agent), William H. Tiffany, and William F. Eaton became part of the freedpeople's lives by officiating at their weddings, teaching them in Sunday school, conducting their weekly religious services, and protecting their claims from white intruders. These men also shared Saxton's desire to continue to settle freedpeople on grants of land within the reservation.[20]

The federal government failed to confirm the titles of the freedpeople who worked land within Sherman's reservation in 1866, thus binding the Bureau's hands and limiting the freedpeople's options there. Restoration of sea island and coastal property began during Tillson's administration and continued into Sibley's administration. This development did not endear the Bureau to the freedpeople, and the agency's reputation was worse on the coast than in most other areas of the state. Freedpeople, deprived of their land, protested. Many refused to sign contracts to remain in the old reservation or to take up property in South Carolina to which the federal government had clear title. Some freedpeople were arrested by Tillson, whereas Sibley used troops to force others to live by their contracts. In the end, the alliance that appeared so promising turned into bitter confrontation.

As for distributing land gratis to the rest of the freedpeople of Georgia, the Bureau had no choice in the matter. Congress and the president made land policy; the Bureau was only the executor of the national will. By September 1865, when Tillson replaced Saxton, President Andrew Johnson's liberal pardon policy had deprived the agency of the opportunity to lease (as the Bureau law allowed the agency) any abandoned or confiscated property to the freedpeople. None remained beyond the boundaries of Sherman's reservation. The best option left open to the freedpeople, as far as the Bureau was concerned, was that provided by contract-regulated labor arrangements, which, according to Bureau doctrine, would allow the agency to protect the interests of all involved parties.[21]

The Georgia Bureau had greater control over its personnel than it did over national land policy, and its intentions are better judged in this area. Throughout the summer of 1865, most white and black Georgians only heard or read about the agency, so slow was Saxton to make the Bureau's presence felt beyond the coast and a few towns. The lack of resources, the uncertainty of the breadth of the agency's authority, conflict with local army commanders, and a leave induced by illness all conspired against Saxton's desire to do more.

Beginning in September 1865, Tillson did better as far as expanding the Bureau's authority across Georgia, but, even as he established something of an organization, the assistant commissioner began to shape a controversial legacy for the agency when he appointed native white Georgians as Bureau agents.

Tillson turned to native white Georgians for a number of reasons but certainly not to return the freedpople to the absolute control of their ex-masters. He fully understood the reality of his situation but completely misjudged the response of white Georgians when he presented them with what today would be considered modest challenges to the racial status quo. Tillson's expectations were threefold. First, Tillson realized that the Bureau would never have the resources required to set up an extensive network of paid northern agents; Congress would not allow it. Second, because of the time limits placed on the Bureau's life expectancy by Congress, Tillson realized that, to secure the freedpeople in their new status, he had to persuade white Georgians of the benefits of a Union-defined Reconstruction that would guarantee the rights of the freedpeople. Third, he assumed that he could rely on the "better sort" of white Georgians to look after the interests all Georgians once he had indoctrinated them. Given these expectations, Tillson assumed that he could solve his personnel problem while instructing a key group of presumably intelligent, reasonable white Georgians in the intricacies of the new relationship between the races.

Another group of individuals could have filled out the ranks of the Bureau, but Tillson never gave any serious thought to appointing black subordinates as field agents (nor, for that matter, did his successors). Ex-slaves still needed guidance and education, as far as he was concerned, so they were unqualified for the responsibility. Tillson probably assumed that northern blacks would do more harm than good if they were anything like Saxton's black agent Campbell, the assistant commissioner's nemesis on the Sherman reservation. If he had appointed blacks to Bureau agencies, given the limited military resources at the Bureau's disposal and the determination of the white population to resist Reconstruction, he would have been condemning their agencies to failure and probably sentencing the black agents to death.[22]

Tillson's approach to overcoming his Bureau's institutional limitations failed. Although a few of his white southern agents accepted

Tillson's concerns for justice for black Georgians as a valid point of departure for Reconstruction, most of them were never greatly influenced by the free-labor ideology that Tillson assumed would be so appealing. Rather, most of Tillson's citizen agents continued to think like their white neighbors; their inability to act as advocates for the ex-slaves was more a reflection of white Georgia's inability to accept Tillson's ideas than of the Bureau's lack of desire to do right by the freedpeople.[23]

During 1867, Sibley removed most of Tillson's citizen agents but only after a number of those agents had the opportunity to turn some freedpeople against the Bureau. Freedpeople who encountered the worst of Tillson's citizen agents had serious grievances, which would certainly be sufficient, if repeated frequently, to convince the freedpeople of Georgia that their alleged guardian was, in fact, in league with their ex-masters and intent on forcing them into another kind of servitude. Yet, generally, the freedpeople understood that the Bureau was there to help them. They might have held individual agents in contempt, but they expected the Bureau to work for them. They demanded better, and the Bureau tried to accommodate them.

During 1865 and 1866, even as he reviewed recommendations from white Georgians for appointments to agencies, Tillson had willingly listened to freedpeople who expected to have a say in their own government, which reinforced their assumptions that the Bureau was there to work for them. On the Fourth of July in 1866, the freedpeople of Washington County planned to hold an election to pick their Bureau agent. When informed that this course of action was beyond their power, they urged James R. Smith, the local physician who was teaching a freedmen's school at the time, to take on the task; within two weeks, Tillson appointed him.[24] In late 1865, Clarke County whites nominated a former slave trader and marshal for the county agency, much to the alarm of the local freedpeople who learned of this nomination through Subassistant Commissioner Sprague. The black community leaders of Athens, the county seat, entered a strong protest. Tillson listened and appointed the white man that the freedpeople had recommended to him.[25]

Tillson seriously considered the freedpeople's complaints about the white citizen agents he appointed, investigated their accusations, and did not hesitate to act decisively when the evidence warranted it. In Polk County, for example, the freedpeople had lost all confidence in their agent, Stephen B. Pearce, who could not stem the tide of abuse being dispensed by white planters. Their complaints led to his removal after Subassistant Commissioner C. A. de la Mesa completed an investigation of the agent's activities.[26]

The corollary to this action is that Tillson did not blindly accept the word of white Georgians against that of the freedpeople. During the summer of 1866, when Griffin whites tried to convince Tillson to remove J. Clarke Swayze from his Bureau agency, freedpeople successfully petitioned the assistant commissioner to keep Swayze on duty. In this case, however, Tillson eventually had to replace Swayze for the good of the Bureau and the freedpeople that it served. Swayze had honed a fine antagonistic relationship with his ex-Confederate neighbors—he once had to deal with a gang of whites who confronted him on the streets of Griffin "to put [him] out of the way." Further, it became apparent to Tillson, who always believed that agents should act within prescribed guidelines, that Swayze was overstepping his authority. In August, Tillson asked Swayze to resign, and the agent turned his attention to recruiting labor for employers beyond Georgia's boundaries.[27]

Tillson had not completely lost faith in Swayze at the time of his resignation; the assistant commissioner selected James S. Boynton, another white Georgian, for the Spalding County agency on Swayze's recommendation. His appointment was probably also endorsed, if not advocated, by the local freedpeople, who had developed a good working relationship with Swayze. After Boynton accepted the appointment, freedman G. W. Pills informed Tillson that the freedpeople were pleased with his choice. It appears that the ex-slaves had not misjudged their man. Within a month, Boynton reported that he had collected more than $400 in back wages for the freedpeople.[28]

Agent Boynton had become actively engaged in making the contract system work by confronting planters who failed to honor their obligations to the freedpeople. It was in this area of activity—contract-regulated labor relations—that the Bureau did some of its hardest and most dangerous work for the freedpeople. The freedpeople appreciated these efforts, in part, because they already had come to see a contract system as something that could work to their benefit even before the end of their first season as free laborers.

In August 1865, for example, freedpeople on John A. Cobb's family plantation in Sumter County "seemed dissatisfied," the plantation manager wrote to Cobb, "because you have not come down & made a contract with them" even though Cobb had promised to pay the freedpeople better than some other planters who had accepted the contracting procedure.[29] In this case, the freedpeople also might have assumed that a written document negotiated and signed face-to-face with their old master would not only confirm that they were free but also that they were equal to their employer, at least in the eyes of contract law.

Freedpeople watched landowners compete for their labor, learned that work could bring them "greenbacks," and vexed their ex-masters by bargaining for the most favorable terms. Labor agents looking for workers for planters with land beyond Georgia's borders also convinced many ex-slaves that their labor was a valuable commodity. This competition made the freedpeople, according to planter Howell Cobb, Jr., "high in their self-esteem."[30] "I can see a change taking place in the condition of the freedmen," Bureau surgeon George O. Dalton observed from his post in Albany in early 1867. "Since freedom & the surrender the laborer is learning to go where he can improve his condition, get good wages & be well treated."[31]

The Bureau's contract system provided the freedpeople with opportunities to negotiate with their employers under the supervision of a third party that the ex-slaves assumed was formally bound to be their advocate in the enforcement of those agreements. This assumption was reinforced when the freedpeople learned initially during Tillson's administration that the Bureau insisted on workers holding the first lien on crops that they raised.[32] Agent A. Leers of Halcyondale, for example, made it clear that he expected the freedpeople to be paid for their labor before their employers' other creditors when he encouraged workers "not to suffer any part of the crop to be removed from the plantations, out of their reach, until they received their full shares, as stipulated in their contracts."[33]

Such actions as Leers's convinced many of Georgia's freedpeople to insist on having the Bureau involved in their work arrangements. During late 1866, when the freedpeople of Walton County learned that the county judge would be approving contracts for the next season, they objected because they preferred to have Bureau-supervised documents.[34] In 1867, LaGrange-area freedpeople continued to distrust their old masters, but they accepted work arrangements that were not as favorable as they had hoped because they had the Bureau agent's explanation that the poor harvests of past years made times hard for all concerned. "They will listen to no argument of reason, nor believe anything that may be told them by any person but an Ag[en]t of the Bureau, who has heretofore acted as their Guardian agent & advisor," explained W. E. Wiggins, their agent. "Without his assurance & promise of protection they have no idea they would ever realise any thing from their employers for their labor."[35]

In southwest Georgia, freedpeople also were evidencing an early faith in the federal government during 1865 when they expressed their dissatisfaction with crop settlement procedures "unless some United States officer or bureau agent were present."[36] Ex-slaves quickly learned, however, that having an agent or officer at hand at settlement time was more of a necessity than they might have imagined because of their ex-masters' reluctance to meet their obligations. Ex-slaves, as Augusta agent John Emory Bryant's long workdays proved during the summer of 1865, were beginning to look to the Bureau and their labor contracts for help in protecting their economic rights as early as the summer of 1865, when "planters were turning away their hands without pay in hundreds of cases."[37]

Bryant was not the only overworked Bureau official. Although the freedpeople apparently expected the Bureau to function almost indefinitely, white northerners and southerners always knew that the Bureau was a temporary agency and treated it accordingly. The federal government's most telling example of the shortsightedness stemming from the understanding that the Bureau was not to be a long-term fixture in the South was its unwillingness to provide the agency with a staff adequate for meeting the demands of black petitioners. In August 1867, for example, the freedpeople of Calhoun petitioned Assistant Commissioner Sibley because they believed that Agent C. B. Blacker, a former officer of black troops, was neglecting them. The problem arose not because of Blacker's unconcern or incompetence but because the agent simply did not have the time to cope with the extraordinary amount of work presented to him by the freedpeople.[38]

Other agents and officers failed to satisfy their black constituents' needs because they had little in the way of military resources to make their decisions effective. Rarely could the Bureau leave behind a sizable force for a long period because there were so few soldiers stationed in the state, and rarely could Union soldiers reach a troubled area with any degree of immediacy because the Georgia command lacked cavalry.[39] Consequently, when Bureau officers investigated complaints, their influence generally lasted only as long as they remained on the scene. In July 1866, when Captain George R. Walbridge, the Georgia Bureau's inspector general, investigated a complaint lodged by Spalding County agent Swayze, he extracted a promise from the citizens of Griffin that they would mend their ways and protect Swayze and the freedpeople from violence. But once the white citizens erroneously believed that Walbridge had left town, they "commenced their abuse firing upon a negro for no other purpose as they stated than to see him run."[40] It was no wonder that Tillson, as early as December 1865, even as he hoped to convince whites of the benefits of Bureau policy, had concluded that Reconstruction would not succeed without the support of armed force.[41]

A temporary, inadequately staffed Bureau deprived of a strong arm for enforcing its will encouraged many white Georgians either to ignore the agency or to bide their time. Local officials arrested agents and officers who pursued their duties; such examples further encouraged planters to offer the Bureau little respect.[42] After more than two years of Bureau activity in Georgia, whites still boasted "openly that they will have their day when the Bureau is ceased to exist." As one agent observed in January 1868, those whites were "just as much embittered against the government today as when General Lee was at the head of his army."[43]

New Jersey native, journalist, and wartime Georgia Unionist Swayze witnessed similar white attitudes in Griffin, Spalding County, after the war.[44] "There is a great need of some agency here to protect the Freedmen against the impositions of their former masters and now inveterate persecutions, the more so since the [army] garrison formerly at this place have left," he informed Lieutenant Colonel D. C. Poole, the subassistant commissioner located not too far north along the rail line at Atlanta. "All manner of inhuman treatment is being perpetrated," including shootings and whippings.

The civil authorities were of no assistance in dealing with these problems; according to Swayze, they were "disposed to accept, the general sentiment, which is 'Ho! Ho! now the Yankees are gone, we'll give you hell.' " He warned the Bureau officer that "this country cannot be left to its own government yet, nor until the proper status of the black man is acknowledged and universally accepted."[45] No wonder that he concluded: "The proper status of the Freedmen as designed by the Government, is not, nor will not be appreciated by the people here, unless troops are kept here to force them to yield obedience to the laws." White Georgians did "not seem to comprehend that a negro can be his own free agent."[46]

Freedpeople developed strong feelings about such men as Swayze who worked for their cause. They praised them, showed them respect, and willingly stood up for them when white Georgians tried to derail their work. John Trowbridge, who traveled through Georgia after the war, observed: "The reverence shown by the colored people toward the officers of the bureau was often amusing. They looked to them for what they had formerly depended upon their masters for. If they had lost a pig, they seemed to think that such great and all-powerful men could find it for them without any trouble. They cheered them in the streets, and paid them at all times the most abject respect."[47]

In 1866, a few months after Swayze had joined the agency, the *Griffin Star* mockingly reported that a group of freedpeople returning from a meeting passed the Griffin Bureau office and "exhibited their high appreciation of this institution in the following manner: The hemales gave the military salute, tipping the beaver in the highest style of the art, while the females waved their snowy kerchiefs in the most 'gushing' manner."[48] Regardless of the source, the freedpeople apparently appreciated Swayze. Ex-slaves from beyond Swayze's jurisdiction began to travel to his office to vent their grievances after the grapevine spread the word that, as Swayze boasted, "the Bureau at Griffin protects them in their rights."[49]

Some freedpeople showed their appreciation for their Bureau allies by trying to keep them out of harm's way. In January 1867, freedpeople in Kingston probably saved Rome Subassistant Commissioner Carlos A. de la Mesa's life. De la Mesa was investigating an incident of white violence against a freed family. The local magistrate dismissed the case, and the brother of the defendant threatened to kill de la Mesa. Apparently, the Bureau agent did not seriously consider the threat until the freedpeople learned that there was indeed a plot against him. "I intended returning to Rome that night," de la Mesa explained to his superior officer, "but I was prevented from doing so by the Freedmen and the proprietor of the Hotel who informed me that I would probably be assassinated if I left the house." Not only did the freedpeople warn him; they also "guarded the house through the night."[50]

Freedpeople also took an active part in protecting Major John J. Knox, the Athens subassistant commissioner. Knox, a Michigan native, had been seriously hurt when a bullet passed through his neck during the battle at Fair Oaks, Virginia, on May 31, 1862, a wound that crippled his right arm, induced chronic throat problems, and would eventually contribute to his death in April 1877. A member of the Veteran Reserve Corps, Knox came to Georgia as a recent widower, the lack of family perhaps allowing him to take a strong stand against hostile whites without fear of endangering loved ones.[51] He also brought with him some formative experiences accumulated during his first Bureau assignment in Mississippi. On May 4, 1866, several white Mississippians, who were fed up with Knox's efforts to secure the rights of the area's freedpeople, attacked him and his associate, Superintendent of Education Joseph Warren, in his office at Meridian. As they broke down the door, the Mississippians shouted, "Get out of here you d—d Yankees." They fired at Knox and Warren, who both returned fire, but Knox had to report with regret that he failed to hit anyone.[52]

Knox believed that he had a critical job to perform because, in his experience, white southerners had shown no signs of acknowledging the rights of the freedpeople. When confronted with the possibility that Congress would not continue the Bureau beyond the end of June 1868, Knox admitted that it saddened him to think that the freedpeople "this large class of industrial loyal people" would be "left entirely to the tender mercies of a wicked rebellious people who get glory in their shame." Indeed, Knox was angered by President Andrew Johnson's lenient policies toward the South because they encouraged whites to commit outrages against the freedpeople, "who stand nobly by the principles [of] union[,] Liberty[,] and equal rights to all."[53] The subassistant commissioner had suffered much for the Union cause, which, to him, included civil rights for the ex-slaves, and he was now unwilling to watch unreconstructed southerners mock his sacrifice.

After his appointment to the Bureau in February 1867, Major Knox quickly made friends among the city's freedpeople, who named a schoolhouse in his honor.[54] He took the time to visit black churches and schools ("the best I have seen," he admitted); acknowledged the freedpeople's basic intelligence; and, as one of their teachers noted, "insisted on making known to the colored people their rights as Freedmen."[55] The respect that the freedpeople held for Knox grew as they came to observe him in action. In late December 1868, the subassistant commissioner, with the assistance of six soldiers, courageously dispersed a mob of college students who intended to do harm to "the Negroes[,] the Yankees[,] and government officers." In turn, Knox aggravated the ill will of the whites within his jurisdiction.[56]

The political excitement of the 1868 electoral campaign brought things to a head. Knox suffered numerous insults and threats, including some from an ex-Confederate named Tom Frierson, as he monitored the polls on election day. Shortly thereafter, a drunken Frierson confronted Knox at his office. Knox had endured Frierson's insults at the polls because he wished to avoid provoking violence, "but when he was coming into my room swearing he would beat my brains out," Knox admitted, "I had no alternative left." After warning Frierson several times to leave, Knox shot him in self-defense. "[A]nd if I had not been quite sure that I had killed him," Knox later noted, "I should have shot him again."[57]

Major Knox was confident that he was the wronged party, so he surrendered to the civil authorities. While the Bureau officer was in custody, a vengeful mob gathered and threatened to exercise lynch law. Knox later admitted that the situation worried him, but his friends in the black community came to his rescue. Soon after Knox was taken into custody, about 200 freedmen appeared. Knox later learned that some of his protectors "boldly asserted that if the mob molested me the town would be in ashes—this fact alone saved me."[58]

The freedpeople had a friend in Knox, and they were willing to take risks to protect him. In this instance, however, the white malcontents ultimately had their way. Knox asked to be relieved of his Bureau duties because, as the soldiers sent to Athens in the wake of this incident confirmed, his life would never be safe without constant military protection. "I know the citizens (white) will rejoice to know that the Bureau was closed up before the time fixed by law," Knox wrote. "The colored people will feel sad to know that I have to go at all, yet I shall always remember their kindness in standing by me during the darkest hours of my existence in Georgia."[59]

Ex-slaves were clearly aware of the shifting fortunes of local agencies, in particular, and of the Georgia Bureau, in general. In December 1868, freedpeople in Dougherty County in southwest Georgia, for example, petitioned Congress with their grievances and revealed that they had a good notion of the ebb and flow of Bureau power in their region of the state. They had been unhappy with the citizen agents first appointed by Tillson, they allowed, but agreed that, when these ex-slaveholders "were discharged and better men substituted," there was a beneficial change. The new Bureau men "despatch[ed] business rapidly and equitably" with the help of Military Reconstruction. The petitioners remembered General John Pope, the first commander of the Third Military District, which included Georgia, as the head of a "wise and patriotic administration" that allowed the Bureau "to attend to its own business, only furnishing sufficient military for the enforcement of its decrees." General George Gordon Meade, Pope's successor, on the other hand "assumed arbitrary power over the Bureau," thus limiting its effectiveness and making it difficult for the freedpeople to obtain justice. Although the story of Military Reconstruction is more complex than the freedpeople allowed, its rendering by the petitioners of southwest Georgia was not far off the mark. Further, their use of Bureau reports in the writing of the petition indicates that they had the cooperation of sympathetic Bureau men who were watching their own presence become moot.[60]

The reaction of some freedpeople to the news of the agency's contraction and termination provided further witness to their understanding that the Bureau was an ally in their efforts to secure rights commensurate with their new status. In October 1867, agent Edwin Belcher was relieved of his duties with the Bureau at Forsyth, Georgia, and the vacancy went unfilled. Raised in Philadelphia, Belcher had served as a Union officer during the war. He was wounded and taken prisoner at Chancellorsville in 1863, paroled, and, continuing his run of bad luck, wounded and taken prisoner a second time in 1864 at Rocky Falls Ridge, Georgia. After the war, he taught at the freedmen's school in Augusta, Georgia. It was not until after he began his duties as a Bureau agent that he learned that he had been born in South Carolina and was a mulatto. Belcher had been a sympathetic advocate of the freedmen and would go on to become a Republican politician, but, in the meantime, the ex-slaves of Monroe, Pike, and Upson Counties expected the agency to replace him with someone of like mind.[61]

In November 1868, freedman George H. Clower wrote a desperate letter, at least his second, to Assistant Commissioner Lewis and urged him to send a replacement for Belcher as soon as possible because the freedpeople were "in A Bad fix." Since the Bureau had left the area and because of the political excitement of the times, he informed Lewis, white employers had driven freedpeople from their homes without their pay or justice. Clower was near despair because he believed that only the presence of the Bureau could improve the freedpeople's situation. "I have [done] all I can do," he wrote.[62]

About a week later, Clower, still waiting to hear from Lewis, again wrote to the Bureau and reminded Lewis of his unanswered pleas for assistance and the bad times the freedpeople were enduring. "Genral I want you to help us here," he again implored. "Genral Send us A Bureau if you pleas to do so now soon as you can for we need it here soon as We can Get one."[63] Again, on December 4, 1867, Clower pleaded for an agent because "when Capt. Belcher Was here We don Well but sense he is Goin We has don bad so Genral send a Bureau here."[64] Finally, a Bureau officer arrived on the scene in the hope that "by rendering prompt Justice to the freed people in these cases it will deter other employers from swindling their employees out of their hard earnings."[65]

As the Bureau began to curtail its activities, other freedpeople worried about their future without the agency. As early as November 1867, the freedpeople in the Carnesville area "began to express their feelings of forelorn hope since they heard the Bureau was to cease next year."[66] And, as late as January 1870, the freedpeople at a meeting in Augusta expressed their desire to keep the Bureau in Georgia after they learned that it would be abolished.[67]

In August 1868, when they learned that the return to civilian government would severely restrict the Bureau's authority, the freedpeople in the Butler area became "full of cares about their wages and part of the crop for this year." To vent their anxiety, they held a two-day "Prayer and Revival" meeting "with large attendance." The Butler agent observed that the news of the Bureau's changing status "spred very quickly" among the freedpeople who were "well informed" of the Bureau's affairs even though their employers were yet unaware of the new situation.[68] Such activity led the Hawkinsville agent to conclude: "The freedmen in this section of the county look to me for protection."[69]

When the agency announced that it was terminating its duties, Georgia freedpeople protested the loss of a valuable ally. The freedpeople confirmed that, despite decisions made in Washington, despite the agency's flaws, and despite the complaints of a few black politicians, they considered the Bureau to be their agency. As Rome Subassistant Commissioner de la Mesa had learned, the freedpeople offered no better favorable testimony for the agency than their continued use of the Bureau, even as it began to wind down its operations. In January 1868, the Athens agent reported his office "every day . . . crowded with freedmen women and children . . . demanding justice."[70] To the last, Georgia's ex-slaves turned to the Bureau to resolve all types of complaints ranging from the trivial to the serious. Freedpeople in the Hawkinsville area continued to ask the Bureau to help them collect debts, and those in the counties around Columbus looked to the Bureau for solutions to problems concerning spouses, employers, pilfered watches, unsound horse flesh, and borrowed clothing.[71]

Immediate problems—problems that the Bureau could handle because it still had agencies in the state—gave way to the realities of the future, and freedpeople had to begin to adjust to them. The fact that the Bureau's short lifetime had been common knowledge to white southerners and northern policymakers from its inception had always limited the agency's effectiveness. When it became clear that, despite the pleas of the freedpeople, there would be no reprieve for the Bureau, ex-slaves came to grips with the fact that their futures would be negotiated between themselves and their exmasters. In the spring of 1868, freedpeople in the Crawfordville area indicated that they preferred to work under Bureau-supervised contracts, but they did not have them. Their employers pointed out that the Bureau would not be around to enforce those documents at the end of the season because of its reduction in force. The freedpeople probably concluded that it would be best not to antagonize their employers by insisting on something that, in the long run, was of little worth.[72]

Certainly, there was a pragmatic side to the freedpeople's relationship with the Freedmen's Bureau, but at least that pragmatism suggested that the agency had something real to offer them. Still, there was more than calculation in the freedpeople's dealings with the agency. Freedpeople realized that they could find allies in the Bureau because so many of the agency's personnel had allowed their northern beliefs to shape their workaday lives. Of course, Bureau rhetoric also had helped. Requested by Athens freedpeople to address one of their gatherings, Gilbert L. Eberhart, the Georgia Bureau's first school superintendent, told the freedpeople which party was responsible for the Emancipation Proclamation and the legislation that established the Bureau, and he delineated their civil rights.[73] Even common Bureau lectures on the obligations of freedom cast the freedpeople in roles that placed them in promising positions and urged them to understand that, at least in the economic, legal, and civic spheres, they had the potential to become their former masters' equals. Such rhetoric propelled the Bureau's message across Georgia.

The message was appealing to the freedpeople, at least once they realized that the distribution of their ex-masters' land was not going to come to pass. Just consider Tillson's speech in which he told black Georgians in early 1866 that "A single year of patient, honest, steady work and the fortunes of your people are established forever."[74] Or Crawfordville agent John Barney's words to a planter that "the days for whipping colored people for amusement & gratification of passion &c have passed away. Moral Law, has superceded, lynch law in this country," which undoubtedly made their way to the local freedpeople in the spring of 1868.[75] Or the exhortation of Thomasville Subassistant Commissioner William F. White, a veteran whose health had been ruined by the war, that the freedpeople must vote or again become slaves.[76]

Such words were appealing, and the Bureau tried to give meaning to them. Enforcing the message of hard work and education, Bureau personnel made it clear that they expected the freedpeople to be given the same consideration before the law as were their white neighbors.[77] Telling freedpeople to vote was one thing, but making sure that polls were open to the freedpeople, as did Major Knox and also agent William C. Morrill, who successfully forced a crowd of armed whites to open the polls to freedmen voters in Americus in November 1868, was something else.[78] Claiming that the Bureau, the Republican Party, or the federal government stood for justice was an important message, but intervening in an improperly heard case and then securing an acquittal for the defendant, as Albany Subassistant Commissioner O. H. Howard did, put substance in the message.[79] To the ex-slaves who witnessed these actions—who watched these men put themselves in harm's way to carry out a mission that coincided with the goals of the ex-slaves themselves— the Freedmen's Bureau in Georgia was an ally in the struggle to define a meaningful freedom.

NOTES

1. George P. Rawick, ed., *The American Slave: A Composite Autobiography*, 19 vols. (Westport, Conn.: Greenwood Press, 1972), vol. 8: *Arkansas Narratives*, pt. 1, 68.

2. B. Phinizy Spalding, "Georgia," in *The Encycopedia of Southern History*, ed. by David C. Roller and Robert W. Twyman (Baton Rouge: Louisiana State University Press, 1979), 537.

3. For a complete treatment of the Georgia Bureau, see Paul A. Cimbala, *Under the Guardianship of the Nation: The Freedmen's Bureau and the Reconstruction of Georgia, 1865–1870* (Athens: University of Georgia Press, 1997). Much of the material used in this essay is drawn from the book with permission from the University of Georgia Press, for which the author is grateful.

4. For a discussion of the ideology of the Georgia Bureau men, see Cimbala, *Under Guardianship of the Nation*, chap. 1. For antebellum and wartime ideological roots of the northern Bureau men, see Herman Belz, *A New Birth of Freedom: The Republican Party and Freedmen's Rights, 1861–1866* (Westport, Conn.: Greenwood Press, 1976); Eric Foner, *Free Soil, Free Labor, Free Men: The Ideology of the Republican Party before the Civil War* (New York: Oxford University Press, 1970); Earl J. Hess, *Liberty, Virtue, and Progress: Northerners and Their War for the Union* (New York: Fordham University Press, 1997); and James M. McPherson, *What They Fought For, 1861–1865* (Baton Rouge: Louisiana State University Press, 1994).

5. Richard Zuczek argues in *State of Rebellion: Reconstruction in South Carolina* (Columbia: University of South Carolina Press, 1996) that whites in South Carolina considered the years of Reconstruction as a continuation of

the Civil War by other means. White Georgians seemed to have shared this view. I have found that northern Bureau men and, in particular, northern Bureau men who had served in the Union Army's Veteran Reserve Corps (those men who had been wounded during the war but could still do some type of valuable military work) had a comparable view of Reconstruction and saw their work in Georgia as critical for securing the fruits of Union victory.

6. Douglas G. Risley, Civil War Pension Files, Records of the Veterans Administration, Record Group 15, National Archives, Washington, D.C. For Risley's and the Bureau's education work, see Cimbala, *Under Guardianship of the Nation*, 105–30.

7. D. G. Risley to E. P. Smith, Aug.23, 1867, reel 3, American Missionary Association Papers, Georgia, Amistad Research Center, Tulane University, New Orleans, Louisiana (microfilm) (hereinafter cited as AMA-Ga).

8. D. G. Risley to C. C. Sibley, June 24, 1867, reel 19, Records of the Assistant Commissioner for the State of Georgia, Bureau of Refugees, Freedmen, and Abandoned Lands, National Archives Microfilm Publication M798 (hereinafter cited as BRFAL-Ga [M798]).

9. Subassistant commissioners were army officers or ex-army officers and, more likely than not, were or had been members of the Veteran Reserve Corps. During Davis Tillson's administration, they had an advisory relationship with agents who reported directly to Tillson. After Tillson's successor, Caleb C. Sibley, reorganized the Bureau, subassisant commissioners had command authority over agents and acted as part of the hierarchy between agents and the assistant commissioner. The figure given in the text includes "assistant subassistant commissioners," who were also army officers serving in the Bureau with powers and duties that combined aspects of the agents and the subassistant commissioners but in a subordinate position. For the organization of the Bureau in Georgia, see Cimbala, *Under Guardianship of the Nation*, chap. 2. For the number of subassistant commissioners and their backgrounds, see ibid., 271 n.25.

10. Abijah P. Marvin, *History of Worcester in the War of the Rebellion* (Cleveland: Arthur H. Clark Company, 1880), 181; Homer B. Sprague, Civil War Pension Files, Records of the Veterans Administration, Record Group 15, National Archives, Washington, D.C.

11. H. B. Sprague to D. Tillson, Nov. 24, 1865, reel 13, BRFAL-Ga (M798).

12. H. B. Sprague to D. Tillson, Jan. 10, 1866, reel 29, BRFAL-Ga (M798).

13. R. Saxton, Circular No. 2, Aug. 16, 1865, U.S. House, *Executive Documents*, 39th Cong., 1st sess., no. 70 (serial 1256), 92–9.

14. For example, see "General Tillson's Speech Delivered before the Freedmen's Convention, *Augusta Loyal Georgian*, Jan. 20, 1866.

15. J. R. Lewis, "Annual Report," Nov. 1, 1866, U.S. Senate, *Executive Documents*, 39th Cong., 2nd sess., no. 6 (serial 1276), 130–1, 140.

16. For more information on the ideological parameters of the Georgia Bureau assistant commissioners, see Cimbala, *Under Guardianship of the Nation*, chap. 1.

17. D. Tillson to O. O. Howard, Dec. 20, 1865, reel 20, Registers and Letters Received by the Commissioner of the Bureau of Refugees, Freedmen, and Abandoned Lands, National Archives Microfilm Publication M752 (hereinafter cited as [LR]BRFAL [M752]).

18. For example, see how Tillson adjusted his views about which party was the most eager to accept his direction for labor arrangements, in Cimbala, *Under Guardianship of the Nation*, 138–44.

19. Ibid., 24.

20. Special Field Orders, No. 15, Jan. 16, 1865, in *The War of the Rebellion: A Compilation of the Official Records of the Union and Confederate Armies*, 70 vols. in 128 (Washington, D.C.: Government Printing Office, 1880–1901), ser. 1, vol. 47, pt. 2, 60–2; W. H. Tiffany to H. F. Sickles, Nov. 27, 1865, Unregistered Letters Rec'd, Savannah Subassistant Commissioner, Records of the Subordinate Field Offices for the State of Georgia, Bureau of Refugees, Freedmen, and Abandoned Lands, Record Group 105, National Archives, Washington, D.C. (hereinafter cited as BRFAL-Ga); W. F. Eaton to G. Whipple, May 15, 1866, reel 1, AMA-Ga.

21. See the problems of land claims along the Georgia coast in Cimbala, *Under Guardianship of the Nation*, 166–92. For a different interpretation of the Bureau's role in the reservation, see Russell Duncan, *Freedom's Shore: Tunis Campbell and the Georgia Freedmen* (Athens: University of Georgia Press, 1986). For the various shifts in Bureau administrations in Georgia and their reasons, see Cimbala, *Under Guardianship of the Nation*, 22–49.

22. At this point, the Georgia Bureau, because of the limits placed on it by meager congressional appropriations, appointed unsalaried agents who relied on fees collected for performing their various duties. Given this situation, it was unlikely that Tillson would have had much luck in finding northern civilians to staff his Bureau. It was after the reorganization in early 1867 that the Bureau began to pay salaries and its staff became much more northern in nature. See Cimbala, *Under Guardianship of the Nation*, 5–9, 22–49. On Campbell's troubled relations with Tillson, see Cimbala, ibid., 174–88.

23. For the problems that the Bureau experienced with native white Georgians, see ibid., 41–4, 51–2, 55–8.

24. It is Dr. Smith's word that the freedpeople wanted him, but his record was such that Caleb Sibley, in the midst of removing almost all of Tillson's native agents, continued to carry him on the rolls as a paid agent.

Although Tillson was willing to listen to the freedpeople and frequently accepted their recommendations, he did not always do their bidding. Tillson appointed James G. Brown as an agent in Washington County along with Dr. Smith even after Dr. Smith informed him that the freedpeople did not want Brown. In this case, Tillson was probably trying to please both blacks and whites by balancing his appointments at a time when he still hoped to convince white Georgians of the benefits of Reconstruction. It should be noted that Tillson's successors did not appoint all individuals recommended for agencies by freedpeople. See J. R. Smith, July 4, 1866, reel 29; Register of Civilian Agents, 1865–1867; Station Books, vol. 1, 1867–1868, reel 35; Petition of Rev. Adam N. Burton and others, Dec. 4, 1867, Registers of Letters Rec'd, reel 17, BRFAL-Ga (M798).

25. H. B. Sprague to M. Davis, Dec. 1, 1865; M. Davis and others to H. B. Sprague, Dec. 3, 1865, reel 31; Register of Civilian Agents, 1865–1867, reel 35, BRFAL-Ga (M798). Into the next year, Tillson continued to show some sensitivity to the freedpeople's feelings about his appointments. In the spring of 1866, Tillson appointed Allen G. Bass as agent for McIntosh County and Sapelo Island but removed him within two weeks. Tillson probably did so because he had learned that Bass had been an overseer before the war and continued to act as one on the estate of Thomas Spalding. See also Special Field Orders, No. 7, March 16, 1866, Special Field Orders, No. 9, March 27, 1866, reel 34, BRFAL-Ga (M798); list of payments to A. G. Bass, "overseer," Oct. 30, 1862; Feb. 5, 1863; Jan. 13, 1864; and June 11, 1866, in Journal of William Cooke, University of Georgia, Athens; Robert Manson Myers, ed., *The Children of Pride: A True Story of Georgia and the Civil War* (New Haven: Yale University Press, 1972), 1683.

26. C. A. de la Mesa to S. B. Pearce, July 31, 1866, enclosed in C. A. de la Mesa to D. Tillson, Oct. 3, 1866; C. A. de la Mesa to D. Tillson, Oct. 3, 8, 28, 1866, reel 13; C. A. de la Mesa to D. Tillson, Oct. 19, 1866, reel 26; E. Pickett to C. A. de la Mesa, Nov. 7, 1866, reel 4; Registers of Civilian Agents, 1865–1867, reel 35, BRFAL-Ga (M798).

27. G. H. Pratt to J. C. Swayze, March 21, 1866, Unregistered Letters Rec'd, Griffin Subassistant Commissioner, BRFAL-Ga; G. Walbridge to D. Tillson, July 23, enclosed in J. C. Swayze to D. Tillson, July 18, 1866, reel 29; E. M. L. Ehlers to W. W. Dane, July 23, 1866, reel 26; D. Tillson to C. Peebles, Sept. 12, 1866, reel 3; C. Peebles to D. Tillson, Sept. 15, 1866, reel 28; J. C. Swayze to D. Tillson, Sept. 28, Oct. 14, 1866, reel 29, BRFAL-Ga (M798). For the details of Swayze's life before and after he served as a Bureau agent, see Richard H. Abbott, "Jason Clarke Swayze, Republican Editor in Reconstruction Georgia, 1867–1873," *Georgia Historical Quarterly* 79 (summer 1995): 337–66. For the controversy stirred up by Swayze's emigration agent activities, see Cimbala, *Under Guardianship of the Nation*, 149.

28. J. C. Swayze to D. Tillson, July 20, 1866, reel 29; T. F. Forbes to G. W. Pills, Oct. 3, 1866, reel 3; J. F. Boynton to D. Tillson, Nov. 1, 1866, reel 25; Register of Civilian Agents, 1865–1867, reel 35, BRFAL-Ga (M798).

29. T. J. Mount to John A. Cobb, Aug. 27, 1865, Cobb-Erwin-Lamar Collection, University of Georgia, Athens.

30. Howell Cobb, Jr., to father, Jan. 3, 1866, Cobb-Erwin-Lamar Collection.

31. G. O. Dalton to J. V. De Hanne, Feb 7, 1867, reel 1, Unregistered Letters Rec'd, Records of the Surgeon-in-Chief for the State of Georgia, Bureau of Refugees, Freedmen, and Abandoned Lands, Record Group 105, National Archives, Washington, D.C., microfilm located at University of Georgia Science Library, Athens.

32. E. Pickett to J. J. Bradford, Nov. 22, 1866, reel 4, BRFAL-Ga (M798); endorsement of F. A. H. Gaebel, July 20, 1867 on C. Raushenberg to F. A. H. Gaebel, July 20, 1867, Letters Rec'd, Albany Subassistant Commissioner; and J. Leonard to J. B. Davenport, Jan. 10, 1868, vol. 223, Letters Sent, Columbus Subassistant Commissioner, BRFAL-Ga.

33. A. Leers to J. M. Hoag, Sept. 30, 1868, Unregistered Letters Rec'd, Savannah Subassistant Commissioner, BRFAL-Ga.

34. J. W. Arnold to [W. W. Deane], Dec. 22, 1966, reel 25, BRFAL-Ga (M798).

35. W. E. Wiggins to T. D. Elliot, Dec. 30, 1867, vol. 288, Letters Sent, LaGrange Agent, BRFAL-Ga.

36. C. H. Howard, Inspection Report for South Carolina, Georgia, and Florida, Dec. 30, 1865, U.S. House, *Executive Documents*, 39th Cong., 1st sess., no. 70 (serial 1256), 357.

37. J. E. Bryant to R. Saxton, Aug. 4, 1865, reel 7, Records of the Assistant Commissioner for the State of South Carolina, Bureau of Refugees, Freedmen, and Abandoned Lands, National Archive Microfilm Publication M869. For the Bureau's efforts to enforce the contract system, see Cimbala, *Under Guardianship of the Nation*, 131–65.

38. C. C. Sibley to O. O. Howard, Apr. 15, 1867, reel 16; J. R. Hill and others to [C. C. Sibley], Aug. 19, 1867, reel 12, BRFAL-Ga (M798).

39. In October 1866, for example, there were only 850 infantrymen in Georgia; there were no cavalry troops stationed in the state. See James E. Sefton, *The United States Army and Reconstruction, 1865–1877* (Baton Rouge: Louisiana State University Press, 1967), 261–2; Cimbala, *Under Guardianship of the Nation*, 61–2.

40. G. R. Walbridge to D. Tillson, July 26, 1866, reel 29, BRFAL-Ga (M798).

41. D. Tillson to O. O. Howard, Dec. 20, 1865, reel 20, (LR)BRFAL (M752).

42. For the problems Bureau men had with local officials, see Cimbala, *Under Guardianship of the Nation*, 66–7.

43. H. G. Flournoy to T. D. Elliot, Jan. 9, 1868, vol. 171, Letters Sent, Athens Agent, BRFAL-Ga.

44. Endorsement of G. R. Walbridge to D. Tillson, July 30, 1866, on J. C. Swayze to D. Tillson, July 18, 1866, reel 29, BRFAL-Ga (M798).

45. J. C. Swayze to D. C. Poole, Jan. 21, 1866, reel 31, BRFAL-Ga (M798).

46. J. C. Swayze to D. Tillson, Jan. 21, 1866, reel 29, BRFAL-Ga (M798).

47. John Townsend Trowbridge, *The South: A Tour of Its Battlefields and Ruined Cities, a Journey through the Desolated States, and Talks with the People* (Hartford, Conn.: L. Stebbins, 1866), 465.

48. *Griffin Star*, n.d., reprinted in *Augusta Daily Constitutionalist*, May 3, 1866.

49. J. Clarke Swayze to D. Tillson, July 20, 1866, reel 29, BRFAL-Ga (M798).

50. C. A. de la Mesa to D. Tillson, Jan. 6, 1867, reel 30, BRFAL-Ga (M798).

51. J. J. Knox, Civil War Pension Files, Records of the Veterans Administration, Record Group 15, National Archives, Washington, D.C.

52. John A. Carpenter, "Agents of the Freedmen's Bureau," unpublished book manuscript, Manuscript, Archives and Rare Books Division, Schomberg Center for Research in Black Culture, New York Public Library.

53. J. J. Knox to T. D. Elliot, Dec. 30, 1867, vol. 169, Letters Sent, Athens Subassistant Commissioner, BRFAL-Ga.

54. American Missionary Association, *Twenty-Second Annual Report* (New York: American Missionary Association, 1868), 47.

55. Register of Complaints, Feb. 15, 1867, vol. 174, Athens Subassistant Commissioner, BRFAL-Ga; F. E. Sautell to E. P. Smith, Dec. 1, 1868, reel 4, AMA-Ga.

56. H.G. Flournoy to T. D. Elliot, Jan. 9, 1868, vol. 171, Letters Sent, Athens Agent, BRFAL-Ga.

57. J. J. Knox to R. B. Bullock, Nov. 9, 1868, vol. 170, Letters Sent, Athens Subassistant Commissioner, BRFAL-Ga; F. A. Sautell to E. P. Smith, Dec. 1, 1868, reel 4, AMA-Ga; J. J. Knox to M. F. Gallagher, Nov. 24, 1868, reel 58, (LR)BRFAL (M752); E. Whittlesey to J. R. Lewis, Dec. 15, 1868, reel 23. For the white Georgia version of the incident and the assessment of Clarke County residents' feelings toward the Bureau, see Fan [Atkisson] to [M. Blackshear], Nov. 22, 1868, Baber-Blackshear Papers, University of Georgia, Athens, and the testimony of John H. Christy, given on July 24, 1871 in *Testimony Taken by the Joint Select Committee to Inquire into*

the Condition of the Affairs in the Late Insurrectionary States, 13 vols., serials 1484–1496 (Washington, D.C.: Government Printing Office, 1872), vol. 6: *Georgia,* 233–35.

58. J. J. Knox to M. F. Gallagher, Nov. 24, 1868, reel 58 (LR)BRFAL (M752).

59. J. J. Knox to M. F. Gallagher, Nov. 24, 1868, and all endorsements and enclosures (LR)BRFAL (M752); Station Books, vol. 1, 1867–1868, reel 35, BRFAL-Ga (M798); John J. Knox, Civil War Pension Files, Records of the Veterans Administration, Record Group 15, National Archives, Washington, D. C.

60. Lee W. Formwalt, ed., "Petitioning Congress for Protection: A Black View of Reconstruction at the Local Level," *Georgia Historical Quarterly* 73 (summer 1989): 303–22. Formwalt suggests that the extensive use of Bureau material in the petition indicates a good working relationship.

61. E. Belcher to C. C. Sibley, April 28, May 14, 1867, reel 14; E. Belcher to J. R. Lewis, Oct. 23, 1867, reel 17; Station Books, vol. 1, 1867–1868, reel 35; E. Belcher to [C.C. Sibley], March 12, 1867, Register of Letters Rec'd, reel 11, BRFAL-Ga (M798); J. R. Lewis to O. O. Howard, Sept. 26, 1867, reel 49, (LR)BRFAL (M752); Edwin Belcher, Civil War Pension Files, Records of the Veterans Administration, Record Group 15, National Archives, Washington; Edmund L. Drago, *Black Politicians and Reconstruction in Georgia: A Splendid Failure,* 2nd ed. (Athens: University of Georgia Press, 1992), 69–70.

62. G. H. Clower to J. R. Lewis, Nov. 19, 1867, enclosed in G. H. Clower to J. R. Lewis, Nov. 29, 1867, reel 17, BRFAL-Ga (M798).

63. G. H. Clower to J. R. Lewis, Nov. 29, 1867, reel 17, BRFAL-Ga (M798).

64. G. H. Clower to J. R. Lewis, Dec. 4, 1867, enclosed in G. H. Clower to J. R. Lewis, Nov. 29, 1867, reel 17, BRFAL-Ga (M798).

65. J. Leonard to J. R. Lewis, Dec. 16, 1867, enclosed in G. H. Clower to J. R. Lewis, Nov. 29, 1867, reel 17, BRFAL-Ga (M798).

66. J. J. Knox, Contract Report for Nov. 1867, Contract Reports, Athens Subassistant Commissioner, BRFAL-Ga.

67. J. W. Alvord to O. O. Howard, Jan. 17, 1870, in John W. Alvord, *Letters from the South Relating to the Condition of the Freedmen Addressed to Major General O. O. Howard, Commissioner B. R., F., and A. L.* (Washington, D. C.: Howard University, 1870), 16.

68. [A. Pokorny] to J. Leonard, Aug. 31, 1868, vol. 195, Letters Sent, Butler Agent, BRFAL-Ga.

69. Endorsement of L. Lieberman to C. C. Sibley, Aug. 10, 1868, on L. Lieberman to N. S. Hill, June 29, 1868, reel 21, BRFAL-Ga (M798).

70. H. G. Flournoy to T. D. Elliot, Jan. 9, 1868, vol. 171, Letters Sent,

Athens Agent, BRFAL-Ga. Any number of agents' complaint registers will confirm this statement, but especially see vol. 344, Register of Complaints, Rome Agent, BRFAL-Ga, which covers a period from June 1866 through the end of November 1868.

71. L. Lieberman to N. S. Hill, Apr. 4, 1868, Unregistered Letters Rec'd, Hawkinsville Agt; and the numerous entries in the agent C. W. Chapman's journal for the latter part of 1868, vol. 226, Columbus Agent, BRFAL-Ga.

72. W. B. Moore to H. Catley, May 31, 1868, reel 21, BRFAL-Ga (M798).

73. G. L. Eberhart to O. O. Howard, June 17, 1867, reel 46, (LR)BRFAL (M752). For the Bureau men and their politics, see Cimbala, *Under Guardianship of the Nation*, 67–72.

74. "General Tillson's Speech Delivered before the Freedmen's Convention," *Augusta Loyal Georgian*, Jan. 20, 1866.

75. J. W. Barney to J. Scott, May 15, 1868, vol. 211, Letters Sent, Carnesville Agent, BRFAL-Ga.

76. William Warren Rogers, *Thomas County, 1865–1900* (Tallahassee: Florida State University Press, 1973), 15; William F. White, Civil War Pension Files, Records of the Veterans Administration, Record Group 15, National Archives, Washington, D.C.

77. W. W. Deane to J. W. Arnold, Jan. 19, 1866, reel 1; T. F. Forbes to J. D. Harris, June 9, 1866, reel 3; J. R. Lewis to F. A. H. Gaebel, May 28, 1867, reel 5, BRFAL-Ga (M798).

78. W. C. Morrill to [J. R. Lewis], Nov. 3, 4, 1868, reel 23, BRFAL-Ga (M798); *Testimony Taken by the Joint Select Committee to Inquire into the Condition of Affairs in the Late Insurrectionary States*, vol. 7: *Georgia*, 1087.

79. O. H. Howard to M. F. Gallagher, April 16, 1868, reel 21, BRFAL-Ga (M798).

Afterword

James McPherson

THE AMERICAN CIVIL WAR abounds in ironies. A nation born of secession fought a war against secession four score and seven years later to preserve the entity created by the first secession from dismemberment by the second. The commander in chief of the victorious army had no military training and once joked that his only military experience had consisted of "charges upon the wild onions" and "a good many bloody struggles with the mosquitoes" as a militia captain in the Black Hawk War.[1] His rival commander in chief was a West Point graduate and a combat veteran, who had been a superb secretary of war. Yet most historians agree that Abraham Lincoln proved to be a better strategist and military leader than Jefferson Davis. Both sides in the war initially tried to keep the issue of slavery in the background, yet defense of that institution was the mainspring of secession and its abolition one of the most important results of the war. If the conflict had ended in the summer of 1862, which appeared imminent after a remarkable string of Union victories in the winter and spring of that year, plantation slavery and the social structure of the Old South would have survived the war. But the advent of Robert E. Lee as the Confederacy's premier military commander reversed the initial momentum of northern success, prolonged the war for three years, and ensured that Union victory would destroy slavery, the Old South, and almost everything for which Lee had fought.

The reputation of the Freedmen's Bureau, created during the final months of the war to help harvest one of the fruits of victory, emancipation, offers another example of irony. Welcomed as a much-needed ally by the freedpeople, the Bureau reaped abuse and ridicule from southern whites, especially former slaveholders. They denounced it as a "vicious institution," "a curse," a "ridiculous folly."

The ex-Confederate cavalry leader Wade Hampton, formerly the largest and wealthiest slaveholder in the South, wrote of the Bureau in 1866: "The war which was so prolific of monstrosities, new theories of republican government, new versions of the Constitution . . . gave birth to nothing which equals in deformity and depravity this 'Monstrum horrendum informe ingens.' " Planters maintained that they could "make the niggers work" if interfering Bureau agents would leave them alone. "The Bureau doesn't seem to understand the possibility of a white man's being right in a contest or difference with a negro," complained one planter. Another declared, "The fairest minded of all the [Bureau] officials seemed not to be able [to] comprehend the difference between the 'nigger' freedman and the white northern laborer."[2]

The Dunning school of Reconstruction historiography echoed these judgments. "The administration of justice by Bureau agents gradually became a petty persecution of whites," wrote Walter L. Fleming. "[T]heir interference between the races caused lasting discord" and set back southern economic recovery because the Bureau's efforts to enforce contracts between freedpeople and planters left labor "disorganized for several years." If the supervision of labor "had been carried out by people who knew as much about Negroes and conditions in the South as did the Southerners," all might have been well, according to E. Merton Coulter. But the "Northern placemen and former Federal soldiers" who ran the Bureau "took up all matters relating to freedmen and if a white man were concerned especially in the matter of contracts the Negro usually came out winner." The Bureau's favoritism toward blacks thus produced "suspicion which ripened into racial hostility." Even as late as 1955, George R. Bentley concluded his scholarly study of the Freedmen's Bureau with the judgment that the agency "sought too much for the Negro too soon."[3]

Wherein lies the irony? In the 1960s, a 180-degree shift in historiographical winds laid the Bureau on its beam ends. It was now damned for not doing what a previous generation of historians had damned it for doing. Several historians now saw its efforts to restore order and stability in the South as an effort to promote "social control" of blacks and even its support for freedmen's schools as a form of paternalism that fostered black subordination to the repressive values and institutions of capitalism. These historians also criticized the white male Bureau agents for socializing with southern whites and adopting their racial attitudes, at the cost of equal justice to the freedpeople.

The Freedmen's Bureau had the "resources for achieving much economic and social reform for the freedmen," insisted William S. McFeely in 1968, "but failed them by substituting paternal supervision for man to man respect," "banked the fires of the freedmen's aspirations," and failed to stop "the delivery of the Negro labor force into the hands of [Andrew] Johnson's planter and business allies." Conceding that "some" agents did what they could "to protect the freedmen from fraud, harassment, and violence," Leon F. Litwack nevertheless found that "many" others "coveted acceptance by the communities in which they served and became malleable instruments in the hands of the planter class, eager to service their labor needs and sharing similar views about the racial character and capacity of black people and the urgent need to control them . . . embracing a paternalism and a contract-labor system that could only perpetuate the economic dependency of the great mass of former slaves."[4]

Were contemporaries who denounced the Bureau for its pro-black policies and historians who criticized it for its anti-black shortcomings speaking of the same institution? If so, do we have here a case analogous to the blind men touching different parts of an elephant and each describing a different animal? The paradox can be resolved, the irony explained, by recognition that the perspectives of white southerners in the 1860s and radical historians a century later were poles apart. Both were describing the same elephant, but each had contrasting opinions about the merits of the elephant.

Missing is the perspective of the freedpeople themselves. That too consisted of a range of attitudes, as the essays in this volume make clear. Some freedpeople praised Bureau agents for what they did, or tried to do, to help them receive their just wages, obtain justice in legal disputes, or acquire an education. Others criticized agents for failures to achieve these goals, perhaps even their failure to try. If any one comment can stand as representative, perhaps it is the plea of the Georgia freedman George Clower for a replacement agent at Forsyth: "When Capt. Belcher War here We don Well but sense he is Goin We has don bad so Genral send a Bureau here."[5]

Whatever the Bureau's shortcomings, it surely accomplished more for the freedpeople than if there had been no Bureau.

The foregoing essays, on balance, confirm in their range of details and interpretations the general conclusions offered nearly a century ago by W. E. B. Du Bois: "this Bureau set going a system of free labor, established a beginning of peasant proprietorship, secured the recognition of black freedmen before courts of law, and founded the free common school in the South." At the same time, however, "it failed to . . . guard its work wholly from paternalistic methods which discouraged self-reliance, and to carry out to any considerable extent its implied promises to furnish the freedmen with land." The Bureau was "not perfect, indeed, notably defective here and there," wrote Du Bois, "but on the whole successful beyond the dreams of thoughtful men."[6]

By now, American society has had a great deal of experience with the problems of race, class, and their intersections with free labor in South and North and in rural and urban areas. The architects of a transition from slave to free labor in the devastated South of 1865 had no such experience. The emancipation of the four million slaves and the reconstruction of a society torn apart by a terrible civil war were totally new experiences. No models existed to guide those who had to deal with them. There was no tradition of government responsibility for a huge refugee population and no bureaucracy to administer a large welfare, employment, and land reform program. Congress and the army and the Freedmen's Bureau were groping in the dark. They created the precedents. And, in doing so, they had to overcome the determined opposition of the president and the bitter resistance of many southern whites. No other society in history had liberated so many chattel slaves in so short a time at such a cost in lives and property. No other country had established a Freedmen's Bureau to help the transition from slavery to freedom. No other society had poured so much effort and money into the education of freed slaves. If the result fell short of entire success, the alternative might well have been total failure.

NOTES

1. Roy P. Basler, ed., *The Collected Works of Abraham Lincoln*, 9 vols. (New Brunswick: Rutgers University Press, 1953–5), 1:510.

2. Unattributed quotations from George R. Bentley, *A History of the Freedmen's Bureau* (Philadelphia: University of Pennsylvania Press, 1955), 104, 159; and from James L. Roark, *Masters without Slaves: Southern Planters in the Civil War and Reconstruction* (New York: W. W. Norton, 1977), 154; Hampton quoted in Walter L. Fleming, ed., *Documentary History of Reconstruction*, 2 vols. (Cleveland: Arthur H. Clark Co., 1906), 1:368.

3. Fleming, *Documentary History*, 1:316; E. Merton Coulter, *The South during Reconstruction* (Baton Rouge: Louisiana State University Press, 1968), 74, 79, 89; Bentley, *History of Freedmen's Bureau*, 214.

4. William S. McFeely, *Yankee Stepfather: General O. O. Howard and the Freedmen* (New Haven: Yale University Press, 1968), 3, 7, 328; Leon F. Litwack, *Been in the Storm So Long: The Aftermath of Slavery* (New York: Alfred A. Knopf, 1979), 382–3, 386.

5. Paul A. Cimbala, "Reconstruction's Allies: The Relationship of the Freedmen's Bureau and the Georgia Freedmen," in this volume on page 332.

6. W. E. B. Du Bois, *The Souls of Black Folk* (New York: Signet Classics, New American Library ed., 1969), 74, 70.

CONTRIBUTORS

Paul A. Cimbala, professor of history at Fordham University in the Bronx, received his Ph.D. from Emory University. He is the author of *Under the Guardianship of the Nation: The Freedmen's Bureau and the Reconstruction of Georgia, 1865–1870*, winner of the Georgia Historical Society's 1999 Malcolm and Muriel Bell Barrow Award. With Randall M. Miller, he edited *American Reform and Reformers: A Biographical Dictionary* and *Against the Tide: Women Reformers in American Society*. He also edited (with Robert F. Himmelberg) *Historians and Race: Autobiography and the Writing of History*. He is currently writing *Jester, Trickster, Priest: Black Musicians from Slavery to Freedom in the Rural American South* and has begun research on a book about the Union Army's Veteran Reserve Corps during the Civil War and Reconstruction. He is the editor of two Fordham University Press book series, *The North's Civil War* and *Reconstructing America*.

Randall M. Miller, professor of history and director of American Studies at Saint Joseph's University in Philadelphia, received his Ph.D. from Ohio State University. He has published numerous books, including the award-winning *"Dear Master": Letters of a Slave Family*; (with John David Smith) the award-winning *Dictionary of Afro-American Slavery*; and (with Harry S. Stout and Charles Reagan Wilson) *Religion and the American Civil War*. His latest book is a study of immigrants in the American South. He is coeditor of the University Press of Florida book series, *Southern Dissent*, and editor of two book series, *Historic Guides to the Twentieth Century* and *Major Issues in American History*, at Greenwood Press.

Caryn Cossé Bell, assistant professor of history at Worcester State College in Massachusetts, received her Ph.D. from Tulane University. She is author of *Revolution, Romanticism, and the Afro-Creole Protest Tradition in Louisiana, 1718–1868,* winner of the Jules and Frances Landry Award for 1996, and (with Joseph Logsdon) of "The Americanization of Black New Orleans, 1850–1900" in *Creole New Orleans: Race and Americanization.* She is currently writing a book on New Orleans spiritualism, which sets the nineteenth-century phenomenon in an international context.

Barry A. Crouch, professor of history at Gallaudet University in Washington, D.C., received his Ph.D. from the University of New Mexico. He is the author of numerous articles on the Freedmen's Bureau and African Americans. He also has published *A Place of Their Own: Creating the Deaf Community in America, The Freedmen's Bureau and Black Texans,* and (with Donaly E. Brice) *Cullen Montgomery Baker, Reconstruction Desperado.* He is presently working on several book-length projects, including a history of Reconstruction in Texas and a collection of essays about African Americans in Texas.

Mary J. Farmer is a doctoral candidate in history at Bowling Green State University. Her dissertation is entitled "Freed*women* and the Freed*men*'s Bureau: Race, Gender, and Public Policy in the Age of Emancipation." Her publications include a forthcoming article (with Donald G. Nieman), titled "Race, Class, Gender, and the Unintended Consequences of the Fifteenth Amendment," in *The Unintended Consequences of Constitutional Amendments,* edited by David Kyvig, and essays in both *The Oxford Companion to American Military History* and the *Encyclopedia of Violence in the United States.* She received a Mellon Research Fellowship from the Virginia Historical Society.

Randy Finley is an assistant professor of history at Georgia Perimeter College in Dunwoody, Georgia. He received his Ph.D. from the University of Arkansas and is the author of *From Slavery to Uncertain Freedom: The Freedmen's Bureau in Arkansas, 1865–1869.* He is currently working on a study of Albany, Georgia, in the 1960s.

Michael W. Fitzgerald is an associate professor of history at St. Olaf College in Northfield, Minnesota. He received his Ph.D. from the University of California at Los Angeles. He is the author of *The Union League Movement in the Deep South: Politics and Agricultural Change* *during Reconstruction.* He also has published three articles in the *Journal of Southern History*, most recently on African American political factionalism in Reconstruction Alabama. The subject of his next book is black politics in Mobile after emancipation.

Richard Paul Fuke is an associate professor of history at Wilfrid Laurier University in Waterloo, Ontario, Canada. He received his Ph.D. from the University of Chicago. He is the author of numerous articles on the Freedmen's Bureau, Republican ideology, and the freedpeople in Maryland. He recently published *Imperfect Equality: African Americans and the Confines of White Racial Attitudes in Post-Emancipation Maryland.* Currently, he is working on a study of racial attitudes and urban reform in postemancipation Baltimore.

Michael L. Lanza received his Ph.D. from the University of Chicago. He is the author of *Agrarianism and Reconstruction Politics: The Southern Homestead Act,* the chapter on the 1898 Louisiana constitution in *In Search of Fundamental Law: Louisiana's Constitutions,* and several articles. He has taught at the University of New Orleans, Virginia Polytechnic Institute and State University, Middlebury College, George Mason University, and Prince George's (Maryland) Community College. He is currently a senior officer in the Federal/State Partnership at the National Endowment for the Humanities.

James M. McPherson is the George Henry Davis '86 Professor of History at Princeton University. Since receiving his doctorate from Johns Hopkins University, he has published *The Struggle for Equality: Abolitionists and the Negro in the Civil War and Reconstruction* and *The Abolitionist Legacy: From Reconstruction to the NAACP* as well as numerous books on the Civil War. He won the Pulitzer Prize for *The Battle Cry of Freedom: The Civil War Era,* a volume in the Oxford History of the United States, and the Lincoln Prize for *For Cause and Comrades: Why Men Fought in the Civil War.*

E. Allen Richardson is an associate professor of religious studies at Cedar Crest College in Allentown, Pennsylvania. With a Ph.D. in Oriental Studies from the University of Arizona, he has specialized in South Asian history, devotional Hinduism (*bhakti*), and the transplantation of Asian religions in the United States. He is the author of *East Comes West: Asian Religions and Cultures in North America* and *Strangers in This Land: Pluralism and the Response to Diversity in the United States*. Continuing an additional interest in American history, his current research is focused on Michael E. Strieby, abolitionist minister and executive secretary of the American Missionary Association from 1876 to 1895.

John C. Rodrigue, assistant professor of history at Louisiana State University in Baton Rouge, received his Ph.D. from Emory University. From 1992 to 1996, he was a member of the Freedmen and Southern Society Project at the University of Maryland at College Park. He is coeditor of *Freedom: A Documentary History of Emancipation, 1861–1867*, Series 3, Volume 1: *Land, Labor, and Capital: 1865*. He is now completing a study of the transition from slavery to free labor in the Louisiana sugar region during the Civil War and Reconstruction.

James D. Schmidt is an assistant professor of history at Northern Illinois University. He received his Ph.D. from Rice University. He has published several articles and presented numerous papers on nineteenth-century labor law and work. He has recently published *Free to Work: Labor Law, Emancipation, and Reconstruction, 1815–1880*. Currently, he is working on an investigation of the role of the state in the creation of bourgeois childhood and on a project exploring legal campaigns against subsistence in the nineteenth-century United States.

Brooks D. Simpson, professor of history and humanities at Arizona State University, received his Ph.D. from the University of Wisconsin at Madison. Among his books are two History Book Club selections, *Let Us Have Peace: Ulysses S. Grant and the Politics of War and Reconstruction, 1861–1868*, and *The Reconstruction Presidents*. He is also the author of *The Political Education of Henry Adams* and *America's Civil War* and the editor of several volumes. Currently, he is engaged in writing a biography of U. S. Grant.

Hans L. Trefousse, Distinguished Professor Emeritus at Brooklyn College and the Graduate Center of City University of New York, received his Ph.D. from Columbia University. The author of biographies of Ben Butler, Ben Wade, Carl Schurz, Andrew Johnson, and Thaddeus Stevens, he has also written, among other works, *The Radical Republicans: Lincoln's Vanguard for Racial Justice* and *Impeachment of a President: Andrew Johnson, the Blacks, and Reconstruction.* He is now writing a book about Abraham Lincoln's reputation during the Civil War.

INDEX

Montgomery (Alabama), 53
Moore, Orlando, 242
Moore, William G., 42
Morrill, William C., 335

National Freedmen's Relief Association (NFRA), 123, 289
Nelson, Samuel, 16
New England Freedmen's Aid Society, 289
New Orleans, 19, 140–56, 195
New Orleans Freedmen's Aid Association, 148
New Orleans Tribune, 141
New Smyrna (Florida), 81–82
New South, 233–34
New York Herald, 39
New York Tribune, 145
New York World, 37
Nicholson, A. O. P., 37
Nieman, Donald G., 29
North Carolina, conditions in, 38
North Carolina Proclamation, 31

Oberlin Institute, 121, 124, 133
O'Brien, Edward F., 249
Ohio Liberty Party, 123
Oneida College, 133
Ord, Edward O. C., 21, 73, 75, 96
orphans, 268–71
Orr, James, 227, 231, 243
Owen, Robert Dale, 32

Parker, Ely S., 13
Parsons, Lewis E., 58, 59–60
Patton, Robert M., 12
Pease, W. B., 275
Pennsylvania Freedmen's Relief Association, 289
Perkins, William, 292
Phillips, Wendell, 226, 233
Pierpoint, Francis, 31

Pingree, George, 239–41
planters. *See* whites
Poole, D. C., 327
Pope, John, 331
Porter, Byron, 264
Port Royal Experiment, xx–xxi, 123, 125, 224
Proclamation of Pardon and Amnesty, 31
Purman, W. J., 81
Putnam, Joseph R., 72

race riots, 16, 19–20, 101
Randolph, Paschal B., 39
Rapier, John T., 269
Reconstruction: historiography of, ix–xi; 3, 46, 344–46; and Freedmen's Bureau, xiii–xxxi, 4; Lincoln's plan of, xiv–xv; and Union Army, xxi–xxiii, 3–4; and Andrew Johnson, 5, 10, 31, 32–33, 40–42, 50, 60, 126, 131, 225, 263, 321
Reconstruction Act, 22, 23
Reed, Mary, 126
Regulators, the, 109–10
Remley, Jacob, 78
Republican Party, x, xvii, xxi, xxiii, xxviii, 18, 56, 155; and Freedmen's Bureau, ix, xvi, xviii; and Free Labor ideology, xix, 68, 122, 130, 133, 145; and civil rights, 15, 22, 263, 266; and Andrew Johnson, 29, 33, 36–38, 40–41; and Southern Homestead Act, 68
Richardson, Joe M., 137*n*1
Risley, Douglas G., 316–17
Rose, Willie Lee, 33
Roudanez, Jean-Baptiste, 141, 143
Roudanez, Louis Charles, 143
Runkle, Benjamin P., 234–35
Rutherford, George, 103
Rutherford, R. G., 294